the EVERYDAY
BAKER

Recipes & Techniques for Foolproof Baking

Breads | Pastries | Cakes | Pies | Cookies and More

Abigail Johnson Dodge

The Taunton Press

With a nod to a loving, supportive past: David Clayton Johnson Jr. and Margaret Gordon Johnson;
and a toast to a brilliant, joyful future: Alexander Timothy Dodge and Margaret Tierney Dodge
My love forever.

> >

Text © 2015 Abigail Johnson Dodge

The Taunton Press, Inc., 63 South Main Street, PO Box 5506, Newtown, CT 06470-5506
Email: tp@taunton.com

Editor: Carolyn Mandarano
Copy Editor: Li Agen
Indexer: Heidi Blough
Cover and Interior design: Carol Singer
Layout: Carol Singer, Sandy Mahlstedt
Photographers: Sloan Howard © The Taunton Press, Inc., except for pp. 91–102, 104–106,
171–186, 251–266, 331–346, 411–418, 420–426 © Tina Rupp; 75, 81, 133, 212, 352, 364–365,
510–511, 549 Shaffer Smith © The Taunton Press, Inc.
Author photo: Winnie Abramson
Food Stylist (finished dish photos): Adrienne Anderson
Prop Stylist (finished dish photos): Pam Morris

The following names/manufacturers appearing in *The Everyday Baker* are trademarks:
Bacardi®, Baking Steel®, Boursin®, Cabot™, Calphalon®, Cinnabons®, Coco Lopez®,
Crisco®, Cuisinart®, Diamond®, Divine®, DuFour®, Effie's™, Frangelico®, Ghirardelli®,
Gold Medal®, Grand Marnier®, Grandma's®, Guittard®, Hershey's®, Jell-O®, Jif®,
Kahlúa®, KerryGold®, King Arthur®, KitchenAid®, Knox®, Kraft®, Land O' Lakes®, Lindt®,
McCormick®, Microplane®, Myers's®, Nabisco® Famous®, Nordic Ware®, Nutella®, Oxo®,
Pabst Blue Ribbon®, Pepperidge Farm®, Pillsbury®, Play-Doh®, Pyrex®, Red Star®, San
Pellegrino®, Scharffen Berger®, Spice Islands®, Sugar in the Raw®, Sunbeam®, Swans
Down®, Thomas'®, Trader Joe's®, Tupperware®, Valrhona®, Waring®, Wheat Thins®

LIBRARY OF CONGRESS CATALOGING-IN-PUBLICATION DATA

Dodge, Abigail Johnson, author.
  The everyday baker : recipes & techniques for foolproof baking breads, pastries, cakes,
pies, cookies, and more / Abigail Johnson Dodge.
    pages cm
  ISBN 978-1-62113-810-5
1. Baking. 2. Desserts. 3. Bread. I. Title.
  TX765.D599 2015
  641.81'5--dc23

                        2015032688

PRINTED IN THE UNITED STATES OF AMERICA
10 9 8 7 6 5 4 3 2 1

ACKNOWLEDGMENTS

I am forever grateful for the privilege of working in a field that inspires, invigorates, humbles, and, at times, intimidates me. Every situation, every chef, every teacher, every writer, every editor, every success, and every failure has influenced who I am as baker, writer, and human.

The making of this book spanned well over three years, otherwise known as an eternity in the book publishing world. Between planning, researching, developing and testing recipes, writing, photographing finished dishes as well as thousands of process shots (still and video), design, graphics, editing, layouts, and more, this book has literally taken a village of talented people who worked together with precision and in perfect harmony.

Once again, it was an honor and a pleasure to work side by side with my wonderful editor, Carolyn Mandarano. Thank you, Carolyn, for allowing me the privilege to author this dream project, involving me in every aspect of it, and steadfastly supporting and guiding me through it. You are a true collaborator, gifted editor, and a generous, kind person.

My trusted colleague and friend Claire Van de Berghe has worked on every aspect of this project. Claire was an instrumental voice in conceptual discussions, testing recipes, assisting at the process shoots, reviewing cover design, editing text, inputting metric conversions, and doing a final read before layout. Thank you, Claire, for your patience, taste buds, and keen attention to detail, as well as your hard work. Her friends call her Claire "Van-wonderful" for good reason.

> > > >

>>>>

Few cookbook authors are fortunate to have a true home with their publisher, and I am one of them. The Taunton Press has published three of my cookbooks, but I began working for *Fine Cooking* magazine (published by Taunton) with their first issue, published in 1994, and I have loved and learned from every issue and every person who has graced their staff. With heartfelt thanks to Maria Taylor, Kathy Kingsley, Jennifer Armentrout, and the entire Taunton family—your work is an inspiration.

Included in my Taunton/*Fine Cooking* family are the other team members that made this book come alive. Thank you ladies and gentleman for your time, talents, and good humor. Sloan Howard led the process photography shoots with his unflappable nature and his instinctive and talented photographic sensibilities for capturing recipes in process. Keeping track of all the images, Erin Giunta and Linda Carter lent their keen eyes on each one. Dianna Andrews and Claire spent days planning, shopping, and prepping, rolled with the ebb and flow of long shoot days, and were always two steps ahead of me. Carolyn was at every shoot and was, as always, the voice of reason and, sometimes, sanity, especially on those long shoot days when mine came into question. Art director Rosalind Wanke was also "keeper of the costumes"—the double set of shirts and faux aprons I wore for the shoots. Thanks to the stellar video team of Sarah Breckenridge and Gary Junken. We worked hard but shared plenty of laughs, as well as delicious lunches from the T-room. Am I the only one who misses hearing what the daily specials are and then comparing notes on who's having what?

Thanks to the effervescent Juli Roberts and her *Fine Cooking* test kitchen staff for letting "the band" crash their dance space for the countless (and I do mean countless) process and video shoot days. The sights, sounds, and nibbles coming from your happy kitchens brightened our days and filled our bellies.

Thanks to the all-star art, design, and production team for working your magic on this book. Carol Singer created the beautiful look, cover design, and layout of this book. It's gorgeous and exactly as we imagined it. Li Agen is a longtime friend, a trusted colleague, and a true goddess of a copy editor. I am indebted to finished food photographer Tina Rupp, food stylist Adrienne Anderson, and prop stylist Pam Morris for their hard work creating and staging the glorious color photos that bring so many of these recipes to life.

Susie Middleton and Juli Roberts were a constant source of information and support throughout this long dance. Not only did they read and comment on *The Everyday Baker* basics chapter, but they also answered endless queries like, "How much does your 1 cup of spinach weigh?" In the *FC* test kitchen, Juli was ever gracious when I peppered her with things like, "Do you have any Rainier cherries I can borrow—and by 'borrow' I mean 'have'?," and "Do you mind if I steal just a bit more of your counter space?" Thank you, ladies, for your brilliance, patience, and kindness.

With thanks to my long-time agent, Stacey Glick, for always keeping it real, pushing me to do better, and protecting me along the way.

I'm blessed to have many close friends. We met in conventional ways (childhood, school, work) and unconventional ways (Twitter, Facebook, Instagram). I wish there was space to name you all. Thankfully, you know who you are. No matter how near or far we live from each other, you guys dole out buckets of laughter, friendship, and support.

Through the course of developing, testing, and retesting these recipes, my kitchen and counters have been flooded with literally hundreds of baked goods. Leftovers found their way to neighbors, friends, and, where appropriate, the local shelter. My brother, Tim Johnson, also swooped in and collected the goods to share with colleagues, though I think a few stayed behind for him and his lovely wife, Allyn Chandler, to nibble on.

Thanks to the cast and crew of "cabana one" for tasting and critiquing all that I put before you. We are all a bit heavier for it, and I appreciate your sacrifice for the greater good.

I am fortunate to count Larry Norton as a trusted friend. Along with being a "cabana one" charter member, he is a highly regarded publishing professional, and I sought his counsel often. Thanks, Larry, for your guidance and support throughout all stages of this project.

Lastly and lovingly, to my husband, Chris, and my smart, strong babies, Alex and Tierney. I hope you've enjoyed this sweet ride as much as I have loved sharing it with you.

INTRODUCTION

The Everyday Baker is my tenth cookbook and by far the most important and personal of my career. With each recipe, both sweet and savory, I share with you my personal baking journey. You'll discover that I began baking at my mother's side and learned from her gentle, warm instruction. When I was older, I moved to Paris for culinary training then into professional kitchens and bakeries before focusing on recipe development, teaching, and writing. You get the idea—I've been baking a long time. My goal with this book is to demystify baking and empower you with all the techniques, skills, and information that I have culled through my personal and professional baking life.

Through my recipes and from my experiences, you'll learn that baking is more than a science assignment where you simply follow steps leading to a finished project. It's also definitely not about creating something that is perfect. (Perfection is unattainable so let's agree to let go of that goal.) With my guiding hands in every recipe, you will bake confidently and successfully through this book just as if we were baking together. I'll encourage you to engage all of your senses (sight, smell, touch, taste) and remind you that baking takes some patience, trust in your instincts, and, sometimes, a little courage to try something new. It doesn't matter a lick if your finished product looks exactly like mine (remember, I've been doing this for eons), if the bread is lopsided, or if the frosting is speckled with cake crumbs. What you handcrafted with care will still taste delicious and allow you a chance to take pride in your effort.

Like me, you'll have some awesome baking days and some when things don't turn out exactly as you planned. Maybe you are distracted, tired, rushed, or, most likely, all three. It's ok. We all have those days, but don't let that discourage or stop you from baking. Acknowledge what's going on, let it go, and bake on. If you let go of the need to be perfect along with as much outside noise as humanly possible, working through a recipe can be remarkably soothing and rewarding. As for those not-so-great baking days, rest assured that they will make the times when you are rockin' n rollin' through a recipe even sweeter.

While the vast majority of the recipes were developed specifically for this book, I pulled some directly from my mother's tiny metal recipe box, tweaking them as needed to modernize them to today's tastes and appliances; others I adapted from my restaurant and bakery days. My techniques are based on classic methods that I have tweaked and honed throughout my baking years. This isn't meant to take away from the original version—any variance was designed to streamline and, on occasion, update some older styles. Each recipe includes a road map for baking success: an ingredient list given in volume and weight measures, directions that encompass how-to, step-by-step technique photos to guide you along your way, and numerous variations to satisfy every palate. One note about measurements: I test and develop all my recipes using ounce weights in ⅛-oz. increments; for those who prefer metric, I have converted those ounces to grams (hence the non-rounded gram measures).

It is my honor and privilege to share my baking life with you, and I hope this book inspires you to tell your own baking story. I look forward to hearing from you as we bake together.

Chapter 1

EVERYDAY BAKING BASICS

>>>>

No matter whether you're a newbie or a pro, read through this section before you start baking. Here you'll discover everything you need to know to get ready to bake, from ingredients to stock in your pantry to tools and equipment and important information to know before you dive in. For those new to baking, you'll find this information invaluable to get you set up. But seasoned bakers will benefit too, and hopefully you will uncover a new gem or two. In either case, think of me as being by your side in the kitchen, working together with you.

Everyday Ingredients

Keeping a variety of these ingredients stowed in your fridge, freezer, and pantry will guarantee you'll be ready to bake at a moment's notice. By no means do you need to have every item listed, nor do you need to keep large amounts of anything—no one has that much space in their kitchen. Feel free to stow away smaller amounts or stock up on them depending on your storage space and baking frequency.

IN THE PANTRY
Flour

There are many types of flour these days, and it can be confusing as to which to buy and why. Breaking down the difference between all-purpose, cake, bread, and whole-wheat begins with the gluten-forming protein content within each type and brand of flour. I like to think of the protein content as the "muscle" within the flour.

Proper measuring of all types of flour is of the utmost importance to ensure accurate and consistent baked results. I use weight measurements, included in every recipe, so I urge you to buy a digital kitchen scale. If you don't use a scale, use the spoon-and-swipe method: Stir the flour in its container, lightly spoon into the appropriate metal measuring cup (avoid the cute-shaped variety and stick to the basic), and swipe off the excess with a flat edge (a ruler or spatula handle).

Using the dip-and-swipe method for measuring (dipping the measure directly into the flour container and scooping up flour) will result in adding more (sometimes much more) flour to the recipe, resulting in tougher, drier baked goods.

Bread flour The higher the protein content in a type of flour, the more gluten (or "muscle") it brings to your baking. For example, yeast breads tend to be long-risers with chewy interiors and a crusty exterior. So for them we want a harder or stronger wheat flour with a higher protein content, like bread flour, in order to supply the amount of muscle power the yeast needs to be successful. For recipes calling for bread flour, I have used King Arthur® (12.7% protein) and Gold Medal® (12.2% to 12.7%) interchangeably with great results.

Cake flour On the other end of the spectrum, for soft-textured, tender cakes like angel food, the muscle of a high-protein flour would be counterproductive and weigh down a delicate cake, causing it to be dense and tough. Instead, a softer wheat flour with a lower protein content, like cake flour, is a better fit. I use Swans Down® (6% to 8% protein), and I always sift it (in some cases more than once) after measuring.

All-purpose flour The middle-of-the-road flour that you'll use most often—unbleached all-purpose flour—is the workhorse of a baker's pantry and the one I use in the majority of my baking, including some of my bread recipes. My top three choices for unbleached all-purpose flours are King Arthur (11.7% protein), Gold Medal (9.8% to 11%), and Pillsbury® (10.5%). They all differ slightly in their protein content, but I have used them interchangeably in these recipes with good results. Because of the chemicals that are used to whiten bleached flour, I prefer to use unbleached all-purpose in my baking.

All flours should be stored in separate airtight containers (I use Tupperware®) at room temperature in a cool, dark place to keep them fresh and bug-free.

Sugars

To prevent clumping, drying out, hardening, and other unhappy results, all sugars should be stowed in airtight containers (I use Tupperware) in a cool, dry place.

Granulated sugar The most commonly used type of sweetener in baking (and in this book), granulated, or white, sugar is refined cane (sometimes beet) sugar. Because the hard granules are free flowing and don't compact when pressed, you can scoop up the sugar and swipe the top to level for volume measuring.

Superfine sugar Also known as bar sugar or caster sugar, these finely ground sugar crystals dissolve quickly, making them ideal for meringue and candy making. If you can't find superfine sugar in your grocery store, make your own by whizzing the same amount (volume or weight) of granulated sugar in a food processor until the granules are pulverized (see p. 589).

Confectioners' sugar Also known as powdered, 10X, or icing sugar, confectioners' is granulated sugar that has been crushed into a very fine and powdery sugar with some cornstarch added to prevent it from clumping when stored. That said, tiny to small lumps will inevitably form, so you should always sift it before using. If measuring by volume, use the stir-spoon-swipe method. In the unlikely event that the lumps are very pronounced, sift before measuring.

Coarse sanding sugar These large, crunchy crystals, also known as decorating, demerara, or turbinado sugar, range in color from pure white to dark brown depending on the amount of residual molasses still clinging to them. The crystals with the darker color, as in demerara sugar, will have more molasses flavor, but the flavor won't be overpowering. I use these sugars primarily as a dusting on muffins, scones,

and cookies just before baking. I like the sweet crunch they add to each bite, and the glittery appearance is always delightful. In my recipes, all of these coarse sugars can be used interchangeably. The most common brand available is Sugar in the Raw®.

Brown sugar Adding varying amounts of molasses to granulated sugar makes both light and dark brown sugar. Light brown sugar contains about 3% to 12% molasses, and the dark variety contains about 6% to 12%. In most recipes, the two are interchangeable, with the exception that dark brown sugar will give a slightly spicier flavor and a deep color to your baked goods. Both types must be stored in an airtight container in a cool, dark place. Exposed to even the slightest amount of fresh air, brown sugar will dry out and harden. If this happens, tuck a slice of bread in the container and leave overnight. Unlike measuring granulated or confectioners' sugar, for accurate volume measuring, you must firmly pack brown sugar into the appropriately sized volume (not liquid) measuring cup.

Salt

Table salt I call for table salt—not coarse kosher—in all of my recipes. Unlike the random-sized bits of kosher, table salt granules are fine and relatively uniform, so I get a consistently accurate measurement every time. The grains also dissolve faster and more evenly in my batters.

Coarse sea salt In many of my recipes, I add a sprinkle of coarse sea salt as a finishing touch to cast a spotlight on the dessert's flavor. Sea salt is very coarse, in some cases even flaky, in texture and, because of the sand collected with salt, it can often have a slight gray tinge. Its intriguing flavor comes from the minerals. It's available in a number of forms and flavors, and you can find it in specialty stores and online. Buy a small quantity of a few varieties so you can sample and choose one or two to always have on hand. It's expensive, so use appropriately and judiciously.

Oil

All but the most perishable nut oils can be stowed at room temperature for 3 to 6 months. If you aren't a frequent oil user, give it the sniff and taste before using it in a recipe. If it smells or tastes even a little "off," crack open a new bottle.

Olive Pressing and extracting the oils from ripe olives without using heat or chemicals make extra-virgin and virgin olive oils. The resulting flavor-rich, fragrant oil will vary from deep golden to dark green depending on the type of olive used and its place of origin. Heating or cooking with this oil will negate the flavor and aroma, so it's best to use it in dressings and drizzled over foods or breads.

"Pure" olive oil is made from subsequent pressings and usually involves heat and/or chemicals in the extraction and is good to use in general cooking.

Neutral-flavored oil For the majority of recipes in this book that call for an oil other than olive, I use the term "neutral-flavored" because any one of many oils—safflower, canola, pure vegetable, corn, and even grape seed—will work well. Made from pressing seeds, nuts, grains, etc., the oil is filtered and refined, resulting in a very mild flavor that's good for baking and cooking. Unless I am deep-frying and need a large quantity, I stow a smaller-sized bottle in a dark cool space. Before I use it, I'm sure to give it the sniff test to make sure it has a clean, fresh aroma.

Shortening

Made by hydrogenating vegetable oil, shortening is a milky-white, flavorless solid fat. Shortening has a higher melting temperature than butter, so I add a small amount in combination with butter to my pie dough to help give it a flakier crust. An equal amount of unsalted butter can be substituted, though the crust will be a bit less flaky. Shortening can also be used for deep-frying.

Cornmeal

While yellow and white cornmeal can be used interchangeably, I use yellow in my baking. I like the sunny tone it adds to my cakes and breads. It's available in many grinds or textures and, while I use coarse for dusting yeast breads, I prefer to use stone-ground for the majority of my baking. Similar to finely ground, stone-ground retains tiny nubbins of corn (the germ) but adds a wonderful, slightly gritty texture. As cornmeal can go rancid, tuck a small bag in an airtight container and stow in your fridge. It will keep for months.

Cornstarch

Also known as cornflour in the UK, cornstarch is made by finely grinding and refining the heart of the corn—the endosperm—into a paper-white powder. After cooking or boiling, thickened cornstarch is shiny and translucent, making it a nice choice to thicken pie fillings and puddings. I also use it in combination with other ingredients like sugar to make a dry, crispy meringue or all-purpose flour to reduce the protein content for a softer, lighter finish.

Double-acting baking powder

This chemical leavener reacts with liquid and heat to release carbon dioxide within the batter to cause it to rise during baking. Double-acting baking powder is a mixture of an alkaline and two acids that activate twice for a double punch of leavening power. The first trigger is liquid (during the mixing process) and the second is heat (during the baking process). While single-acting baking powders exist, make sure to only purchase and use double-acting for my recipes. Baking powder can be used with baking soda or separately in a recipe, depending on the other ingredients.

Baking soda

Also a chemical leavener, baking soda (bicarbonate of soda) is an alkaline that activates when paired in a recipe with an acidic ingredient like buttermilk or sour cream. When activated, baking soda releases carbon dioxide, causing the batter to rise during baking.

Yeast

Yeast is a living, microscopic organism and it's the dynamo behind many types of fermentation, most commonly beer, wine, and bread. Not only does it do the heavy lifting in the bread recipes, but it also gives them their earthy, yeasty flavor and aroma. Available in many forms, I use active dry and quick-rise (instant) for the recipes in this book. Both are sold in jars and small envelopes (look in the baking aisle or the refrigerated case). A few things to watch for when using yeast: Before buying and using, check the expiration date, take care to use the proper liquid temperature as noted in each recipe, and keep it away from salt when measuring, as salt can damage or "kill" the yeast. I use Red Star® Yeast for all my baking; check out their website for more information (redstaryeast.com).

For the majority of my recipes, I use quick-rise (instant) yeast. Not only can it be added directly to the dry ingredients without dissolving in liquid ahead of time, but it also shortens the bread dough rising times. I use active dry yeast in bread recipes that might need a longer rise time for flavor, as well as those that stow in the fridge for resting. In these cases, I begin the dough with a starter to hydrate and activate the yeast.

Oats

There are many types of processed oats available: groats, steel-cut, whole rolled/old-fashioned, quick/quick-cooking, instant. The one thing they have in common is that they all start out as whole oat seeds. Groats are made when the seeds are cleaned and the thick outer hull is removed. When groats are cut, they are referred to as steel-cut or Irish oats. But if the groats are rolled and steamed, they become whole rolled or old-fashioned oats. Quick or quick-cooking oats are similar to old-fashioned oats but they've been cut before the steaming and rolling step so they are thinner flakes and, therefore, cook in about a third of the time.

Rolled oats and quick-cooking rolled oats can often be substituted for one another in recipes. However, instant oats cannot be substituted for either. Instant oats are oat groats that have been cooked and dried before being rolled. When adding these to your baked goods, they will turn lumpy and unpleasant.

While available in every grocery store in the cereal aisle, I prefer to use the Trader Joe's® gluten-free oats, as some oats are processed in gluten facilities and include trace amounts. Tightly sealed containers can be stored at room temperature, but I prefer to stow mine in the fridge to all but guarantee freshness.

Pure maple syrup

While maple trees grow all around the world, only ones that grow in cold, long winter climates like New England and Canada produce sap that can be collected and boiled down to varying grades of syrup. The longer the boiling, the more water is cooked away, resulting in a progressively thicker and darker maple syrup. For baking and cooking, I prefer the stronger, more robust flavor of grade B, but grade A (medium or dark amber) can be substituted. Once opened, stow the container in the fridge and bring back to room temperature before using. To speed this process along, I soak the jar in a pot of hot water. Be sure not to substitute "maple-flavored" or pancake syrup.

Honey

I prefer to use local honey in my baking, and I encourage you to seek out what's available in your neck of the woods or even your neighbor's backyard. Unlike some store-bought honeys that can include other ingredients such as water, buying local will guarantee a pure, unadulterated product. I like mild-flavored honeys like orange blossom or clover, but there are many more to choose from, so I urge you to sample the offerings at your farmers' markets and roadside stands. Honey's flavor profile as well as color will vary depending on the local flowers your neighborhood bees select—imagine the choices!

Molasses

Molasses is a natural byproduct of sugar refinement. Refining sugar is done in three stages, with each one producing distinct types of molasses. Light molasses, from the first stage, is lightest in color and flavor. Dark molasses from the second stage, is thicker, darker, and stronger in flavor. The final stage produces blackstrap, which is the thickest, darkest, and most bitter. I use Grandma's® brand light molasses in my baking with great, flavorful results.

Jam, preserves, and lemon curd

Don't be reluctant to tuck a jar of your favorite store-bought jam or preserves—and a jar of lemon curd—into your pantry. Sure it's wonderful (and delicious) to make these ingredients from scratch, but think of the store-bought jars as a baker's safety net. They can save you time and energy when you are in need of a last-minute homemade treat.

Peanut butter

When it comes to peanut butter, I keep two types on hand. For spreading on toast or apple slices, I like the flavor of natural PB, but when using this type in baking, the nut purée and oils tend to separate, making them difficult to mix and measure accurately. I get the best, most consistent baking results using widely available brands like Jif®, which are emulsified and stabilized so the oil won't separate. Available in crunchy or smooth, emulsified PB can be stowed in the pantry for up to 6 months, while natural/organic brands should be stored in the fridge after opening.

Nuts

For baking, I prefer unsalted (raw) or lightly salted nuts because the nut flavors are bolder and cleaner than the dry-roasted varieties. If using lightly salted nuts, the added salt kicks up the sweet flavors in the dessert to push the sweet-savory line.

To keep nuts tasting fresh and to protect them from turning rancid, tuck a small stash in a heavy-duty zip-top bag and pop it into the freezer. Nuts thaw quickly so you don't need to plan ahead. Just give one a quick taste to be sure the nut oils haven't turned. Unless otherwise indicated, nuts are easily swappable. Here are a few that I always have on hand: pecans, walnuts, macadamia (especially when I find them on sale), almonds (slivered, sliced, and whole), peanuts (lightly salted, not dry roasted), hazelnuts, and cashews.

Dried fruit

Vast varieties of dried fruits are available nationwide. Choose fruits with vibrant colors and plump flesh and avoid packages where you can't see the fruit. Dried fruit that is past its prime will look dry and especially pruney, and the sugars will have crystallized, giving the fruit an unpleasant granular texture. For the freshest flavor and best texture, buy just slightly more than the amount called for in the recipe (extras make great nibblers) and keep them stowed in airtight containers in your pantry, replenishing when necessary.

Spices

As a frequent (okay, maybe constant) baker, I keep a collection of small (2 oz./57 g or more) jars tucked into my spice drawer. If you have limited storage space, smaller jars (about 1 oz./28 g) are very handy.

Well-sealed ground spices (cinnamon, ginger, cardamom, etc.), dried herbs (herbes de Provence, thyme, etc.), and seasonings (anise, ground cumin or pods, smoked paprika, cayenne, etc.) will taste vibrant for 3 to 6 months if stored at room temperature in your pantry. Before using, check the spice for a strong, aromatic fragrance and a bright, unfaded color. If the smell and look aren't up to snuff, ditch it and head to the store for a fresh supply, or your baked good's flavor will be limp and weak.

Gelatin

Unflavored powdered gelatin is used to thicken and set many chilled desserts. I use Knox® brand gelatin. Each ¼-oz. (7 g) envelope contains 2½ teaspoons of powdered gelatin. Soften the granules in liquid, as directed, until plump and moist (see p. 378). Unless otherwise directed in a recipe, heat gently in a microwave or over simmering water until the liquid is clear and no granules remain. Avoid boiling, as that can adversely affect its thickening power. Don't use fresh kiwi, papaya, pineapple, prickly pears, or figs in gelatin mixtures. These fruits contain protease enzymes that destroy protein and, therefore, prevent the gelatin from gelling.

While I don't use leaf (sometimes called "sheet") gelatin in the book, it is commonly used in Europe. Instead of softening the powdered gelatin granules in cold liquid, the paper-thin, transparent sheets are soaked in cold water, squeezed dry (water discarded), and added to hot liquid to dissolve. The general rule for substitution is 5 leaves (2⅞ x 8½ inches/7.3 x 21.5 cm) have the same gelling power of 1 envelope of Knox.

Chocolate

Bittersweet (extra dark) and semisweet (dark) chocolate I like to bake with (and nibble on!) chocolate that contains about 60% to 62% chocolate solids. Most brands, but not all, will call this "bittersweet," but do check labels. For example, Scharffen Berger®'s (one of my favorites) "semisweet" is 62% chocolate, which is the same percentage as Ghirardelli® bittersweet (the brand I use in all my primary testing). The higher-percentage choices will have more cacao and less added sugar, giving a stronger, more bitter flavor to the chocolate. Within the 60% to 70% range, bittersweet and semisweet are interchangeable. Unless otherwise directed, avoid using chocolates with any higher percentage chocolate as the chemistry can be thrown off and your results could be disappointing. All chocolate should be well wrapped (or kept in an airtight container) and stowed in a cool, dark place. To learn how to melt chocolate, see p. 250.

Unsweetened chocolate Unlike bitter and semisweet varieties, unsweetened chocolate is 99% to 100% cacao with no added sugar and cannot be directly substituted for bittersweet or semisweet chocolate. You can find more good information about swapping and substituting chocolates in baking at the following website: ghirardelli.bayareacreativeservices.com/recipes-tips/working-ghirardelli/substitutions.

White chocolate White chocolate is faux chocolate—it doesn't contain any cocoa solids at all. According to the FDA, white chocolate must contain 20% cocoa butter, 14% milk solids, 3½% milk fat, and no more than 55% sugar or other sweeteners. It also contains vanilla and lecithin (an emulsifier). Flavors between brands vary widely from very sweet to nutty. A few that I like are Valrhona®, Lindt®, and Scharffen Berger. Do not substitute white chocolate chips for chopped.

Chips (bittersweet, semisweet, and white) For chips, I like Guittard® and Ghirardelli brands. There are many bittersweet and semisweet chocolate varieties out there, so I encourage you to sample often and make note of your favorites. I prefer not to substitute chips for chopped bittersweet or semisweet chocolate (the chips have added ingredients to stabilize them), but, in most cases, it can be done successfully. (On average, you can substitute 1 cup of chips for 6 oz. of chocolate.) The exception is white chocolate chips—they are not a substitute for chopped chocolate, because they will not melt properly. So please chop up a bar instead.

Cocoa powder Made from roasted cocoa beans pulverized into a paste and then dried and ground, this fine powder is unsweetened. Not to be confused with sweetened cocoa mix, it is available in natural or Dutch-processed forms. Dutch-processed cocoa is treated with an alkaline to neutralize the acid, giving it a smoother taste and darker appearance. This makes it perfect for icings and frostings, as well as truffles. The varieties aren't always interchangeable, so it's best to use what's called for in the recipe. Natural cocoa is lighter in color, has a fruitier, more acidic, stronger chocolate flavor; it is my choice for baking. Unless otherwise noted, I have tested the recipes here using natural Hershey's® brand as it's the most commonly available. But feel free to experiment with other brands. If your cocoa is lumpy, always sift before measuring. And when using volume measuring, use the spoon-and-swipe method.

Cookies

Tuck a box or two of one of the following crisp cookies in your pantry: graham crackers, chocolate wafers, vanilla cookies, amaretti cookies. While they make good nibblers, they are perfect for a dessert accompaniment or grinding and making crumb crusts (see p. 330).

Liqueurs and brandies

I use spirits, liqueurs, and wines throughout the book. If you aren't interested in building a collection, most of them can be purchased in the small nips size.

Instant espresso powder and instant coffee granules

While not a good choice for your morning coffee, instant espresso powder adds rich, roasted coffee flavor to many desserts. Already-brewed espresso grounds are dried and pulverized into a very fine powder that dissolves easily in batters. In a pinch you can substitute instant coffee granules, but the dessert might lack the robust flavor of the espresso.

Vanilla

There are three types of vanilla you can use in a recipe: pure vanilla extract, the seeds of a vanilla bean pod, and pure vanilla bean paste. Always keep vanilla extract on hand and follow the recipe for how much to add to flavor the recipe—more is not better and instead will lend a medicinal flavor to your desserts. Extract, like paste, should be added after any cooking (which will reduce flavor); the two can be used interchangeably and in the same amounts. If using a vanilla bean pod, you'll need to split it and scrape the beans (see p. 275). One 2- to 3-inch (5 to 7.5 cm) vanilla bean is equal to 1 teaspoon extract. If using in a custard or other infused mixture, add the split pod directly to the pot. If using in a batter, add only the scraped seeds, saving the pod for another use.

Essential oils

Use only pure oils and pass over the subpar imitation varieties. Orange and lemon oils are ones that I always have on hand.

IN THE FRIDGE

Milk

I use whole or full-fat cow's milk when developing and testing recipes, and I urge you to follow my lead. That said, 2% milk will yield similar yet less interesting and flavorful results, but I wouldn't go any lower than that, as any lower fat content will adversely affect the texture and depth of flavor of whatever you are baking.

Heavy cream

Heavy cream and whipping cream are not the same thing. Well, not exactly the same thing. Heavy cream has a higher percentage of fat—between 36% and 40%—while whipping cream contains somewhere between 30% and 36% fat. Both will whip up to firm peaks. But with more fat, heavy cream whips up faster and holds firmer, more stable peaks. For all my recipes, I call for heavy cream but, in a pinch, you can substitute whipping cream.

Half-and-half

Half-and-half is a combination of milk and heavy cream with a fat content between 10% and 18%. In a pinch, I make my own by using 3 parts milk to 1 part heavy cream (1 cup half-and-half equals ⅔ cup whole milk plus ⅓ cup heavy cream). If using 2% milk, use ½ cup 2% and ½ cup heavy cream for 1 cup of half-and-half. You can also substitute an equal amount of evaporated milk, though the taste will be somewhat altered. Do not, however, substitute half-and-half for heavy cream—it can't be whipped.

Buttermilk

Buttermilk is a tangy, slightly thickened liquid that is available in whole, low-fat, and fat-free, and though I'm partial to the full-fat variety, I use them all interchangeably in these recipes. In a pinch, you can make your own soured milk by replacing 2 tablespoons of 1 cup of whole milk with 2 tablespoons freshly squeezed lemon juice, stirring and letting sit for a few minutes before using. Buttermilk powder can also be added to the dry ingredients with whole or 2% milk as the liquid.

Sour cream and yogurt

Sour cream is made from cultured cream (usually heavy cream) and allowed to ferment to make a thick, tangy cream.

Less sour and, depending on the variety, less thick than sour cream, *yogurt* is made in a similar style using milk (whole or with lesser percentages of fat) instead of cream. For these recipes, use whole fat, unflavored sour cream and yogurt. In a pinch, they make a suitable substitution for one another.

Mascarpone

One of my favorite dairy products, mascarpone is a very creamy double or triple cow's milk cheese. Known for its lusciously thick and smooth consistency, it has a mildly tangy, rich flavor. This Italian cheese plays a starring role in Tiramisu (see p. 374), a classic dessert from the same country. I also use mascarpone to lend much greater stability (and more flavor) to whipped cream. And I add it to many of my creamy desserts, like Raspberry Zebra Cheesecake (see p. 218).

Unsalted butter

I use only unsalted butter in my recipes. Without the salt, the butter lacks the longer shelf life of its salted counterpart, all but ensuring that the grocery store's unsalted butter is fresher. Salted butter also contains a higher percentage of water and a lower percentage of butterfat, which can affect the results you get when baking. Stow butter away from the fridge door, where the temperature rises and falls when it opens.

Using unsalted also means I can accurately control the salt level in my recipes. Don't be tempted to leave out or reduce the salt—it's imperative to the flavor, and your recipes will taste flat without it. When I'm developing and testing recipes, I use store-brand butter as well as Land O'Lakes® in the first tests, and sometimes butters like KerryGold® in secondary rounds. Much like chocolate, there are many types of butters available and all with subtle flavor characteristics. So feel free to experiment.

Don't be tempted to substitute other butter-like products (spreads and margarines). Not only will copycats not perform properly in my recipes, but the taste and texture will also be subpar and not worth your time, money, and effort. Stick to the real thing. When butter is on sale at my market, I buy a few extra pounds and stow it in my freezer, where it will keep for months.

Eggs

Size matters. Eggs are sized from medium to jumbo—a range of 1¾ oz. to 2½ oz. per egg. That's a huge spread, especially if you're making a recipe that calls for 3 or more eggs. Using a different size egg than what is called for can drastically alter your baked results. For example, let's say a recipe calls for 4 large eggs (8 oz.) and you use 4 jumbo (10 oz.). That is the equivalent of adding one additional egg—not a good idea in baking. For this reason, I prefer that you use only large eggs in my recipes, but if you would like or need to substitute eggs of differing sizes, use the chart on p. 12 and your scale as a guide. I also spot-check the size of my large eggs and randomly weigh them. The USDA requires only that the dozen weigh in at 24 oz., so that means the eggs within can vary in size—a weight between 1⅞ and 2⅛ oz. will work. I've been known to return upwards of 5 dozen eggs that were labeled "large" but most actually weighed 2½ oz. or even more. Thankfully, the on-duty store manager was a baker and completely understood my concern.

> Medium = 1¾ oz.

> Large = 2 oz.

> Extra Large = 2¼ oz.

> Jumbo = 2½ oz.

Unless otherwise directed, eggs should be used at room temperature. If you are in a rush and your eggs are cold, take a few minutes to warm them in a bowl of warm water. Stow eggs away from the fridge door, where the temperature rises and falls when it opens.

Fresh herbs

Look for brightly colored, robust, perky fresh herbs and avoid those that are limp or dry looking. I treat long-stemmed (tender) herbs like mint, parsley (I prefer flat-leaf, or Italian), and cilantro just like cut flowers. Trim the stems and put in a tall glass filled with some water, loosely cover the tops with plastic, and refrigerate. When it comes to basil, I rely on my friend, trusted colleague and ultimate farmer, Susie Middleton. She believes that basil, if it hasn't been previously refrigerated, should ideally stay out, standing in water—if uncovered in the fridge, it can blacken from cold. If it is already in a plastic pack, it will have to be refrigerated.

For other (hardy) herbs like oregano, sage, and thyme or even chives, remove them from any packaging, stow them in plastic bags with a few holes punched out, and tuck into the crisper section of the fridge. Before using, rinse with cold water and arrange in an even layer on several layers of paper towels or a clean dishtowel. Top with another layer of paper towels and pat dry.

Fresh ginger

When choosing fresh ginger (also known as ginger root) at the grocery store, select pieces that are hard and smooth, not shriveled and dry looking. For the longest holding time, I store mine in a small plastic bag that I've poked a few holes in and tuck into the crisper section of my fridge. Before grating, slicing, or chopping, remove the thin silver-gray peel by running the edge of a spoon in short strokes over the ginger until the peel is scraped off (see p. 312).

Fruit

Fresh, ripe fruit is the star ingredient in many recipes. Choose ripe, seasonal fruit and use it quickly. Check out the produce at your local farmers' markets, pick-your-own farms, and green markets; even better, consider joining a CSA (Community-Supported Agriculture). "Going local" is a great way to support your community and get some of the best regional varieties. The best ways to check for ripeness depend on the type of fruit you're using, but here are some general guidelines.

> *Tree fruit (pears, apricots, peaches, plums, nectarines):* Choose firm but not hard fruit. The shoulders (just below the stem) should give slightly when pressed. Give the fruit a good sniff—the more fragrant, the better the taste.

> *Berries and cherries:* Look for firm, plump fruit with bright coloring, and avoid any with a hint of mold or moisture. Just before using (or freezing), pick through and discard any leaves and stems, as well as any berries or cherries that are bruised or moldy. Put in a colander and rinse with cold water. Line a baking sheet with several layers of paper towel or a clean dishtowel, and arrange the fruit in an even layer. Top with another layer of paper towels and pat dry.

> *Tropical fruit (mangos, papayas, bananas, kiwi):* Choose firm but not hard fruit and avoid any with bruises or wrinkles. Bananas and papayas are ready to eat when yellow or as directed in the recipe.

> *Citrus:* Select heavy, firm fruit without soft spots or bruises. The rind's color should be vibrant, and the fruit should have a strong citrus fragrance.

> *Individually quick-frozen fruit (IQF):* IQF fruit is widely available, and while not a substitute for what's on your counter, it will whip up into some terrific recipes. You can make your own IQF fruit in a snap. Arrange rinsed and dried berries and pitted cherries in a single layer on a baking sheet or large plate lined with parchment, plastic wrap, or foil for easy cleanup. Freeze until very firm, then transfer to freezer bags or containers and keep frozen until ready to use or for up to 6 months.

Coconut (sweetened vs. unsweetened)
Throughout the book, you'll find recipes calling for both sweetened and unsweetened coconut. You'll recognize the long shredded strips of the sweetened variety. Unsweetened coconut, also known as desiccated, is characterized by its short, flaky appearance. To preserve freshness, both should be stowed in the refrigerator in a sealed bag.

IN THE FREEZER
Phyllo (or filo)
This flour-based, commercially made dough is carefully stretched and pulled until it's so thin that it's practically transparent. Cut into rectangles, the layers or sheets are stacked and rolled together and frozen. Recipes typically use many sheets layered with butter (or other fat) and sometimes sugar, which bake up into crisp, flaky pastries, shells, or toppings. A cautionary word: When working with phyllo, cover any dough sheets not in use with plastic wrap to keep them from drying out and becoming brittle.

Store-bought pie dough and puff pastry
Both of these pastry doughs can be made from scratch—and I offer you great ways to do both (see p. 361 and p. 502). I really much prefer to make these doughs at home, because the taste and texture of pre-made, store-bought varieties just aren't comparable to homemade. But that said, if time is short, you can certainly find some premade options that are not bad. Before buying, check the ingredient list on the package and try to stick with brands that use butter and lack preservatives. Trader Joe's makes a decent premade pie dough with Pillsbury coming in second place (the latter has some artificial ingredients). For premade puff pastry, I use DuFour® (all butter) and Pepperidge Farm®, and I keep a box in my freezer for "emergency" use. All are "prerolled," but you will likely need to roll further depending on the recipe directions.

Equipment and Tools

BAKING PANS AND DISHES
I've developed and tested these recipes with specific pans, and while it might seem like I'm being a stickler, it's imperative to your success that you use the same size and shape listed in the recipes. I understand the temptation to use the 8-inch cake pan that you have on hand instead of the 9-incher called for in the recipe, but the batter will bake up and out of the smaller pan, creating a small oven disaster. Likewise, if you have a 9-inch pan but the recipe calls for an 8-incher, the cake won't fill the pan properly and will therefore bake up faster and into a thinner, most likely disappointing layer.

Like other kitchen equipment, baking pans (see the photos on pp. 14 and 15) are meant to give you a lifetime of baking enjoyment, so select heavy-duty, high-quality options. Metal pans should be washed by hand and never in the dishwasher. Pyrex® and ceramic dishes are dishwasher-safe and, in most cases, are microwave-safe.

Large roasting pan
Not only will you roast up a beautiful chicken in this classic pan, but you will also use it as the base of a water bath when slow-cooking puddings and custards.

Ceramic ramekins
Available in many colors, 6 oz. (180 ml), which is 3½ inches wide and 1⅔ inches high/9 cm wide and 4.25 cm high, is the size you'll use most often for custards, mousses, mini flourless cakes, and soufflés.

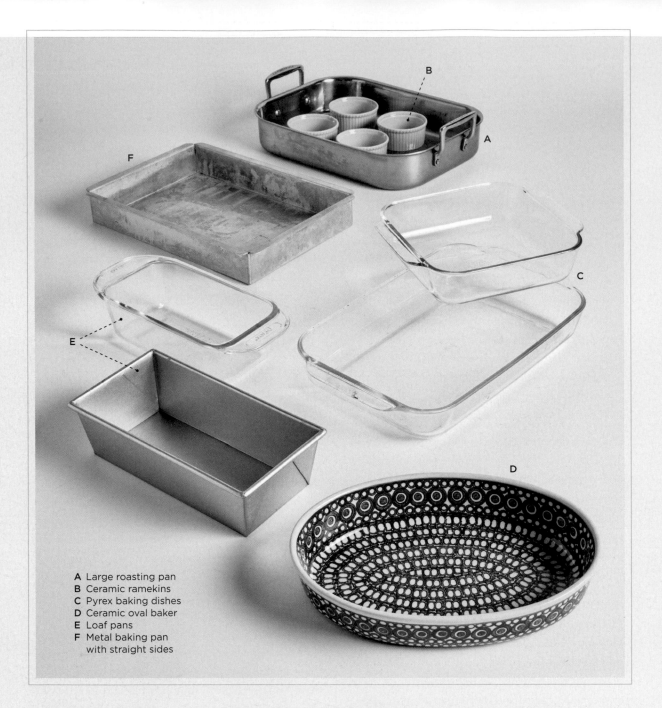

A Large roasting pan
B Ceramic ramekins
C Pyrex baking dishes
D Ceramic oval baker
E Loaf pans
F Metal baking pan
   with straight sides

Pyrex baking dishes

Available in many sizes, the 8-inch (20 cm) square (8 cup) and 9 x 13 x 2-inch (23 x 33 x 5 cm) rectangular (12 cup) are workhorse pieces in a baker's kitchen. Pyrex dishes are inexpensive and typically oven- and microwave-safe.

Ceramic baking dishes

Oval bakers, like the one shown above, are a decorative alternative to Pyrex when baking puddings and crisps. Before using, check the volume by measuring 1 or 2 cups of water at a time into the vessel until it is filled to the brim. It should be just about the same volume as the one called for in the recipe.

Loaf pans

A 10 x 5 x 3-inch (25 x 12 x 7.5 cm), 8-cup rectangular loaf pan is often used for large yeast and quick breads. For consistent baking, choose ones that are light-colored and not nonstick.

A 6-cup Pyrex loaf pan is also used often; it measures 8 1/2 x 4 1/2 x 2 3/4 inches (21.5 x 11 x 7 cm), smaller than its metal counterpart.

A Bundt pan
B Metal cake pan
  with straight sides
C Muffin tins
D Metal baking pan
  with straight sides
E Springform pan
F Angel food cake pan
G Cake boards

Metal baking pan

The straight sides of a 9 x 13 x 2-inch (23 x 33 x 5 cm) pan produce crisp edges for bars and cakes.

Bundt pan

Made by Nordic Ware®, this solid, cast aluminum fluted pan is a classic. I like the original 10-inch (25 cm), 12-cup model shown, but this type of pan is available in many styles and sizes. If you are using a small size, make sure to adjust your batter amounts and plan on less baking time.

Metal cake pans

Straight-sided, light-colored (not dark or nonstick) metal cake pans are a staple in the baker's arsenal. I keep two of each on hand: round and square— 8 x 2 inch (20 x 5 cm) and 9 x 2 inch (23 x 5 cm).

Muffin tins

Not just for cupcakes, you'll find muffin tins in standard, mini, and jumbo sizes. But even those designations vary in size. My standard-size muffin cup is 2¾ x 1⅛ inches (7 x 2.9 cm); mini is 1¾ x ¾ inches (4.5 x 2 cm), and jumbo is 3½ x 1¾ inches (9 x 4.5 cm). It's important to use the size called for in your recipe.

Springform pan

This lightweight two-piece metal pan has a bottom and a tall (3-inch/7.5 cm) wrap-around exterior ring with a grooved bottom edge to lock in the bottom and secures with a spring clasp. You'll use this type of pan for cakes with a high profile (like cheesecakes). This way, the cake remains top side up (no inverting needed) and can even be served with the bottom piece in place. You'll also use just the ring portion of the pan for molding cakes with a tall straight side. Secure the ring closed and set on a serving plate, then layer cake and mousse filling. To prevent dings or, worse, warping, it's best to stow the pan with the outer ring secured to the bottom. Pans are available in 8- and 9-inch (20 and 23 cm) diameters.

Angel food cake pan

This unusual cake pan is used to bake chiffon, sponge, and, as the name alludes, angel food cakes. I prefer an aluminum pan that is 10 x 4 inches (25 x 10 cm) with a removable bottom and inner tube. These pans are also available in silicone models, but I haven't had success with this variety. Some angel food cake pans, like mine, come with short legs on the edges to hold the pan steady when inverted. If your pan doesn't have them, while the cake is baking, have a bottle (a beer bottle works well) or metal funnel ready in a level position on your counter to invert the cake while cooling.

Cake boards

Cake boards are an invaluable baking assistant, so I keep a few of these corrugated rounds (8-, 9-, and 10-inch/20, 23, and 25 cm) tucked away in the pantry. Slide them under cake layers to aid in frosting and decorating or use them to invert cakes. They also make for an easy, disposable transporter and server—not very elegant, but certainly practical.

Muffin tin foil and paper liners

Like their pan counterparts, liners for muffin tins are available in standard, mini, and jumbo sizes, as well as in colorful paper and foil. Keep some of each on hand; your recipe will specify which should be used.

Cookie sheets and half and quarter sheet pans

Cookie sheets and baking sheets are not the same thing! *Baking sheets* (known in the restaurant world and this cookbook as full, half, or quarter sheet pans) have four 1-inch (2.5 cm) high sides with rolled edges. *Cookie sheets* have one raised edge for easy handling in and out of the oven, and the remaining rimless edges allow for even heat circulation and uniform cooking. Choose both types made from heavy-duty, shiny (not dark) aluminum. Insulated cookie sheets are also readily available and help distribute heat to cookies and other baked goodies evenly.

Nonstick baking liners

These nonstick mats are made of silicone-coated fiberglass and used to line cookie sheets and pans to keep the baked goods from sticking. Heatproof up to 450°F (230°C), they come in many sizes and are sturdy and reusable. Use a damp, very slightly soapy paper towel to wipe down after using (especially when baking strong flavors), repeat if necessary, and layer with paper towels and stow flat. Note that they should not be used as a cutting surface.

Parchment

Indispensable in a baker's kitchen, parchment serves double duty as a top-notch assistant in rolling as well as baking dough (it's silicone-coated and can withstand oven temperatures up to 450°F/230°C). Parchment is available in rolls at the supermarket or flat sheets from restaurant- and paper-supply stores;

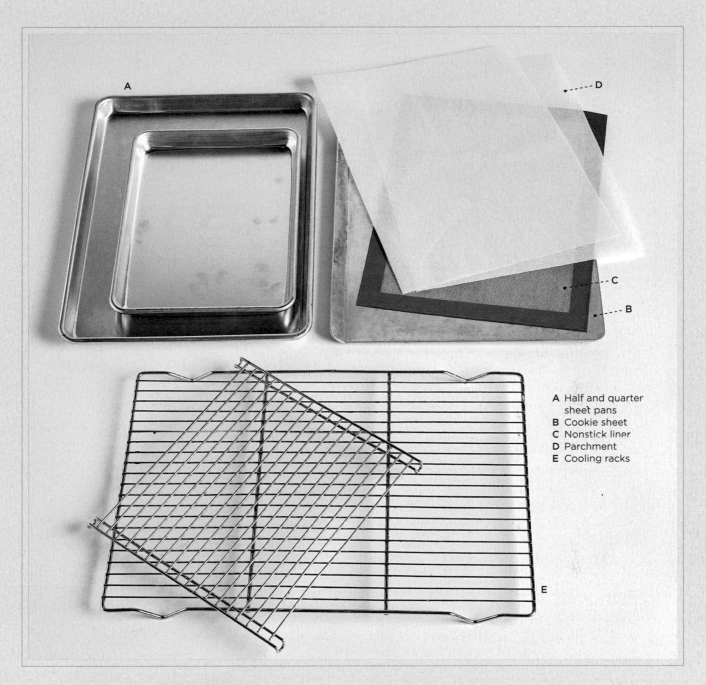

A Half and quarter
  sheet pans
B Cookie sheet
C Nonstick liner
D Parchment
E Cooling racks

I find the flat sheets the easiest to work with. I buy the full sheet pan size, stow them flat in the drawer below my oven, and cut to fit any pan as needed. Unless otherwise noted, for baking, parchment and silicone mats are interchangeable. P.S.: Waxed paper is not a substitute!

Cooling racks (small and large)

If I'm baking just one sheet of cookies or one small baking dish, I'll occasionally let my cold cooktop stand in as a cooling rack. But you can't always count on a cold cooktop or only needing room for one hot-from-the-oven item. When inverting cake layers, the cooktop can't help. I recommend two small and two large racks at the ready. If storage is an issue, go with two large ones and stow them in the oven when not in use. Sturdy metal racks are inexpensive and will last a lifetime.

Pie plates and tart pans

The backbone of pie and tart making begins with a 9¼-inch (23.5 cm) *fluted tart pan* with removable

A Fluted tart pan with removable bottom
B Pie plate
C Pie weights (beans) and foil

bottom and a *9-inch (23 cm) pie plate.* For the pie plate, I prefer Pyrex so I can visually gauge the browning of the crust and because it delivers consistent results. For blind-baking (partial and complete, see p. 51), you'll need foil and pie weights (I use a combination of dried beans and uncooked rice, but you can use one or the other interchangeably).

HAND TOOLS AND EQUIPMENT
Bowls

You'll use bowls of all sizes for every recipe, so keep at least one of each size—small, medium, and large—on hand. *Glass bowls,* like the nesting variety shown on the facing page, are great for mixing. If heatproof (check the label), they can go in the microwave, on top of gently simmering water, and in the dishwasher. *Metal bowls* are good, too. They're lighter weight than the glass but aren't microwave-safe. Stay away from plastic bowls, as they aren't as sturdy, they stain easily, and they can hold onto strong odors. *Ramekins* (small, medium, large) are great for *mise en place,* melting small amounts of butter or chocolate in the microwave, and are also used as baking vessels.

Scrapers

Rectangular bench scrapers are made of stainless steel with a sturdy wooden or plastic handle. You'll use them to scrape dough from the counter, cut dough into portions, and score or mark rolled dough into strips. A similarly shaped plastic version (I know it as a "corne," French for horn) has one straight side for scraping counters, smoothing frosting on a cake, or marking dough and one rounded side for scraping the inside of a bowl or scooping up batter. A more modern version of this tool, made by Oxo®, is smaller and sleeker but performs similar tasks.

Offset spatulas

Tuck a wide *offset silicone or nonstick spatula* in your drawer. You'll use it to flip pancakes and other items when cooking on a nonstick pan. Using a metal one will scrape and damage the surface. *Offset pie servers* are just the tool needed to lift up pieces of pie or cake for clean serving. The metal blade of an *offset spatula* jogs out from its handle at about a 45-degree angle and then continues out to a flat, dull blade. I have long and short as well as wide and narrow ones in my

A Glass bowls
B Metal bowls
C Ramekins

drawer. Nothing is better for spreading a soft dough, creamy filling, batter, frosting, or glaze.

Metal whisks

Keep a few thin-wired whisks with wooden or metal handles (the latter being more dishwasher safe than the former); you'll find that they are excellent multitaskers in a baker's kitchen. A *very small whisk* is ideal for whisking dry ingredients until well blended as well as combining wet ingredients in small vessels. *Small whisks* are perfect for mixing dry ingredients. *Medium-sized and elongated models* are excellent at whisking many things. The slightly pointy end gets into the bottom edges of a saucepan when making custards as well as serving a multitude of other purposes.

Cookie press and die plates

If you have an old cookie press languishing in your cabinet, it's probably because you find it frustrating to use. Treat yourself to a new one! The modern versions, like the one shown on p. 20, are much easier to use and with the right dough (see Anise Spritz cookies on p. 191), you'll be baking buttery, rich-flavored spritz cookies all year long.

Round wooden toothpicks

I keep them in their original box from the grocery store and use them for a number of baking purposes like testing cakes for doneness and decorating cookies.

Silicone pastry brush

I like the multi-layer of silicone bristles in the Oxo offset brush shown on p. 20. It spreads glaze or egg wash smoothly and easily and it's also dishwasher-safe.

Mini scoops

In many of my recipes, I ask you to portion dough using a 1-tablespoon, 2-tablespoon, or 3-tablespoon mini scoop. While this makes your cookies visually similar (pastry shop worthy), more importantly, it also means that they will bake up evenly and your yield will match mine. Using a mini scoop will also make quick and clean work of the task.

Spoons

When you need to mix, stir, scrape, and scoop, you'll reach for one of these: The Asian-inspired *Chinese skimmer,* also known as a spider skimmer or strainer, retrieves items from boiling water or hot oil. Available with a stainless or bamboo handle, it is interchange-

A Scrapers
B Nonstick spatula
C Offset pie server
D Small wide offset metal spatulas
E Small offset metal spatula
F Long offset metal spatula
G Metal whisks

H Cookie press and die plates
I Round wooden toothpicks
J Silicone pastry brush
K Mini scoops
L Chinese skimmer
M Silicone spatula
N Angled wooden spatula
O Ladle

P Slotted spoon
Q Long-handled spoon
R Handheld cherry pitter
S Citrus juicer
T Metal tongs
U Potato masher
V Fine-mesh medium sieve
W Fine-mesh mini sieve

able with a *slotted spoon.* A stainless *long-handled spoon* is one of the most all-purpose utensils in the baker's kitchen. I bet you already have one in your drawer.

Spatulas

You'll use a spatula for many tasks, from scraping batter from beaters and bowls to stirring a pot of pudding or custard. Long-handled *silicone spatulas* are the newest and most durable on the market. They are heatproof, unless otherwise labeled, up to 500°F/260°C. Other than my treasured rolling pin, an *angled wooden spatula* is the only wooden tool left in my arsenal. The straight bottom edge set on an angle can easily and efficiently scrape and glide across the bottom of a saucepan while getting into the bottom's edges, making it ideal for mixtures like puddings and custards that might burn easily on the bottom of the pan.

Ladle

While it's ideal to have a variety of ladle sizes, from small to large, you'll get the most use from a medium-sized one.

Handheld cherry pitter

There's nothing like the taste of fresh cherries, and I've captured their deliciousness in a couple of recipes (see pp. 320 and 577). Of course, you'll need to remove pits before using them, so invest in a handheld pitter; it's easy to use and quick to clean up (see p. 322).

Citrus juicer

Freshly squeezed juice can make all the difference in a recipe; plus, you won't get any of the preservatives from bottled varieties. Stow a citrus juicer in your drawer for quick work of juicing lemons, limes, and other citrus.

Metal tongs

I keep two sets of tongs in my drawer—one medium one to turn and flip everything from bacon to flat-breads, and one smaller set with wide rubber bands wrapped around the claws for a slip-proof grip (see p. 400).

Potato masher

A potato masher does more than just mash potatoes! Use this tool for mashing fruits, too.

Sieves

You'll use a sieve for more than rinsing fruit. A *fine-mesh medium sieve* will be put to work sifting dry ingredients and straining liquids. A *fine-mesh mini sieve* is great for sifting when garnishing desserts with confectioners' sugar and the like.

Pastry cutter

Use a pastry cutter with a fluted or plain blade to aid in cutting out pastry and dough. See p. 28 for more information.

Small paring knife

A key tool for scoring, marking, and cutting all types of doughs and pastries when rolling out. You'll use the tip as well as dull and sharp edges of this little knife.

Rulers

When it comes to baking, a ruler is your best friend. Using a ruler to measure your lengths, widths, and slices is the only way you'll know that your pan or pastry dough is the same size that's called for in the recipes and will ensure your results are similar to mine. I keep both a 12- and 20-inch (30.5 and 50 cm) and use them frequently.

Straight wooden rolling pin (non-tapered edges)

My pin of choice is a straight wooden cylinder without handles or slightly tapered ends. Before you purchase a new pin, make sure it's even with no warped spots. The best way to do so is to set the pin on a flat surface, get down to eye level, and roll the pin on the surface, making sure the pin evenly touches the surface without gaps all the way around. This might seem odd and you might feel awkward doing this, but baked results will be happy you did. To keep the wood's patina and smooth surface, use a slightly dampened towel to clean. If dough is stuck to the pin, rub with extra flour to release it (see p. 501). Resist washing a wooden pin and never scour.

Rolling pin bands

Rolling bands are silicone "bracelets" for a rolling pin. When positioned on the pin, they ensure you roll to an even thickness. The bands come in a variety of thicknesses. Position the bands 2 to 3 inches (5 to 7.5 cm) in from the ends of the rolling pin. (For more information, see p. 150.)

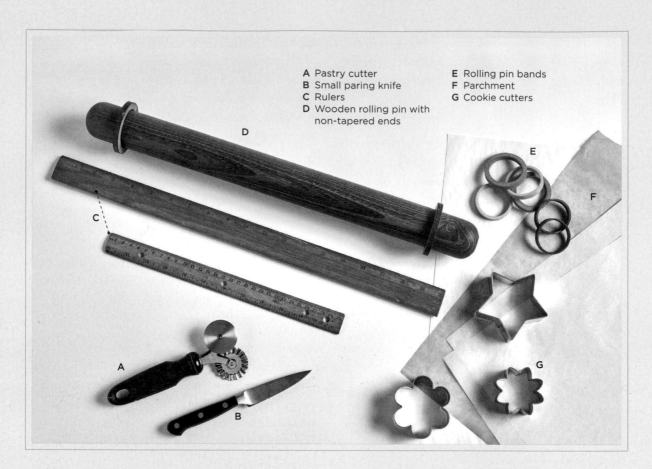

A Pastry cutter
B Small paring knife
C Rulers
D Wooden rolling pin with non-tapered ends
E Rolling pin bands
F Parchment
G Cookie cutters

Assorted cookie cutters

If you are new to baking, start with a set of graduated round cutters and grow your collection as inspiration and recipes warrant. I stow mine in a large (ok, very large) glass apothecary jar.

POWER TOOLS AND EQUIPMENT
Blender and food processor

It's close to impossible for me to choose between these two power tools. They both have a place in my kitchen. I use a ***blender*** for mixing thin batters (crêpes and popovers) and puréeing fruits and soups. That said, a ***food processor*** may be more versatile for a baker's kitchen. For the most flexibility, choose one that has a variety of work bowl sizes (my Cuisinart® has three: small, medium, and large) and blades. I use it to cut butter into flour, grind nuts, chop, and purée (though I think a blender does a better job with the latter task.)

Whenever I use either machine, I cover the top of the work bowl with plastic wrap before securing the lid. This way, the lid stays clean—no washing needed.

Electric mixers (handheld or stand)

Every baker needs one or the other, but you don't have to break the bank to get a good-quality model. If you have the counter space, I urge you to buy a ***freestanding mixer.*** While it was a significant initial investment, my KitchenAid® has been working hard for over 30 years. It comes with attachments (paddle, whisk, and dough hook); if you have that brand, I would urge you to purchase the flex-edge beater blade. Used in place of the paddle attachment, one side has a rubber blade that scrapes the bowl's bottom and sides when mixing. You'll still need to stop and scrape down the bowl sides and beater, but you will do it less often.

If a ***handheld mixer*** fits your space and budget restrictions, look for one with a comfortable handle, sturdy beater blades, and multiple speeds. I have a KitchenAid, but Cuisinart makes a great one as well.

Waffle iron

Another power tool in my baker's pantry is a good waffle iron. Mine is a single round one, but there are plenty of quality shapes, sizes, and brands available.

A Blender
B Food processor
C Stand mixer with attachments
D Handheld mixer
E Waffle iron

If you are looking for one that successfully cooks two at a time, try the Waring® Pro Double Waffle Maker.

Be sure to read the instructions and baking guidelines before you start cooking and be flexible with your timing and temperatures (if available) once you start cooking. As you and your waffle iron get to know each other, make some notes about amounts and timing in the margins of recipes here so that you'll remember for the next time.

MEASURING TOOLS
Kitchen scale

For the most accurate measuring of dry ingredients and portioning of doughs, I strongly urge you to have and use a scale. My Oxo has a flat surface to set a bowl or plate for weighing ingredients, a button to reset the scale to zero (tare), and measures in ⅛-oz. increments up to 5 pounds.

Measuring cups

For measuring liquids, use *glass* (Pyrex) and/or *plastic* (Oxo) measures. I keep a graduated set. Before using, double-check the accuracy of the lines on both by placing the measures, one at a time, on your scale, zeroing the scale, and filling with water to the 1-cup demarcation. If the line is accurate, it should weigh 8 oz. Oxo measures have the added bonus of lines marked on the sides as well as inside the cup. You'll want to double-check that both lines are accurate.

For those whom I haven't yet convinced that weighing ingredients is the easiest, most accurate, and consistent method of measuring ingredients, also have on hand a set of *metal measuring cups* (sized from ¼ to 1 cup). You can use them for measuring dry ingredients (see p. 5) and thicker creamy items like yogurt, crème fraîche, and mascarpone. They will also come in handy when portioning batter and dough.

I have two sets of standard graduated *measuring spoons* (sized from ⅛ tsp. to 1 Tbs.)—one for liquids and one for small amounts of dry ingredients like spices and leaveners. The elongated style fits easily into narrow spice jars.

Thermometers

Used to monitor the temperature of liquids in deep-frying (oil) and candy making (usually sugar syrup),

a *candy thermometer* attaches to the side of a pot with an adjustable clip. Before you use it in a recipe, check its accuracy. Fill a pan with 2 to 3 inches of water. Clip the thermometer to the side of a pan and adjust the probe so that it is in the middle of the water and not touching the bottom; bring the water to a boil. Once boiling, the reading should be 212°F (for sea level).

The same test can be done to check the accuracy of an *instant-read thermometer*, used to check the temp of finished baked goods. Dip the probe end of the instant-read thermometer into the same pan of boiling water. Again, it should read 212°F (for sea level). Make note of any inaccuracies and adjust your recipe temperature to reflect any differences.

Make sure you're cooling, freezing, and baking at the correct temps by investing in one thermometer each for the *fridge, freezer, and oven*. Be warned that just because you have your fridge, freezer, or oven set to a certain temperature, it doesn't mean that it's accurate. In all cases, especially your oven, this can have a major impact on your timing and, worse, results. Set one in the middle, away from the door, of your fridge, freezer, and heated oven and check back in 15 to 20 minutes. Adjust your temperatures up or down as needed. You can also have your appliances calibrated professionally. (For more, see Take the Temperature of Your Oven, Fridge, and Freezer, on p. 30.)

POTS AND PANS

Obviously you'll need various pots and pans when baking, as much a staple in your kitchen as flour and sugar. Here are the pieces I recommend, as well as those you'll need for recipes in this book:

> Dutch oven (5-quart)

> Medium saucepan (with lid)

> Medium stainless steel skillet

> Nonstick skillets (ovenproof, in both small and large sizes)

> Large cast iron skillet

> Double griddle

> Small saucepan (with lid)

> Large straight-sided skillet (with lid)

A Kitchen scale
B Glass measuring cups
C Plastic measuring cups
D Metal measuring cups
E Measuring spoons
F Candy thermometer
G Instant-read thermometer
H Fridge/freezer/oven thermometer

A 5-quart Dutch oven
B Medium saucepan with lid
C Medium stainless steel skillet
D Nonstick skillets
E Cast iron skillet
F Double griddle
G Small saucepan with lid
H Large straight-sided skillet with lid

A Cutting board
B Large chef's knife
C Long serrated knife
D Hollow-blade slicing knife
E 9-inch utility knife
F Short serrated knife
G Small paring knife
H Kitchen shears/scissors
I U-shaped peeler
J Box grater
K Handheld Microplane zester
L Zester/channel knife
M Melon baller
N Pizza wheel
O Pastry cutter
P Pastry blender

KNIVES AND OTHER TOOLS FOR CUTTING

Cutting board

Have a large and small cutting board on hand. I prefer the silicone, skid-proof types, as they stay put when being used and are dishwasher-safe. If you have wooden boards, you can make them skid-proof by placing a folded damp paper towel underneath. If the board still wiggles, double up on the paper towels.

Knives

Yup, even bakers need a few good knives. I suggest you stow these in your drawer or block and keep them sharp. A dull knife causes more injuries than a sharp one, and it will only slow your work. I take my knives to my local butcher when they need a new edge or just a quick professional sharpening.

> Large chef's knife, for chopping and prepping veggies and fruit

> Long serrated knife, for slicing bread and cutting cake

> Hollow-blade slicing knife, for slicing and chopping fruits and veggies

> 9-inch utility knife, my go-to knife for heating to use for slicing and serving desserts

> Short serrated knife, ideal for slicing small breads and cakes

> Small paring knife, my go-to knife for marking rolled-out dough and pastry

> Kitchen shears/scissors, great for everything from opening packages to snipping herbs

> U-shaped (sometimes called a Y-shaped) peeler with a swivel ceramic blade, with an almost ever-sharp blade, this peeler affords the greatest control over veggies and fruit; it's also great for creating chocolate curls (see p. 381)

Graters

The traditional multi-sided box grater works well for shredding (coarse or fine) cheese as well as carrots, squash, and other veggies.

Handheld Microplane® zester

While they come in a variety of shapes and sizes, I like a wide, stainless steel blade with very small and extremely sharp holes or rasps for finely grating citrus zest or fresh ginger. A rubber-coated grip keeps this very sharp tool in control. See p. 138 for how to use.

Zester/channel knife

This is a nifty little two-in-one tool for zesting citrus. The top has small holes for scraping citrus zest into very thin strips, and the single notch on the side (the channel) is great for thicker, longer zests to use as garnishes (see p. 138). It has a comfortable round, slip-proof handle and is dishwasher safe.

Melon baller

I use a melon baller to scoop out the cores from peeled and halved apples and pears. It takes out only the core, leaving behind all the fruit.

Pizza wheel

Large and in charge, this round-bladed wheel cuts pizza in a jiff and, in a pinch, can substitute for a plain-blade pastry wheel.

Pastry cutter

This fun little gadget has two cutting blades—plain or fluted—and makes quick work of cutting dough or pastry into strips or shapes. The fluted blade should only be used for pie dough (see p. 326), as it will compress the layers of rough puff pastry or other laminated, flaky dough.

Pastry blender

This horseshoe-shaped tool has a straight handle and curved, parallel tines and is great for cutting butter into flour if you don't own a food processor. Hold it with both hands, as you'll need to chop the butter into the flour until you get pieces the size called for in your recipe. (For how to use this tool, see p. 502.)

COOKIE DECORATING

Beginning bakers and cookie decorators will want to start with a small selection of cookie decorating items. Add the following to your collection as your interest and needs develop.

> Gel food coloring
> Round wooden toothpicks (to help move royal icing)
> Disposable clear plastic pastry bags
> Various pastry tips
> Couplers (to attach small tips to a pastry bag; large tips don't need them to fit comfortably in the bag)
> Squeeze bottles (small and medium-sized)

SPECIALTY TOOLS

Cast iron molds

Available in various shapes and sizes, most models are preseasoned, making them virtually nonstick.

Popover pan

Popovers puff up best when baked in a proper popover pan. The deep cups give the batter plenty of room to climb up and rise to form beautiful crowning domes. These pans have a dark, nonstick finish and are available with 6 standard or 12 miniature cups.

Donut pan

I try to avoid using highly specialized baking pans, but nothing bakes up small donuts quite as well as this little gem of a pan. It has a dark, nonstick finish and is available with 6 standard or 12 miniature donut molds.

PIZZA AND BREAD MAKING GEAR

When a crusty finish is what you are looking for when baking up pizza or bread, here are two essential tools you'll need for success:

Baking Steel® and baking stone

New to the pizza and bread baking game, a *Baking Steel* is heavy and extremely durable. It is super heat-conductive and, because it's made of steel, the company even suggests that you turn on your broiler for a few minutes to crisp the top of the pizza. I've tested the bread and pizza recipes with both the Baking Steel and traditional *ceramic baking stones* employing traditional methods. Both produced wonderful results.

A Gel food coloring
B Round wooden toothpicks
C Disposable clear plastic
    pastry bags
D Pastry tips
E Couplers
F Squeeze bottles

Wooden peel

A wooden peel coaxes the dough into and out of the oven, keeping your hands a healthy distance from the heated stone. In a pinch, you can use an inverted cookie sheet, but a peel is much more effective.

Pasta roller

Not just for pasta making, you'll use this machine for rolling cracker dough into even, paper-thin sheets. Available in hand-crank models like the one on the facing page, an attachment for the KitchenAid stand mixer is also available, as shown.

Create a Foundation for Success

Over the years I've learned some important points to help make baking—or any type of cooking for that matter—a successful and fun time.

BEFORE STARTING, GAUGE YOUR AVAILABLE TIME

The last thing you want is to be halfway through baking a cake before having to pick up the kids. Before diving full speed into a recipe, make sure you choose one based on the time you have available. Trying to squeeze too much into a limited time will only make you feel crazed and your results will suffer. There are plenty of recipes that can be made simply and quickly. For those time-pressed bakers or those that want or need to plan ahead, take a look at the Make Ahead section of each recipe where I've broken down the recipe, when possible, into manageable steps.

READ THE RECIPE, THEN READ IT TWO MORE TIMES

While reading a new recipe three times before you begin baking might sound like overkill, it's crucial to your baking success. The first read-through will give you a feel for how long the recipe will take. Don't forget to read the Make Ahead section to help you break the recipe into manageable steps, if needed. Grab a pencil and paper for the second read-through and jot down the ingredients and equipment you will need. You might need to run to the store before rolling up your baking sleeves. For your final read, pay close attention to the directions and look up any techniques

that are new to you (see the cross-references in the recipe) or ones that you might want to brush up on.

FOLLOW THE RECIPE

Until you are very familiar with a recipe, please follow the recipe exactly as I have written it. This sounds simplistic and fundamental, but you'd be shocked by the amount of emails I receive regarding recipes that home bakers have followed "exactly" only to uncover that a step had been overlooked, an ingredient substituted or omitted entirely, or a different pan or mold used.

THAT SAID, MAKE THE RECIPE YOUR OWN

Once you've made the recipe exactly as directed a few times, play around with it to make it your own. In the Twists section of each recipe, I offer a few options for switching up the flavor combinations and/or size and shape of the recipe. From there, feel free to experiment with your own ideas, keeping in mind that the base of the recipe—flour, butter, liquid amount (the type of liquid can sometimes be changed), and leaveners—are best kept the same; otherwise, the balance or chemistry of the ingredients can be thrown off.

If you're new to baking, start with simple substitutions or additions. Adding nuts instead of chopped chocolate to a batter or swapping lemon zest for vanilla extract are good starting points.

TAKE THE TEMPERATURE OF YOUR OVEN, FRIDGE, AND FREEZER

Sadly, all appliances are not created equal. Because temperatures are so important in baking, it's not enough to trust the digital read-out on your oven. Place a thermometer (preferable mercury filled) in the center of your oven, heat the oven, and check the temp occasionally to be sure it's in sync. Adjust the controls as needed until the temp on the thermometer is accurate. You can also have your oven tested by a service repairperson and recalibrated if necessary. Burt from All American Appliance tests my ovens regularly.

Keep an eye out for hot spots in your oven. Those pockets are hotter than other areas in your oven and can cause overcooking and even burning. No repairman (even Burt) can fix them, so you'll need to rotate your pans about halfway through the baking time.

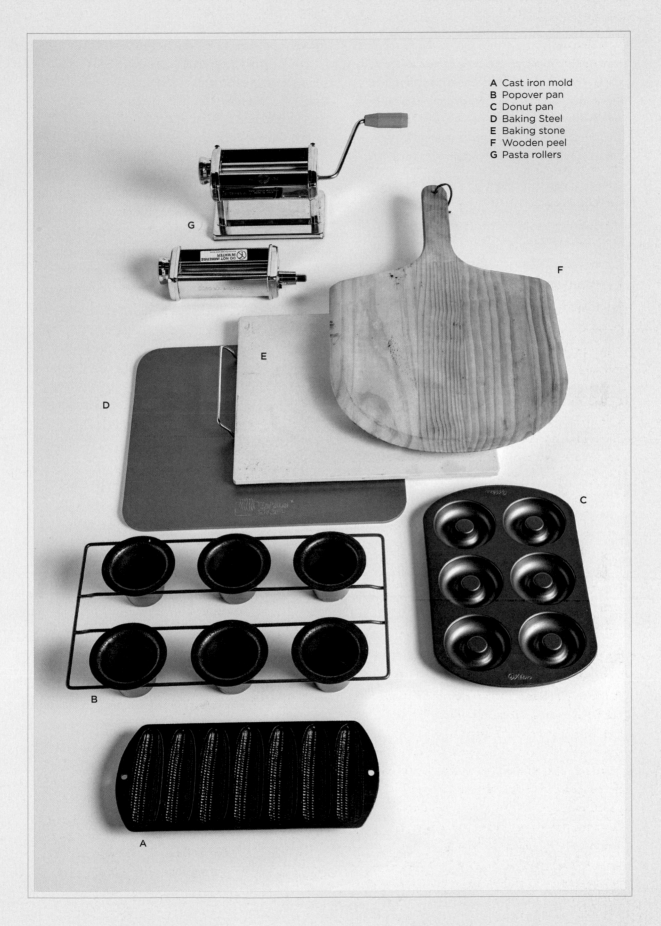

A Cast iron mold
B Popover pan
C Donut pan
D Baking Steel
E Baking stone
F Wooden peel
G Pasta rollers

Fridge and freezer temps should also be monitored to make sure your perishables hold well and so that your recipes chill and/or freeze in about the same time frame as mine. Place a thermometer away from the door and in the center of the fridge and freezer. The temperature in the fridge should be 38°F and the freezer 0°F. If not, adjust the controls accordingly.

SUBSCRIBE TO THE RITUAL OF *MISE EN PLACE*

Have you ever made a stir-fry? If so, you know how important it is to have all the ingredients prepared and measured before you start cooking. The same holds true for baking. *Mise en place*—French for "put in place"—is the process of organizing and prepping your ingredients (and equipment too) so that you are 100% sure you have everything and can work through the recipe smoothly and efficiently.

WHISK DRY INGREDIENTS TO COMBINE

The majority of my recipes begin with whisking all the dry ingredients together in a bowl until well blended. While this seems easy enough, I can't emphasize enough how important it is to disperse the leaveners, flavoring, and salt throughout the flour so that the batter will be evenly flavored and rise properly. The trick is to use a small whisk (see p. 20) and fold the ingredients beginning from the center and moving outward toward the edge of the bowl, dragging the outer ingredients toward the center and vice versa.

Here's a good test: Imagine you have a bowl of flour with a pile of cocoa powder in the center. To combine completely, you'll not only need to stir the bottom of the bowl with the whisk, but also to use the whisk to fold or pull in the flour from the edge and continue whisking until there are no streaks of cocoa and flour (see p. 570).

SCRAPE THE BOWL AND BEATERS

Whether you are mixing using a stand mixer, electric handheld mixer, or spoon, some of the batter inevitably splatters against the sides of the bowl. In order to combine the ingredients thoroughly, it's important to occasionally stop mixing and scrape the batter from the beater (especially if you are using a paddle attachment) and the sides of the bowl (see p. 289).

BAKE ONE SHEET AT A TIME FOR EVEN RESULTS

For greater control and more consistent results, bake one sheet at a time. That said, there are times when you might need to hurry things along. For those times, arrange one rack in the upper third and one in the lower third of the oven. Halfway through baking, rotate the pans (front to back) and swap their positions on the racks and continue baking. Keep in mind that you'll most likely add more baking time, as the oven temp drops considerably when the door is open.

For those of you who have ovens with convection options, you can bake several sheets at one time by setting the racks in the upper third, center, and lower third of the oven and adjusting the temperature down by 25°F (-3.6°C). For baking times, begin by reducing it by 25% and, as always, use the doneness tests (see below) as your guide and make a note of the timing in the margin of your recipe. Most convection baking will not require that pans be turned and repositioned, but if uneven baking is problematic, simply swap the pans halfway through baking.

CHECK DONENESS TESTS AND TIME FRAMES

In all my recipes, I give you sensory clues, known as doneness tests, along with a suggested time frame to help you gauge when a recipe is done cooking, baking, or chilling. While the time frame is helpful, it is not definitive and should be used as a general guide. I can't emphasize this enough: the time frame is only there to steer you in the right direction. It is not the rule. I have given you a baker's roadmap to success, but it's you and you alone who is smelling, tasting, touching, and looking at what you are making. Using the doneness clues, engage and trust your senses to determine when the recipe is ready.

MAKE NOTES IN THE MARGINS—I DO!

When I'm baking and cooking, I use those side margins in magazines and cookbooks (not just mine) to make note of all kinds of info that will come in handy the next time around. I jot down the date I've made it along with additional doneness tests, time changes, and ingredient sub-ins as well as notes about serving and ideas for future revisits. I encourage you to follow suit. Not only will these notes help you the next time around, but you will also begin to tell your own story through these musings.

FOLLOW PROPER MEASURING FOR CONSISTENT, SUCCESSFUL RESULTS

For the most successful and consistent results, how you measure dry ingredients (flours and sugars, especially) is critical. It's important that all measurements are accurate. If you measure by volume, the weight of 1 cup of flour can vary by as much as 2 oz. depending on the method you use (dip-and-sweep or spoon-and-sweep; more below). That's a huge swing in any recipe and can make pie dough crumbly and dry or wet and pasty. All my recipes are based on flour being measured by weight with a baseline of 1 cup unbleached all-purpose flour weighing 4½ oz.

If you don't use a scale, use the spoon-and-sweep method for all dry ingredients except for granulated sugar (you can dip and sweep—it will weigh the same) and brown sugars (firmly packed is a must for consistency). Here's how: Stir the flour (or cornstarch or confectioner's sugar) in the container, lightly spoon into the appropriate metal measuring cup—no scooping, packing, or tapping—and sweep off the excess with a flat edge (a ruler, knife, or spatula handle).

USE A SCALE

While I have given volume measurements in all of the recipes, I also include weight measurements (in ounces as well as grams) for the flour as well as all the ingredients so you can easily adopt the weighing technique. For the most consistent and successful results, I urge (implore) you to buy a digital kitchen scale (see p. 25) as it is important to ensure accurate measurements. Digital scales are inexpensive and easy to use. Simply put your bowl on the scale, press the tare button so the scale registers zero, and then spoon in your ingredients until the scale reads the appropriate weight. To add other ingredients, keep the bowl on the scale and return your scale to zero by pressing the tare button between each addition.

SOFTEN BUTTER, DON'T MELT IT

Many of my recipes call for butter to be softened to a malleable state so that the batter aerates and mixes together properly. Straight from the fridge, your butter will be too hard and, as some recipes instruct, "room temperature" butter will be too soft, as kitchen temperatures vary greatly. If you haven't been able to plan ahead and your butter is still cold from the fridge, use the microwave, but use it judiciously. Put the wrapped butter on a plate and microwave in short 5-second blasts, turning and rotating, until the butter is soft enough to give slightly when pressed with a finger. If you've gone too far, start again with a fresh stick.

SEPARATE EGGS WHEN THEY'RE COLD

While it's easiest to separate the egg whites when the eggs are cold, they get the most volume when at room temperature. So, separate first and then warm to room temp before beating. Tap the eggshell against the rim of a small bowl or ramekin. Working over the bowl, separate the shell into two halves, being careful to keep the yolk in one half. Pass the yolk from shell to shell, allowing the white to drop into the bowl (see p. 371). Put the yolk and white in separate mixing bowls. Using the same method, separate any remaining eggs over an empty bowl or ramekin before adding to the mixing bowl to avoid any yolk contamination.

BEAT EGG WHITES WITH CLEAN TOOLS

Impeccably clean beaters and a stainless steel or glass bowl are a must for beating egg whites—even a touch of grease makes whites unbeatable. To ensure that my bowls and beaters are spotless, after cleaning with warm soapy water, I pour a good splash of white distilled vinegar into the bowl along with some fresh water (it should smell vinegary), add the beaters, and swish the water around the bowl a few times. Rinse and dry well with a clean dishtowel.

Beat slowly at first, until the whites are foamy, then gradually increase the speed and proceed as directed in the recipe. Be careful not to overbeat or the whites will be dry and possibly deflate.

TOAST NUTS TO DEEPEN THEIR FLAVOR

Always toast nuts when directed, as it heightens their flavor. Heat the oven to 350°F (180°C/gas 4). Spread the nuts on a quarter or half sheet pan in an even layer. Bake, stirring once or twice, until golden brown and fragrant, 7 to 12 minutes (depending on the size and variety). Let cool completely before using.

Chapter 2

MORNING FOOD

> > > >

Individual Roasted Carrot Jalapeño Soufflés

Serves 6

I've been serving this soufflé every Thanksgiving for as long as I can remember. For those harboring soufflé anxieties, let me put you at ease. First off, making the base of the soufflé is similar to making pudding; it comes together easily and can be done days—yes, days—in advance. Make sure the base is well seasoned with plenty of salt and pepper, fresh lemon juice, and as much spicy jalapeño as you like before stowing it in the fridge. This way, you aren't tasting with the raw egg yolks, and all that is left to do is whip the whites and fold them in (just like making the Classic Strawberry Mousse on p. 405). Go ahead—you can do it!

Nonstick cooking spray or softened butter, for preparing the ramekins
16 oz. (454 g) carrots, peeled and cut into uniform pieces about ½ to ¾ inch (12 mm to 2 cm) thick and about 1½ inches (4 cm) long
1 Tbs. olive oil

Kosher salt and freshly ground black pepper
1 cup (240 ml) whole milk + more as needed
3 Tbs. (1½ oz./42 g) unsalted butter, cut into 3 pieces
5 Tbs. unbleached all-purpose flour
2 Tbs. thinly sliced fresh chives
½ to 1 tsp. granulated sugar

2 tsp. freshly squeezed lemon juice + more to taste
1 to 2 tsp. minced jalapeño (see p. 83)
4 yolks from large eggs (see p. 371)
5 whites (5 oz./142 g) from large eggs, at room temperature

Make the carrot purée

1. Position a rack in the center of the oven and heat the oven to 425°F (220°C/gas 7). Put the carrot pieces, oil, and a pinch of salt and pepper in an 8-inch (20 cm) square baking dish and toss until evenly coated. Spread in an even layer and bake, turning once or twice, until the carrots are golden brown and tender when pierced with a knife, 25 to 35 minutes, depending on the size of the pieces. Move the baking dish to a rack and let cool slightly. Leave the oven on.

2. Put the carrots and milk into a blender and process until smooth, scraping down the sides once or twice. Scrape into a 2-cup (480 ml) glass measure and add enough milk to make 2 cups (480 ml).

Make the soufflés

1. Lightly grease six 6-oz. (180 ml) ramekins (3½ inches wide x 1⅔ inches high; 9 cm x 4.2 cm) and arrange on a quarter or half sheet pan.

2. Whisk the butter in a medium saucepan over medium heat until melted and bubbling. Add the flour and cook, whisking constantly, until smooth, bubbling, and pale golden brown, about 2 minutes. Pour in the carrot–milk mixture and continue cooking, whisking constantly, until very thick and boiling. Cook, whisking constantly for 1 minute, then slide the pan off the heat and scrape the mixture into a large bowl. Add the chives, sugar, lemon juice, jalapeño, and salt and pepper to taste and whisk

MAKE AHEAD

The carrot mixture can be prepared, covered, and refrigerated for up to 2 days before bringing to room temperature and adding the egg yolks and beaten whites.

BAKER'S WISDOM

Buying carrots

The soufflés' flavor relies heavily on the carrots. Save those dry-looking, beefy carrots for the horses and reach for the sweeter ones with the greens still attached. Buy a test bunch in advance of your soufflé making or, better yet, ask for a sample—the flavor should be sweet and bright and the texture crispy. Roasting the carrots adds extra sweetness as well as an earthy, potato-like flavor. I think it's worth the extra effort, but if you are short on time, I've given directions for boiling as well (see Twists on p. 36).

(Carrot Jalapeño Soufflés continued)

TWISTS

Flavor swap

> Instead of the whole milk, use the same amount of carrot juice.

> Instead of the jalapeño, add 1½ to 2 tsp. minced fresh ginger.

> Instead of roasting the carrots, boil them. Put the carrot pieces in a medium saucepan, cover with about 1 inch (2.5 cm) of water, and add a big pinch of salt. Bring to a boil over high heat, reduce the heat to medium, and boil until the carrots are tender when pierced with the tip of a knife, 8 to 12 minutes. Drain well and set aside to cool slightly before proceeding with the recipe.

You'll need less additional milk to total 2 cups (480 ml), as boiled carrots will retain more of their liquid than roasted carrots. Purée the carrots with a little milk, measure, and add more if needed.

until blended. Taste and adjust seasonings as needed. The flavors should be prominent as they will soften with the addition of the yolks and whites. Add the egg yolks and whisk until well blended.

3. Put the egg whites in a clean bowl. Beat with an electric handheld mixer fitted with wire beaters on medium speed until the whites are frothy, 30 to 45 seconds. Increase the speed to medium high and beat until the whites form medium-firm peaks, 2 to 3 minutes.

For more about beating egg whites, see p. 212.

4. Scoop about one-quarter of the whites into the carrot mixture and, using a silicone spatula, gently stir until blended to lighten the mixture. Add the remaining whites and gently fold in until just blended. Ladle evenly into the ramekins. Discard any excess batter. Using a small offset spatula, smooth the tops and run your thumb around the inside rim to help a "hat" form while baking (see the Essential Technique below). Bake until puffed and browned, 14 to 16 minutes. Move the pan to a rack, then use rubber band–coated tongs to carefully move the ramekins to serving plates and serve immediately.

For more about folding, see p. 270.

For more about using rubber band–coated tongs, see p. 400.

ESSENTIAL TECHNIQUE

Fill the ramekins and make a "hat"

A Ladle the soufflé mixture into the ramekins, portioning it evenly among them. Don't worry if the edges get messy—they'll be cleaned up later.

B Smooth the tops of the ramekins using a small offset spatula. Be sure the ramekins are filled to the rim. Wipe all around the outsides with a paper towel to remove excess, which will burn while baking if left on the ramekin.

C Working with one filled ramekin at a time, hold the sides with one hand and use the thumb of your other hand to form a "hat" by running your thumb around the inside of the rim. This "hat" will help the soufflés puff during baking.

Zesty Lemon Artichoke Frittata

Serves 4 to 6

Satisfying morning, noon, and night, a frittata is an Italian version of an omelet or crustless quiche. It's easy to prepare and adapt to whatever my fridge and cupboard hold. For this version, I use canned artichoke hearts brightened with lemon juice for a zesty flavor along with scallions, fresh herbs, and mozzarella and Parmigiano cheeses. Once you've made this recipe a few times, feel free to swap in your own ingredients.

For lunch and dinner, I serve wedges alongside an herb-filled green salad with a light vinaigrette (see the recipe on p. 40). This big frittata can also be cut into bite-sized squares and served as a crowd-pleasing appetizer, warm or at room temperature.

1 can (14 oz./397 g) quartered artichokes, rinsed and drained
8 large eggs
¾ cup (180 ml) half-and-half or whole milk
1 Tbs. Dijon mustard
2 tsp. Worcestershire sauce
Few drops of hot sauce + more to taste

Table salt and freshly ground black pepper
3 Tbs. olive oil, divided
⅓ cup (¾ oz./20 g) chopped scallions, white and most of the green part
1 tsp. minced garlic
2 Tbs. chopped fresh basil
2 Tbs. chopped fresh flat-leaf parsley

1 Tbs. freshly squeezed lemon juice + more to taste
¾ cup (3 oz./85 g) shredded mozzarella cheese (fresh or packaged)
⅓ cup (1⅜ oz./39 g) ground Parmigiano Reggiano cheese, divided (see p. 38)

1. Position a rack in the center of the oven and heat the oven to 375°F (190°C/gas 5). Spread the rinsed artichokes onto a paper towel–lined plate, cover with more paper towels, and press to get rid of excess water. Scrape the artichokes onto a cutting board and coarsely chop.

2. Put the eggs, half-and-half, mustard, Worcestershire, hot sauce, ¾ tsp. salt, and a good pinch of black pepper in a medium bowl and whisk until well blended.

3. Pour 1 Tbs. of the oil in a 10-inch (25 cm) ovenproof nonstick skillet and cook over medium heat until hot but not smoking. Add the chopped artichokes, scallions, garlic, and a pinch each of salt and pepper and cook, stirring frequently with a silicone spatula, until fragrant and heated through, about 3 minutes. Slide the pan off the heat, add the basil, parsley, and lemon juice and stir until blended. Taste and adjust the seasonings as needed—the mixture should be lemony and well seasoned. Scrape onto a plate.

4. Reduce the heat to medium low, add the remaining 2 Tbs. oil, and, using a spatula, nudge and loosen any nubbins that may have stuck to the pan. Swirl the pan to coat with the oil, give the egg mixture a quick whisking, and pour into the skillet. Scatter the artichoke mixture, mozzarella, and ¼ cup (1 oz./28 g) of the Parmigiano over the top.

(continued)

MAKE AHEAD

> The artichoke mixture and egg mixture can be prepared and stowed separately in the refrigerator for up to 1 day.

> Leftovers can be covered and refrigerated for up to 2 days; reheat in the skillet, microwave, or oven until a fork inserted in the center comes out warm to the touch.

BAKER'S WISDOM

Caring for nonstick pans

The coating on the inside of nonstick pans is fragile and needs to be protected. To avoid scratches, use only silicone spatulas and utensils—avoid using anything metal. To clean the pans, use only nonabrasive sponges and a mild detergent. Once dry, I line the inside of my nonstick pans with paper towels before stacking.

(Lemon Artichoke Frittata continued)

TWISTS

Flavor swap

> Instead of the mozzarella, use the same amount of shredded pepper Jack or sharp Cheddar cheese.

> Instead of the artichokes, add 1½ cups coarsely chopped roasted vegetables or diced ham to the scallions and garlic. Omit the lemon juice.

Cook, giving the mixture a few stirs in the beginning to distribute the ingredients, until the eggs are just barely set around the edges but still very loose in the center, 2 to 4 minutes (see the Essential Technique below).

5. Sprinkle the remaining Parmigiano over the frittata, then slide the skillet into the oven and bake until the frittata is puffed, browned around the edges, and firm in the center when gently pressed, 22 to 25 minutes. Let cool for 10 minutes (just enough time to dress and toss a salad), then run a silicone spatula between the frittata and the pan to loosen, slide onto a serving plate, and cut into wedges.

For more about removing the frittata, see p. 40.

For more about removing the frittata, see p. 40.

ESSENTIAL TECHNIQUE

Assembling and cooking a frittata

A Once the egg mixture is in the skillet, scatter the artichoke mixture evenly over the top.

B Scatter the mozzarella and some of the Parmigiano evenly over the top of the artichoke mixture, then use a silicone spatula to gently stir in the ingredients to distribute them evenly throughout the eggs.

C The frittata is ready for the oven when the eggs are just barely set around the edges but still very loose in the center. You will be able to see the difference in color and texture.

Grinding Parmesan cheese

The weight of a volume measure of grated Parmesan will depend on what method you use to grate it. 2 oz. (57 g) Parmesan cheese coarsely ground in a food processor will be nubby and compact (far left) and give you a volume measure of ½ cup. However, if you use a microplane or rasp-style grater to grate the same amount of cheese, you'll end up with a light, fluffy pile (near left) with a volume measure of almost 2 cups. For my recipes, I prefer the ground method, but either grating method will work as long as you use the weight as your guide.

Mushroom Chicken Sausage Frittata

Serves 2 to 3

Similar to the larger Artichoke Frittata (see p. 37), this smaller version finds its way to my breakfast, lunch, or dinner plate especially when I'm looking at an almost empty fridge or I'm short on preparation time. It's the ideal size for two served with a simple tossed salad with an easy vinaigrette (see p. 40) or even when it's just me. I'll slide any leftovers into the fridge and happily reheat and enjoy the following day.

4 large eggs
½ cup (120 ml) half-and-half or whole milk
1 tsp. Worcestershire sauce
Few drops of hot sauce + more to taste
Coarse salt and freshly ground black pepper
2 Tbs. olive oil, divided

3 oz. (85 g) chicken breakfast sausage, halved lengthwise and cut into ½-inch (12 mm) pieces (about ¾ cup)
2 medium button, cremini, or shiitake mushrooms, thinly sliced
1 Tbs. finely chopped shallots
1 tsp. minced garlic

1 Tbs. dry sherry (optional)
⅓ cup (2⅜ oz./67 g) cooked orzo or other small or medium pasta
⅔ cup (2⅝ oz./74 g) coarsely shredded Cheddar cheese
2 Tbs. ground Parmigiano Reggiano cheese, divided (see p. 38)

1. Position a rack in the center of the oven and heat the oven to 375°F (190°C/gas 5). Put the eggs, half-and-half, Worcestershire, hot sauce, ½ tsp. salt, and a good pinch of black pepper in a medium bowl and whisk until well blended.

2. Put 1 Tbs. of the oil in an 8-inch (20 cm) ovenproof, nonstick skillet and cook over medium heat until hot but not smoking. Add the sausage and mushrooms and cook, stirring frequently with a silicone spatula, until the mushrooms are lightly browned and the sausage is barely cooked, 3 to 4 minutes. Add the shallots, garlic, a pinch or two of salt and black pepper and cook, stirring, until fragrant, about 1 minute. Taste and adjust the seasonings as needed. Sprinkle the sherry over the mixture and gently shake the pan. The liquid will evaporate almost immediately. Scrape the mixture onto a plate.

3. Reduce the heat to low, add the remaining 1 Tbs. oil, and, using a spatula, nudge and loosen any nubbins stuck to the pan. Swirl the pan to coat with the oil, give the egg mixture a quick whisking, and pour into the skillet. Scatter the sausage mixture, cooked pasta, Cheddar, and 1 Tbs. of the Parmigiano over the top. Cook, giving the mixture a few stirs in the beginning to distribute the ingredients, until the eggs are set around the edges but still very loose in the center, 3 to 4 minutes.

For more about assembling and cooking a frittata, see the facing page.

4. Sprinkle the remaining Parmigiano over the frittata, then slide the skillet into the oven and bake until the frittata is puffed, browned around the edges, and firm in the center when gently pressed, 12 to 15 minutes. Let cool for 5 minutes, then run a silicone spatula between the frittata and the pan to loosen, slide onto a serving plate, and cut into wedges.

(continued)

MAKE AHEAD

> The sausage mixture and the egg mixture can be prepared and stowed separately in the refrigerator for up to 1 day before proceeding.

> The frittata is best served warm. If you're not serving within 1 hour, let cool completely, cover the skillet, and refrigerate for up to 1 day; reheat in the skillet or oven until a fork inserted in the center is warm to the touch.

TWISTS

Flavor swap

> Instead of the sausage and mushrooms, add the following to the shallot and garlic: 3 oz. (85 g) thickly sliced pancetta, chopped; ¼ lb. (113 g) asparagus, trimmed and cut into 1-inch (2.5 cm) pieces; and ½ tsp. chopped fresh thyme.

> **Spicy:** Instead of the Cheddar, use the same amount of shredded pepper Jack cheese; instead of the chicken sausage, use the same amount of chorizo.

BAKER'S WISDOM
Easy vinaigrette

For a quick and versatile vinaigrette, whisk 2 Tbs. vinegar (balsamic or red or white wine), 1½ tsp. Dijon mustard, ½ tsp. minced garlic, ¾ tsp. kosher salt, and several grinds of black pepper in a small bowl until blended. Whisking constantly, add 6 Tbs. olive oil in a slow and steady stream until completely blended. Taste and adjust the seasonings as desired.

ESSENTIAL TECHNIQUE

Removing the frittata from the pan

Let the frittata cool for about 5 minutes when it comes out of the oven, then run the edge of a silicone spatula between the frittata and pan to loosen it.

Slide the spatula under the frittata and guide the frittata onto a serving plate.

Baked Double Chocolate Donuts

Serves 6

Biting into a warm, intensely chocolate donut is a happy and satisfying way to begin any day. Because this recipe makes just six small donuts, the overindulging risk is minimized. Donut lovers, you are welcome!

The batter whips up easily while the oven heats up, pipes evenly into the pan with little fuss and mess with the help of a handy zip-top bag, and bakes to perfection in about 12 minutes. Although the recipe requires a specialty pan, the baked results are well worth the small investment for this inexpensive and easy-to-store pan.

If you are a donut perfectionist, cut out any extra cake clogging the center of the baked donut to create a more visible center hole. The extras make a great chef's nibbler.

For the donuts

Nonstick cooking spray or
softened butter, for preparing
the pan

⅔ cup (3 oz./85 g) unbleached
all-purpose flour

¼ cup (¾ oz./20 g)
unsweetened natural cocoa
powder, sifted if lumpy

½ cup (3½ oz./99 g)
granulated sugar

1 tsp. baking powder

⅛ tsp. baking soda

½ tsp. table salt

½ cup (4 oz./113 g) sour cream,
at room temperature

1 large egg, at room temperature

1 tsp. pure vanilla extract

⅓ cup (2 oz./57 g) finely
chopped milk or bittersweet
chocolate

4 Tbs. (2 oz./57 g) unsalted
butter, melted and cooled

For the glaze

½ cup (2 oz./57 g) confectioners'
sugar, sifted if lumpy

2 Tbs. heavy cream + more
as needed

Colored sprinkles (optional)

Make the donuts

1. Position a rack in the center of the oven and heat the oven to 350°F (180°C/gas 4). Lightly grease the bottom and sides of a 6-cup donut pan.

For more about greasing the pan, see p. 83.

2. Whisk the flour, cocoa powder, sugar, baking powder, baking soda, and salt in a medium bowl until well blended. Put the sour cream, egg, and vanilla in a small bowl and whisk until well blended. Pour the liquid over the dry ingredients along with the chopped chocolate and melted butter. Using a silicone spatula, gently fold (no stirring) until just blended.

For more about folding batter, see p. 53.

3. Scrape the mixture into one corner of a heavy-duty zip-top bag. Snip off the corner and pipe the dough into the donut cups (see the Essential Technique on p. 42). No need to spread evenly or smooth the tops. Bake until a pick inserted in the center comes out clean, 11 to 13 minutes.

For more about filling a zip-top bag, see p. 170.

4. Move the pan to a rack and let cool for about 5 minutes. Invert the pan onto a rack, lift off the pan, and let the donuts cool, rounded side up, until warm (if not glazing) or room temperature (if glazing), 10 to 30 minutes.

Make the glaze

1. Put the confectioners' sugar and heavy cream in a small bowl and stir with a spoon. Add more heavy cream, a little at a time, until the glaze is smooth, very thick, and shiny.

For more about correct glaze consistency, see p. 78.

2. Using a small offset spatula, spread some of the glaze over the tops of the completely cooled donuts and scatter some sprinkles on top, if desired.

(continued)

MAKE AHEAD

The donuts can be covered and stowed at room temperature for up to 5 days.

TWISTS

Flavor swap

> Instead of the glaze and sprinkles, dust the tops with confectioners' sugar before serving.

> **Buttermilk:** Omit the sour cream and use ½ cup (120 ml) buttermilk.

> **Cinnamon:** Add ½ tsp. ground cinnamon to the flour mixture.

ESSENTIAL TECHNIQUE

Piping the dough

A Firmly grasp a filled zip-top bag of dough as you pipe the dough into the prepared donut pan. Work all the way around the donut cup to evenly fill it.

B Once the donuts are completely cool, use the tip of a paring knife to cut out the cake clogging the centers. Hold the knife straight up and down and use a sawing motion to cut your way around the inside of the donut.

Summer's Finest Veggie Gratin

Serves 4 to 6

I make this veggie side dish often throughout the summer and every time I do, I think of my friend and colleague Susie Middleton. Like me, Susie is a *Fine Cooking* alum (she's a former editor in chief, as well as a noted cookbook author and farmer), and she loves making gratins or, as she calls them, "tians."

Like me, Susie would remind you that the flavor of this dish relies heavily on the produce you use. Unlike Susie, I don't have my own farm, so I rely on my farmers' market and a few favorite local shops to choose fragrant, ripe tomatoes (even slightly overripe is ok for this recipe), along with fresh herbs and any type of summer squash. If the corn is fresh and local, use it; if not, just omit it.

Wonderfully versatile, this gratin can be made in any shallow casserole—round, square, oval, or rectangle—and is delicious served warm or at room temperature as a side dish. It also makes a terrific main dish served warm with a soft-boiled or fried egg on top, along with some fresh bread.

Nonstick cooking spray or softened butter, for preparing the pan

5 Tbs. olive oil, divided

1 large yellow or red onion (about 8 oz./227 g), halved, peeled, and thinly sliced (see p. 518)

2 ears of sweet corn, kernels removed (see p. 90)

1 garlic clove, minced

1 tsp. chopped fresh thyme or basil leaves

Coarse salt and freshly ground black pepper

¾ cup (2 oz./57 g) fresh breadcrumbs (I like to use English muffins)

¼ cup (1 oz./28 g) ground Parmigiano Reggiano cheese (see p. 38)

2 to 3 (20 oz./567 g total) ripe tomatoes (multicolored is pretty but not mandatory)

1 medium (8 oz./227 g) zucchini

Make the caramelized onions

1. Put 2 Tbs. of the oil in a medium skillet (nonstick is best) and heat over medium heat. Add the onions and cook, stirring frequently until they're beginning to brown, 10 to 15 minutes. Reduce the heat to medium low and continue cooking and stirring (more toward the end of cooking) until the onions are deep brown and reduced down, another 5 to 8 minutes.

For more about making caramelized onions, see p. 518.

2. Add the corn kernels, garlic, thyme, and a good pinch or two of salt and pepper and continue to cook, stirring, until fragrant, 30 to 60 seconds. Slide the skillet off the heat and set aside to cool slightly.

Assemble and bake

1. Position a rack in the center of the oven and heat the oven to 375°F (190°C/gas 5). Grease a shallow 2- to 2½-quart (2 to 2.5 liters) baking dish. In a small bowl, mix the breadcrumbs and Parmigiano with a fork. Drizzle 1 Tbs. of the oil over the crumbs and stir until well blended. Put the remaining 2 Tbs. olive oil in a small ramekin.

2. Core the tomatoes and cut crosswise into thin slices (a scant ¼ inch/ 6 mm thick). Arrange on several layers of paper towels and let drain while preparing the remaining ingredients. Cut the zucchini on a slight diagonal into thin slices (a scant ¼ inch/6 mm thick).

3. Arrange a row of the sliced tomatoes, slightly overlapping, down one edge of the pan. Sprinkle with salt and pepper and drizzle with a little olive oil. Scatter about a third of the onion mixture along the bottom edge of the tomatoes. Layer a row of zucchini slices slightly overlapping each other and the tomatoes. Sprinkle with salt and pepper and drizzle with a little olive oil. Repeat the layering with rows of tomatoes, onions, and zucchini, seasoning and drizzling with oil until you have 3 rows of tomatoes, onions, and zucchini. Use your fingers to adjust the slices to fit the bottom of the pan. Most likely, you won't use all the slices. Sprinkle with salt and pepper and drizzle any remaining oil evenly over the top (see the Essential Technique on p. 44).

4. Bake for 30 minutes. Move the pan to a rack, sprinkle the crumb mixture evenly over the veggies, return the pan to the oven, and continue to bake

MAKE AHEAD

The onion mixture can be prepared, covered, and refrigerated for up to 2 days or frozen for up to 1 month. Thaw and bring to room temperature before using.

BAKER'S WISDOM

Making fresh breadcrumbs

Any variety of bread will work for crumbs. I like English muffins, but sourdough, egg, or whole wheat also works.

Tear the bread into 1- or 2-inch (2.5 to 5 cm) pieces and put a few handfuls in a food processor. Don't overcrowd or the crumbs will end up pasty. Pulse until broken down into coarse crumbs somewhere between small peas and flakes of oatmeal. Dump out and repeat, if necessary. Store crumbs in a zip-top bag in the fridge for up to 1 week or in the freezer for up to 3 months and thaw before using.

until the top is golden brown and the juices are reduced and bubbly, another 40 to 45 minutes. Move to a rack and let cool for at least 15 to 20 minutes. The gratin is best when served the same day (the top stays nice and crunchy) and can be warmed slightly in a 300°F (150°C/gas 2), if desired.

TWISTS

Flavor swap

Instead of using Parmigiano in the topping, use one of the following: ¼ cup (1⅛ oz./32 g) crumbled feta cheese, ¼ cup (1⅛ oz./32 g) crumbled goat cheese, or ¼ cup (1⅛ oz./32 g) crumbled blue cheese.

Layering the gratin

A Starting at one end of the baking dish, arrange a row of tomatoes so they're slightly overlapping. Snug them up to the edge of the dish, then sprinkle with salt and pepper and drizzle with a little oil. Heirloom tomatoes, while not necessary, add a beautiful color and deep flavor to the gratin.

B Scatter some of the onion mixture over the lower edge of the tomato layer. Use a fork and your fingers to evenly spread the mixture along the length of tomatoes.

C Follow the layering with a row of zucchini slices, overlapping one another as you did with the tomatoes. Use your fingers to help position the zucchini on top of the onion mixture and slightly overlapping the tomatoes.

D Because the vegetables shrink and reduce while cooking, it's important to include as many layers as possible for a hearty gratin. But that means there's a lot to fit in the dish. Use the palm of your hand held firmly against one of the zucchini layers to slide the vegetables toward the edge to make room for more. Be sure the layers remain intact.

E Once all vegetables are layered, add a final sprinkling of salt and pepper, then drizzle with the last of the oil.

Make-Ahead Chocolate French Toast

Serves 4 [PHOTO ON P. 91]

I'm a firm believer that chocolate is the ultimate comfort food and that it may even have medicinal qualities. Well, the latter might be wishful thinking on my part, but chocolate is the first ingredient that pops into my mind when I'm planning on serving something sweet. This easy-to-assemble French toast is deeply chocolaty and equally satisfying as a party dessert or afternoon snack as it is a special breakfast treat. Each bite holds a prescription-strength dose of chocolate and is guaranteed to cure even the biggest chocolate craving.

While chocolate for breakfast is always a treat, the real beauty of this recipe is that it can and should be made well ahead of time, giving the bread plenty of time to soak up all the custard flavors.

⅔ cup (4⅝ oz./131 g) granulated sugar
⅓ cup (1 oz./28 g) unsweetened cocoa powder (natural or Dutch-processed), sifted if lumpy
⅛ tsp. baking powder

¼ tsp. table salt
4 large eggs
1 cup (240 ml) whole milk
1 tsp. pure vanilla extract
6 thick slices soft-crusted bread, such as challah or brioche, preferably stale

3 Tbs. (1½ oz./42 g) unsalted butter, cut into small pieces, for the griddle

1. Whisk the sugar, cocoa powder, baking powder, and salt in a medium bowl until well blended. Add the eggs and whisk until blended. The mixture will be very thick. Slowly pour in the milk and vanilla, whisking constantly until blended and smooth.

2. Arrange the bread slices in a 9 x 13 x 2-inch (23 x 33 x 5 cm) baking dish in a single layer and pour the cocoa mixture over the top. Turn the slices once or twice to coat both sides. Poke the slices with the tines of a fork in several places, cover, and refrigerate for 4 hours or overnight. Turn the slices during this time to ensure the bread is evenly soaked (see the Essential Technique on p. 46).

3. Heat a large, double stovetop griddle (mine is a double-burner Calphalon®) or large (12-inch/30.5 cm) heavy-duty pan (like a cast iron skillet) over medium heat until a droplet of water immediately evaporates upon hitting the pan. Put a couple of the butter pieces on the griddle and, using the tip of a heatproof spatula, spread the melting butter. Using your fingers and a large silicone spatula, carefully move the soaked bread slices, one at a time, onto the griddle.

For more about testing a griddle for heat, see p. 65.

4. Cook until the underside of the bread is nicely browned and the edges look set and dry, 3 to 4 minutes. If the bread is overbrowning, reduce

---

MAKE AHEAD

> The batter can be covered and refrigerated for up to 12 hours.

> To keep the French toast warm, arrange a clean, heatproof rack in the center of the oven and heat the oven to 250°F (120°C/gas ½). As the toast comes off the griddle, slide it onto the rack in a single layer.

TWISTS

Flavor swap

Add to the batter along with the vanilla one of the following: ¼ tsp. pure almond extract, 2 tsp. finely grated orange zest (see p. 138), or ¼ tsp. ground cinnamon.

(Chocolate French Toast continued)

FINISHING TOUCHES

Serve with cut-up fresh fruit, confectioners' sugar, chopped and toasted nuts, granola, or maple syrup.

the heat to low. Using a wide, offset silicone spatula, flip and cook on the other side until the bread is puffed in the center and the top springs back when lightly pressed, 3 or 4 minutes. If cooking in batches, repeat with the remaining bread, lightly greasing the griddle with more butter pieces between batches. Serve immediately.

BAKER'S WISDOM

Choosing bread for French toast

I like using thick slices of eggy, soft bread for this recipe, but I don't always have a loaf on hand. When I do, I slice off a few thick slices and stow them in the freezer so I'm ready when this craving hits.

ESSENTIAL TECHNIQUE

Soaking the bread

A

B

Arrange the thick bread slices in a baking dish like puzzle pieces; edges touching is fine, but be sure the slices lay flat on the bottom of the dish. Then pour the cocoa mixture evenly over the top of all the slices.

With the help of a fork and your fingers, turn the slices over in the pan so that both sides of the bread are fully drenched with the liquid. Again, be sure the slices are lying flat in the liquid, poke them with the tines of a fork, and refrigerate for 4 hours.

C

After the 4-hour soak time, the bread slices should have completely absorbed the liquid, as shown on the left; if the bread has not been evenly soaked (like the piece on the right), the inside will be dry—and so will your French toast. Turn the slices over and let soak a bit longer, if necessary.

Best-Ever Crunchy Maple Granola Clusters

Makes about 8 cups (1 lb. 7 oz./ 652 g)

These buttery, crispy-crunchy clusters of oats and meaty almonds have a mellow maple flavor and a hint of cinnamon. They are delicious stirred into yogurt, sprinkled over or mixed into ice cream, or layered with a fruity mousse for a parfait. They also make a fab daytime snack.

  I make this granola often, but, because I find it so deliciously addictive, I make sure to give away about three-quarters of the batch. It's a welcome gift any time of the year and ships well, too. Care packages for your college-aged kids never tasted so wonderful.

Nonstick cooking spray or softened butter, for preparing the pan
¾ cup (180 ml) pure maple syrup (preferably grade B)
4 Tbs. (2 oz./57 g) unsalted butter, melted

¼ cup (60 ml) neutral oil (safflower, canola, vegetable, or corn)
2 tsp. pure vanilla extract
1 tsp. ground cinnamon
¼ tsp. pure almond extract
½ tsp. table salt

3½ cups (10½ oz./298 g) rolled or old-fashioned oats
1 cup (3¾ oz./106 g) slivered almonds

1. Whisk the maple syrup, melted butter, oil, vanilla, cinnamon, almond extract, and salt in a large bowl until well blended. Add the oats and almonds and stir until blended and the oats are evenly coated. Set aside, stirring frequently. (This allows the oats to soak up the maple syrup mixture.)

2. Position a rack in the center of the oven and heat the oven to 325°F (165°C/gas 3). Line a 9 x 13 x 2-inch (23 x 33 cm x 5 cm) baking pan (I like the straight-sided kind) with foil, leaving about a 1-inch overhang on two sides. Lightly grease the bottom and sides.

For more about lining a straight-sided pan with foil, see p. 135.

3. Scrape the oats mixture and any remaining liquid into the prepared pan and spread evenly. Cover the surface of the mixture with a piece of plastic and, using your hands, press down firmly to make an even, compact layer (see the Essential Technique on p. 48). Remove the plastic and bake until the top is browned and the nuts and oats are very fragrant, 44 to 46 minutes. (If you prefer a less crunchy granola, bake until golden brown, 40 to 42 minutes.)

4. Move the pan to a rack and let cool completely. Use the foil "handles" to lift the entire layer from the pan. Break apart the granola until it crumbles with some large pieces and some loose (I like to leave a lot of large pieces).

(continued)

MAKE AHEAD

The granola can be covered and stowed at room temperature for up to 2 weeks.

TWISTS

Flavor swap

> Instead of the almonds, use the same amount of walnuts, pistachios, peanuts, macadamias, or pecans and omit the almond extract.

> **Fruity:** Add up to 1½ cups (10 oz./283 g) dried fruit (chopped, if large) to the baked, cooled, and crumbled granola.

(Crunchy Maple Granola Clusters continued)

Press firmly for big clusters

To ensure lots of chunky clusters, it's important to press firmly on the oat mixture before baking. After baking and cooling completely, break apart the granola in large pieces and stow in an airtight container. I like to mix the smaller shards into my morning yogurt, saving the larger pieces for snacking.

ESSENTIAL TECHNIQUE

Pressing the mixture into the pan

Using a silicone spatula, scrape the oats mixture into a lightly greased, foil-lined pan and spread evenly. Be sure to nudge the mixture into the corners and edges.

Cover the oats mixture with a large piece of plastic wrap, then use one hand to press the mixture into a firm layer. Remove the plastic before baking.

Removing from the pan and crumbling

Once the baked granola is cool, grip the foil handles and lift the granola from the pan. Some of the granola will break apart into small, loose pieces.

Break off chunks of granola and crumble it over a bowl, leaving some larger pieces and some smaller bits as well.

Broccoli, Red Pepper, *and* Cheddar Quiche

Serves 8

I'm a big believer in re-inventing leftovers, and quiche is a frequent destination for any combination of cooked veggies and meats that might otherwise languish in my fridge. Pairing one or two cooked veggies, cheese, and something from the onion or pepper family—in this case, broccoli, Cheddar, and roasted peppers—is easy enough. The trick is to not overlook the custard base of this savory pie. Enhancing the primary ingredients—half-and-half and eggs—with herbs, Dijon mustard, roasted garlic, and salt and pepper elevates the filling to a whole new level of deliciousness.

For the pie dough
8 Tbs. (4 oz./113 g) unsalted
   butter
2 Tbs. very cold water
1 Tbs. freshly squeezed
   lemon juice
1⅓ cups (6 oz./170 g)
   unbleached all-purpose flour
1 tsp. granulated sugar
½ tsp. table salt

For the filling
3 whole large eggs
2 yolks from large eggs (see p. 371)
1 Tbs. Dijon mustard
1 or 2 roasted garlic cloves,
   mashed with a fork (optional
   but very tasty) (see the Baker's
   Wisdom on p. 50)
½ tsp. chopped fresh rosemary
½ tsp. table salt
Freshly ground black pepper
   (about 5 twists of the grinder)

Pinch of ground cayenne pepper
2⅓ cups (560 ml) half-and-half
1½ cups (10 oz./283 g) cooked
   broccoli florets
1 cup (4 oz./113 g) coarsely
   shredded extra-sharp
   Cheddar cheese
⅓ cup (2 oz./57 g) diced roasted
   red peppers, fresh roasted or
   jarred and well drained
2 Tbs. ground Parmigiano
   Reggiano cheese (see p. 38)

Make the dough

1. Cut the butter in half lengthwise and then cut each strip into 8 pieces. Pile the butter onto a plate and slide into the freezer until ready to use. Measure the water, add the lemon juice, and refrigerate until ready to use.

2. Whisk the flour, sugar, and salt in a large bowl until well blended. Add the cold butter pieces and, using a pastry blender or two knives, cut them into the flour mixture until the pieces are pea-sized, about 3 minutes. (You can also do this in a food processor using short pulses, scraping the blended mixture into the large bowl before proceeding.)

For more about cutting butter and flour together until the butter is pea-sized, see p. 80.

3. Pour the water over the flour and, using a silicone spatula, stir and fold until it forms a shaggy, moist dough with some floury bits remaining (I like to use one hand to help mix while keeping the other working the spatula). Scrape the dough and any remaining floury bits onto the counter and gather into a mound. Starting with the top of the mound and using the heel of your hand, smear a section of the dough down the side and along the work surface away from you to blend the butter pieces into the dough. Repeat with the remaining dough in sections. Using a bench scraper, fold the dough together (the mixture will be rough and crumbly).

(continued)

MAKE AHEAD

> The pie dough can be prepared, wrapped, and refrigerated for up to 2 days or frozen for up to 1 month.

> The dough-lined pie plate can be covered and refrigerated for up to 1 day or frozen for up to 1 month.

> The baked crust can be covered and stowed at room temperature for up to 1 day.

> If you're not serving the quiche within 2 hours, let cool completely, cover, and refrigerate for up to 3 days and reheat (whole or in slices) in the oven or toaster oven until a fork inserted in the center is warm to the touch. Avoid the microwave for reheating—it will make the crust soggy and unappealing.

(Broccoli, Red Pepper, and Cheddar Quiche continued)

Flavor swap

> **Roasted veggie:** Instead of the broccoli, red pepper, Cheddar, and Parmigiano, use 1¾ cups (about 12 oz./340 g) mixed roasted vegetables, very coarsely chopped (any combo will work well, but include some roasted onions or scallions, if possible); ¾ cup (3 oz./85 g) shredded Gruyère or Swiss cheese; ¼ cup (2 oz./57 g) ground Parmigiano cheese; and 2 Tbs. chopped fresh parsley.

> **Potato-bacon-brie:** Instead of the broccoli, red pepper, Cheddar, and Parmigiano, use 1 cup (7 oz./198 g) cooked diced potato, ½ cup (3 oz./85 g) cooked crumbled bacon, ¼ cup (1¼ oz./35 g) diced shallot or onion, 1 cup (4 oz./113 g) diced Brie cheese (without the rind), and ¾ tsp chopped fresh thyme.

Roasting garlic

Separate one head of garlic into cloves, leaving on the silvery paper jackets. Arrange the cloves in the center of a large piece of foil, drizzle with a little olive oil, gather the edges together on top to form a parcel, and set on a small baking sheet or pie plate. Bake at 375°F (190°C/gas 5) until the cloves are tender when pieced with the tip of a knife, about 50 minutes.

When cool enough to handle, squeeze one end to push out the garlic and discard the skin. Cover and store unused garlic, still in their skins, in the refrigerator for up to 4 days or in the freezer for up to 1 month.

Turn the pile about 90 degrees and repeat the smearing process until the mixture just comes together into a cohesive dough (this is a technique called *fraisage*). Be careful not to overwork the dough because that will make the crust dense. Shape the dough into a 7-inch (17 cm) disk. Wrap in plastic and refrigerate until firm, about 2 hours.

For more about using your hand to help mix, see p. 85.

For more about *fraisage*, see p. 549.

Line the pan and blind-bake the crust

1. Remove the dough from the refrigerator and, if it's very cold, set it out at room temperature until it's just pliable enough to roll, 10 to 20 minutes. Arrange a large piece of parchment on a work surface, put the unwrapped dough in the center, and cover with another piece of parchment. Using a rolling pin, roll the dough between the parchment to a 14-inch (35.5 cm) round, lifting, turning, and repositioning the parchment and lightly flouring throughout the rolling.

For more about rolling dough between parchment, see p. 133.

2. Peel away the top parchment and carefully roll the dough around the pin, leaving the bottom parchment behind. Position the dough over a 9-inch (23 cm) pie plate and unroll it onto the plate, gently nudging it into the bottom and sides of the plate. Now, gently but firmly press the dough against the sides and bottom, being careful not to stretch or tear the dough, allowing the excess dough to hang over the edges. Trim the dough so there's about ¾ inch (2 cm) left hanging over the edge of the plate. Roll the overhang under itself to shape a high-edge crust that rests on top of the rim. Crimp the edge, then cover and refrigerate the crust while the oven heats.

For more about rolling dough over a pie plate and preparing the edges, see p. 364.

3. Position a rack in the center of the oven and heat the oven to 375°F (190°C/gas 5). Use two long pieces of foil to line the pie shell, overlapping the foil to form a cross, then fill with pie weights (I use a combination of dried beans and uncooked rice). Bake until the crust is light brown around the crimping but still pale and moist on the bottom, 22 to 25 minutes. Carefully remove the foil and weights and return the crust to the oven and bake until it looks dry and light golden, another 3 to 6 minutes. (It will bake further with the filling.) Move the pan to a rack and let cool while you make the filling. If you notice any small cracks in the crust (it's rare but it does happen), pinch off some of the reserved dough scraps and press gently onto the hot crust to fill. Be careful—the crust will be very hot. Reduce the oven temperature to 350°F (180°C/gas 4). (See the Essential Technique on the facing page.)

Make the filling and bake

Put the eggs, egg yolks, mustard, roasted garlic (if using), rosemary, salt, black pepper, and cayenne in a 1-quart (950 ml) measuring cup (the spout makes it easy to pour the custard into the crust) or a medium bowl and whisk until well blended. Add the half-and-half and whisk until well blended. Evenly scatter the broccoli, Cheddar, and red peppers over the bottom of the crust, then pour in the custard, being careful not to displace the vegetables. Scrape any remaining ingredients from the bowl and scatter over the filling, then sprinkle the Parmigiano over the top. Bake until the top is golden brown and the center jiggles slightly when the pan is nudged, 39 to 41 minutes. Move the pan to a rack and let cool for at least 2 hours before serving.

Blind-baking

A

Form a cross of two long sheets of foil over the top of the chilled pie shell. Use your fingers to push the foil gently into the edges and the bottom of the pie shell. Make sure the foil mimics the shape of the shell.

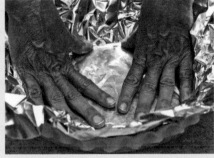

B

Pie weights will prevent the crust from forming air pockets and bubbling up as it bakes, so pour enough weights—I like to use a mixture of dried beans and uncooked rice, though you can buy small metal or ceramic pie weights—into the pie shell to almost completely fill the dish. Spread out the weights so they are evenly distributed and against the sides to prevent the sides from sliding down during baking.

C

To check the pie shell for doneness, pull back one edge of the foil. The crust should look light brown around the crimping but still pale and moist on the bottom. Carefully remove the foil and weights and return the crust to the oven for a few more minutes until it looks dry and light golden.

D

If you notice any cracks in the pie shell when it's done baking, use a small piece of dough scrap to fill the hole, pressing it gently into the hot crust.

Buttermilk–Cornmeal Griddle Cakes

Makes eight 3½-inch (9 cm) cakes

Starting the day with a stack of steaming hot, fluffy pancakes makes even a snowy, frigid winter morning feel like a warm, tropical breeze is floating through the room. This from-scratch recipe is so easy that there's no excuse not to make them every day. A bit of stone-ground cornmeal adds a lovely, slightly gritty texture to the pancakes and helps soak up more of the butter and maple syrup.

1 cup (4½ oz./128 g)
   unbleached all-purpose flour
⅓ cup (1½ oz./42 g) stone-
   ground cornmeal
1 Tbs. granulated sugar

¼ tsp. baking powder
¼ tsp. baking soda
¼ tsp. table salt
1 cup (240 ml) buttermilk
1 large egg

1 Tbs. unsalted butter, melted
½ tsp. pure vanilla extract
2 Tbs. (1 oz./28 g) unsalted
   butter, cut into small pieces,
   for the griddle

TWISTS

Flavor swap

> Add to the batter along with the liquid: ½ cup berries (2½ oz./71 g), lightly crushed; diced ripe pears; peaches; apples; ripe bananas; toasted, chopped nuts; chopped dried fruit; chopped chocolate (bittersweet, semisweet, or white); peanut butter; ¼ cup (1⅛ oz./32 g) chopped crystallized ginger; or ⅓ cup (⅞ oz./25 g) sweetened shredded coconut.

> **Classic buttermilk:** Omit the cornmeal and proceed as directed.

> Along with the vanilla, use one of the following: ¼ tsp. pure almond extract; 1½ tsp. finely grated lemon zest (see p. 138); 2 tsp. finely grated orange zest; or ½ tsp. ground cinnamon.

Re-size it

Silver dollars: Using a 2-Tbs. scoop, drop the batter onto the hot griddle and cook as directed.

1. Whisk the flour, cornmeal, sugar, baking powder, baking soda, and salt in a medium bowl until well blended. Put the buttermilk, egg, melted butter, and vanilla in a small bowl and whisk until well blended. Pour the liquid over the dry ingredients. Using a silicone spatula, gently fold (no stirring) until just blended. The batter will look a little lumpy (see the Essential Technique on the facing page).

2. Heat a large, double stovetop griddle (mine is a double-burner Calphalon) or large (12-inch/30.5 cm) heavy-duty pan (like a cast iron skillet) over medium heat until a droplet of water immediately evaporates upon hitting the pan. Put a couple of the butter pieces on the griddle and, using the tip of a heatproof spatula, spread the melting butter.

3. Ladle or scoop ¼ cup (60 ml) batter (per pancake) onto the griddle, leaving 3 to 4 inches (7.5 to 10 cm) between the pancakes (this will make flipping easier). Reduce the heat to medium low and cook until the undersides are nicely browned and the edges look set and dry, 3 to 4 minutes. Use a wide, offset spatula to gently lift one edge to peek at the color. If the cakes are overbrowning, reduce the heat to low. Using the spatula, flip and cook the other side until the pancakes are puffed and the tops spring back when lightly pressed, 3 or 4 minutes. Repeat with the remaining batter, lightly greasing the griddle with more of the butter pieces between batches. Serve immediately.

For more about heating the griddle and cooking pancakes, see p. 65.

MAKE AHEAD

> The batter can be covered and refrigerated for up to 12 hours ahead.

> To keep the cakes warm, arrange a clean, heatproof rack on the center rack of the oven and heat the oven to 250°F (120°C/gas ½). As the cakes come off the griddle, slide them onto the rack in a single layer.

> Serve with cut-up fresh fruit, confectioners' sugar, chopped nuts, granola, or butter and maple syrup.

> Serve with **Glazed Cinnamon Apples**:

4 Tbs. (2 oz./57 g) unsalted butter

1 tsp. freshly squeezed lemon juice

½ tsp. ground cinnamon

1½ lb. (680 g) firm, sweet apples (about 3 medium-large), peeled, cored, quartered, and thinly sliced

1 Tbs. granulated sugar

2 Tbs. apple brandy or apple cider

Put the butter, lemon juice, and cinnamon in a medium skillet and cook, stirring, over medium heat until melted and bubbling. Add the apples and cook, flipping the slices a few times, until just tender, 3 to 5 minutes. Sprinkle the sugar over the apples and cook, flipping and turning the slices until lightly caramelized, 1 minute. Add the apple brandy or cider and bring to a boil, carefully scraping up any nubbins that might be stuck to the pan. Serve warm. Leftovers can be covered and refrigerated for up to 4 days.

Why lumpy batter

When it comes to quick bread batters (pancakes are essentially a quick bread), lumpy is a good thing! In this type of batter, the dry and wet ingredients are mixed separately before gently folding together, leaving some small lumps of moistened dry ingredients remaining. These little lumps help create light and airy muffins, pancakes, and loaves. Overmixing the batter until it's smooth might look nice, but the gluten in the flour will overdevelop, and the baked results will be tough and dense.

Folding batter until just blended

A silicone spatula is the best tool for folding ingredients together. As opposed to stirring or whisking, folding allows the ingredients to maintain volume and limit gluten development, making the finished cakes light and airy.

The batter should be well blended but lumpy. Overmixing the batter will increase gluten formation, making the cakes flatter and dense.

Cinnamon–Pecan Morning Buns

Makes 8 rolls

While I'm partial to the yeast-risen cinnamon buns like my Hazelnut Sticky Buns on p. 455, there are times where I'm too time-pressed to pull them off. Enter these easy-to-make, buttery biscuit-style buns filled with cinnamon–pecan goodness. I love how quickly the buns come together and fill the kitchen with warm, inviting smells as they bake—a terrific way to start any morning.

P.S. On the rare occasions that I have leftovers, I transform them into a delicious, homey dessert. Gently warmed and topped with a scoop of vanilla ice cream and a drizzle of caramel sauce, they make any evening happier.

Nonstick cooking spray or softened butter, for preparing the pan

For the cinnamon filling
½ cup (3½ oz./99 g) firmly packed light or dark brown sugar
⅓ cup (2⅜ oz./67 g) granulated sugar
⅓ cup (1½ oz./42 g) unbleached all-purpose flour

1 Tbs. ground cinnamon
¼ tsp. ground nutmeg
Pinch of table salt
6 Tbs. (3 oz./85 g) unsalted butter, very soft
¼ cup (1 oz./28 g) chopped pecans, toasted

For the dough
2 cups (9 oz./255 g) unbleached all-purpose flour + more for rolling

¼ cup (1¾ oz./50 g) granulated sugar
1 Tbs. baking powder
½ tsp. table salt
8 Tbs. (4 oz./113 g) unsalted butter, cut into 8 pieces and well chilled
⅔ cup (160 ml) whole milk

Confectioners' sugar, for dusting (optional)

MAKE AHEAD

> The butter can be cut into the dry ingredients, covered, and refrigerated for up to 1 day ahead. When ready to serve, proceed with the recipe while the oven heats up.

> The rolls are best when served warm. If you're not serving them immediately, cover the cooled rolls and stow at room temperature for up to 2 days and reheat in the oven or toaster oven.

Make the filling

Put the brown sugar, granulated sugar, flour, cinnamon, nutmeg, and salt in a medium bowl and stir until blended. Add the butter and mix with an electric handheld mixer fitted with the wire beaters until smooth and well blended. Add the pecans and mix until blended. Set aside.

Make the dough

1. Position a rack in the center of the oven and heat the oven to 425°F (220°C/gas 7). Lightly grease the bottom and sides of 8 muffin cups.

2. Whisk the flour, sugar, baking powder, and salt in a large bowl until well blended. Add the cold butter pieces and, using a pastry blender, cut the butter into the flour mixture until the butter is pea-sized. (You can also do this step in a food processor using short pulses, scraping the blended mixture into a large bowl before proceeding.)

For more about cutting butter and flour together until the butter is pea-sized, see p. 80.

3. Pour the milk over the flour mixture and, using a silicone spatula, stir and fold until you get a shaggy dough that barely hangs together. (I like to use one hand to help mix while keeping the other working the spatula.)

Scrape the dough and any remaining floury bits onto the counter and knead a few times until the dough is evenly moist and holds together. Be careful not to overknead the dough because that will make the buns dense.

For more about using your hand to help mix, see p. 85.

4. Using a rolling pin, roll the dough into a 12 x 10-inch (30.5 x 25 cm) rectangle, lightly flouring the bottom and top of the dough as needed (you can also roll between sheets of parchment). Using a bench scraper to lift the dough and dusting the counter with flour will be helpful. Drop the cinnamon filling by the tablespoon evenly over the dough. Using an offset spatula, spread the filling evenly over the dough, all the way to the edges. Beginning on one long side, roll up the dough, jelly-roll style. Position the roll, seam side down, on the work surface and cut into 8 equal pieces about 1½ inches (4 cm) wide. Arrange the slices, cut side up, in the prepared muffin cups and press down slightly. Bake until the rolls are puffed and brown and a pick inserted in the center of the biscuit layer (not the filling) comes out clean, 24 to 27 minutes.

5. Move the pan to a rack and let cool for about 12 minutes. Invert the pan (use potholders—the pan is too hot to handle safely) onto a rack and lift off the pan. Using another rack or a serving plate, invert the rolls so they are right side up. Serve immediately, dusted with confectioners' sugar, if desired.

For more about inverting a pan, see p. 278.

TWISTS

Flavor swap

> Omit the pecans from the filling and add the same amount of walnuts or slivered almonds.

> Use the same amount of buttermilk instead of the milk.

> **Ginger:** Omit the pecans and add ½ cup (2¼ oz./64 g) chopped crystallized ginger to the filling.

Re-size it

> **One-pan rolls:** Instead of muffin tins, lightly grease the bottom and sides of a 9 x 2-inch (23 x 5 cm) round cake pan and line with parchment or a nonstick liner. Arrange the slices in the prepared pan with one in the center and the rest circling around it (no need to press down) and bake as directed.

> Double the recipe, divide the dough and filling in half, and shape as directed. Bake in a lightly greased 9 x 13 x 2-inch (23 x 33 x 5 cm) baking pan as directed.

(continued)

FINISHING TOUCHES

> Drizzle the top with confectioners' sugar glaze (see p. 77) after baking and cooling slightly.

> Serve with Honey Butter (recipe on p. 85).

> **Top with Honey Glaze:** In a small bowl, combine 2 oz. (57 g) cream cheese (at room temperature), 2 Tbs. heavy cream, and 2 Tbs. honey. Using an electric handheld mixer, beat on low speed until well blended. Increase to medium and continue beating until smooth and shiny. The glaze should be thick but fluid enough to fall from the spoon and form a soft dollop. If it isn't, add more heavy cream 1 tsp. at a time. Spoon the honey mixture into a heavy-duty zip-top bag and seal tightly. Snip off about ¾ inch (2 cm) from one corner and, squeezing gently, move the bag evenly over the top of the rolls in a zigzag pattern to form a thick ribbon. Any extra can be refrigerated for up to 2 weeks.

For more about correct glaze consistency, see p. 78.

(Cinnamon–Pecan Morning Buns continued)

ESSENTIAL TECHNIQUE

Making the rolls

A

With the dough rolled out to a 12 x 10-inch (30.5 x 25 cm) rectangle, drop the cinnamon filling by the tablespoon over the dough. It will be easiest to spread if you drop small amounts of the dough in an even pattern.

B

An offset spatula will help in spreading the filling evenly across the dough. Try to spread the filling all the way to the edges. If needed, scoop a bit of filling with the edge of the spatula and patch any holes.

C

Once the filling is spread, roll the dough jelly-roll style, starting at one long edge. Nudge up the longer edge of the dough (closest to you) with your fingers, then push it forward as you continue to roll.

D

Once rolling is complete, seal the edge of the dough, pressing firmly with one finger all along the edge.

E

Cut the roll into equal slices; a serrated knife and a sawing motion works best. Arrange the slices in the prepared muffin tin.

Salmon- *and* Spinach-Filled Crêpes

Serves 2   [PHOTO ON P. 92]

Buttery in flavor and delicate in texture, crêpes are paper thin, soft, pancake-like wrappers that are the ideal vessel for both sweet and savory fillings. Like my mother, I more often use crêpes for savory fillings, like this salmon-spinach one, but they are just as delicious when reheated in a little butter and sugar, folded, and served with a drizzle of chocolate sauce or filled with Glazed Cinnamon Apples (see p. 53).

Crêpes are traditionally made in special, shallow steel pans, but I find that most home cooks, especially those new to crêperie, have an easier time with a small nonstick pan with sloping sides and an 8-inch-diameter (20 cm) flat bottom—inexpensive and perfect for crêpe-making. If you're new to crêpe-making, I suggest making a double batch of the batter and try using a bit more batter than what's called for (use a smidge over ¼ cup/60 ml) while you get used to rotating and tilting the pan to coat evenly. The crêpes will be a bit thicker but still good. As you move through the batch, reduce the amount of batter until the crêpes are thin and delicate.

For the sauce
1½ Tbs. (¾ oz./20 g)
   unsalted butter
1 Tbs. unbleached all-purpose
   flour
¾ cup + 2 Tbs. (180 ml + 2 Tbs.)
   whole milk
2 to 3 Tbs. freshly squeezed
   lemon juice
Pinch of ground cayenne pepper
Coarse salt and freshly ground
   black pepper

For the filling
1 Tbs. olive oil
1 large garlic clove, minced
4 oz. (113 g) baby spinach,
   trimmed
2 Tbs. sun-dried tomatoes packed
   in oil, drained and chopped
½ tsp. freshly squeezed
   lemon juice
Coarse salt and freshly ground
   black pepper

To assemble
2 crêpes (recipe on p. 58)
Two 4-oz. (113 g each) boneless,
   skinless salmon fillets (1 inch,
   2.5 cm, thick at the center)
1 Tbs. ground Parmigiano
   Reggiano cheese (see p. 38)
2 Tbs. thinly sliced fresh chives,
   for garnish

Make the sauce

Whisk the butter in a small saucepan over medium heat until melted and bubbling. Add the flour and cook, whisking constantly, until smooth and bubbling but not browned, 1 minute. Pour in the milk and continue cooking, whisking constantly, until thickened and boiling. Cook for 1 minute, then slide the pan off the heat. Add the lemon juice, cayenne, and salt and pepper to taste, then whisk until blended. Taste and adjust seasonings as needed. Set aside to cool.

Make the filling and assemble

1. Warm the oil in a medium, ovenproof skillet over medium heat, then add the garlic and cook, stirring frequently, until light brown and fragrant, about 2 minutes. Add the spinach and cook, stirring frequently, until it's wilted and well coated with the oil. Slide the pan off the heat, add the sun-dried tomatoes, lemon juice, and salt and pepper to taste, and toss until blended. Taste and adjust seasonings as needed. Set aside to cool.

(continued)

MAKE AHEAD

> The sauce can be prepared, cooled, covered, and refrigerated for up to 2 days.

> The crêpes can be prepared through Step 3, covered, and refrigerated for up to 1 day.

2. Position a rack in the center of the oven and heat the oven to 425°F (220°C/gas 7). Have ready the crêpes, sauce, and spinach.

3. Arrange the crêpes on the counter. Place a salmon fillet down the center of each crêpe and season with salt and pepper. Spoon the spinach mixture evenly on top of the salmon. Fold one side of the crêpe up and over the filling and repeat with the other side. Arrange seam side up, about ¾ inch (2 cm) apart, in the same skillet.

4. Spoon the sauce evenly over the crêpes and sprinkle with the cheese. Bake until the sauce is bubbling, the top is browned, and the salmon is cooked, 18 to 20 minutes. Move the skillet to a rack, sprinkle with the chives, and serve immediately.

Crêpes

Makes fourteen 8-inch (20 cm) crêpes

1 cup (240 ml) whole milk
1 cup (4½ oz./128 g)
    unbleached all-purpose flour
3 large eggs

7 Tbs. (3½ oz./99 g) unsalted
    butter, melted, divided
¼ tsp. fine sea salt

MAKE AHEAD

> The batter can be prepared through Step 1, covered, and refrigerated for up to 1 day before proceeding. Bring to room temperature before proceeding with the recipe.

> The crêpes can be prepared through Step 2, wrapped in plastic, and then stowed in a zip-top bag and refrigerated for up to 3 days before proceeding.

> The crêpes can be frozen for up to 6 weeks. Lay a piece of plastic or waxed paper in between every 6 crêpes, wrap the whole stack in plastic, and slide into a heavy-duty zip-top freezer bag. Bring to room temperature before using.

1. Put the milk, flour, eggs, 5 Tbs. (2½ oz./71 g) of the melted butter, and the salt in a blender. Blend until very smooth, about 1 minute, stopping once or twice to scrape down the sides. Pour the batter into a medium bowl, cover, and set aside at room temperature for about 30 minutes.

2. If the batter has been refrigerated, allow it to come to room temperature. Set a 10-inch (25 cm) nonstick skillet with sloping sides and an 8-inch (20 cm) bottom over medium heat until droplets of water immediately evaporate upon hitting the pan. Using a folded paper towel, coat the skillet with a little of the remaining melted butter. Working quickly, pour a scant ¼ cup batter (60 ml) into the center of the pan while lifting the pan and rotating and tilting it clockwise to cover the bottom evenly with the batter. Cook until lacy golden brown on the bottom, about 1 minute. Carefully slide a heatproof spatula under the crêpe and turn it over, then continue cooking for another 30 seconds, until the crêpe is just beginning to brown in spots. Slide the crêpe onto a wire rack. Repeat with the remaining batter, lightly greasing the pan when necessary (about every other crêpe) and stacking the crêpes as they are cooked.

Making crêpes

As you pour batter into the center of the hot buttered pan, rotate the pan clockwise to evenly coat the bottom with batter.

Use the tip of a silicone spatula to lift the edge of the crêpe to check for doneness. When it's golden brown, use the spatula and your fingers to flip the crêpe over gently.

> >

Classic Waffles

Makes eight 6 ½-inch (16.5 cm) waffles

The key to crispy, flavorful waffles is using a combination of neutral-flavored oil and melted unsalted butter. The oil helps the waffles cook up with a delicate crispy exterior, and the butter lends its flavor to these lightly sweetened waffles. The recipe is easily accomplished any day of the week.

These waffles have a big-time make-ahead factor. You can store extras in your fridge or freezer and pull them out one at a time for a last-minute breakfast heated up in the microwave or toaster oven.

2½ cups (11⅜ oz./322 g) unbleached all-purpose flour
¼ cup (1¾ oz./50 g) granulated sugar
4 tsp. baking powder

1 tsp. table salt
2 cups (240 ml) whole milk
4 large eggs, at room temperature
6 Tbs. (3 oz./85 g) unsalted butter, melted

6 Tbs. (89 ml) neutral oil (safflower, canola, vegetable, or corn) + 2 Tbs. for the iron

1. Whisk the flour, sugar, baking powder, and salt in a large bowl until well blended. Put the milk, eggs, melted butter, and oil in a medium bowl and whisk until well blended. Pour the liquid over the dry ingredients. Using a silicone spatula, gently fold (no stirring) until just blended. The batter will look a little lumpy.

(continued)

TWISTS

Flavor swap

> Instead of apple cider and apples, use the same amount of pear cider and pears.

> Instead of topping with the apple cider glaze, roll the very warm donuts in 1½ cups (10½ oz./298 g) coarse sanding sugar mixed with 2 Tbs. ground cinnamon.

BAKER'S WISDOM

Deep frying can be intimidating, but it's a crucial step for donut making. I use as little oil as possible and give step-by-step instructions along with tips to help you master the art of cooking with oil (see the Essential Technique on the facing page). As far as what oil to use, I like a solid vegetable shortening like Crisco®. It lends barely any taste to the donut and gives the exterior a wonderful crispy consistency. You can also use canola or any neutral-flavored oil.

2. Whisk the flour, brown sugar, baking powder, salt, baking soda, cinnamon, and nutmeg in a large bowl until well blended. Put the buttermilk and eggs in a small bowl or 2-cup (480 ml) measure and whisk until well blended. Pour the egg mixture along with the melted butter and apple concentrate over the flour and, using a silicone spatula, stir and fold until it forms a moist dough (I like to use one hand to help mix while keeping the other hand working the spatula).

3. Arrange a piece of parchment on your work surface, generously coat with flour, and put the dough in the center. Using floured hands and starting in the center and moving outward toward the edges, gently pat and shape the dough into an even ⅔-inch (17 mm) thick round, flouring your hands as needed. Dust the top of the dough with flour, cover with another piece of parchment, and flip the dough.

4. Peel away the top piece of parchment. Using a 3-inch (7.5 cm) cookie cutter, cut out rounds, dipping the cutter in flour as needed. Using a 1⅛-inch (2.9 cm) plain round cookie cutter, cut out the centers of the rounds and remove. Arrange the rounds and centers, using a floured offset spatula if needed, on the prepared cookie sheet. Stack the scraps and gently press together. Re-roll as directed, chill the dough for about 10 minutes, and cut.

Make the glaze

Put the confectioners' sugar and 3 Tbs. of the apple cider concentrate in a medium bowl and stir with a spoon. Add more cider concentrate, a little at a time, until the glaze is smooth, very thick, and shiny.

Cook the donuts

1. Have ready a large rimmed baking sheet lined with several layers of paper towels and a Chinese-style skimmer (spider) or slotted spoon. Pour enough oil into a large pot (I use a 4-quart/950 ml Dutch oven) to fill it to a 2½-inch (6 cm) depth and clip a candy thermometer to the side of the pan, making sure it doesn't touch the bottom. Heat the oil to 360°F (182°C) over high heat.

2. Using a long, wide spatula, carefully slip a few donuts and donut holes (don't fry too many at one time or the temperature of the oil will drop and the donuts will be greasy) into the oil and cook, turning once with the skimmer, until deep golden brown, 65 to 70 seconds per side. With a skimmer or slotted spoon, remove the donuts from the pan and drain on the paper towel–lined baking sheet. Keep an eye on the oil temperature and adjust the heat up or down accordingly while cooking, making sure to bring the temperature back up to 360°F (182°C) before cooking subsequent batches.

3. When cool enough to handle, arrange the donuts rounded side up and, using a small offset spatula, spread the tops with some of the cider glaze and dip and roll the donut holes to coat completely. Repeat with the remaining donuts. Serve warm. These donuts are best the day they're made.

Cutting and deep-frying donuts

A Using a 3-inch (7.5 cm) cookie cutter, cut out rounds from the rolled-out dough, dipping the cutter in flour as needed. Cut out the centers of the rounds with a 1⅛-inch (2.9 cm) cutter.

B Transfer the rounds and centers to the prepared cookie sheet. A floured offset spatula makes it easy. Use the small cutter to help lift out the centers.

C Once the oil is hot (check with a candy thermometer clipped to the pot), use a long, wide spatula to slip a few donuts and holes into the oil. Don't overcrowd the pot or the oil temperature will drop.

D A Chinese skimmer works well to turn the donuts once the first side is cooked, as well as to remove the donuts to a rack or paper towel–lined baking sheet.

Raspberry–Ginger Ricotta Pancakes *with* Lemon Curd

Makes twenty 4-inch (10 cm) pancakes [PHOTO ON P. 94]

These airy, brightly flavored pancakes are drop-dead gorgeous all on their own but when served with a dollop of lemon curd and fresh berries, they are close to having dessert for breakfast.

⅔ cup (3 oz./85 g) unbleached
    all-purpose flour
3 Tbs. granulated sugar
½ tsp. baking powder
¼ tsp. table salt

1½ cups (13½ oz./383 g)
    ricotta (whole or part skim; to
    make your own, see the Baker's
    Wisdom below)
4 large eggs, separated (see p. 371)
1 Tbs. finely grated fresh ginger

1 cup (5 oz./142 g) fresh
    raspberries + more for serving
3 Tbs. (1½ oz./42 g) unsalted
    butter, cut into small pieces,
    for the griddle
Lemon Curd (recipe on the facing
    page), for serving

For more about folding, see p. 270.

BAKER'S WISDOM

Homemade ricotta

Stir 5¾ cups (1360 ml) whole milk, ¾ cup (180 ml) heavy cream, and ½ tsp. table salt in a large nonreactive (stainless steel or enamel) pot. Bring to a boil over medium heat, stirring with a silicone spatula, first occasionally and then more frequently as the mixture thickens, scraping the side and bottom to prevent scorching. Once the mixture is boiling, slide the pot off heat and stir in 3 Tbs. freshly squeezed lemon juice until the mixture begins to separate. Set aside for 10 minutes.

Unfold, if necessary, and lightly dampen two long pieces of cheese-cloth. Arrange in an X pattern, overlapping the pieces in the center, in a large, fine-mesh sieve set over a large bowl. Using a large spoon or ladle, transfer the milk mixture into the sieve, pouring in the remaining bits. Set aside for 60 minutes to drain, emptying the whey from the bowl as needed. At this point the ricotta will be soft and still wet looking. For a drier, firmer ricotta, let drain for another 45 to 60 minutes.

Use immediately or spoon into a container, cover, and refrigerate until ready to use or up to 3 days. After refrigerating, the ricotta will be drier and firmer. Makes about 1¾ cups (about 16 oz./454 g).

1. Whisk the flour, sugar, baking powder, and salt in a medium bowl until well blended. Add the ricotta, egg yolks, and grated ginger and whisk until well blended.

2. Put the egg whites in a medium bowl and beat with an electric handheld mixer fitted with wire beaters on medium-low speed until foamy. Increase the speed to medium high and beat until the whites form medium-firm peaks when the beater is lifted. (The tips of the peaks should droop over just slightly.) Do not overbeat. Scoop about one-third of the whites into the egg mixture and, using a silicone spatula, stir gently until blended. Add the remaining whites and gently fold in until just blended. Add the raspberries and gently fold into the batter (one or two folds should do it).

3. Heat a large stovetop griddle (mine is a double-burner Calphalon) or large (12-inch/30.5 cm) heavy-duty pan (like a cast iron skillet) over medium heat until a droplet of water immediately evaporates upon hitting the pan. Put a couple of the butter pieces on the griddle and, using the tip of a heatproof spatula, spread the melting butter.

4. Using a ¼-cup (60 ml) mini scoop or ladle, drop the batter (do not spread it out) onto the griddle, leaving about 2 to 4 inches (5 to 10 cm) between the pancakes (this will make flipping easier.) Reduce the heat to medium low and cook until the undersides are well browned, 3 to 4 minutes. If the cakes are overbrowning, reduce the heat to low. Using a wide offset spatula, flip the pancakes and cook on the other side until they are puffed and the tops spring back when lightly pressed, 3 to 4 minutes. Repeat with the remaining batter, lightly greasing the griddle with more of the butter pieces between batches. Serve immediately with the lemon curd and more raspberries. To keep the cakes warm, arrange a clean, heatproof rack on the center rack of the oven and heat the oven to 250°F (120°C/gas ½). As the cakes come off the griddle, slide them onto the rack in a single layer.

Lemon Curd

Makes 1 cup (240 ml)

6 Tbs. (3 oz./85 g) unsalted butter
½ cup (3½ oz./99 g)
   granulated sugar
⅓ cup (80 ml) freshly squeezed
   lemon juice

2 Tbs. finely grated lemon zest
   (see p. 138)
Pinch of table salt
6 yolks from large eggs (see p. 371)
   or 3 whole large eggs

1. Put the butter in a large saucepan and melt over medium heat. Slide the pan off the heat and whisk in the sugar, lemon juice, zest, and salt. Whisk in the yolks until well blended. Cook over medium-low heat, whisking constantly, until the mixture is thick enough to coat a spatula and hold a line drawn through it with a finger, 4 to 6 minutes. Don't let the mixture boil.

2. Set a medium-fine sieve over a small bowl and pour in the curd, straining it without pressing. Discard the zest and cover the surface directly with plastic wrap. Let cool to room temperature, then refrigerate until chilled or for up to 3 weeks.

FINISHING TOUCHES

Instead of the lemon curd and fresh raspberries, serve with one or two of the following: chopped fresh fruit, confectioners' sugar, chopped nuts, granola, chopped chocolate, or maple syrup.

TWISTS

Flavor swap

Instead of the ginger, use one of the following: ¼ tsp. pure almond extract, ¾ tsp. pure vanilla extract, 2 tsp. finely grated lemon zest (see p. 138), ½ tsp. ground cinnamon, or 2 or 3 swipes of freshly grated nutmeg (fresh really makes a difference in flavor).

BAKER'S WISDOM

Lightening up

Gently stirring some of the beaten whites into the egg mixture will "lighten" the mixture before folding in the remaining whites. Doing this makes it easier for the thicker batter to incorporate the whites without deflating them, ensuring your pancakes will be light and fluffy.

ESSENTIAL TECHNIQUE

Heating the griddle and cooking pancakes

A The griddle is hot enough to cook the pancakes when a droplet of water evaporates instantly when it hits the pan.

B A ¼-cup (60 ml) mini ice cream scoop is the perfect tool for dropping batter on the griddle. For the fluffiest cakes, you want a fairly tall mound, so don't spread it out.

C Using a wide offset spatula, peek to see if the cakes are done cooking on the first side—they should be well browned—then flip to cook the other side.

Cinnamon Swirl Crumble-Topped Ricotta Coffee Cake

Serves 12 to 16 [PHOTO ON P. 95]

As a kid I picked off the cinnamony sweet crumb layer of our store-bought coffee cake and left the naked cake behind. I'll be honest—I still like to pick off the crumbs from coffee cakes.

With three essential components, this coffee cake is every bit as delicious as the topping. I've made this one with cake flour for added tenderness and ricotta for added richness. Cocoa-laced cinnamon-sugar adds an intriguing layer of flavor to the sweet filling. (If you want a more traditional cinnamon filling just leave out the cocoa.) The topping is the crown jewel and all that's needed to satisfy even this crumb aficionado!

For the crumb topping

1¼ cups (5⅝ oz./159 g) unbleached all-purpose flour
⅔ cup (4⅝ oz./131 g) firmly packed light or dark brown sugar
1½ tsp. ground cinnamon
¼ tsp. table salt
4 Tbs. (2 oz./57 g) unsalted butter, melted
¼ cup (60 ml) neutral oil (safflower, canola, vegetable, or corn)

For the streusel filling

1 cup (7 oz./198 g) firmly packed light or dark brown sugar
2 Tbs. unsweetened natural cocoa powder (optional), sifted if lumpy
4½ tsp. ground cinnamon
¼ tsp. table salt

For the cake

Nonstick cooking spray or softened butter + flour, for preparing the pan

3 cups (12 oz./340 g) cake flour, sifted
1½ tsp. baking powder
¾ tsp. baking soda
¾ tsp. table salt
16 Tbs. (8 oz./227 g) unsalted butter, softened
1½ cups (10½ oz./298 g) granulated sugar
3 large eggs, at room temperature
2 tsp. pure vanilla extract
1¾ cups (15¾ oz./446 g) ricotta (whole or part skim)

MAKE AHEAD

> The crumb topping can be made, covered, and refrigerated for up to 1 week.

> The dry ingredients for the dough can be prepared, covered, and stowed at room temperature for up to 3 days.

> The streusel can be made, covered, and stowed at room temperature for up to 1 week.

> The coffee cake can be baked, cooled completely, covered, and stowed at room temperature for up to 5 days.

Make the crumb topping

Put the flour, brown sugar, cinnamon, and salt in a medium bowl and mix with a fork until well blended. Add the butter and oil and mix until well incorporated; the mixture should be crumbly. Refrigerate the topping while you make the streusel and coffee cake.

Make the streusel filling

Put the brown sugar, cocoa (if using), cinnamon, and salt in a medium bowl and mix with a fork until well blended.

Make the cake

1. Position a rack in the center of the oven and heat the oven to 350°F (180°C/gas 4). Lightly grease and flour the bottom and sides of a 9 x 13 x 2-inch (23 x 33 x 5 cm) baking pan (I prefer the straight-sided type).

For more about preparing cake pans, see p. 232.

2. Whisk the cake flour, baking powder, baking soda, and salt in a medium bowl until well blended. Put the butter in a large bowl. Beat with a stand mixer fitted with the paddle attachment on medium speed until well blended and smooth, about 1 minute. Add the sugar and beat on medium-high speed until well blended, about 2 minutes. Add the eggs, one at a time, beating well after each addition. Add the vanilla with the last egg. Stop to scrape down the bowl and the beater as needed. Add a third of the flour mixture to the sugar mixture and mix on low speed until just blended. Add half of the ricotta and mix until just blended. Add another third of the flour mixture and mix on low speed until just blended. Add the remaining ricotta and mix until just blended. Add the remaining flour mixture and mix on low speed until just blended.

For more about scraping the bowl and beater, see p. 289.

3. Spoon half of the batter into the prepared pan and, using a small offset spatula, spread evenly. Scatter the filling evenly over the batter. Drop large scoopfuls of the remaining batter over the streusel and spread evenly. Break up the crumb topping, if necessary, then scatter evenly over the top. Bake until a pick inserted in the center comes out clean, 50 to 54 minutes.

4. Move the pan to a rack and let cool for 20 minutes, then cut and serve.

For more about scraping the bowl and beater, see p. 289.

TWISTS

Flavor swap

Nutty: Add ⅔ cup (2⅝ oz./74 g) toasted, chopped nuts (almonds, pecans, or walnuts) to the streusel filling and/or the crumb topping.

FINISHING TOUCHES

Sprinkle the top with confectioners' sugar.

ESSENTIAL TECHNIQUE

Layering the batter

A Spread half of the batter into the prepared pan, even into the corners.

B Pour the filling over the batter, then use your hand to help spread it out to completely cover the batter.

C Use a small offset spatula to spread spoonfuls of the top layer of batter. It's easiest to spread the batter evenly if you drop the batter at regular intervals over the filling.

D Scatter the crumb topping over the batter, breaking up some of the larger pieces. Use your hand to distribute it evenly.

Spicy Asparagus Ham Strata

Serves 10 to 12   [PHOTO ON P. 96]

I pack my savory bread puddings, or stratas as they're also known, with tons of flavor and a good hit of spice. Here, I've combined the bright flavors of spring—asparagus, ham, mushrooms, peppers, and basil—with Cheddar and spicy pepper Jack cheese for a lovely, if zippy, brunch or supper dish. I like to serve it with a lightly dressed green salad and a glass (or two) of a crisp, chilled Sauvignon Blanc.

   Because stratas can be served year-round, I've included a few different flavor pairings to swap for this springtime version. Regardless of the season, this dish can and should be made well ahead of time.

Nonstick cooking spray or softened butter, for preparing the pan

3 Tbs. (1½ oz./42 g) unsalted butter

1 lb. (16 oz./454 g) asparagus, trimmed and cut on the diagonal into 1-inch (2.5 cm) pieces

4 oz. (113 g) fresh mushrooms (cremini, baby bella, or button), cleaned and sliced

1 medium red onion, chopped

1 small yellow bell pepper, coarsely chopped

2 medium garlic cloves, minced

Kosher salt and freshly ground black pepper

7 oz. (198 g) thick-sliced baked ham, chopped into ½-inch (12 cm) pieces (1½ cups)

3 Tbs. chopped fresh basil

8 large eggs

2 Tbs. Dijon mustard

1 Tbs. Worcestershire sauce

3 cups (720 ml) half-and-half or whole milk

8 cups (about 12 oz./340 g) cubed (¾-inch/2 cm) pieces) white or whole-wheat country bread

1 cup (4 oz./113 g) coarsely shredded Cheddar cheese

1 cup (4 oz./113 g) coarsely shredded pepper Jack cheese

3 Tbs. ground Parmigiano Reggiano cheese + more for serving (see p. 38)

MAKE AHEAD

> The bread cubes can be cut, covered, and stowed at room temperature for up to 3 days or in the freezer for up to 1 month.

> The veggie–ham mixture and the egg mixture can be prepared and refrigerated separately for up to 1 day.

> The strata is best served warm. If you're not serving within 1 hour, let cool completely, cover, and refrigerate for up to 3 days and reheat (whole or squares) in the oven or toaster oven until a fork inserted in the center is warm to the touch.

1. Heat the butter in a large skillet over medium-high heat until melted and foamy. Add the asparagus, mushrooms, and onion. Cook, stirring occasionally, until the vegetables are crisp-tender, 3 to 5 minutes. Add the yellow peppers, garlic, and a few grinds of salt and black pepper and cook, stirring, over medium heat until fragrant, 1 to 2 minutes. Taste and add more salt and pepper as needed. The mixture should be well seasoned. Slide the pan off the heat, stir in the ham and basil, and set aside, stirring occasionally, until cooled.

2. Lightly grease the bottom and sides of a 9 x 13 x 2-inch (23 x 33 x 5 cm) baking pan with cooking spray. Put the eggs, mustard, and Worcestershire sauce in a 1-quart (960 ml) measuring cup (the spout makes it easy to pour the custard) or a medium bowl and whisk until well blended. Add the half-and-half and whisk until well blended. Spread half of the bread cubes in the prepared pan. Scatter half of the veggie–ham mixture over the bread, sprinkle with half each of the Cheddar and pepper Jack cheeses, and pour over half of the egg mixture. Repeat the layers with the remaining bread, veggie–ham mixture, cheeses, and egg mixture. Cover the surface of the strata directly with plastic wrap and let sit at room temperature, pressing down on the bread occasionally to cover with the custard, until evenly soaked, 45 to 60 minutes or for up to 1 day in the refrigerator (see the Essential Technique on p. 70).

3. Position a rack in the center of the oven and heat the oven to 350°F (180°C/gas 4). If you have refrigerated the strata, let it sit at room temperature while the oven heats. Uncover and sprinkle the Parmigiano evenly over the top. Bake until the strata is set (a knife inserted in the center comes out clean) and the center springs back when gently pressed with a finger, 44 to 46 minutes. If it begins to overbrown, cover loosely with foil. Move the dish to a rack and let cool for at least 15 minutes before serving.

TWISTS

Flavor swap

> **BUTTERNUT SQUASH-WHITE BEAN**
Instead of the veggie-ham mixture use:
3 cups (18 oz./567 g) cooked, diced butternut squash
1½ cups (8¼ oz./234 g) cooked and drained cannellini beans
  (or other small white beans)
1 cup (5 oz./142 g) cooked, squeezed dry, and coarsely chopped spinach
½ cup (1⅛ oz./32 g) thinly sliced scallions (white and light green parts)
2 Tbs. chopped fresh oregano

Instead of the Cheddar and pepper Jack use:
2 cups (9 oz./255 g) crumbled goat cheese or feta

> **SPINACH-BRIE**
Instead of the veggie-ham mixture use:
3 cups (15 oz./425 g) cooked, squeezed dry, and coarsely chopped spinach
8 oz. (227 g) fresh mushrooms, sliced and cooked
1 medium onion, chopped and cooked
1 Tbs. chopped fresh thyme

Instead of the Cheddar and pepper Jack use:
2½ cups (10 oz./283 g) diced Brie cheese (without the rind)

Re-size it

Make a half recipe by reducing all ingredients by half, assembling in an 8- or 10-cup (1.9 to 2.3 l) baking dish, and proceeding as directed.

BAKER'S WISDOM

Bread for strata and bread pudding

Any bread with a clean, simple flavor is a good candidate for this type of sweet or savory pudding. Rustic or country-style breads like ciabatta, baguette, focaccia, or pugliese are good choices. Soft, egg-rich loaves like challah or brioche also make delicious pudding, as do leftover croissants. The only caveat is that the bread should be a bit on the stale side. The drier or older the bread, the more it will absorb the flavorful custard and make for light, fluffy bread pudding.

(continued)

ESSENTIAL TECHNIQUE

Trimming asparagus

  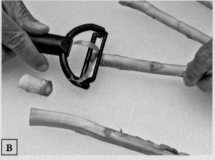

Hold an asparagus spear with both hands and snap off the tough end. If it's fresh, it will break naturally (left); if the spear doesn't break but instead just bends, the asparagus is old and should be discarded (right).

Instead of snapping the ends of thicker spears, cut off the non-green end and use a Y-shaped vegetable peeler to peel off the outer, tough layer at the base of the asparagus. You don't need to peel if you're using young, thin spears.

Assembling the strata

With half of the bread cubes spread out evenly in the prepared pan, layer half of the veggie–ham mixture over the top.

Pour about half of the egg mixture over the cheeses, then finish layering on the remaining bread, veggie–ham mixture, cheeses, and remaining egg mixture.

Cover the strata with plastic wrap and press down directly on the strata to ensure the custard completely covers the filling.

Banana-Stuffed Baked French Toast

Serves 8 to 10

I love making griddled French toast, but it's too time-consuming when I'm feeding a large crowd. Instead, I turn to this recipe for a rich, easy, impressive baked version of the classic that I can make ahead. The latter is a nice perk around the holidays or when you have early-riser houseguests.

The flavor profile is classic Dodge: very ripe bananas and a hint of chocolate teamed up with an egg-rich, creamy custard made with a little mascarpone for good measure. I like to make my Challah (recipe on p. 429) for this recipe, but any good-quality store-bought, soft, egg-rich loaf will be delicious.

Two techniques are important to highlight: cutting a pocket in the sliced bread and piping in the filling (see the Essential Technique on p. 72). Work slowly when cutting the pocket into the slices; keeping the bread intact will help keep the filling inside. You're also working with a very sharp knife in your hands, so be careful. For the filling, I find it easiest and cleanest to fill a zip-top plastic bag (or a pastry bag) to pipe into the pockets, but if preferred, you can spoon it in. Either way, family and friends will be happy you thought ahead and made them this very special meal.

Nonstick cooking spray or softened butter, for preparing the pan
Six 1½-inch (4 cm) thick slices bread (challah, brioche, or other soft-crusted bread), preferably stale
1 medium (6 oz./170 g) very ripe banana
½ cup (4 oz./113 g) mascarpone
¼ cup (1½ oz./42 g) mini chocolate chips or finely chopped bittersweet or semisweet chocolate
4 Tbs. granulated sugar, divided
1 tsp. pure vanilla extract, divided
Pinch or two of table salt
6 large eggs
2 cups (480 ml) whole milk
¾ cup (180 ml) heavy cream

1. Working carefully with the tip of a small serrated knife and using a sawing motion, slice a pocket starting from the top of the crust into the center of each bread slice to within about ½ inch (12 mm) of the edges and the bottom.

2. Peel the banana and mash with a fork in a medium bowl until blended. Add the mascarpone, chocolate, 2 Tbs. sugar, ½ tsp. vanilla, and a pinch of salt and stir until well blended. Scrape into a zip-top plastic bag and, using a bench scraper, push the mixture into one corner, then seal the bag (see the Essential Technique on p. 72).

3. Snip off the corner of the plastic bag. Working with one slice at a time, gently push the tip of the bag into the pocket and slowly fill with about 3 Tbs. of the banana mixture. The bread will expand and some filling will peek out from the top. Holding the bread with the opening up, gently tap on the counter to settle the filling. The exact amount of filling will vary depending on the size of the slice.

4. Lightly grease the bottom and sides of a 9 x 13 x 2-inch (23 x 33 x 5 cm) baking dish and arrange the bread slices in an even layer. Put the eggs, remaining 2 Tbs. sugar, remaining ½ tsp. vanilla, and a pinch of salt in a 1-quart (960 ml) measuring cup (the spout makes it easy to pour the

---

FINISHING TOUCHES

Serve with confectioners' sugar, toasted nuts, and sliced fresh bananas.

custard) or in a medium bowl and whisk until well blended. Add the milk and heavy cream, whisk until well blended, and pour over the slices. Set aside for 10 to 20 minutes, then turn the slices to coat both sides. Cover and refrigerate until the bread is evenly soaked, 6 hours or overnight.

5. Remove the French toast from the refrigerator, uncover, and turn over the slices. Position a rack in the center of the oven and heat the oven to 350°F (180°C/gas 4). Bake the French toast until the top is golden brown and the slices are medium-firm in the center when gently pressed with a finger, 49 to 51 minutes. If it begins to overbrown, cover loosely with foil. Move the dish to a rack and let cool for at least 15 minutes before serving.

Stuffing the bread

A

B

A small serrated knife is the perfect tool to cut a pocket into the center of the bread slices. Start cutting with the bread on a cutting board, then pick up the slice as you finish cutting the pocket to ensure you don't go all the way through to the bottom.

With the filling in a zip-top bag, use a bench scraper to push the filling into one corner, press out any air, and seal the bag. Holding the bag as you would a filled pastry bag, snip off the corner of the zip-top bag.

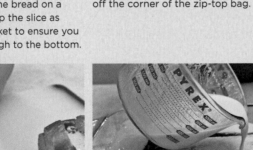

C

D

E

Hold a slice of bread firmly in one hand while you fill the pocket. The bread will expand as filling is piped in.

Position the filled bread tightly together in the prepared baking pan, making sure the slices are laying flat. A large measuring cup makes it easier to pour the custard over the stuffed bread.

After letting the custard-soaked bread sit for about 20 minutes, flip each slice so that the other side gets soaked too. Use both hands so that the stuffing stays in place.

Crumble-Topped Crab *and* Pancetta Mini Quiches

Makes 24 mini quiches [PHOTO ON P. 97]

Two-bite mini quiches are perhaps the most versatile savory recipe in any baker's repertoire. They are perfect for a brunch buffet, holiday party hors d'oeuvres, or Super Bowl snack, and leftovers heat up quickly for a delicious breakfast treat. The rich, custard filling can be easily customized—see the Twists on p. 74. Best of all, these bite-sized gems can be made well ahead of time.

The dough for these quiches owes its delicious flavor to a high amount of butter, which, along with salt and lemon juice, elevates its rich, savory taste. The dough is similar to my classic pie dough, but I've added a touch more water in order to make the dough easy to roll out. A crumble topping, made by grating the leftover dough scraps, adds an additional crunchy and savory flavor to each bite.

Nonstick cooking spray or
softened butter, for preparing
the pan

For the dough
1⅓ cups (6 oz./170 g)
unbleached all-purpose flour
1 tsp. granulated sugar
½ tsp. table salt
8 Tbs. (4 oz./113 g) unsalted
butter, cut into 6 slices,
well chilled
2 Tbs. very cold water
1 Tbs. freshly squeezed
lemon juice

For the crumble topping
2 tsp. unbleached all-purpose
flour
¼ tsp. ground paprika

For the filling
½ cup (2 oz./57 g) finely
chopped, lightly packed
pancetta
⅔ cup (160 ml) half-and-half
1 large egg
2 tsp. Dijon mustard
1 to 4 drops of hot sauce

1 cup (4½ oz./128 g) coarsely
broken, lightly packed lump
crabmeat (picked over and
shells discarded)
½ cup (2 oz./57 g) finely
shredded, lightly packed
Gruyère cheese
3 Tbs. thinly sliced fresh chives
Coarse salt
Freshly ground black pepper
(about 5 twists of the grinder)

Make the dough

1. Whisk the flour, sugar, and salt in a large bowl until well blended. Add the cold butter pieces and, using a pastry blender or two knives, cut them into the flour mixture until the pieces are pea-sized, about 3 minutes. (You can also do this in a food processor using short pulses, scraping the blended mixture into the large bowl before proceeding.)

2. Pour the water and lemon juice over the flour and, using a silicone spatula, stir and fold until you get a shaggy dough that barely hangs together. (I like to use one hand to help mix while keeping the other working the spatula.)

3. Dump the moist crumbs onto a large piece of plastic wrap or an unfloured counter and gather into a pile. Starting on one side of the pile of crumbs and using the heel of your hand, push and gently smear a section of the dough away from you to blend the crumbs together. Repeat with the remaining side of the dough, then fold the dough together using a bench scraper, turn the pile 90 degrees, and repeat the process until the mixture just comes together into a cohesive dough (this is a technique

MAKE AHEAD

> The dough can be prepared, covered, and refrigerated for up to 2 days or frozen for up to 1 month.

> The dough-lined muffin tins can be covered and refrigerated for up to 1 day or frozen for up to 1 month.

> The unbaked quiches can be frozen for up to 1 month. Arrange the filled tins in the freezer until very firm, about 2 hours. Using the tip of a small knife, pop the quiches out of the pan, put them in a zip-top freezer bag or airtight container, and freeze for up to 1 month. To bake, heat the oven as directed, return the quiches to their tins, and bake until the filling is puffed and the crust is browned, 28 to 32 minutes.

Flavor swap

> **CARAMELIZED ONION AND HAM**
Instead of the crab, pancetta, Gruyère, and chives, use:

1 medium onion, chopped (cook, stirring frequently, in a small skillet over medium-low heat until tender and golden brown)

¾ cup (3⅜ oz./96 g) sliced, chopped baked ham

½ cup (3¾ oz./106 g) packed garlic–herb cheese (Boursin®)

1 Tbs. chopped fresh parsley

> **ROASTED RED PEPPER, KALAMATA, GOAT CHEESE, AND BASIL**
Instead of the crab, pancetta, Gruyère, and chives, use:

½ cup (4 oz./14 g) chopped roasted red peppers

¼ cup (2 oz./7 g) chopped pitted Kalamata olives

½ cup (2 oz./57 g) crumbled goat cheese

2 Tbs. chopped fresh basil

TWISTS

> Instead of making the dough, use 2 packages (7 oz./198 g each) premade pie dough and proceed with lining the muffin tins.

---

called *fraisage*). Be careful not to overwork the dough because that would make the crust dense. Shape into a 5-inch (12 cm) disk, wrap tightly in plastic wrap, and refrigerate until firm, about 2 hours, or up to 2 days.

For more about *fraisage*, see p. 549.

Roll out the dough and put in the muffin cups

1. Lightly grease 24 mini (1¾-inch/4.5 cm diameter) muffin cups.

2. If the dough has been chilled longer than 4 hours, set it out at room temperature until it's just pliable enough to roll, 10 to 20 minutes. Arrange a large piece of parchment on a work surface, put the unwrapped dough in the center, and cover with another piece of parchment. Using a rolling pin, roll the dough between the parchment to a ⅛-inch (3 mm) thickness, lifting, turning, and repositioning the parchment and lightly flouring throughout the rolling.

For more about rolling dough between parchment, see p. 133.

3. Peel off the top sheet of parchment and, using a 2½-inch (6 cm) round cookie cutter, cut out as many rounds as possible. Arrange them in a single layer on a parchment-lined cookie sheet. Gather up the scraps, reroll to a ⅛-inch (3 mm) thickness, cut more rounds, and add them to the cookie sheet. Reroll and cut one more round for a total of 24 rounds of dough. (If the dough becomes too soft, slide a cookie sheet under the dough and refrigerate for a few minutes.) Gather the remaining scraps, press into a ball, wrap in plastic, and freeze until firm.

4. Working with one round at a time, use your fingers to gently press the dough into the prepared muffin cups, making sure there are no air bubbles in the bottom and the dough is pressed firmly and evenly up the side and all the way to the top of the cup. Repeat with the remaining dough rounds. Cover with plastic and refrigerate while preparing the filling.

Make the crumble topping and filling

1. For the topping, arrange a box grater over a shallow plate or bowl and coarsely grate the chilled dough ball. Sprinkle the flour and paprika over the shreds, gently toss with a fork (or your fingers) until evenly covered and loose, and refrigerate.

2. For the filling, cook the pancetta in a small nonstick skillet over medium heat, stirring frequently, until evenly browned, 4 to 5 minutes. Using a slotted spoon, move the pancetta to a paper towel–lined plate and let cool completely.

3. Measure the half-and-half in a 2-cup (480 ml) measuring cup (the spout makes it easy to pour the custard into the crust). Add the egg, mustard, and hot sauce and whisk until well blended.

4. Put the crab, cheese, and chives in a small bowl. Add the cooled pancetta and salt and pepper to taste, then use a fork to toss until well blended. Taste and adjust the seasonings.

Fill and bake the quiches

1. Position a rack in the lower third of the oven and set a cookie sheet on the rack. Heat the oven to 425°F (220°C/gas 7).

2. Evenly spoon the crab mixture (about 1 Tbs.) into the dough-lined muffin cups and pour the custard evenly among the cups. Scatter the topping evenly over the filling. Slide the tins into the oven and immediately reduce the oven temperature to 400°F (200°C/gas 6). Bake until the crust and tops are golden brown, 26 to 28 minutes.

3. Move the muffin tins to a rack and let cool for 15 minutes. Using a thin, metal spatula or the tip of a paring knife, carefully remove the tarts from the muffin cups and move them to a rack. Serve warm or at room temperature.

BAKER'S WISDOM

Storing leftovers

The mini quiches are best served warm. If you're not serving the quiches within 20 minutes, let cool completely, cover, and refrigerate for up to 3 days; reheat in the oven or toaster oven until a fork inserted in the center is warm to the touch.

ESSENTIAL TECHNIQUE

Assembling the quiches

A

Using a 2½-inch (6 cm) cookie cutter, cut out as many rounds as possible and move to a parchment-lined cookie sheet. Gather the scraps, reroll, and cut more rounds until you have 24. Save the rest of the dough for the topping.

B

Press each dough round into the cups of a lightly greased mini muffin tin, pressing firmly into the bottom and sides of the cup.

C

Scatter just a bit of crumbled topping evenly over the top of the crab-filled cups.

Chapter 3

QUICK TO MAKE

> > > >

Currant Cream Scones

Makes 8 scones

Homemade scones are easy to make and taste so much better than store-bought. I add just a touch of sugar to these scones to make them slightly sweet, crumbly, and wonderfully delicate. You can add a bit more sugar—up to ½ cup (3½ oz./99 g)—but try them my way first. When teamed with sweet dried fruit (or finely chopped bittersweet chocolate as I sometimes swap in—a guilty pleasure), the flavor is perfectly balanced.

2 cups (9 oz./255 g) unbleached all-purpose flour
¼ cup (1¾ oz./50 g) granulated sugar
1 Tbs. baking powder
½ tsp. table salt

6 Tbs. (3 oz./85 g) unsalted butter, cut into 8 pieces and well chilled
½ cup (2½ oz./71 g) lightly packed dried currants
¾ cup (180 ml) heavy cream, chilled

1 large egg (or 2 yolks from large eggs), chilled
1 tsp. pure vanilla extract

For the confectioners' sugar glaze
1 cup (4 oz./113 g) confectioners' sugar
2 to 4 Tbs. heavy cream or milk
¼ tsp. pure vanilla or almond extract

1. Position a rack in the center of the oven and heat the oven to 375°F (190°C/gas 5). Line a cookie sheet with parchment or a nonstick liner.

2. Whisk the flour, sugar, baking powder, and salt in a large bowl until well blended. Add the cold butter pieces and, using a pastry blender or two knives, cut the butter into the flour mixture until the mixture resembles coarse crumbs. (You can also do this step in a food processor using short pulses, scraping the blended mixture into a large bowl before proceeding.) Add the currants and toss until blended.

For more about cutting in butter, see p. 502.

3. Put the ¾ cup (180 ml) cream, egg, and vanilla in a small bowl (or measure in a 2-cup/480 ml glass measure and add the egg and vanilla) and whisk until well blended. Pour the egg mixture over the flour and, using a silicone spatula, stir and fold until it forms a moist dough with some floury bits remaining. (I like to use one hand to help mix while keeping the other working the spatula.) Scrape the dough and any remaining floury bits onto the counter and knead a few times until the dough is evenly moist and holds together. Be careful not to overwork the dough or the scones will be dense.

For more about using your hand to help mix, see p. 85.

4. Gently pat and shape the dough into a 6-inch (15 cm) disk. With a large knife, cut the dough into 8 wedges. Arrange the wedges about 2 inches apart on the prepared cookie sheet. Bake until the tops are golden brown and a pick inserted in the center comes out clean, 20 to 22 minutes. Move the sheet to a rack and let the scones sit until cool, about 15 minutes.

(continued)

MAKE AHEAD

> The butter can be cut into the dry ingredients, covered, and refrigerated for up to 1 day ahead. The liquid ingredients can be mixed, covered, and refrigerated for up to 1 day ahead. When ready to serve, proceed with the recipe while the oven heats up.

> The scones can be served warm or at room temperature. If you're not serving them immediately, cover the cooled scones and stow at room temperature for up to 2 days; reheat in the oven or toaster oven, if desired.

FINISHING TOUCHES

Instead of drizzling the tops with confectioners' sugar glaze, before baking, brush the tops with heavy cream and sprinkle with sanding sugar.

For more about mixing and shaping, see p. 85.

5. Put the confectioners' sugar, 2 Tbs. cream or milk, and extract in a small bowl and stir. Add more cream or milk, a little at a time, until the glaze is smooth, very thick, and shiny (see the Essential Technique below). Using a teaspoon, drizzle over the top of the cooled scones.

TWISTS

Flavor swap

> Instead of currants, use the same amount of chopped crystallized ginger or other dried fruit or ½ cup (3 oz./85 g) mini chocolate chips or finely chopped chocolate.

> **Almond:** Omit the currants. Add 1 tsp. pure almond extract along with the vanilla extract and top with 1 cup (4 oz./113 g) sliced almonds before baking. Drizzle with almond-flavored glaze.

Re-size it

Mini: Prepare the dough as directed and shape into an 8 x 4-inch (20 x 10 cm) rectangle. With a large knife, cut the dough crosswise into 6 equal strips, then cut each strip into 3 pieces (they'll be about 1⅓ inches/3.4 cm each). Arrange the pieces about 2 inches (5 cm) apart on the prepared cookie sheet. Bake until the tops are golden brown, 19 to 21 minutes. Move the sheet to a rack and let the scones sit until they're cool enough to handle, about 10 minutes.

ESSENTIAL TECHNIQUE

Correct glaze consistency

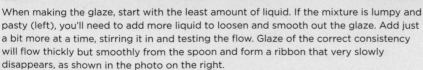

When making the glaze, start with the least amount of liquid. If the mixture is lumpy and pasty (left), you'll need to add more liquid to loosen and smooth out the glaze. Add just a bit more at a time, stirring it in and testing the flow. Glaze of the correct consistency will flow thickly but smoothly from the spoon and form a ribbon that very slowly disappears, as shown in the photo on the right.

Use a teaspoon to drizzle glaze over the top of the cooled scones in a zigzag pattern. If the scone is too warm, the glaze will not hold a ribbon and instead melt off the top.

Mile-High Parmesan–Chive Buttermilk Biscuits

Makes 6 biscuits   [PHOTO ON P. 98]

The scent of these Parmesan-laden biscuits wafting from the oven is swoon-worthy, but one bite proves that they taste even better than they smell.

They come together in the time it takes to heat the oven, making them the perfect side dish for an easy weeknight meal, barbecue, or picnic. With their mile-high appearance, tender, fluffy texture, and bold flavor, they're also sophisticated enough for the most elegant dinner party. Leftovers, if you have any, are great for breakfast, split, toasted, and served with plenty of butter.

For the highest rise and lightest texture, make sure the butter and buttermilk are cold and handle the dough as little as possible. Avoid twisting the cutter when punching out the dough rounds, as that will pinch the dough together and the biscuits won't rise well and will be dense.

2 cups (9 oz./255 g) unbleached
   all-purpose flour
2 tsp. baking powder
¼ tsp. baking soda
¾ tsp. table salt
Pinch of ground cayenne pepper

6 Tbs. (3 oz./85 g) unsalted
   butter, cut into 6 pieces and
   well chilled
½ cup (2 oz./57 g) finely ground
   Parmigiano Reggiano cheese

¼ cup (¼ oz./7 g) lightly
   packed, thinly sliced
   fresh chives
½ tsp. finely grated lemon zest
   (see p. 138)
¾ cup (180 ml) buttermilk, cold

1. Position a rack in the center of the oven and heat the oven to 425°F (220°C/gas 7). Line a cookie sheet with parchment or a nonstick liner.

2. Whisk the flour, baking powder, baking soda, salt, and cayenne in a large bowl until well blended. Add the cold butter pieces and, using a pastry blender or two knives, cut the butter into the flour mixture until the butter is pea-sized. (You can also do this step in a food processor using short pulses, scraping the blended mixture into a large bowl before proceeding.)

For more about cutting butter and flour together until the butter is pea-sized, see p. 80.

3. Add the cheese, chives, and lemon zest and stir until blended. Pour the buttermilk over the flour and, using a silicone spatula, stir and fold until it forms a shaggy, moist dough with some floury bits remaining. (I like to use one hand to help mix while keeping the other working the spatula.) Scrape the dough and any remaining floury bits onto the counter and knead a few times until the dough is evenly moist and holds together. Avoid overworking the dough or the biscuits will be dense.

For more about using your hand to help mix, see p. 85.

4. Gently pat and shape the dough into a 1-inch (2.5 cm) thick slab. Using a 2½-inch (6 cm) round cutter, cut 4 rounds out of the dough. Make sure to press straight down and lift straight up, as twisting the cutter will pinch together the sides and interfere with rising. Arrange

MAKE AHEAD

> Cut the butter into the dry ingredients, cover, and refrigerate along with the mixed wet ingredients up to 1 day ahead. When ready to serve, proceed with the recipe while the oven heats.

> The biscuits are best served warm. If you're not serving them immediately, cover the cooled biscuits and stow at room temperature for up to 2 days or freeze for up to 1 month. Reheat in the oven or toaster oven.

FINISHING TOUCHES

> Serve with a schmear of softened salted or unsalted butter or Honey Butter (recipe on p. 85).

> Split and serve with sliced ham, cucumbers, or bacon.

(Double Corn–Goat Cheese Spoonbread continued)

MAKE AHEAD

The custard can be made without the egg yolks, cooled, covered, and refrigerated for up to 2 days before reheating until warm and then adding the yolks and whipped whites before baking.

TWISTS

Flavor swap

> Instead of the goat cheese, use the same amount of grated pepper Jack or sharp Cheddar cheese.

> Omit the goat cheese, scallions, and basil and add 1 package (5½ oz./156 g) of crumbled herbed garlic cheese (like Boursin).

FINISHING TOUCHES

Add buttered breadcrumbs: Before starting the pudding, put ½ cup (¾ oz./20 g) fresh breadcrumbs, 2 Tbs. grated Parmigiano Reggiano, and a good pinch of salt and pepper in a small bowl and stir until blended. Drizzle 1½ tsp. olive oil over the crumbs and toss until blended. Just before baking, scatter the crumbs over the top of the spoonbread and bake as directed.

1. Position a rack in the center of the oven and heat the oven to 375°F (190°C/ gas mark 5). Lightly grease an 8-inch (20 cm) square pan or another 8-cup (2 liter) vessel about 2 inches (5 cm) tall.

2. Put the milk in a medium saucepan, set over medium heat, and slowly pour in the cornmeal, whisking constantly, until well blended. Cook, whisking constantly, until thickened and boiling, about 3 minutes.

3. Slide the pan off the heat, add the corn kernels, goat cheese, scallions, butter, basil, salt, hot sauce, and black pepper to taste and stir until the butter is melted. Don't worry if the cheese isn't completely melted. Taste and adjust the seasonings—the flavors should be bold. Add the egg yolks and stir until well blended.

4. Put the egg whites in a medium bowl. Beat with an electric handheld mixer fitted with wire beaters on medium speed until the whites begin to foam. Increase the speed to medium high and beat until the whites hold medium-firm peaks when the beater is lifted, 1 to 2 minutes. The tip of the peaks should droop over just slightly. Do not overbeat. Scoop about one-quarter of the whites into the cornmeal mixture and, using a silicone spatula, gently stir until blended. Add the remaining whites and gently fold in until just blended.

For more about beating egg whites, see p. 212.

For more about folding, see p. 270.

5. Pour and scrape the batter into the prepared pan. Bake until the top is puffed and golden and the top springs back when gently pressed with a finger, 35 to 37 minutes. Move the pan to a rack and serve immediately.

ESSENTIAL TECHNIQUE

Stripping the kernels from the cob

Before cutting the kernels from an ear of corn, first remove the husk and as much of the silk as possible. Hold the ear by the stem end, with the tip against the bottom of a bowl. Be sure the bowl is steady, as you will be using it for leverage as you cut. Position a sharp serrated knife about halfway up the ear and cut down the length of the corn, releasing the kernels. You don't want to cut too deeply or you'll get the hard cob along with the kernel. Continue working your way around the ear, then turn the ear over, hold it by the just-cut end, and finish slicing off the kernels.

Make-Ahead Chocolate
French Toast

[PAGE 45]

91

Salmon- *and* Spinach-Filled
Crêpes

[PAGE 57]

92

Apple Cider Donuts

[PAGE 61]

93

Crumble-Topped Crab *and*
Pancetta Mini Quiches

[PAGE 73]

Mile-High Parmesan–Chive
Buttermilk Biscuits

[PAGE 79]

Toasted Pecan Gingerbread
Scones

[PAGE 84]

99

Whole-Wheat Soda Bread
with Pistachios *and* Apricots

[PAGE 86]

Peach-Studded Muffins

[PAGE 107]

101

Double Cranberry
Orange Bread

[PAGE 109]

102

Mom's Popovers

[PAGE 110]

**Double Chocolate Espresso
Wake-Up Bread**

[PAGE 114]

104

Chunky Oatmeal Peanut
Butter Sandwiches

[PAGE 124]

105

Bittersweet Chocolate
Peppermint Thumbprints

[PAGE 126]

Peach-Studded Muffins

Makes 8 muffins   [PHOTO ON P. 101]

This is my go-to fruit-filled muffin recipe. The basic batter is straightforward and foolproof and makes the perfect-sized batch. I've listed a wide variety of fruit and flavorings to add to the batter, but the combinations are endless, so I'll leave it to you to discover your favorite.

Nonstick cooking spray or softened butter, for preparing the pan
1¾ cups (7⅝ oz./216 g) unbleached all-purpose flour
½ cup (3½ oz./99 g) granulated sugar

2 tsp. baking powder
¼ tsp. baking soda
¼ tsp. table salt
¾ cup (180 ml) buttermilk, at room temperature
1 large egg, at room temperature
1 tsp. pure vanilla extract

¾ cup (4 oz./113 g) diced ripe peaches, lightly mashed
6 Tbs. (3 oz./85 g) unsalted butter, melted
Coarse sanding sugar (optional)

1. Position a rack in the center of the oven and heat the oven to 375°F (190°C/gas 5). Lightly grease the top of a standard 12-cup muffin tin (this will keep the muffin tops from sticking to the pan's surface). Line 8 cups with paper or foil baking cups, leaving one empty in between (this gives the muffin tops a nice round shape).

2. Whisk the flour, sugar, baking powder, baking soda, and salt in a large bowl until well blended. Put the buttermilk, egg, and vanilla in a small bowl (or measure the buttermilk in a 2-cup/480 ml glass measure and add the egg and vanilla) and whisk until well blended. Pour the liquid over the dry ingredients along with the peaches and melted butter and, using a silicone spatula, gently fold until just blended. Portion the batter evenly and sprinkle the tops with coarse sanding sugar (if using). The muffin liners will be very full. Bake until a pick inserted in the center comes out clean, 18 to 21 minutes.

For more about folding batter, see p. 53.

For more about portioning muffin batter, see p. 83.

3. Move the pan to a rack and let cool for 10 minutes. Use a table knife to separate the tops (if necessary), then invert the pan to release the muffins.

MAKE AHEAD

The cooled muffins can be covered and stowed at room temperature for up to 2 days. Reheat in the oven or toaster oven if desired.

FINISHING TOUCHES

Instead of coarse sanding sugar, sprinkle the tops with chopped nuts or streusel before baking or drizzle with confectioners' sugar glaze once the muffins are baked and cooled (see p. 77).

TWISTS

Flavor swap

> Instead of the peaches, use the same amount of one of the following: diced ripe pears, apples, or bananas; toasted, chopped nuts; or chopped dried fruit.

> Along with the vanilla, add one of the following: ½ tsp. pure almond extract, 1 tsp. finely grated lemon zest (see p. 138), 2 tsp. finely grated orange zest, or ¾ tsp. ground cinnamon.

> **Sour Cream:** Omit the buttermilk and use ¾ cup (180 ml) sour cream.

Re-size it

> **Mini:** Lightly grease three 12-cup mini muffin tins. Using a 1-Tbs. scoop, portion the batter evenly among the cups and sprinkle the tops with coarse sanding sugar (if using). Bake until a pick inserted in the center comes out clean, 8 to 10 minutes.

> **Big:** Lightly grease the top of a standard 12-cup muffin tin and line 6 cups with paper or foil baking cups, leaving one empty in between (this gives the muffin tops a nice round shape). Bake until a pick inserted in the center comes out clean, 24 to 26 minutes.

(continued)

Preparing the peaches (and other stone fruit)

A To slice a peach, hold the fruit in one hand and use a small paring knife to slice from the stem end to the bottom, right around the pit. Do this on both sides of the pit. The knife is sharp, so be careful of your fingers holding the peach.

B To open the peach, firmly but gently hold it in both hands and twist each half in opposite directions, releasing one half from the pit.

C To cut the fruit, work with the pitless half and hold over a bowl. Working carefully, make horizontal cuts almost completely through the half, then cut lengthwise; release the diced peaches into the bowl.

D To cut the peach half with the pit, make the same horizontal cuts right up to and around the pit, then make lengthwise cuts around the pit, releasing the fruit into the bowl. When most of the fruit is cut off, pull off the pit and finish cutting what's left.

E To mash the peaches, use the back of a fork to press the fruit against the bottom and up the sides of the bowl.

Double Cranberry Orange Bread

Serves 10   [PHOTO ON P. 102]

As I mulled over this recipe, I wondered how I could make this cranberry bread taste even better than the standard cranberry bread recipe. My answer was obvious: more cranberries! Rather than load this tea bread with more tart, fresh berries, I chose to add dried cranberries. They are lightly sweetened and, because they are dried, their flavor is deeper and more intense, giving the baked cake a well-rounded cranberry flavor. A dash of orange zest and a top crust of sliced almonds complete this festive bread that is delicious served plain or toasted with a schmear of butter.

Nonstick cooking spray or softened butter + flour, for preparing the pan

2 cups (9 oz./255 g) unbleached all-purpose flour

¾ cup (5¼ oz./149 g) granulated sugar

1 Tbs. baking powder

¾ tsp. table salt

1 cup (240 ml) buttermilk, at room temperature

2 large eggs, at room temperature

1 tsp. pure vanilla extract

8 Tbs. (4 oz./113 g) unsalted butter, melted and cooled slightly

1 cup (3½ oz./99 g) fresh cranberries, coarsely chopped (see p. 110)

½ cup (2¼ oz./64 g) packed dried cranberries, coarsely chopped

1 Tbs. finely grated orange zest (see p. 138)

½ cup (2 oz./57 g) sliced almonds

1. Position a rack in the center of the oven and heat the oven to 350°F (180°C/gas 4). Lightly grease and flour the bottom and sides of an 8½ x 4½ x 2¾-inch (21.5 x 11 x 7 cm) loaf pan (I use Pyrex).

For more about preparing cake pans, see p. 232.

2. Put the flour, sugar, baking powder, and salt in a medium bowl and whisk until well blended. Put the buttermilk, eggs, and vanilla in a small bowl (or measure the buttermilk in a 2-cup/480 ml glass measure and add the eggs and vanilla) and whisk until well blended. Pour the liquid over the dry ingredients along with the melted butter, fresh cranberries, dried cranberries, and zest. Using a silicone spatula, gently fold (no stirring) until just blended. Scrape into the prepared pan and spread evenly. Scatter the sliced almonds evenly over the top of the batter. Bake until a pick inserted in the center comes out clean, 55 to 60 minutes.

For more about folding batter, see p. 53.

3. Move the pan to a rack and let cool for 15 to 20 minutes. Run a knife between the bread and the pan to loosen the bread, then invert onto a rack and lift off the pan. Arrange the bread right side up and let cool completely.

(continued)

MAKE AHEAD

The bread can be covered and stored at room temperature for up to 4 days. Leftovers are delicious toasted and spread with butter.

FINISHING TOUCHES

Dust the top with confectioners' sugar or omit the nut topping and drizzle with confectioners' sugar glaze (see p. 77) after baking and cooling completely.

ESSENTIAL TECHNIQUE

Gauging banana ripeness

To get the most banana flavor in your recipe, use bananas that are very ripe. The banana on the left still needs a few days to become overripe. The banana in the center is ok to use in a pinch, but the banana on the right is the best overripeness.

To freeze ripe bananas, weigh them with the peels (I do batches of three), mark the weight on a zip-top freezer bag, peel, and pop them into the bag. Push out the air, seal the bag, and freeze for up to 6 months. Thaw at room temperature.

> >

Double Chocolate Espresso Wake-Up Bread

Serves 10 [PHOTO ON P. 104]

As I'm a tea drinker, my coffeehouse orders are straightforward (large black tea, please), which leaves me with plenty of time to listen to all those wacky coffeehouse orders. One such double-triple-blah-blah concoction inspired this single layer cake. While it is simple to make, it is hardly simple in flavor. With cocoa, ground espresso beans, and bittersweet chocolate in the cake and a brewed coffee glaze, this could easily be called a Trenta Double Chocolate with an Extra Shot and a Coffee Whip. The perfect slice of wake-up cake—even for tea lovers.

For the glaze
1 cup (4 oz./113 g) confectioners' sugar
2 to 4 Tbs. brewed coffee, coffee liqueur, or heavy cream, or a combination of two

For the bread
Nonstick cooking spray or softened butter + flour, for preparing the pan
1¼ cups (5⅝ oz./159 g) unbleached all-purpose flour

½ cup (1½ oz./42 g) unsweetened natural cocoa powder, sifted if lumpy
½ cup (3½ oz./99 g) firmly packed light or dark brown sugar
½ cup (3½ oz./99 g) granulated sugar
1 Tbs. finely ground espresso or coffee beans
2 tsp. baking powder
¼ tsp. baking soda
¾ tsp. table salt

1 cup (240 ml) buttermilk, at room temperature
¼ cup (60 ml) neutral oil (safflower, canola, vegetable, or corn)
2 large eggs, at room temperature
1 tsp. pure vanilla extract
¾ cup (4 oz./113 g) chopped chocolate (bittersweet, semisweet, or white)
4 Tbs. (2 oz./57 g) unsalted butter, melted and cooled

Make the glaze

Put the confectioners' sugar and 2 Tbs. coffee, liqueur, or heavy cream in a small bowl and stir with a spoon. Add more coffee, liqueur, or cream, a little at a time, until the glaze is smooth, very thick, and shiny. Set aside.

For more about correct glaze consistency, see p. 78.

Make the bread

1. Position a rack in the center of the oven and heat the oven to 350°F (180°C/gas 4). Lightly grease and flour the bottom and sides of a 9 x 2-inch (23 x 5 cm) round cake pan.

2. Whisk the flour, cocoa, brown sugar, granulated sugar, ground espresso, baking powder, baking soda, and salt in a large bowl until well blended. Put the buttermilk, oil, eggs, and vanilla in a small bowl (or measure the buttermilk and oil in a 2-cup/480 ml glass measure and add the eggs and vanilla) and whisk until well blended. Pour the liquid over the dry ingredients along with the chopped chocolate and melted butter. Using a silicone spatula, gently fold (no stirring) until just blended. Scrape into the prepared pan and spread evenly. Bake until a pick inserted in the center comes out clean, 40 to 42 minutes.

For more about folding batter, see p. 53.

3. Move the pan to a rack and let cool for 15 to 20 minutes. Run a knife between the bread and the pan to loosen the bread. Invert onto a rack and lift off the pan. Invert the bread onto another rack so that the top is facing up and let cool until just warm, 20 to 30 minutes.

4. Scrape the glaze onto the center of the bread and, using a small offset spatula, spread the glaze over the top to within 1 inch of the edges. Let cool completely, about 1 hour.

MAKE AHEAD

The bread can be covered and stowed at room temperature for up to 5 days.

FINISHING TOUCHES

Before baking, sprinkle the top with some chopped nuts or with 2 Tbs. sanding sugar or cinnamon-sugar (see p. 197).

(continued)

TWISTS

Flavor swap

> Instead of the glaze, dust the top with confectioners' sugar before serving.

> For less coffee flavor, omit the ground espresso beans.

> **Almond:** Omit the ground espresso, add ½ tsp. pure almond extract to the liquid mixture, and sprinkle the top of the batter with sliced or slivered almonds before baking. Dust the top with confectioners' sugar instead of the glaze.

> **Peanut:** Omit the chopped chocolate and ground espresso and use ¾ cup (3¾ oz./106 g) coarsely chopped lightly salted peanuts.

> **Sour cream:** Omit the buttermilk and use 1 cup (240 ml) sour cream.

Re-size it

> **Square:** Prepare the batter as directed and scrape into a lightly greased and floured 8-inch (20 cm) square pan. Bake until a pick inserted in the center comes out clean, 39 to 42 minutes.

> **Loaf:** Prepare the batter as directed and scrape into a lightly greased and floured 8½ x 4½ x 2¾-inch (21.5 x 11 x 7 cm) loaf pan (I use Pyrex). Bake until a pick inserted in the center comes out clean, 52 to 56 minutes.

ESSENTIAL TECHNIQUE

Making and spreading glaze

A Pour the glaze onto the center of the cooled bread. It will be thick enough to hold its position without running to the edges.

B Use a small offset spatula to spread the glaze to within an inch of the bread's edges. Be sure the glaze is evenly spread, going back over any spots where the bread shows through. Tilt the spatula's blade to drag the glaze and make it smooth.

Know your sugar

From left to right: confectioners' sugar, granulated sugar, coarse sanding sugar, light brown sugar, dark brown sugar. Superfine can be purchased or made at home by processing granulated sugar until the granules are fine. All sugar should be stored in airtight containers or it will clump or, worse, harden.

Nutty Applesauce Squash Tea Cake

Serves 10

An ideal destination for some of fall's bumper crop of squash, this moist tea cake, made in a loaf shape, is loaded with all things sugar 'n' spice. I like to toast slices for breakfast or an afternoon snack. It's also yummy baked in a square and cut up into lunchbox-sized portions.

For the cake
Nonstick cooking spray or softened butter + flour, for preparing the pan
1 medium (10 oz./283 g) summer squash (yellow or green)
2 cups (9 oz./255 g) unbleached all-purpose flour
¾ cup (5¼ oz./149 g) granulated sugar

1 Tbs. baking powder
¾ tsp. ground cinnamon
¾ tsp. table salt
¾ tsp. ground ginger
¼ tsp. ground nutmeg
1 cup (8½ oz./241 g) applesauce, at room temperature
2 large eggs, at room temperature
1 tsp. pure vanilla extract

½ cup (2 oz./57 g) toasted, chopped pecans (optional)
6 Tbs. (3 oz./85 g) unsalted butter, melted and cooled

For the glaze
¾ cup (3 oz./85 g) confectioners' sugar, sifted if lumpy
2 to 4 tsp. milk, lemon juice, or orange juice

Make the cake

1. Position a rack in the center of the oven and heat the oven to 350°F (180°C/gas 4). Lightly grease and flour the bottom and sides of an 8½ x 4½ x 2¾ inch (21.5 x 11 x 7 cm) loaf pan (I use Pyrex).

For more about preparing cake pans, see p. 232.

2. Coarsely grate the squash, avoiding the center seeds if the squash is very large. You'll need 2 cups (8 oz./227 g) of lightly packed coarsely shredded squash. Line a plate with several layers of paper towels and spread the squash over them in an even layer. Top with a few more layers of paper towels, press gently, and set aside.

3. Whisk the flour, sugar, baking powder, cinnamon, salt, ginger, and nutmeg in a large bowl until well blended. Put the applesauce, eggs, and vanilla in a small bowl and whisk until well blended. Roll the squash in the paper towel and gently squeeze to remove any excess water. Pour the wet ingredients over the flour mixture along with the squash, pecans, and melted butter. Using a silicone spatula, gently fold (no stirring) until just blended. Scrape into the prepared pan and spread evenly. Bake until the top is pale golden brown and a pick inserted in the center comes out clean, 52 to 55 minutes.

For more about folding batter, see p. 53.

4. Move the pan to a rack and let cool for 15 to 20 minutes. Run a knife between the cake and the pan to loosen the cake. Invert onto a rack and lift off the pan. Arrange the cake right side up and let cool completely.

(continued)

MAKE AHEAD

The bread can be covered and stowed at room temperature for up to 5 days.

TWISTS

Flavor swap

> **Lemon:** Omit the spices and add 1½ tsp. finely grated lemon zest (see p. 138) to the liquid mixture.

> Use chunky-style applesauce for the same amount of regular applesauce.

Re-size it

Square or round: Prepare the batter as directed and scrape into a lightly greased and floured 8-inch (20 cm) square pan or 9-inch (23 cm) round pan. Bake until the top is pale golden brown and a pick inserted in the center comes out clean, 34 to 36 minutes.

FINISHING TOUCHES

Dust the top with confectioners' sugar just before cutting and serving.

BAKER'S WISDOM

Cast iron skillet care, aka seasoning

Treat your skillet well and the nonstick-like nature of the pan, known as seasoning or patina, will increase over time. The oil used in cooking seeps into the cast iron, smoothing out any rough spots and making the surface almost 100% nonstick.

Most new cast iron skillets come preseasoned, but if yours did not, it's easy to season or re-season. Simply coat the inside of the skillet with a thin film of oil and bake upside down in a 400°F oven for 1 hour. (Arrange a baking sheet on the rack below.) Turn off the oven and let the skillet cool completely in the oven.

To clean, rinse the skillet with hot water and a nonabrasive sponge. If some food sticks, let it soak in hot water for a bit. To avoid any rusting, dry the skillet well with a towel and set over low heat for a few minutes. Slide off the heat and coat the interior surface with a drop or two of oil.

ESSENTIAL TECHNIQUE

Cutting and coring pears (and apples)

A

Hold the pear firmly in one hand while using a Y-shaped vegetable peeler in the other to peel the skin from the pear. Start at the stem end and work down in long strokes.

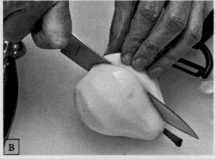

B

To slice a pear in half, place it on a cutting board and hold the pear with the fingers of one hand while cutting through the core with the other.

C

A melon baller is the perfect size to remove the core. Hold the pear in one hand and tilt the baller so that the edge scoops out the bulk of the core along with the bottom stem. Then flip the pear around and slide the edge of the baller through the remaining core and stem.

D

Place half of the pear, cut side down, on a cutting board. Hold one end firmly with the tips of your fingers and cut through the pear to slice. Be watchful of your fingers as you get to the end of the pear.

Chapter 4

COOKIES

> > > >

Chunky Oatmeal Peanut Butter Sandwiches

Makes 34 cookies [PHOTO ON P. 105]

This is my from-scratch homage to the Girl Scouts of America's Do-Si-Do—a cross between an oatmeal cookie and a peanut butter cookie. These gluten-free cookies are chewy-crunchy delicious all on their own, but sandwiching them with a sweet, creamy peanut butter filling takes them to a whole new and decadent level of peanut butter heaven. Be sure to use regular peanut butter, not natural, which tends to separate, making the finished cookies inconsistent in quality.

You can use crunchy peanut butter in this recipe, but it does not take the place of the additional nuts I've called for. The chopped, lightly salted peanuts in the batter not only add extra crunch but they also double up the PB flavor. Don't worry about the extra salt on the peanuts. I've adjusted the salt added to the batter to compensate for their saltiness. Use Virginia peanuts, if you can find them. They are spectacular in size, extra meaty, and pack a boat-load of flavor.

For the cookies
1 cup (3 oz./85 g) certified gluten-free old-fashioned oats
½ tsp. baking soda
¼ tsp. table salt
¾ cup (6¾ oz./191 g) smooth peanut butter, at room temperature
4 Tbs. (2 oz./57 g) unsalted butter, softened

⅔ cup (4⅝ oz./131 g) firmly packed light brown sugar
⅓ cup (2⅜ oz./67 g) granulated sugar
1 large egg
1 tsp. pure vanilla extract
¾ cup (3¾ oz./106 g) lightly salted peanuts, coarsely chopped

For the filling
¾ cup (3 oz./85 g) confectioners' sugar
½ cup (4½ oz./128 g) smooth peanut butter
6 Tbs. (3 oz./85 g) unsalted butter, softened

MAKE AHEAD

> Shape the batter into balls and arrange close together on a flat plate, cover, and refrigerate for up to 1 day or freeze for up to 3 months. Bring to room temperature while the oven heats.

> The cookies can be baked and cooled, then layered between sheets of parchment or waxed paper in an airtight container and stowed at room temperature for up to 5 days or frozen for up to 6 weeks before thawing at room temperature and sandwiching with the filling.

> The filled sandwich cookies can be stowed between sheets of parchment or waxed paper in an airtight container for up to 5 days.

Make the cookies

1. Position a rack in the center of the oven and heat the oven to 350°F (180°C/gas 4). Line two cookie sheets with parchment or nonstick liners.

2. Put the oats in a food processor or blender and pulse until most are coarsely ground (there will still be some larger pieces), 15 to 18 pulses. Put the ground oats, baking soda, and salt in a small bowl and whisk until well blended.

3. Put the peanut butter, butter, brown sugar, and granulated sugar in the bowl of a stand mixer fitted with the paddle attachment (or in a large bowl using an electric handheld mixer fitted with wire beaters). Beat on medium speed until well blended and lighter in color, about 1 minute. Add the egg and vanilla and mix on low speed until just blended. Add the oat mixture and peanuts and beat on low speed until the dough is just blended, about 1 minute.

4. Using a 1-Tbs. mini scoop, scoop into balls and arrange about 1½ inches (4 cm) apart on the prepared cookie sheets. Do not press down. Bake, one sheet at a time, until the cookies are puffed and golden brown around the edges, 12 to 15 minutes. For crispier cookies, bake until the tops are golden brown, another 1 to 2 minutes. Move the cookie sheet to a rack to cool for about 5 minutes, then transfer the cookies from the sheet to a rack until completely cooled.

Make the filling and assemble the sandwiches

1. Put the confectioners' sugar, peanut butter, and butter in a small bowl. Mix with an electric handheld mixer fitted with wire beaters until well blended and fluffy, about 2 minutes.

2. Turn half of the cooled cookies over so they are flat side up. Spoon or pipe 1 Tbs. of the filling onto the center of each cookie. Top with the remaining cookies, flat side down, pressing gently on the top cookie to spread the filling almost to the edge. Set on the rack until the filling is firm, about 1 hour; for faster chilling, refrigerate for about 20 minutes. Serve at room temperature.

For more about sandwiching cookies, see p. 133.

For more about sandwiching cookies, see p. 133.

TWISTS

Flavor swap

> Add 3 oz. (85 g) mini chocolate chips (½ cup) to the cookie batter along with the peanuts.

> **Chocolate filling:** Instead of the peanut butter filling, put 5 oz. (142 g) chopped bittersweet chocolate and 4 Tbs. (2 oz./57 g) unsalted butter into a small heatproof bowl and melt in the microwave or set over a pot of simmering water, stirring with a silicone spatula until smooth (see p. 302). Remove from the heat and set aside until thick enough to hold its shape before filling cookies.

> **Nutella® filling:** Instead of the peanut butter filling, use ¾ cup (7½ oz./213 g) Nutella.

ESSENTIAL TECHNIQUE

Scooping dough

A mini ice cream scoop makes scooping dough and placing it on the prepared cookie sheet a breeze. Scrape the edge of the scoop against the side of the bowl of dough to keep the dough balls even.

Evenly scooped and arranged dough will bake evenly and be uniform in shape. Be sure to position the dough rounded side up and flatten them only if directed in the recipe.

Bittersweet Chocolate Peppermint Thumbprints

Makes 18 cookies   [PHOTO ON P. 106]

These two-bite cookies pack just the right amount of chocolaty richness and minty freshness to cure whatever ails you. With their natural cocoa powder, buttery bittersweet chocolate, and a dash of crunchy peppermint candy, they are the perfect triple-threat treat to satisfy a chocolate-loving crowd.

When it comes to delivering deep, dark chocolate flavor, plain old cocoa powder is hard to beat. For baking, I like to use natural cocoa because it delivers a stronger flavor. For garnishing desserts, like truffles, I prefer Dutch-processed cocoa, as it has a mellower, less acidic flavor.

For the cookies
8 Tbs. (4 oz./113 g) unsalted
   butter, softened
⅓ cup (2⅜ oz./67 g) firmly
   packed light or dark brown sugar
¼ cup (¾ oz./20 g) unsweetened
   natural cocoa powder, sifted
   if lumpy

¼ tsp. table salt
¾ tsp. pure vanilla extract
⅛ tsp. pure peppermint extract
1 cup (4½ oz./128 g)
   unbleached all-purpose flour

For the filling and assembly
⅓ cup (2 oz./57 g) chopped
   bittersweet chocolate (see p. 380)
3 Tbs. (1½ oz./42 g) unsalted
   butter, cut into 4 pieces
⅓ cup (1⅝ oz./46 g) chopped
   peppermint hard candies

TWISTS

Flavor swap

> **Chocolate–caramel:** Omit the peppermint extract from the cookie dough and bake as directed. Instead of the chocolate filling use quick caramel filling (see below). Replace the crushed peppermint candy topping with toasted, chopped nuts.

> **CARAMEL FILLING**

11 small (6 oz.) caramels (I use
   Kraft® brand), unwrapped
3 Tbs. heavy cream

In a small saucepan, combine the caramels and heavy cream. Set the pan over very low heat and cook, stirring constantly, until the caramels have melted and the mixture is smooth, about 2 minutes. (This can also be done in the microwave.) Cover and refrigerate leftovers.

Make the cookies

1. Position a rack in the center of the oven and heat the oven to 350°F (180°C/gas 4). Line two cookie sheets with parchment or nonstick liners.

2. Put the butter, brown sugar, cocoa powder, and salt in the bowl of a stand mixer fitted with the paddle attachment (or in a large bowl using an electric handheld mixer fitted with wire beaters). Beat on medium speed until well blended and smooth, about 1 minute. Add the vanilla and peppermint extracts and beat until well blended, about 1 minute. Add the flour and mix on low speed until a soft dough forms, about 1 minute.

3. Using a 1-Tbs. mini scoop, shape the dough into balls and lightly roll them in your palms to smooth the edges. Arrange them about 1½ inches (4 cm) apart on the prepared cookie sheets. Using a round ½-tsp. measure, press down into the middle of each mound to make a well that is almost as deep as the dough ball. If the dough sticks to the measuring spoon, dip the bottom of the spoon in a little flour. Small cracks in the ball are fine but if the edges break open, reroll and try again. The finished cookies will look better and hold the filling without leaking if the edges are smooth.

4. Bake until the tops look dry, 14 to 16 minutes. Move the cookie sheet to a rack and let cool for about 5 minutes, then transfer the cookies to a rack to cool completely.

Make the filling and assemble

1. Put the chocolate and butter in a small heatproof bowl and melt in the microwave or over a pan of simmering water, stirring until smooth.

(This can also be done in the microwave.) Remove from the heat and set aside until cool and slightly thickened.

For more about melting chocolate, see p. 302.

2. Arrange the cooled cookies on a cookie sheet or sheet pan. Using a small spoon, drizzle the thickened and cooled chocolate into each indentation, filling just to the rim but not to overflowing. Alternatively, scrape the chocolate into one corner of a small zip-top plastic bag, press out the air, and seal. Cut off a small piece of the corner and pipe the chocolate into the indentations. Set the cookies aside until the chocolate filling is set but still tacky to the touch, about 10 minutes. Sprinkle the tops with the chopped peppermint candies. Let cool completely before stowing or serving.

For more about filling a zip-top bag, see p. 170.

For more about melting chocolate, see p. 302.

For more about filling a zip-top bag, see p. 170.

MAKE AHEAD

> The cookies can be baked and cooled, then layered between sheets of parchment or waxed paper in an airtight container and stowed at room temperature for up to 5 days or frozen for up to 3 months before thawing at room temperature and filling.

> The chocolate filling can be prepared and refrigerated for up to 2 weeks. Gently reheat in the microwave or on top of the stove and fill the cookies while the chocolate is still warm.

> The filled cookies can be stowed at room temperature for up to 3 days. To keep the cookies looking their best, arrange them on a half sheet pan in a single layer and cover the pan tightly (avoiding the cookie tops) with plastic.

Shaping the dough and forming the indentation

A

Scoop the dough with a 1-Tbs. mini scoop, then release it into your hand.

B

Form the dough into a smooth ball, rolling it between the palms of both hands (there's no need to flour your hands).

C

Once all the dough balls have been rolled, use a ½-tsp. measure to press down gently into the center of the ball, going almost to the bottom. Dip the measure in flour if it starts to stick to the dough.

D

If big cracks form as you press into the dough ball, reroll the dough and start again.

Rosemary Cornmeal Shortbread

Makes 16 cookies   [PHOTO ON P. 171]

Like most folks, I have a go-to list of tried-and-true cookies that I bake and give year-round. While I like them all, my shortbread cookie is my go-to fave for all occasions—its flavor and shape variations make it truly evergreen. For example, the triangle version was the recipe of choice for my holiday cookie swap, and I brought the round version to The Big Summer Potluck blogger getaway hosted by my talented friends Pam Anderson and her daughters Maggy and Sharon.

The combination of cake flour, cornstarch, and confectioners' sugar adds a tender, meltaway texture to these shortbread cookies. The small amount of stone-ground cornmeal adds a touch of crunchy texture, and the addition of the rosemary and salt makes each bite of shortbread at once slightly sweet, slightly savory, and wonderfully fragrant.

Nonstick cooking spray or softened butter, for preparing the pan
$1^{1}/_{2}$ cups (6 oz./170 g) cake flour, sifted
$^{1}/_{3}$ cup ($1^{1}/_{2}$ oz./42 g) stone-ground cornmeal

2 Tbs. ($^{1}/_{2}$ oz./15 g) cornstarch
$^{1}/_{2}$ tsp. table salt
12 Tbs. (6 oz./170 g) unsalted butter, softened
$^{1}/_{2}$ cup (2 oz./57 g) confectioners' sugar, sifted if lumpy

$1^{1}/_{2}$ tsp. finely chopped fresh rosemary
$^{1}/_{2}$ tsp. pure vanilla extract
Fleur de sel or coarse sanding sugar (optional)

MAKE AHEAD

> The shortbread can be prepared through Step 3 and refrigerated for 1 day or covered and frozen for up to 1 month. If frozen, thaw in the refrigerator overnight before baking.

> Stow the baked and cooled cookies between sheets of parchment or waxed paper in an airtight container for up to 4 days at room temperature or freeze for up to 6 weeks.

1. Lightly grease a $9^{1}/_{4}$-inch (23 cm) fluted tart pan with removable bottom. Whisk the flour, cornmeal, cornstarch, and salt in a medium bowl until well blended.

2. Put the butter and confectioners' sugar in the bowl of a stand mixer fitted with the paddle attachment (or in a large bowl using an electric handheld mixer fitted with wire beaters). Beat on medium speed until smooth and creamy, about 3 minutes. Add the rosemary and vanilla and beat on medium until blended and fragrant, about 1 minute. Add the flour mixture and beat on low speed until the dough forms moist clumps. Dump the dough into the prepared pan. Using lightly floured fingertips, press the dough into the pan to form an even layer. Make sure to press the dough into the scalloped edges to form a clean edge. Sprinkle the fleur de sel or sanding sugar, if using, evenly over the top.

3. Using the tip of a knife or a bench scraper, score the dough all the way through, forming 16 wedges. With the tines of a fork, prick each wedge twice all the way through, starting at the widest part of the wedge and spacing them about $^{1}/_{2}$ inch (12 mm) apart. Lightly flour the tines of the fork as necessary to prevent the dough from sticking. Slide the pan into the freezer or fridge for about 10 minutes while the oven heats.

4. Position a rack in the center of the oven and heat the oven to 300°F (150°C/gas 2).

5. Bake the shortbread until the top looks dry and very pale brown, 39 to 41 minutes. Move the pan to a rack. Using a small paring or serrated knife (I don't use a bench scraper for this because it compresses the cookies' edges), immediately recut the wedges using the scored lines as a guide. Let the shortbread cool completely before removing them from the pan.

FINISHING TOUCHES

Serve the cookies with a dusting of confectioners' sugar.

TWISTS

Flavor swap

INSTEAD OF THE ROSEMARY, USE ONE OF THE FOLLOWING COMBINATIONS:

Double ginger: 2 tsp. finely grated fresh ginger + $1/3$ cup ($1^3/8$ oz./39 g) finely chopped crystallized ginger (add both with the vanilla). See p. 218 for chopping crystallized ginger.

Cinnamon toast: $1/2$ tsp. ground cinnamon added to the flour + 1 Tbs. granulated sugar mixed with $1/2$ tsp. ground cinnamon sprinkled over the shortbread and pressed lightly into the dough before baking.

Espresso chip: $1/2$ tsp. instant espresso powder (dissolved in the vanilla extract) + $1/3$ cup (2 oz./57 g) finely chopped bittersweet chocolate.

Re-size it

> TO MAKE RECTANGULAR COOKIES:

Line the bottom of an 8-inch (20 cm) square baking pan (the straight-sided type makes for a cleaner-looking cookie) with parchment.

For more about lining a pan with parchment, see p. 232.

Prepare the dough as directed. Using lightly floured fingertips, press the dough into the pan to form an even layer. Using the tip of a knife or a bench scraper (my tool of choice), score the dough all the way through, forming 1 x 2-inch (2.5 x 5 cm) bars. With the tines of a fork, prick each bar two or three times all the way through, spacing them evenly and on the diagonal. Lightly flour the tines of the fork as necessary to prevent the dough from sticking. Proceed as directed.

> TO MAKE ROUND COOKIES:

Have ready two cookie sheets lined with parchment or nonstick liners.

Prepare the dough as directed. Arrange a large piece of parchment on the work surface and scrape the dough onto the center. Cover with another piece of parchment and press down on the dough to flatten. Using a rolling pin, roll the dough between the parchment to a $1/4$-inch (6 mm) thickness, turning, lifting, and repositioning the parchment and lightly flouring throughout the rolling. Slide the dough onto a cookie sheet and refrigerate until firm, at least 30 minutes.

For more about rolling dough between parchment, see p. 133.

Remove the top piece of parchment from the chilled dough. Using a $2^1/2$-inch (6 cm) round cookie cutter, cut out rounds. Using the end of a straw, punch out three holes in the center of each round. Arrange about 1 inch (2.5 cm) apart on the prepared cookie sheets. Stack the scraps, gently press together, reroll, chill, and cut as directed. Slide the cookie sheets into the fridge while the oven heats (at least 15 minutes).

Bake, one sheet at a time, until the tops look dry and very pale brown, 26 to 28 minutes.

(continued)

ESSENTIAL TECHNIQUE

Shaping and scoring

A

To make wedges, press the dough evenly into the bottom of a fluted tart pan. Use your fingertips along the fluted edge to ensure the dough completely fills it.

B

A bench scraper works well to score the salt-sprinkled dough. Be sure to press all the way through to the bottom of the pan.

C

With the tines of a fork, prick the wedges twice, starting at the widest part of the wedge. Dip the tines into flour if the dough gets sticky.

D

To make rectangular shortbread, press the dough into a straight-sided pan, then use a bench scraper to score it.

E

Using a fork, press the tines into the scored dough at an angle.

F

To form rounds, roll out the dough evenly and then use a 2½-inch (6 cm) cutter. Press one end of a straw into the cut-out rounds, then transfer the rounds to a baking sheet.

Hazelnut–Raspberry Sandwich Cookie Wreaths

Makes 48 sandwich cookies [PHOTO ON P. 172]

These festive cookies are inspired by the Linzer torte, a famous lattice-topped Austrian pastry made with a rich, buttery nut crust and jam filling. The secret to this cookie's deep, earthy flavor begins with toasting the hazelnuts. This step intensifies the nuts' flavor and is an essential characteristic of a Linzer-inspired cookie. Along with the hazelnuts, this lightly sweetened, buttery dough is laced with cinnamon along with a dash of ground cloves. While the cookies are delicious on their own, sandwiching them with raspberry jelly adds a jewel-toned sparkle as well as a bright, fresh flavor. They are pretty enough for holiday giving but are so delicious they will likely become a year-round favorite— heart-shaped cutters and strawberry or red currant jelly make them Valentine's Day ready!

For the cookies
2 cups (9 oz./255 g) unbleached
   all-purpose flour
¾ cup (3 oz./85 g) hazelnuts,
   toasted, skinned, and
   finely ground
1 tsp. ground cinnamon

½ tsp. table salt
⅛ tsp. ground cloves
16 Tbs. (8 oz./227 g) unsalted
   butter, softened
¾ cup (3 oz./85 g) confectioners'
   sugar, sifted if lumpy
1 tsp. pure vanilla extract

For assembly
Confectioners' sugar
1 cup seedless raspberry jelly

Make the dough

1. Have ready several sheets of parchment and a cookie sheet. Whisk the flour, ground hazelnuts, cinnamon, salt, and cloves in a medium bowl until well blended.

For more about skinning hazelnuts, see p. 457.

2. Put the butter and confectioners' sugar in the bowl of a stand mixer fitted with the paddle attachment (or in a large bowl using an electric handheld mixer fitted with wire beaters). Beat on medium speed until creamy and lighter in color, about 4 minutes. Add the vanilla and beat on medium until blended and fragrant, about 1 minute. Add the flour mixture and beat on low speed until the dough forms moist clumps.

3. Scrape the dough onto the work surface and divide into two approximately equal piles. Put one pile of the dough in the center of a sheet of parchment. Cover with another piece of parchment and press down on the dough to flatten. Using a rolling pin, roll the dough between the parchment to a ³⁄₁₆-inch (4.8 mm) thickness, turning, lifting, and repositioning the parchment and lightly flouring throughout the rolling. Slide the dough and parchment onto a cookie sheet and refrigerate. Repeat with more parchment and the remaining dough, stack on top of the other one, and refrigerate until firm, at least 1 hour.

For more about rolling dough between parchment, see p. 133.

(continued)

MAKE AHEAD

> The rolled cookie dough can be refrigerated for 3 days or wrapped in plastic and frozen for up to 1 month. If frozen, thaw in the refrigerator for 30 minutes before proceeding with the recipe.

> Stow the baked and cooled cookies between sheets of parchment or waxed paper in an airtight container for up to 4 days at room temperature or freeze for up to 6 weeks before thawing at room temperature and sandwiching with the jam.

Flavor swap

> Milk chocolate ganache filling: Omit the cloves from the dough and bake as directed. For the filling, omit the raspberry jelly and put 8 oz. (227 g) chopped milk chocolate (1⅓ cups) and ⅓ cup (80 ml) heavy cream in a small, heatproof bowl. Heat in a microwave until almost melted or set the bowl over a saucepan filled with barely simmering water. Stir until melted and smooth (see p. 302). Set aside until the mixture is thick enough to hold its shape, then fill and sandwich the cookies. Let the cookies sit at room temperature or, for faster cooling, in the fridge until the chocolate is firm.

> Almond-Apricot Sandwich Cookies: Instead of the hazelnuts, use ¾ cup (3 oz./85 g) finely ground blanched and toasted almonds in the dough. Instead of the raspberry jelly, purée 1 cup (11 oz./312 g) apricot jam in a food processor with ⅛ tsp. almond extract for the filling.

Re-size it

Change the shape: Instead of rounds, cut the dough into stars, hearts, or triangles, and make smaller cutouts of the same shape in the center.

Bake and assemble the cookies

1. Position a rack in the center of the oven and heat the oven to 350°F (180°C/gas 4). Line cookie sheets (four, if you have them) with parchment or nonstick liners.

2. Working with one sheet of dough at a time, remove the top sheet of parchment. Using a 2-inch (5 cm) fluted cookie cutter, cut out rounds from the chilled dough. Arrange the rounds about 1 inch (2.5 cm) apart on the prepared cookie sheets. Using a ¾-inch (2 cm) fluted or plain cookie cutter, cut out the centers of half of the rounds and remove. Stack the scraps and gently press together. Reroll, chill, and cut.

3. Bake, one sheet at a time, until the edges and bottom of the cookies are golden brown, 9 to 11 minutes. Move the sheet to a rack and let cool for about 5 minutes, then transfer the cookies to a rack to cool completely. Repeat with the remaining cookie dough using cooled cookie sheets and parchment or liners.

4. Arrange the cookies with the center stamped out, top side up, on a work surface and, using a sifter, dust the tops with confectioners' sugar. Arrange the whole cookies, bottom side up, on the work surface. Put a scant 1 tsp. of the jelly in the center of each cookie. Cover with the confectioners' sugar-coated cookies and press down very gently to evenly spread the jelly until it just reaches the edges. Repeat with the remaining cookies. Serve immediately or cover and stow at room temperature for up to 2 days.

Hazelnuts

Also known as filberts, hazelnuts are a tree nut with a strong, earthly flavor. Not only are they used in many desserts like these cookies, but they are also the central flavor for Frangelico® liqueur and a popular flavor added to brewed coffee. Like all nuts, hazelnuts can go rancid if stored for long periods of time, so keep them tightly wrapped in a heavy-duty zip-top freezer bag in the freezer for up to 6 months. Always taste several nuts from the batch before you use them.

Rolling the dough and making cutouts

A

Roll the dough between two pieces of parchment to ³/₁₆ inch (4.8 mm) thick. Turn and flip the dough and lift the parchment as you go, flouring as needed.

B

Use a 2-inch (5 cm) fluted cookie cutter to cut out rounds from the chilled dough. Using a small offset spatula, arrange the rounds about 1 inch (2.5 cm) apart on a parchment-lined cookie sheet.

C

To create windows in the sandwich tops, use a ³/₄-inch (2 cm) round cutter to remove the centers on half of the cookies.

D

When the cookies are baked and cooled, dust the tops (with the window cutout) with confectioners' sugar.

E

Arrange the remaining cookies bottom side up and put 1 tsp. raspberry jelly in the center of each.

F

Cover the jelly-filled cookie bottom with a cut-out top (hold by the edges) and press down gently to spread the jelly just to the edges.

Double Chocolate Cream Cheese Fudge Brownies

Makes 2 dozen square or 4 dozen triangle brownies   [PHOTO ON P. 173]

On its own, the flavor and texture of the deep chocolate base is everything you could ever wish for in a fudgy brownie. What's even better is that this brownie mixes up in one pot, making it super-efficient and easy. While the brownie is stand-alone fabulous, I just couldn't let it, well, stand alone. It was calling for more—a complementary flavor partner and contrasting textures as well as a stunning presentation. Swirling lightly sweetened cream cheese batter into the base offered all of this and more without overcomplicating the recipe or compromising the original brownie. It's brownie 2.0.

For the cream cheese swirl
8 oz. (227 g) cream cheese, softened
¼ cup (1¾ oz./50 g)
    granulated sugar
2 tsp. unbleached all-purpose flour
1 yolk from a large egg (see p. 371)
1½ tsp. pure vanilla extract
⅓ cup (2 oz./57 g) finely chopped
    bittersweet chocolate or mini chips

For the brownies
Nonstick cooking spray or softened
    butter, for preparing the pan
24 Tbs. (12 oz./340 g) unsalted
    butter, cut into 10 pieces
1¼ cups (3¾ oz./106 g)
    unsweetened natural cocoa
    powder, sifted if lumpy
2 cups (14 oz./397 g)
    granulated sugar

¾ cup (5¼ oz./149 g) firmly
    packed light brown sugar
½ tsp. table salt
4 large eggs, at room temperature
1 tsp. pure vanilla extract
1⅔ cups (7½ oz./213 g)
    unbleached all-purpose flour

MAKE AHEAD

The baked, cooled, and cut brownies can be layered between sheets of parchment or waxed paper in an airtight container and stowed at room temperature for up to 5 days or frozen for up to 1 month.

TWISTS

Flavor swap

> **Almond swirl:** Reduce the vanilla extract to ½ tsp. and add ½ tsp. pure almond extract. Instead of the mini chips, use ⅓ cup (1⅜ oz./39 g) chopped, toasted slivered almonds

> **Mocha swirl:** In a small ramekin, stir together 2 tsp. instant espresso powder and the vanilla until dissolved. Instead of the flour, use 1 Tbs. unsweetened natural cocoa powder (sifted if lumpy).

> **Nutty brownie:** Stir in ¾ cup (3¾ oz./106 g) chopped, toasted nuts to the brownie batter and continue as directed.

Make the cream cheese filling

Put the cream cheese, sugar, and flour in the bowl of a stand mixer fitted with the paddle attachment (or in a large bowl using an electric handheld mixer fitted with wire beaters) and beat on medium speed until creamy and no lumps remain, about 2 minutes. Add the yolk and vanilla and beat on medium until blended, about 1 minute. Add the mini chips and beat on low speed just until blended.

Make the brownies

1. Position a rack in the center of the oven and heat the oven to 325°F (165°C/gas 3). Line the bottom and sides of a 9 x 13 x 2-inch (23 x 33 x 5 cm) baking pan (I like the straight-sided kind) with foil, leaving about a 2-inch (5 cm) overhang on the short sides. Lightly grease the foil.

2. Put the butter in a large saucepan and set over medium-low heat, stirring occasionally, until it is melted, about 2 minutes. Slide the pan off the heat, add the cocoa powder, and whisk until the mixture is smooth. Add the granulated sugar, brown sugar, and salt and whisk until blended and no lumps of brown sugar remain. Using your fingertip, check the temperature of the batter—it should be warm but not hot. If it's hot, set the pan aside for a minute or two before continuing with the recipe.

3. Add the eggs, two at a time, whisking until just blended. Add the vanilla with the final egg addition. Add the flour and stir with a silicone spatula until just blended.

4. Scrape the batter into the prepared pan and, using a small offset spatula, spread evenly. Drop the cream cheese mixture in medium-sized dollops evenly spaced over the batter. You should have a total of 12. Using the tip of the offset spatula, swirl the batters together, leaving large streaks of cream cheese. Bake until a toothpick inserted in the center of the brownie batter comes out with only small bits of brownie sticking to it, 44 to 46 minutes. Move the pan to a rack and let cool completely, about 3 hours.

5. When the brownie is completely cool, use the foil edges on the short sides of the pan to lift it from the pan. Invert onto a cutting board and carefully peel away the foil. Turn the brownie so it is top side up. Run a thin, long knife under hot water, wipe it dry, and, using a long ruler as a guide, cut into 24 squares (cut each square into two triangles, if desired), heating and wiping the knife after every cut.

For more about heating a knife, see p. 248.

FINISHING TOUCHES

Just before baking, sprinkle the top with a little coarse sea salt.

ESSENTIAL TECHNIQUE

Lining the pan

In order to create tight corners on the foil lining, start by placing the pan on a large sheet of foil.

Fold up the foil tight to one short side of the pan first, then fold up on a long side, folding the short side over the long side. Crease to hold the fold.

Continue folding around the other sides of the pan until a tight foil rectangle is formed.

Remove the foil from under the pan. Using your fingertips, guide the foil rectangle into the inside of the pan, pressing the edges into the corners of the pan.

Zesting and peeling citrus

Before zesting, wash and dry the fruit to remove residue. Then hold the fruit firmly in one hand while brushing a handheld grater over the fruit in short strokes. This makes it easy to scoop up and measure the zest. Be sure to remove just the thin, colored layer of rind, not the white bitter pith underneath.

Use a Y-shaped vegetable peeler to remove wide strips of zest, a channel knife (the larger notch on the side of a citrus zester) for thick ribbons, a citrus zester for thin strips, and a handheld grater (or box grater, not shown) for zest. No matter which tool you use, avoid the bitter white pith under the layer of rind.

Lemon curd doneness

Whisk in all ingredients, then cook over low heat, whisking constantly, until the curd holds a line when drawn with a finger. Off the heat, add the vanilla, then strain the curd through a fine-mesh sieve directly over the baked crust.

Apricot Rugelach

Makes 3 dozen cookies   [PHOTO ON P. 175]

I don't know of a more flaky pastry dough than this one, and it bakes up into tender rugelach. Your friends will love them, but I recommend that you tuck a few away for yourself before you give them all away—they make a lovely breakfast treat.

Making this cookie is a two-step process and both can be done well ahead of time. The dough whizzes together easily in the food processor and needs to be refrigerated briefly (2 hours) to firm up the cream cheese and butter before rolling; for those who like to plan ahead, it can also be frozen for up to 1 month. When making the apricot filling, make sure to begin with plump, moist, vibrantly colored apricots. The flavor and color of the baked cookies depend on it.

For the dough
12 Tbs. (6 oz./170 g) unsalted butter
6 oz. (170 g) cream cheese
1⅔ cups (7½ oz./213 g)
   unbleached all-purpose flour +
   more for rolling
3 Tbs. granulated sugar
¼ tsp. table salt

For the apricot filling
1 cup (9 oz./255 g) lightly packed
   dried apricots
3 Tbs. finely chopped fresh ginger
   (see p. 312)
3 Tbs. honey
1 Tbs. freshly squeezed lemon juice
3 Tbs. chopped pistachios

Make the dough

1. Cut the butter into 8 pieces. Cut the cream cheese into 1-inch (2.5 cm) pieces. Pile the butter and cream cheese onto a plate and slide into the freezer until ready to use.

2. Put the flour, sugar, and salt in a food processor and process until well blended. Add the cold butter and cream cheese pieces and pulse until the dough forms moist crumbs.

3. Scrape the dough onto a work surface and knead a few times until the crumbs begin to hold together. Be careful not to overwork the dough because that will make the baked cookie dense. Portion the dough into three equal piles (about 7 oz./198 g each). To make crescents, shape the dough into 5-inch (12 cm) disks. To make mini rolls, shape the dough into 3-inch (7.5 cm) squares. For either shape, wrap the dough in plastic and refrigerate until well chilled, about 2 hours.

For the apricot filling

1. Put the apricots, ginger, honey, and lemon juice in a small saucepan and cover with water. Bring to a boil over medium-high heat. Reduce the heat and simmer until the apricots are tender and the liquid is reduced to about 2 Tbs. Slide the pan off the heat and let cool until warm, about 15 minutes.

(continued)

MAKE AHEAD

> The rugelach dough can be prepared, wrapped in plastic, and refrigerated for 3 days or frozen for up to 1 month. If frozen, thaw in the refrigerator for 30 minutes.

> The apricot filling can be prepared, cooled completely, covered, and refrigerated for up to 1 week before bringing to room temperature.

> Stow the baked and cooled cookies between sheets of parchment or waxed paper in an airtight container for up to 4 days at room temperature or in the freezer for up to 6 weeks. Thaw at room temperature.

TWISTS

Flavor swap

INSTEAD OF THE APRICOT FILLING, MAKE IT CINNAMON–PECAN:

⅓ cup (1⅜ oz./39 g) finely chopped pecans

⅓ cup (2⅜ oz./67 g) firmly packed light brown sugar

1 Tbs. unsweetened cocoa powder (natural or Dutch-processed)

1 tsp. ground cinnamon

3 Tbs. honey

2 Tbs. granulated sugar

Put the pecans, brown sugar, cocoa, and cinnamon in a small bowl and stir until well blended. Drizzle 1 Tbs. honey evenly over the dough and sprinkle a third of the filling (about 1⅜ oz./39 g) evenly over the round or rectangle. Cover with a piece of plastic and, using your fingers, press the filling gently onto the dough. Peel away the plastic and, using a large knife, cut the round into 4 quarters and cut each quarter into 3 triangles. Follow the instructions in Steps 3 and 4 for shaping mini rolls or crescents, sprinkling with some of the granulated sugar before baking. Repeat with the remaining dough and filling.

2. Scrape the apricots and any liquid into a food processor. Process until smooth, stopping to scrape down the sides as necessary. (You can also use a food mill or mini chopper.) Spoon the mixture into a small bowl and set aside, stirring occasionally, until completely cooled.

Assemble and bake the rugelach

1. Position a rack in the center of the oven and heat the oven to 350°F (180°C/gas 4). Line cookie sheets (three, if you have them) with parchment or nonstick liners.

2. Remove one of the dough disks or squares from the refrigerator and, if it's very cold, leave it out at room temperature until it's just pliable enough to roll, 5 to 10 minutes. Arrange a small piece of plastic or parchment on the work surface, put the unwrapped disk or square in the center, and cover with another piece of plastic or parchment. To make crescents, use a rolling pin to roll the dough between the parchment to a 9-inch (23 cm) round, turning, lifting, and repositioning the parchment and lightly flouring throughout the rolling. To make mini rolls, use a rolling pin to roll the dough into a 14 x 5½-inch (35.5 x 14 cm) rectangle, turning, lifting, and repositioning the parchment and lightly flouring throughout the rolling. Peel away the top piece of parchment.

3. For crescents, spread ⅓ cup (80 ml) of the apricot purée evenly over the round. Using a large knife, cut the round into 4 quarters, then cut each quarter into 3 triangles. Working with one triangle at a time and beginning at the wide end, roll up jelly-roll style toward the point. Arrange with the point underneath the roll, about 1 inch apart on a prepared cookie sheet. Repeat with the remaining triangles. Using a small brush or your fingertips, brush a little water over the top of each roll and sprinkle with the pistachios. Repeat with the remaining dough and filling.

4. For mini rolls, spread ⅓ cup (80 ml) of the apricot purée evenly over the rectangle. Starting at one long end, roll the rectangle jelly roll-style using the parchment or plastic if necessary. Arrange the log seam side down and gently press to flatten slightly (it will be about 1¼ inches/3.2 cm wide). Using a sharp knife, cut the log into 1¼-inch (3.2 cm) pieces. Arrange on the prepared cookie sheet. Repeat with the remaining rectangles. Using a small brush or your fingertips, brush a little water over the top of each roll and sprinkle with the pistachios. Repeat with the remaining dough and filling.

5. Bake until the cookies are golden brown, 25 to 27 minutes. Move the sheet to a rack and let cool for about 5 minutes, then transfer the cookies to a rack to cool completely. Repeat with the remaining dough, using cooled cookie sheets and liners.

Spreading the filling and rolling the dough

A For crescents, with the dough rolled out to a 9-inch (23 cm) round, spread the filling to just within the edge.

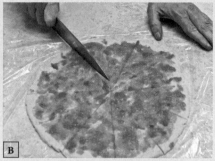

B Cut the prepared dough into 12 even wedges.

C Working with one wedge at a time, start at the wide end and roll up the wedge tightly, then transfer the roll to the prepared baking sheet.

D For a more traditional-looking rugelach, spread filling on a 14 x 5 ½-inch (35.5 x 14 cm) rectangle.

E Using the plastic as a guide and starting on a long side, roll up the dough jelly-roll style, keeping the roll as tight as possible.

F Cut the log into 1¼-inch (3.2 cm) pieces.

Whimsical Vanilla Bean Cutouts

Makes 48 cookies   [PHOTO ON P. 176]

After seeing the picture of these decorated cookies, I bet you think that they look too pretty to eat, but the bottom line is that you must eat them—they are as delicious as they are beautiful. These cookies shine straight from the oven. More often than not, I bake and eat these cookies unadorned just to savor the sweet-salty, buttery crispness of each bite.

Even thickness of the dough is very important. You want the thickness to be ¼ inch (6 mm) to produce a sturdy cookie that can hold up to the decorations and has a nice, meaty bite to it. You also want the dough to be a uniform thickness so the cookies bake up evenly to avoid overbaked patches. I use rolling pin bands (see the Essential Technique on p. 150) and I encourage you to do the same.

For the cookies
2 cups (9 oz./255 g) unbleached
   all-purpose flour
1¼ cups (5 oz./142 g)
   cake flour, sifted
¾ tsp. table salt
¼ tsp. baking powder
18 Tbs. (9 oz./255 g) unsalted
   butter, softened

1¼ cups (8¾ oz./248 g)
   granulated sugar
3 yolks from large eggs (see p. 371)
2 tsp. pure vanilla extract

For the royal icing
2 Tbs. powdered egg whites or
   meringue powder
6 Tbs. warm water

4 cups (16 oz./454 g)
   confectioners' sugar, sifted
   if lumpy
Food coloring, colored sprinkles,
   dragées, or other edible
   decorations, for garnish

MAKE AHEAD

> The cookie dough can be prepared and refrigerated for 3 days or wrapped in plastic and frozen for up to 1 month. If frozen, thaw in the refrigerator for 30 minutes.

> Stow the baked and cooled cookies between sheets of parchment or waxed paper in an airtight container for up to 4 days at room temperature or freeze for up to 6 weeks before thawing and decorating.

Make the dough

1. Have ready several sheets of parchment and a cookie sheet. Whisk the all-purpose and cake flours, salt, and baking powder in a medium bowl until well blended.

2. Put the butter in the bowl of a stand mixer fitted with the paddle attachment (or in a large bowl using an electric handheld mixer fitted with wire beaters) and beat on medium speed until smooth, about 1 minute. Add the sugar and continue beating until fluffy and lighter in color, about 2 minutes. Add the yolks one at a time, beating until just blended before adding the next one. Add the vanilla along with the last yolk and beat on medium until blended and fragrant, about 1 minute. Add the flour mixture and beat on low speed until the dough forms moist clumps.

3. Scrape the dough onto the work surface and portion into two approximately equal piles. Put one pile of the dough in the center of a sheet of parchment. Cover with another piece of parchment and press down on the dough to flatten. Using a rolling pin, roll the dough between the parchment to a ¼-inch (6 mm) thickness, turning, lifting, and repositioning the parchment and lightly flouring throughout the rolling. Slide the dough and parchment onto a cookie sheet and refrigerate. Repeat with more parchment and the remaining dough, stack on top of the other one, and refrigerate until firm, at least 1 hour.

For more about rolling dough between parchment, see p. 133.

Bake the cookies

1. Position a rack in the center of the oven and heat the oven to 350°F (180°C/gas 4). Line cookie sheets (four, if you have them) with nonstick liners or parchment.

2. Working with one sheet of dough at a time, remove the top piece of parchment. Using a 2½-inch (6 cm) cookie cutter, cut out shapes, then arrange them about 2 inches (5 cm) apart on the prepared cookie sheets. Stack the scraps and gently press together. Reroll, chill, and cut.

3. Slide all but one sheet into the refrigerator (if the dough is well chilled, you can stack them two high) and bake, one sheet at a time, until the edges and bottom of the cookies are pale golden brown, 12 to 16 minutes (too little and the texture will be soft and doughy). Move the sheet to a rack, let cool for about 5 minutes, and then transfer the cookies to a rack to cool completely. Repeat with the remaining dough, using cooled cookie sheets and liners and making sure your oven has come back up to temperature.

Make the royal icing

Put the egg white powder and warm water in a large bowl. Let stand, whisking frequently, until the powder is dissolved, about 5 minutes. Using a stand mixer fitted with the whisk attachment (or in a large bowl using an electric handheld mixer fitted with wire beaters), begin mixing on medium-low speed until frothy. Add the confectioners' sugar and continue beating until blended. Increase the speed to high and beat until the mixture is thick and shiny, about 5 minutes. Scrape down the sides and put a damp paper towel directly on the icing to prevent a skin from forming. If not using within 2 hours, cover the bowl with plastic and refrigerate.

Decorate the cookies

1. Arrange the cookies on the work surface. Have ready small-tipped (#2, #3, or #4) pastry tips fitted in small pastry bags or small plastic squeeze bottles and a small offset spatula. Portion the icing into as many small bowls as you like (one for each color) and stir in drops of food coloring to each until the color is to your liking. Check for the proper consistency and add more water, drop by drop, until it is just right (see the Essential Technique on p. 144).

2. Spoon the icings into separate pastry bags or, to fill the squeeze bottles, scrape into small zip-top plastic bags, then snip off one corner and carefully squeeze into the bottles. Have ready any sprinkles or edible decorations you might like to use, along with tweezers and a spatula.

3. For decorating with sprinkles: Pipe small dots or lines on the cookie and dust with edible sprinkles. Set the cookie aside until the icing is hard.

4. For outlined and flooded in the same color: Outline the rim of a cookie with a thin line of the icing to create a border. Using the same color and starting on one edge, squeeze the frosting onto the cookie, keeping the tip close to the cookie (even in the frosting) and moving within the

TWISTS

Re-size it

> **Make them thinner:** Roll the dough as directed but to about a $3/16$-inch (4.8 mm) thickness and bake according to the doneness test, 8 to 10 minutes.

> **Change the shape:** As you can see in the photo on p. 176, any size and shape cutter works well. Depending on what you use, your yield will change but the cookies will still be delicious.

BAKER'S WISDOM

Decorating cookies

For those of you who shy away from the cookie decorating portion of this recipe and look at this picture and say "there's no way mine will look anything like these," fear not. If you look closely at the cookies, the decorations vary from easy (dots and dragées or sprinkles) to more challenging (pipe, flood, and drag or overlay), and I've given you step-by-step directions for all of them (see the Essential Technique on pp. 144–146). My best advice is to remember that perfection is never the goal but rather sharing and eating a yummy cookie!

Decorating with icing (continued)

M

For a distinct outline, wait a few minutes for the outline to firm up before flooding with the same or contrasting color.

N

For a marbled design, pipe one or two lines onto the just-flooded icing. You can also make dots instead of lines, with or without the marbled effect.

O

Using a toothpick, immediately drag the top through one or both lines (or dots), working in the same or opposite directions with each stroke.

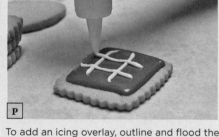

P

To add an icing overlay, outline and flood the cookies and set aside until very firm before piping your design. Sprinkles or dragées can be added to the just-piped icing.

Cardamom Biscotti *with* Dried Fruit *and* Nuts

Makes about 44 cookies

This is my go-to version of classic biscotti. I've scented the base with ground cardamom and loaded it with whole almonds and two of my favorite dried fruits—apricots and cranberries. I like the fruit and nuts to be on the chunky side for the soft, chewy texture they add to the finished product, but you can chop them smaller if you prefer. The only thing not so traditional is my baking process. Unlike most folks, I like my biscotti baked until thoroughly cooked but not super crispy and hard. I can dunk it in my morning or afternoon tea, but it's still soft enough to nibble all on its own.

2 ¼ cups (10 ⅛ oz./287 g) unbleached all-purpose flour + more for shaping

1 cup (7 oz./198 g) granulated sugar

1 ½ tsp. baking powder

1 tsp. ground cardamom (see below for grinding your own)

½ tsp. table salt

1 cup (5 oz./142 g) whole (or slivered) blanched almonds

½ cup (2 ¼ oz./64 g) dried cranberries

½ cup (4 ½ oz./128 g) packed dried apricots, roughly chopped or snipped (see p. 218)

2 large whole eggs, at room temperature

1 white from a large egg (1 oz./28 g), at room temperature (see p. 371)

1 tsp. pure vanilla extract

1. Position a rack in the center of the oven and heat the oven to 325°F (165°C/gas 3). Line a cookie sheet with parchment or nonstick liner.

2. Put the flour, sugar, baking powder, cardamom, and salt in the bowl of a stand mixer fitted with the paddle attachment (or in a large bowl using an electric handheld mixer fitted with wire beaters). Beat on medium-low speed until well blended. Add the nuts and dried fruit and mix briefly to combine.

3. Put the eggs, egg white, and vanilla in a 1-cup (240 ml) measure (the spout makes pouring easier and cleaner) and stir with a fork until well blended. With the mixer on low speed, slowly pour the egg mixture down the side of the bowl. Continue mixing until a moist dough forms, about 1 minute. Dump the dough onto an unfloured work surface and divide into two equal pieces (about 17¾ oz./503 g each). Press and shape each pile into a 10 x 2-inch (25 x 5 cm) log, very lightly flouring your hands if needed, and arrange on the cookie sheet about 4 inches (10 cm) apart (see the Essential Technique on p. 148).

4. Bake until the tops are cracked and the dough inside the cracks no longer looks wet, 38 to 40 minutes. Move the sheet to a rack and let the logs cool until they are just cool enough to handle, 5 to 10 minutes. Keep the oven set at 325°F (165°C/gas 3).

5. Using your hands or an offset spatula, loosen the logs from the liner and set one on a cutting board. Using a serrated knife, cut crosswise at an angle into ½-inch (12 mm) thick slices. Use a gentle sawing motion to break through the crust and then push down firmly on the knife (see the Essential Technique on p. 148). Return the biscotti to the baking sheet and arrange them cut side down—it's fine if they are touching. Repeat with the remaining log. Bake until the biscotti are dried to your taste, 8 to 12 minutes. Move the sheet to a rack and let cool completely before serving.

MAKE AHEAD

Layer the baked and cooled cookies in an airtight container and stow for up to 3 weeks at room temperature or for up to 6 weeks in the freezer.

(continued)

TWISTS

Flavor swap

> **Lemon:** Omit the cardamom, add 1 Tbs. finely grated lemon zest to the egg mixture, and proceed as directed.

> **Chocolate:** Instead of ½ cup (2½ oz./71 g) or all of the nuts, use the same amount of chopped white or bittersweet chocolate.

> Instead of the almonds, use the same amount of any other nut.

> Instead of the cranberries and apricots, use the same amount of any other dried fruit.

BAKER'S WISDOM

Cardamom

This very aromatic spice is commonly found in many Middle Eastern, North African, and Scandinavian sweet and savory dishes. It has a sweet-spicy, somewhat citrusy flavor and a unique, powerful scent. For the very freshest and strongest flavor, buy the green pods and shell and grind your own in a spice or small coffee grinder, but you can also purchase cardamom preground.

Like all ground spices, keep the lid tightly closed, store in a cool dark place, and, for the best flavor, replace your supply after 6 months (at the latest).

FINISHING TOUCHES

Before baking, sprinkle the top of each log with 2 Tbs. coarse sanding sugar, pressing it gently onto the dough.

ESSENTIAL TECHNIQUE

Shaping and cutting

A

Roughly shape a pile of dough, then use the palms of your hands to roll it into a 10 x 2-inch (25 x 5 cm) log.

B

Flatten the top and square up the ends of the log with your hands, then place it on the lined baking sheet.

C

Cut the baked log into angled ½-inch (12 mm) thick slices, then position the slices, cut side down, back on the baking sheet and finish baking.

> >

Gingerbread People

Makes 20 cookies

When Alex and Tierney were young, one of our holiday traditions was to make and decorate big gingerbread houses. After I baked the houses, the kids and I put aside an afternoon for assembling and adorning their houses. These houses served as table centerpieces for weeks on end until the candy embellishments all but disappeared and nothing was left but dried, sad gingerbread that was fit for nothing but the garbage. To make up for the lack of edible holiday gingerbread, I developed this recipe for "people" cookies for us to enjoy and share.

The baked texture is soft and cake-like with a little bit of chewiness mixed in. For folks who like their gingerbread cookies crisper, roll the dough a bit thinner or bake the cookies a bit longer.

A note about the dough: It's dense, so it's best to use a stand mixer for the task. If you only have an electric handheld mixer, consider making a half batch. The dough is also sticky, so be sure to roll between parchment, dusting with additional flour while rolling, to avoid an unfortunate mess on your counter.

3 cups (13½ oz./383 g)
  unbleached all-purpose flour +
  more for rolling
2¼ tsp. ground ginger
2¼ tsp. ground cinnamon
1¾ tsp. baking powder

½ tsp. baking soda
½ tsp. ground nutmeg
½ tsp. table salt
¼ tsp. ground cloves
8 Tbs. (4 oz./113 g) unsalted
  butter, softened

¾ cup (5¼ oz./149 g) firmly
  packed dark or light
  brown sugar
½ cup (6 oz./170 g) light
  molasses
2 Tbs. whole milk

1. Have ready several sheets of parchment and a cookie sheet. Whisk the flour, ginger, cinnamon, baking powder, baking soda, nutmeg, salt, and cloves in a medium bowl and whisk until well blended.

2. Put the butter and brown sugar in the bowl of a stand mixer fitted with the paddle attachment. Beat on medium speed until creamy and lighter in color, about 3 minutes. Add the molasses and milk and beat until blended. Add the flour mixture and beat on low speed until a dough forms.

3. Scrape the dough onto the work surface and divide into two approximately equal piles. Arrange a piece of parchment on the work surface, lightly dust with flour, and put one pile of the dough in the center. Dust the dough with flour, cover with another piece of parchment, and press down on the dough to flatten. Using a rolling pin with bands, roll the dough between the parchment to a ¼-inch (6 mm) thickness, turning, lifting, and repositioning the parchment and lightly flouring throughout the rolling. Slide the dough and parchment onto a cookie sheet and refrigerate. Roll the remaining dough as directed, stack on top of the other one, and refrigerate until firm, at least 1 hour.

For more about rolling dough between parchment, see p. 133.

For more about rolling with bands, see p. 150.

4. Position a rack in the center of the oven and heat the oven to 350°F (180°C/gas 4). Line cookie sheets (four, if you have them) with parchment or nonstick liners.

5. Arrange one sheet of dough on the work surface and remove the top piece of parchment. Using a 4-inch (10 cm) cookie cutter, cut out shapes. Arrange about 1½ inches (4 cm) apart on the prepared cookie sheets. Stack the scraps and gently press together, reroll, chill, and cut.

For more about cutting out shapes, see p. 133.

6. Refrigerate all but one sheet and bake the cookies until the edges are browned, 12 to 14 minutes. Move the sheet to a rack and let cool for 5 minutes, then transfer the cookies to a rack and let cool completely. Repeat with the remaining dough, using cooled cookie sheets and liners.

(continued)

MAKE AHEAD

> The cookie dough can be prepared and refrigerated for 3 days or wrapped in plastic and frozen for up to 1 month. If frozen, thaw in the refrigerator for 30 minutes.

> Stow the baked and cooled cookies between sheets of parchment or waxed paper in an airtight container for up to 4 days at room temperature or freeze for up to 6 weeks.

TWISTS

Re-size it

Change the shape: Any size and shape cutter works well. Depending on what you use, your yield will change but the cookies will still be delicious.

BAKER'S WISDOM

Rolling bands

One word of warning about rolling bands: Don't assume that they are 100% accurate. Before you roll an entire batch of dough, slide the appropriate bands on the ends of your pin and, using a ruler, measure the bands. On occasion, I have found that the bands can stretch and not be the width you are looking for. You might need to use the thicker bands to achieve the correct thickness. It's prudent to double-check the thickness of one of the first cutout cookies before baking. As carpenters say: "Measure twice, cut once" or for bakers, "Measure twice, bake once."

FINISHING TOUCHES

Before baking, sprinkle the tops with coarse sanding sugar or gently press edible dragées, dried currants, or dried cranberries into the dough for eyes and noses.

ESSENTIAL TECHNIQUE

Using rolling bands

Rolling bands come in a variety of thicknesses. When positioned on a rolling pin, they ensure that you roll dough to an even thickness. Position the bands 2 to 3 inches (5 to 7.5 cm) in from the ends of the rolling pin.

With the dough between parchment and rolling bands positioned on the rolling pin, roll out the dough to an even ¼-inch (6 mm) thickness.

> >

Chocolate Coconut Checkerboards

Makes 60 cookies

This is a very organized cookie. Admittedly it's an odd descriptor but let me explain.

A friend of mine, a confident baker, said that she's never been able to make this type of cookie look halfway decent, let alone as good as my batch and she wondered about my secrets to tic-tac-toe success. All you need for first-rate checkerboarding is a delicious butter dough that barely spreads (this one is a winner), a kitchen scale, and a ruler. Dividing the dough into equal portions and measuring the length and width of the ropes while shaping and assembling ensures that your rows will be consistent. It takes some time, patience, and practice, but it's well worth the effort.

If you aren't inclined to use a scale and ruler to make precise rows for a traditional checkerboard, you can get a similar effect using four ropes. The cookies won't be as glamorous but will still taste delicious!

2¼ cups (10 oz./283 g)
   unbleached all-purpose flour
½ tsp. table salt
¼ tsp. baking powder
12 Tbs. (6 oz. /170 g) unsalted
   butter, softened

¾ cup (5 ¼ oz./149 g)
   granulated sugar
1 large egg
1½ tsp. pure vanilla extract
¼ cup (⅝ oz./18 g) sweetened
   shredded coconut, chopped

½ tsp. coconut extract (optional)
3 Tbs. unsweetened natural cocoa
   powder, sifted if lumpy

For more about cocoa powder, see p. 10.

Make the dough

1. Whisk the flour, salt, and baking powder in a medium bowl until well blended. Put the butter in the bowl of a stand mixer fitted with the paddle attachment (or in a large bowl using an electric handheld mixer fitted with wire beaters). Beat on medium speed until creamy and smooth, about 1 minute. Add the sugar and beat until fluffy and lighter in color, 2 minutes. Add the egg and vanilla and beat on medium until blended, about 1 minute. Add the flour mixture and beat on low speed until the mixture is well blended.

2. Scrape the dough onto the work surface and divide into two equal piles (11½ oz./326 g each). Cover one pile with plastic wrap and return the other half of the dough to the bowl. Add the coconut and coconut extract (if using) and beat on medium until blended, about 1 minute. Scrape the dough onto the work surface and cover with plastic wrap. Put the other pile of dough in the bowl, add the cocoa powder, and beat on medium until blended, about 1 minute.

Make a 9-piece checkerboard

1. Working with one pile of dough at a time, shape into a 4-inch (10 cm) square. Using a rolling pin, roll the dough between parchment to a 7½ x 4½-inch (19 x 11 cm) rectangle (about ½ inch/12 mm thick), turning, lifting, and repositioning the parchment throughout the rolling. For the best-looking results, use the flat side of a ruler or bench scraper to make the sides and corners straight. Repeat with the remaining dough.

For more about rolling dough between parchment, see p. 133.

For more about using a bench scraper to square up dough, see p. 549.

2. Using a ruler and a sharp knife, score and cut each rectangle into nine ½-inch (12 mm) wide strips. If the dough is too soft to move, cover and refrigerate for 15 minutes or up to 1 day.

3. Arrange three strips of dough, alternating flavors, next to each other and press together gently. Top with a row of alternating flavors, pressing together gently. Add a final row of alternating flavors and press together gently to form a square. Use the bench scraper or ruler to square off the sides, if necessary. Wrap the log in plastic and refrigerate until firm enough to slice, at least 2 hours or up to 2 days.

4. Repeat with the remaining strips, reversing the flavors.

(continued)

For more about cocoa powder, see p. 10.

For more about rolling dough between parchment, see p. 133.

For more about using a bench scraper to square up dough, see p. 549.

MAKE AHEAD

> The cookie dough can be prepared and refrigerated for 2 days or wrapped in plastic and frozen for up to 1 month. If frozen, thaw in the refrigerator for 30 minutes before proceeding.

> Stow the baked and cooled cookies between sheets of parchment or waxed paper in an airtight container for up to 4 days at room temperature or for up to 6 weeks in the freezer. If frozen, thaw at room temperature.

TWISTS

Flavor swap

Orange: Instead of the coconut and coconut extract, add 1 Tbs. finely grated orange zest to half of the dough and proceed as directed with the other dough and assembly.

Re-size it

CLASSIC CHECKERBOARD, WHICH HAS 4 ROWS; MAKES 40 COOKIES

Divide each pile of dough into two equal piles. Starting with the coconut dough and using your hands, roll each pile back and forth on the counter to form a rope about 10 inches (25 cm) long. Arrange one chocolate and one coconut rope next to each other and press together gently. Top with the remaining two pieces, alternating the flavors, and press gently to form a relatively square log, then roll on the counter to help seal the seams. If you like, use the bench scraper or ruler to square off the sides. Wrap the log in plastic and refrigerate until firm enough to slice, at least 2 hours.

Layering the dough

A

To make the 9-row checkerboard, roll out both piles of dough into 7½ x 4½-inch (19 x 11 cm) rectangles that are ½ inch (12 mm) thick, then use a bench scraper to even up the edges. To ensure exact-size strips, which are necessary to form the best-looking checkerboard, use a ruler to measure out, score, and cut the dough. Before proceeding, refrigerate the dough if it's too soft to move.

B

Working on the counter, arrange three strips of dough next to each other, alternating flavors. Use the sides of your palms or fingers to gently press the strips together, taking care so the outside rows don't become misshapen.

C

Add two more layers to the first one, alternating flavors as you go and using your fingertips to guide the alignment of dough rows. If necessary, use a bench scraper to help straighten the checkerboard log, then wrap in plastic and chill until very firm.

Slice and bake the cookies

1. Position a rack in the center of the oven and heat the oven to 350°F (180°C/gas 4). Line cookie sheets (four, if you have them) with parchment or nonstick liners.

2. Unwrap one of the logs and set on a cutting board. Using a thin, sharp knife, trim one end; measure and score at ¼-inch (6 mm) intervals, then slice and arrange about 1½ inches (4 cm) apart on the prepared sheets. Accurate slicing is important so that the cookies bake evenly. Bake, one sheet at a time, until very pale golden brown around the edges, 13 to 15 minutes. Move the sheet to a rack and let cool for 5 minutes. Using a large spatula, move the cookies from the sheet to a rack until cool enough to eat.

For more about measuring and scoring, see p. 160.

3. Repeat with the remaining dough, using cooled cookie sheets and liners.

D To make the classic 4-row checkerboard, divide each dough in half and roll each into equal-length ropes. Then layer them together in 2 rows, alternating the flavors. Press gently along the logs to secure them to each other.

E Once all 4 rows are added, roll the log on the counter, sealing the seams and gently pressing the ropes together to prevent gaps. If desired, use a bench scraper or ruler to square up the sides.

F Use a sharp knife to score and cut ¼-inch (6 mm) slices, then arrange on the prepared cookie sheets and bake.

> >

Meringue Cookies

Makes 20 to 60 cookies, depending on the shape

I'll bet that you have egg whites in your fridge or freezer aching to be used, but even if you don't, it takes only two egg whites and some sugar to whip up this wonderfully versatile meringue. Piped and slow-baked until crisp and dry, these snow-white cookies/confections can be eaten on their own, served alongside a bowl of fresh fruit or sorbet, or employed as clever cake decorations or garnishes.

I've given you four shape options, but the meringue can be piped into endless variations or even scooped or spooned into large or small mounds with smooth or spiked tops. Mushroom-shaped meringues are a traditional accompaniment for a Bûche de Noël (recipe on p. 225). The directions here are for single mushrooms, but you can make doubles or even clusters by piping the tops close together. While the kisses and swirls make a sweet treat, they are a fun and inexpensive gift when bundled together in cellophane bags or nestled into tissue-lined pint containers or cardboard take-out containers. The sticks can be eaten, given like the swirls and kisses, or used as a cake decoration when pressed around the outside of cake or randomly stuck into the frosted top to mimic candles.

(continued)

¼ cup (1¾ oz./50 g) superfine
  sugar (see p. 589)
⅓ cup (1⅜ oz./39 g)
  confectioners' sugar
Pinch of table salt

2 whites from large eggs
  (2 oz./57 g), at room
  temperature (see p. 371)
¼ tsp. cream of tartar
¼ tsp. pure vanilla extract

Unsweetened natural or Dutch-
  processed cocoa powder, for
  the mushrooms

MAKE AHEAD

Layer the baked and cooled meringues between sheets of parchment or waxed paper in an airtight container and stow for up to 2 weeks at room temperature.

TWISTS

Flavor swap

> **Peppermint:** Add ¼ tsp. pure peppermint extract along with the vanilla and sprinkle finely chopped peppermint candies over the tops before baking.

> **Lemon:** Add ¼ tsp. pure lemon extract along with the vanilla and sprinkle finely chopped pistachios over the tops before baking.

1. Position racks in the top and bottom thirds of the oven and heat the oven to 175°F (80°C). Line two large, heavy baking sheets with parchment (not a nonstick liner).

2. Sift together twice the superfine sugar, confectioners' sugar, and salt onto a sheet of parchment.

3. Put the egg whites and cream of tartar in the bowl of a stand mixer fitted with the whisk attachment (or in a large bowl using an electric handheld mixer fitted with wire beaters). Beat on medium low until frothy and well blended. Increase the speed to medium high and beat until the whites form soft peaks, about 2 minutes. Fold the parchment around the sifted sugars to fashion a chute and gradually add the sugars to the mixer while continuing to beat the whites. When all the sugar is added, increase the speed to high and beat until firm, glossy peaks form, about 3 minutes. Stop the mixer, scrape down the sides, and add the vanilla extract. Beat on medium speed until blended, about 10 seconds.

For more about beating egg whites to firm peaks, see p. 212.

For more about filling and handling a pastry bag, see p. 205.

Make mushrooms

1. Using a wide plastic scraper or silicone spatula, scrape about half of the meringue into a large pastry bag fitted with a ¼-inch (6 mm) wide plain tip (Ateco #803). Holding the pastry bag perpendicular to the lined baking sheet, pipe 60 mounds about 1¼ inches (3.2 cm) in diameter and no higher than ¾ inch (2 cm), spacing them about ½ inch (12 mm) apart on the prepared baking sheets. Using a damp fingertip, lightly press to tap down any meringue peaks. Dust with the cocoa powder.

2. For the stems, use the same bag, tip, and most of the remaining meringue to pipe 60 small mounds with a ½-inch (12 mm) base tapering to a peak about ¾ inch (2 cm) high on the other baking sheets, spacing them about ¼ inch (6 mm) apart. Reserve a little of the meringue.

3. Bake the meringues until the tops are firm enough to lift off the parchment, about 1½ hours. Be gentle with them as they won't be completely dry and can easily mush between your fingers. Move the sheet to a rack and turn over the mounds. With the tip of a small knife, make a small hole in the center, dip the peaked end of one of the stems into some of the reserved meringue, and insert into the hole in one of the mounds. Repeat with the remaining tops and stems (you'll have 12 extra mounds).

Return to the oven and bake until dried and crisp but not browned, about 1 more hour. Turn off the oven (leave the door shut) and let the meringues sit in the oven until cool, about 1 hour. Move to a rack and gently rub the cocoa powder tops to smudge, if desired.

Make sticks

1. Using a wide plastic scraper or silicone spatula, scrape the meringue into a large pastry bag fitted with a ¼-inch (6 mm) wide plain tip (Ateco #803). Holding the pastry bag at about 45 degrees to the lined baking sheet, pipe long sticks about ¼ inch (6 mm) wide and 3 inches (7.5 cm) long, spacing them about ½ inch (12 mm) apart. Using a damp fingertip, lightly press to tap down any meringue peaks.

2. Bake the meringues until dried and crisp but not browned, about 2 hours. Turn off the oven (leave the door shut) and let the meringues sit in the oven until cool, about 1 hour. Remove the baking sheets from the oven and gently lift the meringues off the parchment.

Make swirled strips

1. Using a wide plastic scraper or silicone spatula, scrape the meringue into a large pastry bag fitted with a ½-inch (12 mm) wide fluted tip (Ateco #8). Holding the pastry bag at about 45 degrees to the lined baking sheet, pipe long sticks about 1 to 2 inches (2.5 to 5 cm) wide and 3 inches (7.5 cm) long, spacing them about ½ inch (12 mm) apart.

2. Bake the meringues until dried and crisp but not browned, about 2½ hours. Turn off the oven (leave the door shut) and let the meringues sit in the oven until cool, about 1 hour. Remove the baking sheets from the oven and gently lift the meringues off the parchment.

Make swirled kisses

1. Using a wide plastic scraper or silicone spatula, scrape the meringue into a large pastry bag fitted with a ½-inch (12 mm) wide fluted tip (Ateco #8). Pipe swirled kisses about 1½ inches (4 cm) wide and 2 inches (5 cm) high, spacing them about 1 inch (2.5 cm) apart on the prepared baking sheet.

2. Bake the meringues until dried and crisp but not browned, about 2½ hours. Turn off the oven (leave the door shut) and let the meringues sit in the oven until cool, about 1 hour. Remove the baking sheets from the oven and gently lift the meringues off the parchment.

(continued)

BAKER'S WISDOM

Using a clean bowl and beaters

Impeccably clean beaters and a stainless steel or glass bowl are a must for beating whites—even a touch of grease makes for flat, unbeatable whites. After cleaning the bowl and beater with warm soapy water, add a splash of distilled white vinegar into the bowl along with some hot water. Swirl the mixture around the bowl and beater and pour out. Rinse with fresh water and dry with a clean dishtowel.

ESSENTIAL TECHNIQUE

Making shapes

A

B

C

To make mushroom tops, fit a large pastry bag with a ¼-inch (6 mm) wide plain tip (I use Ateco #803) and fill with meringue. Hold the bag perpendicular to the prepared baking sheet and pipe meringue into a mound that's about 1¼ inches (3.2 cm) in diameter, spacing them about ½ inch (12 mm) apart. The mushroom top should be no higher than ¾ inch (2 cm). Release pressure from the bag and gently swirl the tip while lifting it off the mound. Tap down any pointy tips with a damp finger.

To make the stems, use the same tip and pipe small mounds with a ½-inch (12 mm) base, releasing pressure and lifting the tip straight up for a tapered peak about ¾ inch (2 cm) high. Like the mounds, they will all be slightly different.

To make swirled kisses, fit a large pastry bag with a ½-inch (12 mm) wide fluted tip (I use Ateco #8) and fill with meringue. As with mushrooms, hold the bag perpendicular to the prepared baking sheet and pipe meringue into a swirled mound about 1½ inches (4 cm) in diameter and 2 inches (5 cm) high, releasing pressure at the end and lifting the tip straight up as you finish.

D

For swirled strips, fit a large pastry bag with a ½-inch (12 mm) wide fluted tip (Ateco #8) and fill with meringue. Holding the pastry bag at about 45 degrees to the lined baking sheet, pipe 3-inch (7.5 cm) long swirls that are 1 to 2 inches (2.5 to 5 cm) wide. When you're at the end, release the pressure and gently swirl the tip while lifting it off the meringue.

Orange-Scented Double Chocolate Crackles

Makes about 40 cookies

These cookies speak volumes about the depth of my love for chocolate and my belief in its medicinal values. Riding the line between brownie and cookie, each bite is moist, chewy, and loaded with big chocolate flavor and a burst of orangey freshness. I roll the dough balls in confectioners' sugar for a snowcapped appearance, but they can also be rolled in granulated sugar for an extra sugary crunch. If you're not into the chocolate-orange combo, feel free to omit the zest. Any way you make them, these guys hold the key to satisfying even the biggest chocolate cravings and curing whatever ails you.

¾ cup (3 oz./85 g) confectioners' sugar, sifted if lumpy, for rolling
1¾ cups (7⅞ oz./223 g) unbleached all-purpose flour
½ cup (1½ oz./42 g) unsweetened natural cocoa powder, sifted if lumpy
1½ tsp. baking powder

¼ tsp. table salt
8 Tbs. (4 oz./113 g) unsalted butter, softened
¾ cup (5¼ oz./149 g) granulated sugar
½ cup (3½ oz./99 g) firmly packed light or dark brown sugar

2 large eggs, at room temperature
1 Tbs. finely grated orange zest
1 tsp. pure vanilla extract
3 oz. (85 g) bittersweet, semisweet, or white chocolate, chopped (½ cup) (see p. 380)

1. Position a rack in the center of the oven and heat the oven to 350°F (180°C/gas 4). Line two cookie sheets (or more if you have them) with parchment or nonstick liners. Put the confectioners' sugar in a small bowl.

2. Whisk the flour, cocoa powder, baking powder, and salt in a medium bowl until well blended. Put the butter in the bowl of a stand mixer fitted with the paddle attachment (or in a large bowl using an electric handheld mixer fitted with wire beaters). Beat on medium speed until creamy and smooth, about 1 minute. Add the sugars and beat until fluffy and lighter in color, 2 minutes. Add the eggs, one at a time, beating briefly between additions, adding the orange zest and vanilla with the last egg; beat on medium until blended, about 1 minute. Add the flour mixture and chopped chocolate and beat on low speed until the mixture is well blended.

3. Using a 1-Tbs. mini scoop, shape the dough into balls, roll in the sugar, and arrange about 1½ inches (4 cm) apart on the prepared cookie sheets. Bake, one sheet at a time, until the cookies are puffed and the cracks still look wet, 11 to 13 minutes. Move the sheet to a rack and let cool for about 5 minutes. Using a spatula, lift the cookies from the sheet and onto a rack until completely cooled.

For more about scooping cookie dough using a mini scoop, see p. 125.

(continued)

MAKE AHEAD

> Shape the dough balls and arrange close together on a flat plate, cover, and refrigerate for up to 1 day or freeze for up to 3 months. Bring to room temperature while the oven heats.

> Layer the baked and cooled cookies between sheets of parchment or waxed paper in an airtight container. They can be stowed for up to 6 days at room temperature or frozen for up to 1 month.

TWISTS

Flavor swap

Almond: Along with the vanilla, add ¾ tsp. pure almond extract. Instead of chopped chocolate, use ½ cup (2 oz./57 g) slivered almonds, toasted and chopped (see p. 33).

BAKER'S WISDOM

When to sift

If you're weighing cocoa, it's fine to sift after measuring, as the weight will not change. If you're using volume measures and you have lumpy cocoa, sift it before measuring to avoid any air pockets. By the way, this same concept applies to confectioners' sugar.

ESSENTIAL TECHNIQUE

Sifting cocoa powder

If your cocoa powder is lumpy (as shown on the left), you'll need to sift it before measuring in order to get an accurate measure. Spoon some cocoa powder into a fine-mesh sieve and tap the side. Using your fingers or a silicone spatula, press on any cocoa lumps left in the sieve.

> >

Espresso Chocolate Biscotti Straws

Makes about 16 straw-like cookies

When Claire, my baking partner in crime, first saw this recipe, she exclaimed, "Right up my alley!" I know of no greater fan of biscotti than Claire, and with this biscotti's chocolate–espresso flavor profile, she is doubly pleased.

    Claire and I both buck tradition when it comes to the baked texture of biscotti. Instead of the traditional super-dry and crunchy texture some prefer, we like biscotti a bit on the softer, easier-to-bite side. This recipe is the best of both worlds. The strawlike shape means the biscotti can be baked until crisp according to tradition, but they are thin enough to nibble without dunking in coffee.

1 Tbs. coffee liqueur or water
1 Tbs. instant espresso powder
1⅓ cups (6 oz./170 g) unbleached all-purpose flour
½ cup (3½ oz./99 g) firmly packed light brown sugar
1 tsp. baking powder

⅛ tsp. ground cinnamon
¼ tsp. table salt
1⅝ oz. (46 g) finely chopped bittersweet or milk chocolate (⅓ cup) (see p. 380)
1 large egg, at room temperature

1 white from a large egg (1 oz./28 g), at room temperature (see p. 371)
2 Tbs. coarse sanding sugar, for dusting
White Chocolate Drizzle (see the recipe on the facing page; optional)

1. Position a rack in the center of the oven and heat the oven to 325°F (165°C/gas 3). Line a cookie sheet with parchment.

2. Put the coffee liqueur and espresso powder in a 1-cup (240 ml) glass measure (the spout makes it easy to pour) and stir until dissolved.

3. Put the flour, brown sugar, baking powder, cinnamon, and salt in the bowl of a stand mixer fitted with the paddle attachment (or in a large bowl using an electric handheld mixer fitted with wire beaters). Beat on medium-low speed until well blended. Add the chopped chocolate and mix briefly to combine.

4. Add the egg and egg white to the espresso mixture and stir with a fork until well blended. With the mixer on low speed, slowly pour the egg mixture down the side of the bowl. Continue mixing until a sticky, moist dough forms, about 1 minute. Dump the dough onto the center of the prepared cookie sheet. Using slightly wet hands, press the dough roughly into a rectangle. Cover with a large piece of plastic and, using your hands and a rolling pin, press and roll into a 7 x 10-inch (17 x 25 cm) rectangle. Lift the plastic wrap occasionally and reposition it on the dough until you have an even layer. The flat side of a ruler or bench scraper also helps square off the sides. Sprinkle the top with the sanding sugar and gently press in.

For more about how to use a bench scraper to square up dough, see p. 549.

5. Bake until the rectangle is firm to the touch around the edges and the top looks dry, 24 to 26 minutes. Move the sheet to a rack and set aside until the rectangle is just cool enough to handle, about 10 minutes. Keep the oven set at 325°F (165°C/gas 3).

6. When the biscotti rectangle is cool enough to handle, turn it rounded side down on a cutting board and, starting at one corner, gently but firmly peel away the parchment, steadying the biscotti with the other hand. Arrange it, rounded side up, on a cutting board. Using a serrated knife, cut crosswise into slices about ½ inch (12 mm) thick. I use a gentle sawing motion to break through the crust and then push down firmly on the knife. Return the biscotti to the baking sheet and arrange them cut side down—it's fine if they are touching. Bake until the biscotti are dried to your taste, 10 to 14 minutes. Let cool completely before adding White Chocolate Drizzle, if desired.

For more about how to use a bench scraper to square up dough, see p. 549.

MAKE AHEAD

Layer the baked and cooled straws (without the White Chocolate Drizzle) between sheets of parchment or waxed paper in an airtight container. They can be stowed for up to 3 weeks at room temperature or frozen for up to 6 weeks.

FINISHING TOUCHES

White Chocolate Drizzle

Combine 3 oz. (85 g) chopped white chocolate (not chips) and 2 tsp. canola or vegetable oil in a small heatproof bowl. Melt over a pan of simmering water or in a microwave and stir until well blended.

Scrape the melted chocolate into one corner of a heavy-duty zip-top bag, press out the air, and seal. Arrange the cooled biscotti straws on their sides—they should be touching—on a wire rack or lined cookie sheet. Snip off a small piece of the corner of the bag and drizzle the chocolate casually over the straws. Set aside until the chocolate firms up, about 30 minutes.

TWISTS

Flavor swap

> **Orange:** Instead of using the espresso powder, add 2 tsp. finely grated orange zest to the egg mixture. Instead of using coffee liqueur, use the same amount of orange liqueur or fresh orange juice or water. Omit the cinnamon. Instead of the sanding sugar, sprinkle the top with 2 Tbs. finely chopped nuts just before baking.

> **White chocolate:** Instead of the bittersweet chocolate, use the same amount of white chocolate.

Re-size it

To make shorter straws, cut the baked rectangle crosswise (along the shorter side) and proceed as directed. Your yield will be about 22 strawlike cookies.

(continued)

FINISHING TOUCHES

Set on a rack and drizzle with melted milk, white, or dark chocolate and let sit until the chocolate firms up, about 30 minutes.

BAKER'S WISDOM

Almond flour

Almond flour or very finely ground almonds can be purchased at most health and gourmet food stores, or you can make your own. Start with natural (with skins) or blanched (skinless) whole almonds and, using a food processor and short pulses, chop the nuts until finely ground. Be careful not to overprocess or the nuts will release their oils and you'll end up with almond butter which, while delicious, is not a substitute for almond flour.

ESSENTIAL TECHNIQUE

Browning the butter and forming the cookies

To make brown butter, cook the butter over medium heat, swirling over the heat as it melts, until it smells nutty and the milk solids are dark brown (shown left). If the milk solids turn black (shown right), you've cooked the butter too much and need to start over.

Slide the pan off the heat, let cool slightly, about 5 minutes, then add the dry ingredients, stirring until well blended before adding in the egg and extracts.

The dough will spread as the cookies bake, so arrange the dough 3 inches (7.5 cm) apart. Flatten the dough with lightly dampened fingers, forming 2¼-inch (5.5 cm) rounds. Use a ruler to measure for accuracy. Re-wet your fingers as needed to prevent sticking.

The cookies are done when the edges are golden brown.

Sparkling Orange–Apricot Pinwheels

Makes 44 cookies   [PHOTO ON P. 177]

This crisp sugar cookie is not just another "pretty face." It is also bursting with orangey apricot flavor thanks to the hefty amount of puréed dried apricots and orange zest. The technique for making these pinwheels might look daunting but, because the dough is pliable and shaped before chilling, the cookie construction project moves along quickly and easily.

For the dough
1/3 cup (3 oz./85 g) lightly packed dried apricots
12 Tbs. (6 oz./170 g) unsalted butter, softened
1 cup (4 oz./113 g) confectioners' sugar, sifted if lumpy
1 yolk from a large egg (see p. 371)

1 1/2 tsp. pure vanilla extract
1/2 tsp. table salt
2 cups (9 oz./255 g) unbleached all-purpose flour
2 tsp. finely grated orange zest (see p. 138)
2 to 4 drops orange gel paste (optional)

For assembly
1 white from a large egg (1 oz./28 g)
1 tsp. water
Scant 1/2 cup (3 1/2 oz./99 g) white, clear, or orange coarse sanding sugar or a combination

Make the dough

1. Put the apricots in a food processor and pulse until very finely chopped. Alternatively, use a large chef's knife to chop into very, very tiny pieces. Using scissors, cut an empty paper towel roll lengthwise.

2. Put the butter and confectioners' sugar in the bowl of a stand mixer fitted with the paddle attachment (or in a large bowl using an electric handheld mixer fitted with wire beaters). Beat on medium speed until creamy and lighter in color, about 3 minutes. Add the yolk, vanilla, and salt and beat on medium speed until blended and fragrant, about 1 minute. Add the flour and beat on low speed until the dough forms moist clumps.

3. Scrape the dough onto the work surface and divide into two equal piles (10 oz./283 g each). Wrap one pile in plastic and set aside. Return the other half of the dough to the bowl. Add the apricots, orange zest, and gel paste, if using, and beat on medium until blended, about 1 minute. Arrange a piece of plastic wrap on the work surface and put the orange-flavored dough in the center and wrap to cover.

4. Working with one dough at a time, unwrap it and shape into a 4-inch (10 cm) square. If the dough is crumbly, gently knead on the counter a few times. Flatten the plastic wrap (use a fresh piece if it's too wrinkled) and arrange the dough in the center. Using a rolling pin, roll the dough between the plastic (or you can use parchment) to a 7 x 5-inch (17 x 12 cm) rectangle, turning, lifting, and repositioning the plastic throughout the rolling. For the best-looking results, use the flat side of a ruler or bench scraper to make the sides and corners straight. Roll the remaining dough in the same way.

For more about rolling dough between parchment (or plastic), see p. 133.

For more about using a bench scraper to square up dough, see p. 549.

(continued)

MAKE AHEAD

> The cookie dough can be prepared and refrigerated for 2 days or wrapped in plastic and frozen for up to 1 month. If frozen, thaw in the refrigerator for 30 minutes before proceeding with the recipe.

> Stow the baked and cooled cookies between sheets of parchment or waxed paper in an airtight container at room temperature for up to 4 days or freeze for up to 6 weeks.

ESSENTIAL TECHNIQUE

Piping the filling

A

Fold the open end of a large heavy-duty zip-top bag over your hand to form a cuff. Using a silicone spatula, scoop the filling into the bag, scraping it against the top edge. Reposition the bag over your hand as needed as it becomes full.

B

Using the edge of a bench scraper, push the filling into one corner of the bag, press out the air, then seal the bag. Twist the top of the bag against the filling and snip off the corner as directed in the recipe.

C

Squeeze about 1½ tsp. of filling in the center on the flat side of half of the meringue shells. Add a top shell, flat side down, and gently press the shells together until the filling just reaches the edges.

Rosemary Cornmeal
Shortbread

[PAGE 128]

171

**Hazelnut–Raspberry
Sandwich Cookie Wreaths**

[PAGE 131]

172

**Double Chocolate Cream
Cheese Fudge Brownies**

[PAGE 134]

Creamy Meyer Lemon–Lavender Squares

[PAGE 136]

Apricot Rugelach

[PAGE 139]

175

Whimsical Vanilla Bean
Cutouts

[PAGE 142]

176

Sparkling Orange–Apricot Pinwheels

[PAGE 163]

177

Candied Rose Macarons
with White Chocolate Filling

[PAGE 203]

**Espresso–Hazelnut
Meringue Cake *with*
Espresso Buttercream *and*
Milk Chocolate Ganache**

[PAGE 208]

179

Flourless Raspberry–Orange
Chocolate Decadence

[PAGE 213]

180

**Raspberry Zebra
Cheesecake**

[PAGE 218]

181

Chocolate–Mocha
Marshmallow Cake

[PAGE 221]

Three-Layer Carrot Cake
with **Vanilla Cream Cheese Frosting**

[PAGE 230]

Sparkling Coffee-Marbled
Bundt Cake

[PAGE 235]

Creamy Peanut Butter-Filled Devil's Food Cupcakes *with* **Milk Chocolate Ganache**

[PAGE 244]

185

Big-Time Orange Angel
Food Cake *with* Winter
Fruit Compote

[PAGE 267]

186

Strawberry Crumble-Topped Bars

Makes 16 squares

In need of a destination for your homemade preserves or your favorite jam? Look no further than this lightly sweetened, subtly nutty, crumbled-topped square. I most often use strawberry or raspberry—I always have both in my fridge—but guava, apricot, rhubarb, or Concord grape will also hit the spot.

While the jam takes center stage in this cookie, the supporting role of the crust and the crumble top shouldn't be overlooked. Both crust and crumble are made from one easy dough—half pressed into the bottom of the pan and the other half mixed with nuts (or you can leave them out) to make a loose, crumbly topping. It's a terrific recipe to make for and with kids. I've made these bars for bake sales, picnics, and snacks, but I'll admit that I've also enjoyed one or two for breakfast—I call them my breakfast bar of champions.

A note about the timing window: Claire likes these squares to be slightly underbaked for a soft, almost melty texture, and I prefer mine to have a bit more crunch. The timing window and doneness test reflect both our preferences.

Nonstick cooking spray or softened butter, for preparing the pan
12 Tbs. (6 oz./170 g) unsalted butter
1 large egg, at room temperature

1 tsp. pure vanilla extract
2 cups (9 oz./255 g) unbleached all-purpose flour
2/3 cup (4⅝ oz./131 g) granulated sugar
1½ tsp. baking powder
¼ tsp. table salt

1 cup (11 oz./312 g) strawberry jam
1/3 cup (1⅜ oz./39 g) medium-finely chopped walnuts (optional)
Confectioners' sugar, for dusting (optional)

1. Position a rack in the center of the oven and heat the oven to 350°F (180°C/gas 4). Line an 8-inch (20 cm) square baking pan (I like the straight-sided kind) with foil, leaving about a 1-inch (2.5 cm) overhang on two opposite sides. Lightly grease the foil.

For more about lining a straight-sided pan with foil, see p. 135.

2. Cut the butter in half lengthwise and then cut each strip into 6 pieces. Pile onto a plate and slide into the freezer until ready to use.

3. Put the egg and vanilla in a ramekin or small bowl and use a fork to mix until well blended. Put the flour, sugar, baking powder, and salt in a food processor. Process until blended, about 2 seconds. Scatter the chilled butter pieces over the flour mixture and pulse until the mixture forms coarse crumbs and the butter is in very small pieces. Drizzle the egg mixture over the flour mixture, then pulse just until the dough forms moist crumbs and the butter is incorporated, about 20 seconds. Remove the dough from the bowl and divide in half (about 10⅞ oz./308 g each).

For more about mixing butter and flour together until the butter is pea-sized, see p. 80.

MAKE AHEAD

> The bars can be prepared through Step 3, covered, and frozen for up to 1 month before baking. Thaw in the refrigerator overnight before baking.

> The baked bars can be covered and stowed at room temperature for up to 2 days.

(continued)

TWISTS

Flavor swap

> In place of the walnuts, use the same amount of any nut—even lightly salted peanuts are delicious in these cookies, especially when using grape jelly or jam.

> In place of the strawberry jam, use the same amount of any flavor fruit jam or preserves.

4. Scatter half of the dough in the prepared pan and, using lightly floured fingertips if necessary, pat it down into the bottom and corners of the pan to make an even layer. Using a spoon or small offset spatula, spread the strawberry jam evenly over the dough. Add the walnuts (if using) to the remaining dough and, using your fingers, mix and gently pinch the dough until it forms crumbles (there will be some big crumbles but mostly small). Scatter the crumbles evenly over the jam.

5. For a soft texture, bake until the top is pale golden, 36 to 38 minutes. For a crunchy texture, bake until the top is golden brown and the jam is bubbling around the edges, 40 to 42 minutes. Move the pan to a rack and let cool completely.

For more about cutting bar cookies, see p. 167.

6. To cut, use the foil edges on the sides of the pan to lift the cookie from the pan. Carefully peel away the foil from the sides and set the cookie on a cutting board. Using a ruler as a guide and a serrated knife, cut crosswise into 4 equal strips and then cut each strip into 4 squares (about 2 inches/ 5 cm). I use a gentle sawing motion to break through the top crust and then firmly push down on the knife. Dust lightly with confectioners' sugar just before serving, if desired.

ESSENTIAL TECHNIQUE

Layering the dough and crumbles

A Scatter half of the dough in the prepared pan and press into the bottom and corners to form an even layer. Lightly flour your fingertips if needed. Use a small offset spatula (a spoon works, too) to spread the jam evenly across the dough layer.

B Mix and gently pinch the remaining half of the dough and walnuts, if using, to form crumbles. They should mostly be small, but a few larger ones are fine too.

C Scatter the crumbles loosely and evenly across the jam-topped dough. Don't press down.

Lemon Drop Snaps

Makes 24 cookies

When I ran the bakery at Hay Day Country Market (now owned by Balducci's), new product development was one of my favorite parts of the job. We already had a very successful line of cookie classics like oatmeal and peanut butter, so coming up with a something different was challenging. I decided to take a slightly more sophisticated approach and, with the help of my stellar staff, the crisp, snappy cookie line was born. The lemon and coffee snaps were wildly popular and, in fact, Balducci's still sells them.

In most recipes, I call for whisking the flour with other dry ingredients like salt, spices, and leaveners before proceeding with the recipe. For cookies that don't have leaveners or added spices, like this cookie, you can skip the step (no need to dirty an extra bowl if you don't have to) and simply add the salt along with the sugar and then add the flour as directed.

For crispy, snappy cookies, make sure to follow the doneness test and bake until the cookie edges have a deep browned edge.

6 Tbs. (3 oz./85 g) unsalted butter, softened
⅔ cup (4¼ oz./120 g) granulated sugar

1½ tsp. finely grated lemon zest (see p. 138)
½ tsp. pure lemon extract or oil
¼ tsp. table salt

1 large egg, at room temperature
¾ cup (3⅜ oz./96 g) unbleached all-purpose flour

1. Position a rack in the center of the oven and heat the oven to 350°F (180°C/gas 4). Line cookie sheets (three if you have them) with parchment or nonstick liners. Nonstick liners will make a flatter cookie; the parchment will make the cookies a bit thicker (see the Essential Technique on p. 190). Both are delicious, but I prefer the nonstick liner for this cookie.

2. Put the butter in the bowl of a stand mixer fitted with the paddle attachment (or in a medium bowl using an electric handheld mixer fitted with wire beaters). Beat on medium speed until creamy, about 1 minute. Add the sugar, lemon zest, lemon extract, and salt and continue beating until the mixture is fluffy and lighter in color, about 2 minutes. Add the egg and beat until well blended. Add the flour and mix on low speed until just blended.

3. Using a 2-tsp. mini scoop, scoop and level the dough and arrange about 2½ inches (6 cm) apart on the prepared cookie sheets. Bake, one sheet at a time, until the cookies are deep golden brown around the edges, 11 to 13 minutes. Move the sheet to a rack and let cool for 5 minutes. Using a large spatula, move the cookies from the sheet to a rack until cool enough to eat or cooled completely. Repeat with the remaining dough, using cooled cookie sheets and liners.

For more about scooping cookie dough using a mini scoop, see p. 125.

(continued)

MAKE AHEAD

Stow the baked and cooled cookies between sheets of parchment or waxed paper in an airtight container at room temperature for up to 5 days.

TWISTS

Flavor swap

> Orange: In place of the lemon zest and extract, use the same amount of orange zest and extract.

> Coffee: In place of the lemon zest and extract, dissolve $1\frac{3}{4}$ tsp. instant coffee granules or espresso powder in 1 tsp. pure vanilla extract.

Re-size it

> If you don't have a 2-tsp. mini scoop, use a 1-Tbs. mini scoop, arrange about 3 inches (7.5 cm) apart on the prepared cookie sheets, and bake for the same amount of time. The cookies will be bigger and the yield lower but still delicious.

> Make and bake the cookies as directed. Immediately after baking, use a wide metal spatula to lift the cookies, one at a time, from the cookie sheet and arrange over a rolling pin to shape as tuiles (for more about how to do this, see p. 194).

ESSENTIAL TECHNIQUE

Checking doneness

In order for the cookies to be really crisp and snappy, the edges must be a deep golden brown. In the photo on the left, the cookies on parchment bake up a bit thicker. The cookies on the right are baked on silicone liners and are a bit thinner. Both have the browned-edged ring, and both are delicious.

> >

Anise Spritz Cookies

Makes about 50 cookies

Anise has a very distinct aroma—it smells like licorice but tastes even better and stronger. Adding it to a traditional cream cheese–butter spritz elevates the baked cookie to a whole new level of deliciousness. Crack open a fresh jar of anise for the best and strongest flavor and make the cookies a few days before serving or sharing, as the flavor grows and improves with time.

If you haven't used a cookie press lately or if this is your first try at making spritz cookies, treat yourself to one of the new models out there. They are sleek and easy to handle, and they produce beautiful cookies with little fuss. Because the equipment varies between brands, it's important to read the instructions thoroughly before you start baking.

14 Tbs. (7 oz./198 g) unsalted butter, softened
4 oz. (113 g) cream cheese, softened
1 cup (7 oz./198 g) granulated sugar

¾ tsp. ground anise
½ tsp. table salt
1 yolk from a large egg
1 tsp. pure vanilla extract

2⅓ cups (10½ oz./298 g) unbleached all-purpose flour + more as needed
Colored sanding sugar (optional)

1. Position a rack in the center of the oven and heat the oven to 350°F (180°C/gas 4). Line cookie sheets (three if you have them) with parchment or nonstick liners.

2. Put the butter, cream cheese, and sugar in the bowl of a stand mixer fitted with the paddle attachment (or in a large bowl using an electric handheld mixer fitted with wire beaters). Beat on medium speed until creamy and smooth, about 2 minutes. Add the anise and salt and beat until well blended, about 1 minute. Add the yolk and the vanilla and beat until blended. Add the flour and mix on low speed until a soft dough forms, about 1 minute.

3. Scrape the dough onto a lightly floured work surface and portion into four approximately equal (no need to be perfect) piles. Shape each pile into a log about 1¼ inches (3 cm) in diameter or slightly narrower than your cookie press, lightly flouring as needed. Cover three logs with plastic.

4. Fit the cookie press with a die plate (concave side out, for my press) as directed. Slide one log into the cookie press and close the press. Shape the cookies directly onto the baking sheets about 1½ inches (4 cm) apart, as directed by the manufacturer (two clicks works on my press). (If using parchment, dab a bit of the batter between the parchment and cookie sheet to help secure the paper.) Sprinkle with colored sugar, if desired. Repeat with the remaining dough.

(continued)

MAKE AHEAD

Stow the baked and cooled cookies between sheets of parchment or waxed paper in an airtight container for up to 5 days at room temperature or freeze for up to 6 weeks.

TWISTS

Flavor swap

> **Almond:** Omit the ground anise and add ½ to ¾ tsp. pure almond extract along with the vanilla extract.

> **Vanilla bean:** Omit the ground anise and use 1½ tsp. vanilla bean paste instead of the vanilla extract.

(Anise Spritz Cookies continued)

5. Bake, one sheet at a time, until the edges and bottoms of the cookies are golden brown, 12 to 14 minutes (too little and the texture will be soft and doughy). Move the sheet to a rack and let cool for 5 minutes. Using a large spatula, move the cookies from the sheet to a rack and let cool completely. Repeat with the remaining dough, using cooled cookie sheets and liners.

ESSENTIAL TECHNIQUE

Working with a cookie press

 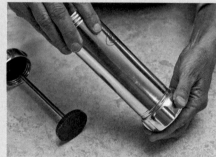

Follow the manufacturer's instructions to fit the your cookie press with a die plate.

Portion the dough into 4 piles and roll each into a log that's slightly narrower than the cookie press. Cover three logs with plastic, slide the remaining one into the press, and screw on the top lever.

Working directly on the prepared cookie sheet, press and shape the cookies according to the manufacturer's instructions. I use two clicks on my press. I prefer nonstick liners when working with a cookie press, as the liners stay in place, but you also can use parchment. To help secure parchment to the baking sheet, dab a bit of dough between the corners of the paper and the cookie sheet to help secure it.

Brown Butter–Pecan Tuiles

Makes about 20 cookies

Shaped like the curved terra-cotta roofing tiles that are common in the south of France, tuiles (French for tiles) are paper-thin wafer cookies. The not-so secret technique to creating their elegant shape is to drape them over a rolling pin while still hot from the oven; they collapse around the pin and cool into a crispy, bowed cookie.

   While the cookies are special in appearance, using brown butter in the batter adds a toasty, nutty essence. Don't be intimidated by making brown butter. It takes only a few extra minutes to go from melted butter to melted brown butter, and it makes the cookies' flavor much more complex and interesting.

7 Tbs. (3½ oz./99 g) unsalted butter
2 egg whites from large eggs (2 oz./57 g), at room temperature

½ cup (3½ oz./99 g) granulated sugar
Pinch of table salt
½ tsp. pure vanilla extract or paste

⅔ cup (3 oz./85 g) unbleached all-purpose flour
3 Tbs. finely chopped pecans (see p. 304)

1. Position a rack in the center of the oven and heat the oven to 350°F (180°C/gas 4). Line two cookie sheets (or more if you have them) with nonstick liners (parchment won't work). Steady a rolling pin between two bottles or cans so that it's secure and ready to shape the cookies.

2. Put the butter in a medium skillet or saucepan. Cook, swirling the pan, over medium heat until nutty brown and the milk solids are dark brown (not black), 6 to 7 minutes. Slide the pan off the heat and let cool slightly, about 5 minutes.

For more about making brown butter, see p. 162.

3. Put the egg whites, sugar, and salt in a medium bowl and whisk by hand until blended and a bit foamy, about 1 minute. Add the warm brown butter and the vanilla and whisk until blended. Pour in the flour and continue to whisk until smooth and blended.

4. Using a 1-Tbs. mini scoop, drop the batter by a scant 1 Tbs. about 4 inches (10 cm) apart onto the prepared cookie sheets (I can fit 5 on one sheet). Using a small offset spatula, spread each round of batter into a 3½-inch (9 cm) round. Sprinkle about ¼ tsp. of the pecans over each cookie. If the batter becomes too thick to spread, set the bowl over a pot of simmering water and stir until it loosens. Bake, one sheet at a time, until the cookies are golden brown around the edges, 9 to 11 minutes.

For more about scooping cookie dough using a mini scoop, see p. 125.

For more information on doneness, see p. 190.

(continued)

MAKE AHEAD

Stow the baked and cooled cookies between sheets of parchment or waxed paper in an airtight container at room temperature for up to 3 days.

TWISTS

Flavor swap

Spicy: Add ⅛ tsp. Chinese five-spice powder to the flour before whisking into the brown butter.

BAKER'S WISDOM

Practice makes perfect

Because the cookies firm up very quickly and can only be shaped when hot from the oven, start off by baking only one or two at a time until you get the hang of shaping them over the rolling pin. Also be sure to have a metal spatula and rolling pin at the ready, so you're ready to transfer the cookies from the cookie sheet to pin.

5. Working quickly, move the cookie sheet to a rack. Using a wide metal spatula and working with one cookie at a time, lift off the hot cookie and immediately drape it over the rolling pin. Let cool until set, about 1 minute. Carefully remove the tuiles from the rolling pin and set them on a rack to cool completely.

Spreading the dough

Scoop a scant 1 Tbs. dough onto the prepared cookie sheet and, using a small offset spatula and a circular movement, spread the dough into a thin 3½-inch (9 cm) round. Size is important with these cookies, so measure with a ruler.

Sprinkle finely chopped pecans evenly over the top of each cookie, then bake.

Forming the curved shape

These cookies must be shaped immediately after baking or they become rigid and crisp, so work quickly and carefully (they are very hot) to place them on a waiting rolling pin. Use a wide metal spatula to transfer a hot cookie to the pin, nudging it off the spatula with your fingertips.

As you place the cookies over the pin, use your fingers and the edge of the spatula to help shape them over the curve. After about a minute, the cookies will be cool and the tuile shape formed; remove them carefully and place on a rack to cool completely.

Chewy Molasses Ginger Cookies

Makes 46 cookies

My son Alex is a molasses-cookie junkie, so he takes special interest when I'm developing and testing a new version. He scrutinizes and critiques each incarnation, and I take his suggestions seriously. This cookie is no exception. With more ground ginger and slightly less sugar per Alex's request, this cookie has his official seal of approval.

Like other spice cookies, the flavors deepen and develop after a day or two, making them a terrific make-ahead treat.

½ cup (3½ oz./99 g) coarse
   sanding sugar, for rolling
2⅓ cups (10½ oz./298 g)
   unbleached all-purpose flour
1 Tbs. ground ginger
1 tsp. baking soda

¼ tsp. table salt
12 Tbs. (6 oz./170 g) unsalted
   butter, softened
½ cup (3½ oz./99 g) firmly
   packed light or dark
   brown sugar

½ cup (3½ oz./99 g)
   granulated sugar
1 large egg, at room temperature
¼ cup (60 ml) light molasses
3 Tbs. finely chopped
   crystallized ginger (see p. 218)

1. Position a rack in the center of the oven and heat the oven to 350°F (180°C/gas 4). Line two or more cookie sheets with parchment or nonstick liners. Put the coarse sanding sugar in a small bowl.

2. Whisk the flour, ground ginger, baking soda, and salt in a medium bowl until well blended. Put the butter in the bowl of a stand mixer fitted with the paddle attachment (or in a large bowl using an electric handheld mixer fitted with wire beaters). Beat on medium speed until creamy and smooth, about 1 minute. Add the brown and granulated sugars and beat until fluffy and lighter in color, 2 minutes. Add the egg and molasses and beat on medium until blended, about 1 minute. Add the flour mixture and crystallized ginger and beat on low speed until the mixture is well blended.

3. Using a 1-Tbs. mini scoop, shape the dough into balls, roll in the sanding sugar, and arrange about 1½ inches (4 cm) apart on the prepared cookie sheets. Bake, one sheet at a time, until puffed and the dough in the cracks still looks wet, 12 to 14 minutes. Move the sheet to a rack to cool for about 5 minutes. Using a spatula, move the cookies to a rack until completely cooled.

For more about scooping cookie dough using a mini scoop, see p. 125.

(continued)

MAKE AHEAD

> Shape the dough into balls and roll in the sanding sugar, then arrange them close together on a flat plate; cover and refrigerate for up to 1 day or freeze for up to 3 months. Bring to room temperature while the oven heats.

> Stow the baked and cooled cookies between sheets of parchment or waxed paper in an airtight container at room temperature for up to 6 days or freeze for up to 1 month.

Rolling the dough and scoring

A

Draw a 13¾ x 9-inch (35 x 23 cm) rectangle on parchment, turn it over, and roll out the dough into a rectangle slightly larger than the drawn lines. Roll between parchment (see p. 133) and flour the dough as needed.

B

Once the shape is close to size, trim off any overhang following the pencil lines on the parchment. Patch bald spots with the trimmed dough to complete the dough rectangle and roll once or twice to even out the dough.

C

Once all areas are patched and the entire drawn rectangle is covered, use a ruler as a guide and trim the dough to form an exact 13¾ x 9-inch (35 x 23 cm) rectangle. Discard the excess dough.

D

Sprinkle the cinnamon-sugar over the top of the dough. Don't worry about getting it close to the edges—you'll use your fingers to spread it out in an even layer. As you spread, press the cinnamon-sugar gently into the dough.

E

Score the dough into 2¾ x 3-inch (7 x 7.5 cm) cookies; a bench scraper works well to do this, but you can also use a knife. Before scoring, measure out with tick marks along the edges to ensure the correct size.

F

Use a fork to prick each square. Space the indentations evenly in 4 or 5 rows. If desired, use the bench scraper to score (not all the way through) the squares in half, then slide the parchment on a cookie sheet and chill before baking.

Sugar 'n' Spice Press-Down Cookies

Makes 36 cookies

Snickerdoodles never make it to my top ten all-star cookie list. While the cinnamon-sugar flavoring is enticing, I prefer a more complex complement of spices along with meatier, sink-my-teeth-into texture, so I've done some remodeling for this cookie. I've upped the spice ante by adding nutmeg and ginger to the base of a more traditional butter cookie batter and added a cinnamon-sugar coating for a little crunch. The baked texture is soft and slightly chewy and the flavor is buttery and spiced.

1⅓ cups (9⅜ oz./266 g) granulated sugar, divided

2½ tsp. ground cinnamon, divided

2 cups (9 oz./255 g) unbleached all-purpose flour

1 tsp. cream of tartar

¾ tsp. ground ginger

½ tsp. baking powder

½ tsp. table salt

⅛ tsp. ground nutmeg

12 Tbs. (6 oz./170 g) unsalted butter, softened

1 large egg, at room temperature

1½ tsp. pure vanilla extract or vanilla bean paste

1. Position a rack in the center of the oven and heat the oven to 350°F (180°C/gas 4). Line two cookie sheets (or more if you have them) with parchment or nonstick liners. Put ⅓ cup (2⅜ oz./67 g) of the sugar and ¾ tsp. of the cinnamon in a small bowl and stir until well blended. Set aside.

2. Put the flour, the remaining 1¾ tsp. cinnamon, the cream of tartar, ginger, baking powder, salt, and nutmeg in a medium bowl and whisk until well blended.

3. Put the butter in the bowl of a stand mixer fitted with the paddle attachment (or in a large bowl using an electric handheld mixer fitted with wire beaters). Beat on medium speed until creamy and smooth, about 1 minute. Add the remaining 1 cup (7 oz./198 g) sugar and beat until fluffy and lighter in color, 2 minutes. Add the egg and vanilla and beat on medium speed until blended, about 1 minute. Add the flour mixture and beat on low until the mixture is well blended.

4. Using a 1-Tbs. mini scoop, shape the dough into balls, roll the rounded top in the cinnamon-sugar, and arrange about 2 inches (5 cm) apart on the prepared cookie sheets. Using the bottom of a glass or mug, flatten the cookies to ¼ inch (6 mm) thick (see the Essential Technique on p. 200). You can expect the edges to crack slightly. Bake, one sheet at a time, until the tops look dry and the edges are tinged light brown, 10 to 13 minutes. Move the cookie sheet to a rack to cool for about 5 minutes. Using a spatula, move the cookies to a rack until completely cooled.

For more about scooping cookie dough using a mini scoop, see p. 125.

(continued)

MAKE AHEAD

> The dough can be shaped into balls but not rolled in cinnamon-sugar or flattened. Arrange the dough balls close together on a flat plate, cover, and refrigerate for up to 1 day or freeze for up to 3 months. Bring to room temperature while the oven heats. Just before baking, roll in cinnamon-sugar and flatten as directed.

> Stow the baked and cooled cookies between sheets of parchment or waxed paper in an airtight container at room temperature for up to 3 days or freeze for up to 1 month.

(Toasted Coconut Meltaways continued)

Flavor swap

> **Vanilla:** Omit the toasted coconut and coconut extract and increase the vanilla extract to 2 tsp.

> **Lemon:** Omit the toasted coconut, vanilla extract, and coconut extract and add 2½ tsp. finely grated lemon zest and 2 tsp. freshly squeezed lemon juice.

> **Nutty:** Omit the coconut extract. Instead of the toasted coconut, use the same amount of finely diced nuts (walnuts, pecans, hazelnuts, or pistachios) and increase the vanilla to 1½ tsp.

ESSENTIAL TECHNIQUE

Checking for doneness and rolling in sugar

To test for doneness, use a spatula to peek at the color of the bottom. The cookies are done when the bottoms are light golden brown, like those on the right. The cookies on the left are overcooked.

While the cookies are still warm, roll them in confectioners' sugar, then set on a rack, rounded side up, to cool completely.

Candied Rose Macarons *with* White Chocolate Filling

Makes 35 sandwich cookies (70 shells)   [PHOTO ON P. 178]

There's no question in my mind that homemade macarons are served for very important occasions. Using candied (sugared) rose petals as the flavor base elevates these precious cookies to an even higher level. Although the candied rose petals are expensive, the sophisticated floral fragrance and flavor and their elegant appearance make them even more special than their traditionally flavored cousins. Candied rose petals can be purchased online, but I find the best prices when I shop in larger spice stores and buy in large quantities.

The ground candied petals add a touch of pink to the macaron shells. For an extra color boost, add a drop or two of pink gel paste. Gel paste colors are more intense than the grocery store food colorings.

For the candied rose shells
½ cup (2½ oz./71 g) candied rose petals
1½ cups (6 oz./170 g) confectioners' sugar, divided
¾ cup (2½ oz./71 g) almond flour (see p. 162)

3 whites from large eggs (3 oz./85 g), at room temperature (see p. 371)
Pinch of table salt
¼ tsp. rose water (optional)
1 or 2 drops pink gel paste (optional)

For the filling
6 oz. (170 g) white chocolate, chopped (1 cup)
¼ cup (60 ml) heavy cream
Pinch of table salt

Make the shells

1. Line three cookie sheets with nonstick liners or parchment (I prefer nonstick liners for this job).

2. Put the candied rose petals in a food processor and process until they are mostly finely ground (some larger bits are all right), about 3 minutes. Add 1 cup (4 oz./113 g) of the confectioners' sugar and the almond flour and process until the almond flour is very fine, 45 to 60 seconds. Set a fine-mesh sieve over a medium bowl and add the confectioners' sugar mixture. Sift and then press and scrape the rose bits against the sieve (see the Essential Technique on p. 206); set aside any remaining bits (2 to 3 Tbs.).

3. Put the egg whites and salt in the bowl (make sure the bowl and beater are clean; see p. 33) of a stand mixer fitted with the whisk attachment (or in a large bowl using an electric handheld mixer fitted with wire beaters). Beat on medium speed until frothy and opaque, about 1 minute. Increase the speed to medium high and beat until the whites form medium-soft peaks, about 2 minutes. Continue beating while gradually sprinkling in the remaining ½ cup (2 oz./57 g) confectioners' sugar, 1 Tbs. at a time. When all the sugar is added, add the rose water and gel paste (if using), increase the speed to high, and whip until firm, glossy peaks form. Use a spatula to scrape down the sides of the bowl, then beat until just barely blended (it will mix more when you are folding), about 10 seconds.

For more about beating egg whites to firm peaks, see p. 212.

For more on scraping the bowl and beater, see p. 289.

(continued)

MAKE AHEAD

> Stow the shells, unfilled, layered between sheets of parchment or waxed paper in an airtight container for up to 1 month.

> The filled sandwiches can be stowed at room temperature for up to 1 day. The longer the macarons sit, the softer the shells will be.

TWISTS

Flavor swap

> Raspberry filling: Instead of white chocolate ganache, substitute ²/₃ cup (160 ml) seedless raspberry jam, using about ¹/₂ tsp. jam per sandwich.

> Instead of the candied rose petals, use the same amount of one of the following: candied violets (¹/₈ tsp. violet water and 1 to 2 drops violet food gel paste, optional); candied lavender (¹/₄ tsp. lavender water and 1 to 2 drops purple food gel paste, optional); or candied orange blossoms (¹/₈ tsp. pure orange extract and 1 to 2 drops orange food gel paste, optional).

FINISHING TOUCHES

Just before baking, sprinkle the tops of half of the shells with a little finely crushed fleur de sel along with the rose bits and use these for the tops of the macaron sandwiches.

4. Add half of the confectioners' sugar–almond flour mixture to the meringue and, using a large silicone spatula, fold until most of the mixture is combined. Add the remaining sugar–flour mixture and 1 Tbs. of the reserved petal bits and continue folding until completely combined and the meringue is no longer stiff. It should be glossy and slowly flow off the spatula when lifted.

For more about folding, see p. 270.

5. Using a wide plastic scraper or silicone spatula, scoop the meringue into a large pastry bag fitted with a ¹/₂-inch (12 mm) wide plain tip (Ateco #806, or a coupler without a tip) (see the Essential Technique on p. 205). Holding the pastry bag perpendicular to a lined baking sheet, pipe small flat mounds (about 1¹/₂ inches/4 cm in diameter and no higher than ¹/₃ inch/8 mm) about 1¹/₂ inches (4 cm) apart onto the prepared sheet. Release the pressure on the bag and flick the tip away from the batter. When the cookie sheet is filled (I get 24 mounds on each sheet), firmly rap it on the counter several times to release any air bubbles and to flatten the mounds slightly. Don't be too timid with this step or your shells won't rise evenly and will crack. Any tips should have smoothed out to form an even top on the mounds. Repeat with remaining meringue and baking sheet. Sprinkle the tops with a little of the remaining rose bits (see the Essential Technique on p. 206).

6. Set the cookie sheets aside on the counter, uncovered, until the meringue is no longer sticky when lightly pressed with a finger, 30 minutes to 2 hours (depending on the humidity). If some meringue still sticks to your finger, continue to let the mounds dry out before baking.

7. Position racks in the top and bottom thirds of the oven and heat the oven to 300°F (150°C/gas 2). Bake two sheets of meringues for 9 minutes, rotating the sheets halfway through baking, and then continue to bake until the meringues are very pale golden brown, another 5 to 6 minutes. Move the sheets to racks and set aside until completely cool.

Make the filling and assemble the sandwiches

1. Put the chopped chocolate, heavy cream, and salt in a small heatproof bowl. Melt in the microwave or set over a pot of simmering water and stir until well blended. Set aside, stirring frequently, until the mixture firms up. For faster chilling, refrigerate the bowl, stirring frequently.

2. Scrape the ganache into one corner of a large heavy-duty zip-top bag, press out the air, and seal. Arrange half of the cooled shells with their flat sides up—they can be touching—on a wire rack or lined cookie sheet. Snip off a small piece of the corner of the bag and pipe about 1 tsp. of ganache onto the center, then gently press another shell, flat side down, onto the filling until it just reaches the edge.

For more about filling a zip-top bag, see p. 170.

Assembling and filling a pastry bag

A

Insert the tip into the pastry bag and use your fingers to guide it as close to the tip of the bag as possible. With scissors, snip off the corner of the bag; don't snip too much— the tip needs to fit tightly into the corner so the batter doesn't leak out.

B

Using your fingers, push the tip toward the opening. Snip off a bit more of the bag if needed to allow the tip to poke through the corner of the bag but still be held snug. Twist the bag at the top of the tip and use your thumb to push it into the tip. This keeps the batter from flowing out when filling the bag.

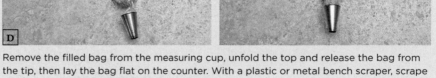

C

Place the bag, tip down, in a 2-cup (480 ml) measure and fold over about half of the bag. The cup will hold the bag upright as you fill it. The batter should flow easily from the spatula into the bag.

D

Remove the filled bag from the measuring cup, unfold the top and release the bag from the tip, then lay the bag flat on the counter. With a plastic or metal bench scraper, scrape the filling down into the bag, working it into the tip.

(continued)

ESSENTIAL TECHNIQUE

Making meringue shells

A

Twist the top of the pastry bag closed and hold the twisted top between the thumb and forefinger in one hand as you guide the bag with the fingers of the other hand. Hold the bag perpendicular to the sheet, putting pressure on the top of the bag (not down by the tip) as you pipe small mounds. When the mound is almost complete, release the pressure on the top of the bag and gently swirl and flick the tip to release the batter.

B

C

Hold the cookie sheet with two hands and rap it on the counter several times. This necessary step will release air bubbles from the mounds, allowing them to rise evenly. Dip your finger in water and dab it on any peaks or ridges.

Sprinkle the tops with reserved bits of rose petals, then bake.

D

Grind the large candied rose petals (on the left) in a food processor until they are finely ground (right). Once you sift through a fine-mesh sieve, you'll be left with bits (center).

Chapter 5

CAKES

> > > >

Espresso–Hazelnut Meringue Cake
with Espresso Buttercream *and* Milk Chocolate Ganache

Serves 12 to 14   [PHOTO ON P. 179]

Special occasions call for spectacular desserts, but that doesn't mean you have to be a trained pastry chef to make them. This four-layer masterpiece of crunchy meringues, moist hazelnut cake, rich milk chocolate ganache, and silky espresso buttercream is a guaranteed showstopper. Best of all, it is easy enough for a beginning baker. The secrets to success are to plan ahead (the components can and, in some cases, should be made in advance) and put aside plenty of time for assembly (rushing through this stage will end in disappointment).

Combining strong flavors like hazelnut, milk chocolate, and espresso in one cake might seem to be a flavor overload, but when paired with the varying textures of the meringue, cake, ganache, and buttercream, they complement one another beautifully. Hazelnuts (see p. 457 for how to skin hazelnuts) are the star ingredient of both the crispy meringue and tender cake layers. Using milk chocolate for the ganache rather than a more traditional bittersweet chocolate gives the cake a mellow chocolate profile.

The buttercream here will become your new go-to frosting recipe. It's rich and creamy yet contains no eggs. Instead, the base of this buttercream is half-and-half (or milk) thickened with a touch of flour. It's just as delicious as a classic buttercream but much simpler to prepare.

For the meringue layers
1 cup (4 oz./113 g) confectioners' sugar, sifted if lumpy
⅓ cup (2⅜ oz./67 g) superfine sugar (see p. 589)
Pinch of table salt
3 whites from large eggs (3 oz./85 g), at room temperature (see p. 371)
½ tsp. cream of tartar
1 tsp. pure vanilla extract
½ cup (1¾ oz./50 g) finely ground hazelnuts (see p. 304)

For the cake
Nonstick cooking spray or softened butter, for preparing the pan
¾ cup (3⅜ oz./96 g) unbleached all-purpose flour + more for preparing the pan
⅓ cup (1⅜ oz./39 g) finely ground hazelnuts
¾ tsp. baking powder
¼ tsp. table salt
2 whole large eggs
2 yolks from large eggs (these can be saved from the meringue whites)
½ cup (3½ oz./99 g) firmly packed light brown sugar
2 Tbs. neutral oil (safflower, canola, vegetable, or corn)
1 Tbs. hazelnut liqueur or 1 tsp. pure vanilla extract

For the milk chocolate ganache
10 oz. (283 g) milk chocolate, chopped (see p. 380)
6 Tbs. (3 oz./85 g) unsalted butter, cut into 6 pieces
Pinch of table salt
⅔ cup (160 ml) heavy cream

For the espresso buttercream
2 Tbs. unbleached all-purpose flour
1 cup (240 ml) half-and-half or whole milk
1⅓ cups (9⅜ oz./266 g) firmly packed light brown sugar
5 tsp. instant espresso powder
Pinch of table salt
28 Tbs. (14 oz./397 g) unsalted butter, softened
½ cup (2 oz./57 g) finely ground hazelnuts, for garnish

Make the meringue layers

1. Position racks in the upper and lower thirds of the oven and heat the oven to 175°F (80°C).

2. Using a pencil, trace an 8-inch (20 cm) circle on each of two sheets of parchment. Place the parchment sheets pencil side down on two cookie sheets. Sift together the confectioners' sugar, superfine sugar, and salt onto another sheet of parchment. Put the egg whites and cream of tartar in the bowl of a stand mixer fitted with the whisk attachment (or in a large bowl using an electric handheld mixer fitted with wire beaters) and beat on medium low until frothy and well blended. Increase the speed to medium high and beat until the whites form soft peaks, about 2 minutes. Fold the parchment around the sifted sugars to fashion a chute and gradually add the sugars to the mixer while continuing to beat the whites. When all the sugar is added, increase the speed to high and beat until firm, glossy peaks form, about 3 minutes. Stop the mixer, scrape down the sides, and add the vanilla extract. Beat on medium speed until blended, about 10 seconds. Scatter the hazelnuts over the meringue and use a silicone spatula to fold until just blended.

For more about beating egg whites, see p. 212.

For more about tracing on parchment, see p. 232.

For more about folding, see p. 270.

3. Divide the meringue evenly between the circles. Using a small offset spatula, spread the meringue in an even layer (about ½ inch/12 mm thick) within the lines. Bake until the meringues are dried and crisp on top but not browned, about 3 hours. Turn off the oven and let the meringues cool completely in the oven.

4. Carefully lift the meringues off the parchment (see the Essential Technique on p. 212).

Make the cake

1. Position a rack in the center of the oven and heat the oven to 350°F (180°C/gas 4). Lightly grease the bottom and sides of an 8 x 2-inch (20 x 5 cm) round cake pan and line the bottom with parchment. Lightly dust the sides with flour, tapping out any excess.

For more about preparing cake pans, see p. 232.

2. Put the flour, ground hazelnuts, baking powder, and salt in a medium bowl and whisk until well blended. Put the eggs and yolks in the bowl of a stand mixer fitted with the whisk attachment (or in a large bowl using an electric handheld mixer fitted with wire beaters). Beat on medium-high speed until pale and foamy, about 2 minutes. Add the brown sugar and continue beating until thick enough to form a ribbon when the whisk is lifted, about 3 minutes. Add the oil and the hazelnut liqueur and beat until blended, 1 minute. Sprinkle the flour mixture over the egg mixture

MAKE AHEAD

> The meringue layers can be baked and stowed in an airtight container for up to 2 weeks.

> The ganache can be made, covered, and refrigerated for up to 4 days. Bring to room temperature before proceeding with the recipe.

> The unfrosted cake can be cooled, covered, and stowed at room temperature for up to 1 day.

TWISTS

Flavor swap

> **Almond–amaretto meringue cake:** Substitute finely ground toasted almonds for the finely ground hazelnuts, and substitute amaretto liqueur for the hazelnut liqueur.

> **Bittersweet chocolate ganache:** Instead of the milk chocolate, use 10 oz. (283 g) bittersweet chocolate.

> **White chocolate ganache:** Instead of the milk chocolate, use 12 oz. (340 g) white chocolate and reduce the heavy cream to ½ cup (120 ml).

Re-size it

MAKE IT A RECTANGLE

> **For the meringue:** Using a pencil, trace two 12 x 4-inch (30.5 x 10 cm) rectangles about 1 inch (2.5 cm) apart on a sheet of parchment. Put the parchment, pencil side down, on a baking sheet. Proceed as directed.

> **For the cake:** Lightly grease the bottom and sides of an 8½ x 12-inch (21.5 x 30.5 cm) jelly-roll pan with 1-inch (2.5 cm) sides (a quarter sheet pan) and line the bottom with parchment. Lightly dust the sides with flour, tapping out any excess. Proceed as directed, baking the cake for about 15 minutes. Using a serrated knife, cut the cake lengthwise into two long halves. Assemble the four rectangular layers (two cake, two meringue) as directed in the recipe on a long, flat plate or wooden board.

and gently fold using a silicone spatula until just blended. Scrape the batter into the prepared pan and spread evenly with an offset spatula.

For more about folding, see p. 270.

For more about beating until the batter forms a ribbon, see p. 243.

For more about scraping the bowl and beater, see p. 289.

3. Bake until the top springs back when gently touched, 17 to 19 minutes. The center will be slightly sunken. Move to a rack to cool, 15 to 20 minutes. Run a small knife around the cake to loosen it, then invert onto a wire rack and carefully peel off the paper. Let the cake cool completely.

For more about inverting a cake onto a rack, see p. 278.

Make the ganache

Put the chocolate, butter, and salt in a medium bowl. Put the cream in a small saucepan set over medium heat and bring to a boil. Pour over the chocolate mixture and whisk until well blended and smooth. Set aside, stirring occasionally, until thick enough to spread. For faster cooling, set the bowl over a larger bowl filled with ice, stirring and scraping the sides frequently until chilled and thick enough to spread.

Make the buttercream

1. Put the flour in a medium saucepan. Tipping the pan to one side, add about 2 Tbs. of the half-and-half and whisk until the mixture is a thick, smooth paste. Add another 2 Tbs. and whisk until blended. Set the pan flat on the counter and gradually add the remaining half-and-half, whisking until the mixture is smooth and well blended. Cook, whisking constantly, over medium heat until boiling, then continue to boil, whisking constantly, until thick, 1 minute. Slide the pan off the heat, add the brown sugar, instant espresso, and salt and whisk until the sugar is dissolved.

2. Pour the mixture through a fine-mesh sieve set over a medium bowl to strain out any small floury bits (do not press down). Scrape the underside of the sieve into the bowl and discard the floury bits. Set aside, stirring occasionally, to cool completely. For faster cooling, set the bowl over a larger bowl filled with ice, stirring and scraping the sides frequently until cooled to room temperature.

3. Put the butter in the bowl of a stand mixer fitted with the paddle attachment (or in a large bowl using an electric handheld mixer fitted with wire beaters). Beat on medium speed until well blended and smooth, about 2 minutes. With the mixture on medium low, gradually add the cooled espresso mixture and beat on medium speed until light and fluffy, about 2 minutes. Cover with plastic and keep at room temperature until ready to assemble the cake.

Assemble the cake

1. Using a serrated knife, slice the cake horizontally into two layers. Brush away any crumbs with your hands.

2. Reserve about ⅓ cup (80 ml) of the chocolate ganache for decorating the top. Put a few small dabs of buttercream in the center of a flat serving plate or board and carefully arrange one cake layer, cut side down, on the plate. To protect the plate from frosting smears, slip small strips of foil or parchment between the edges of the cake and the plate. Using a small offset metal spatula, spread half of the remaining ganache evenly over the cake. Place a meringue layer, top side down, on the ganache. Align the sides and then gently press down on the top layer. Spread with 1 cup of the buttercream, top with the remaining cake layer, cut side up, and press down gently. Spread with the remaining ganache. Top with the final meringue layer, top side up, and press down gently.

For more about prepping a cake for frosting, see p. 224.

3. Spread a thin layer of the remaining buttercream over the entire cake to seal in any crumbs and fill in any gaps between layers. Refrigerate until the frosting is cold, 10 to 15 minutes. Spread the remaining frosting evenly over the top and sides, leaving a smooth finish. Refrigerate until the frosting is firm, about 30 minutes.

For more about creating a crumb coat, see p. 293.

4. In a small, heatproof bowl set over a pan of simmering water, warm the reserved ganache until partially liquid, about 1 minute. Remove from the heat and stir the ganache until just thin enough for drizzling. This can also be done in the microwave. Let cool slightly. Spoon the ganache into a small zip-top bag, then scrape it into one corner, press out the air, and seal. Snip off a small bit of the ganache-filled corner and pipe horizontal lines decoratively across the top of the cake. Sprinkle the ground hazelnuts in a narrow band (½ to ¾ inch/12 mm to 2 cm) around the top edge of the cake. Remove the foil or parchment strips and refrigerate the cake for at least 6 hours (it needs time for the layers to soften and the flavors to blend) or up to 1 day. The cake is best when served slightly chilled but not cold. Let sit at room temperature for 1 hour before serving.

For more about filling a zip-top bag and piping, see p. 170.

To serve

Run a thin, serrated knife under hot water, wipe it dry, and, using a sawing motion, cut the cake into slices, heating and wiping the knife after every slice.

For more about heating a knife, see p. 248.

(continued)

BAKER'S WISDOM

The new buttercream

Classic buttercream frostings owe some of their rich, creamy consistency to either egg yolks or egg whites. The yolks or whites are whipped with boiling hot sugar syrup and, once cooled, mixed with plenty of softened butter. Delicious indeed, but it is concerning for those who don't like the partially cooked eggs or who are afraid of using the cooked sugar syrup.

My goal with this frosting was to create one that still had the same luscious, rich, thick texture and taste as the classic version but without using eggs or a boiled sugar syrup. Thickening half-and-half with a little flour and then straining to make a smooth paste takes the place of the egg-sugar mixture. Once you add the butter, no one will be the wiser.

Making the meringue disks

In a stand mixer, beat the egg whites and cream of tartar on medium speed until soft peaks form.

Use a sheet of parchment to gradually funnel the sifted sugars into the mixer as you continue beating the egg whites.

Beat until firm, glossy peaks form, then add the vanilla and beat until just incorporated.

Gently fold in the ground hazelnuts by hand with a silicone spatula.

Using a small offset spatula, spread half of the meringue to the edges of an 8-inch (20 cm) circle drawn on parchment. Repeat with the other half of the meringue and a second sheet of parchment.

Once the meringue disks are baked and completely cooled, carefully peel them off the parchment. Go slowly, lifting the meringue up with one hand and pulling down on the parchment with the other.

Flourless Raspberry–Orange Chocolate Decadence

Serves 6 [PHOTO ON P. 180]

I love flourless chocolate cake as much today as I did when it was the new "it" dessert. In my mind (and on my plate), it is the ideal blank canvas of chocolate desserts. In its purest form, it was Chocolate Decadence—one of my signature desserts from my days at Hay Day Country Market. This "little black dress" of desserts can change flavor pairings quickly—think caramel, mocha, or almond for starters. It can be dressed down and served with a glass of cold milk and a sprinkle of graham cracker crumbs. Or, as I've done here, it can be served as a glamorous dessert partnered with a creamy raspberry filling and served in a pool of ruby red berry sauce. Add a glass of Prosecco and a candle or two and you have one timeless, elegant dessert.

For the raspberry batter
4 oz. (113 g) cream cheese, softened
⅓ cup (2⅜ oz./67 g) granulated sugar
1 yolk from a large egg, at room temperature (see p. 371)
1 Tbs. orange liqueur or water
1 tsp. pure vanilla extract
Pinch of table salt
½ cup (2½ oz./71 g) raspberries, rinsed and dried

For the cake
Nonstick cooking spray, for preparing the ramekins
6 oz. (170 g) bittersweet chocolate, coarsely chopped
6 Tbs. (3 oz./85 g) unsalted butter, cut into 6 pieces
2 large eggs, at room temperature
¼ cup (1¾ oz./50 g) granulated sugar
2 tsp. finely grated orange zest (see p. 138)

½ tsp. pure vanilla extract
Pinch of table salt
2 Tbs. unsweetened natural cocoa powder, sifted if lumpy + more for the ramekins (see p. 158)

Double Raspberry Sauce (recipe on p. 215), for serving

Position a rack in the center of the oven and heat the oven to 300°F (150°C/gas 2). Lightly grease six 4-oz. (120 ml; 3½ inches wide and 1⅔ inches high/9 cm wide and 4.25 cm high) ramekins and dust with cocoa powder (or unbleached all-purpose flour). Arrange on a small baking sheet and set aside.

Make the raspberry batter

Put the cream cheese in a small bowl and beat with an electric handheld mixer fitted with wire beaters until smooth. Add the sugar and continue beating until well blended and no lumps remain. Add the egg yolk, orange liqueur, vanilla, and salt and beat until just blended. Add the raspberries and gently fold in with a silicone spatula just until the raspberries are covered with batter. Some berries will be lightly crushed. Set aside.

For more about folding, see p. 270.

Make the cake

1. Put the chocolate and butter in a medium heatproof bowl and melt in the microwave (or put in a medium metal bowl set in a skillet of barely simmering water), stirring with a silicone spatula until smooth. Set aside to cool slightly.

(continued)

MAKE AHEAD

Line a large flat plate with parchment or plastic wrap. Unmold the cakes and set on the plate (they can be close together). Cover with plastic and refrigerate until firm and well chilled, as directed or up to 2 days. To freeze, slide the cakes from the plate and wrap in more plastic. Freeze for up to a month. To serve, unwrap the cakes and set on serving plates. Cover loosely but completely with plastic wrap and thaw in the refrigerator overnight or at room temperature for an hour or two.

(Sugar-Crusted Triple Ginger Pound Cake continued)

Chopping crystallized ginger or dried fruit

To avoid a sticky mess when chopping crystallized ginger or dried fruit, spray a chef's knife with nonstick spray, then use a folded paper towel to wipe the excess, leaving a thin film of oil on the blade. Or use a paper towel to wipe the blade with a neutral oil and repeat as needed.

> >

Raspberry Zebra Cheesecake

Serves 12 to 16   [PHOTO ON P. 181]

This decadent raspberry–vanilla zebra cheesecake is a showstopping, sophisticated version of one of America's favorite desserts, and it's deceivingly easy to prepare. Both the crisp, nutty crust and smooth, airy mascarpone–cream cheese filling mix up quickly before assembling and baking. Plus, this cake can be made several days in advance, making it a perfect party dessert.

The creamy vanilla batter owes its flavor to a healthy dose of pure vanilla extract. Use the highest quality you can afford and avoid the imitation extract, which is less expensive and will result in a disappointing flavor for this cheesecake (and all your other baked goods). The deep, fresh flavor of the raspberry batter comes from boiling puréed raspberries until reduced and thickened. This step intensifies the berries' flavor and deepens their ruby red color, which maximizes the contrasting colors of the zebra stripes.

Don't be intimidated by the zebra-striped design—it's easier than it looks. Just put aside plenty of time for assembly and review the photos in the Essential Technique on p. 221. Keep in mind that "perfection" is not the goal. Your first attempt might not produce a beautiful bulls-eye top, but rest assured that the side view of each slice will have wonderful stripes and the taste will wow your guests.

Toasted Co...

Serves 12 to 16

Any Southerner wi...
This born-and-rais...
The flavor and text...
and frosting, I've v...
luscious, rich whit...
jewel of any cocon...
flavor is deeper an...

   Another reaso...
ins, it turns into a...
See p. 234 for all t...

For the cake
Nonstick cooking sp...
   softened butter + f...
   preparing the pan...
2½ cups (10 oz./283...
   cake flour
1 Tbs. baking powd...
¾ tsp. table salt
12 Tbs. (6 oz./170 g...
   butter, softened
1½ cups (10½ oz./...
   granulated sugar
3 large eggs, at room...

Make the cake
1. Position a rack i...
(165°C/gas 3). Ligl...
(23 x 5 cm) round...
Lightly flour the si...

For more about pre...

2. Sift the flour, ba...
until well blended....
the paddle attachm...
fitted with wire be...
and smooth, about...
medium-high spee...
the eggs, one at a ti...
and the coconut ex...
down the bowl and...

For the crust
2 cups (8 oz./227 g) finely
   crushed chocolate cookie
   crumbs (I like Nabisco® Famous®
   cookies) (see p. 330)
¾ cup (3 oz./85 g) finely
   chopped pecans (see p. 304)
2 Tbs. granulated sugar
Pinch of table salt
4 Tbs. (2 oz./57 g) unsalted
   butter, melted

For the filling
2½ cups (12½ oz./354 g) fresh
   or thawed frozen raspberries
3 packages (8 oz./227 g each)
   cream cheese, slightly softened
1 cup (8 oz./227 g) mascarpone
2 Tbs. unbleached all-purpose
   flour
1½ cups (10½ oz./298 g)
   granulated sugar
2 tsp. finely grated lemon zest
   (see p. 138)
¼ tsp. table salt
4 large eggs, at room temperature
1 Tbs. pure vanilla extract

Make the crust
1. Position a rack in the center of the oven and heat the oven to 350°F (180°C/gas 4). Have ready a 9 x 3-inch (23 x 7.5 cm) springform pan.

2. Put the cookie crumbs, pecans, sugar, and salt in a medium bowl and stir until blended. Pour the melted butter over the crumbs and, using a silicone spatula, mix until well blended and the crumbs are evenly moist. Dump the mixture into a 9-inch (23 cm) springform pan and put a large piece of plastic on top of the crumbs. Using your fingers directly on the plastic, press the crumbs evenly onto the bottom and about 2¼ inches (5.5 cm) up the sides of the pan. (A straight-sided, flat-bottomed coffee mug or a measuring cup works well at the end to ensure the crumbs are tightly packed on the bottom.) Remove the plastic and bake the crust until darkened and fragrant, 12 to 14 minutes. Move the pan to a rack to cool. If the crust bubbles, use a measuring cup or coffee mug to gently press it back into an even layer on the bottom.

For more about making a press-in crust, see p. 360.

Make the filling and bake
1. Reduce the oven temperature to 300°F (150°C/gas 2). Purée the raspberries in a food processor or blender until smooth, 1 to 2 minutes. Strain the mixture through a fine-mesh sieve over a medium saucepan, pressing firmly on the seeds. Scrape the underside of the sieve into the pan and discard the seeds. Bring to a boil over medium-high heat, stirring occasionally, then reduce the heat to low and cook, stirring often, until very thick and reduced to ⅔ cup (160 ml), 10 to 15 minutes. Slide the pan off the heat and let cool completely.

2. Put the cream cheese, mascarpone, and flour in the bowl of a stand mixer fitted with the paddle attachment (or in a large bowl using an electric handheld mixer fitted with wire beaters). Beat on medium speed until very smooth, scraping down the sides of the bowl and paddle frequently, 2 to 3 minutes. Add the sugar, lemon zest, and salt and continue beating on medium-high speed until well blended and smooth. Add the eggs, one at a time, beating briefly after each addition, and beat until just blended. Add the vanilla with the last egg and beat until

MAKE AHEAD

> The crust can be baked, cooled, covered, and stowed at room temperature for 2 days before proceeding with the recipe.

> The cheesecake can be refrigerated for up to 4 days or frozen for up to 1 month. To freeze, put the unmolded, cooled cheesecake in the freezer, uncovered, until the top is cold and firm, and then wrap it in two layers of plastic and one layer of foil. Thaw in the refrigerator overnight.

ESSENTIAL T...

Preparing cal...

Not all recipes call fo...
so provides extra insu...
piece. Precut cake pa...
make my own. Set th...
For the best fit, posit...
up and down) under...
around the pan.

Lightly and evenly c...
thin layer of spray o...
parchment liner, pos...
call for lightly greas...

The pan on the left...
pan on the right is...
will leave a thick, h...

ESSENTIAL TECHNIQUE

Making chocolate shards

Melt $^2/_3$ cup (4 oz./113 g) chopped semisweet, bittersweet, milk, or white chocolate in a heatproof bowl set over a pot of barely simmering water, stirring with a silicone spatula until it's melted and smooth.

Tear off two 12 x 12-inch (30.5 x 30.5 cm) pieces of waxed paper and arrange one on the work surface. Pour the melted chocolate onto the center of the paper and use a small offset spatula to evenly spread the chocolate to within an inch of all edges of the paper.

Place the second sheet of waxed paper on top of the still-warm chocolate, aligning the edges and using your hands to gently press and smooth the paper over the chocolate to release most of the air bubbles.

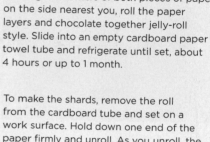

Holding the corners of both pieces of paper on the side nearest you, roll the paper layers and chocolate together jelly-roll style. Slide into an empty cardboard paper towel tube and refrigerate until set, about 4 hours or up to 1 month.

To make the shards, remove the roll from the cardboard tube and set on a work surface. Hold down one end of the paper firmly and unroll. As you unroll, the chocolate will crack and split, forming the shards. Peel away the top layer of paper and slide a long offset spatula under the chocolate to release the shards. Use the spatula to move the shards to the dessert or to a large plate and refrigerate until ready to use.

Dried Fruit Upside-Downer

[PAGE 271]

251

Mom's Lemony Roll Cake *with* **Blueberry Goat Cheese Filling** *and* **Crushed Blueberry Sauce**

[PAGE 279]

Snow White Layer
Cake *with* Strawberry
Mascarpone Frosting

[PAGE 290]

Spicy Lemon Meringue Pie

[PAGE 313]

254

Tropical Fruit Tart

[PAGE 317]

255

Triple Cherry Galette

[PAGE 320]

Lattice-Topped
Mixed Berry Pie

[PAGE 323]

257

Banana Rum Truffle Tart

[PAGE 347]

258

Maple Pear Slab Pie

[PAGE 349]

Sugar-Coated Strawberry
Mini Turnovers

[PAGE 353]

260

Roasted Butternut Squash Pie *with* **Pecan Praline**

[PAGE 356]

Almond Caramel Tart

[PAGE 358]

262

Caramel Velvet Apple Pie

[PAGE 361]

263

Chocolate–Bourbon
Croissant Pudding

[PAGE 372]

264

Individual Tiramisu

[PAGE 374]

Ricotta Panna Cotta *with* **Raspberry "Brezza Fresca" Sauce**

[PAGE 376]

Big-Time Orange Angel Food Cake
with Winter Fruit Compote

Serves 12 to 16   [PHOTO ON P. 186]

Angel food cake is one of the first cakes that I learned to bake. Mom said she chose it for one of our Sunday afternoon baking sessions because "baking with egg whites is magical." Armed with our trusted Sunbeam® electric handheld mixer and an angel food pan (I still use this same pan today), we made the batter and filled the pan. After sliding the pan into the oven, Mom pulled a stool close to the oven so I could peer in through the window and told me to "watch as the magic happens." And watch I did as the batter rose up high and puffy, filling the pan and beyond. It was one of many magical baking moments with my mom both in and out of the oven. Her words of wisdom were every bit as good as the wonderful things we baked up together.

The mixing technique called folding is often used to prevent the baked item (cakes, cookies, quick breads, etc.) from being tough. It's crucial to maintain the volume of the whipped egg whites in soufflés, mousses, and chiffon and angel food cakes, so it's essential to fold—not stir—the flour mixture into the whites. This will keep the air in the batter, and the cake will bake up light and rise high. For this cake, the flour is added in four parts but not all recipes are the same, so it's important to follow the specific recipe instructions while using this same technique when directed to "fold."

This cake can be flavored in many ways. I've listed a few options on p. 268, and I encourage you to experiment with others; just be sure to fold gently or the magic might not happen.

1 cup (4 oz./113 g) cake flour
1¼ cups (5 oz./142 g) confectioners' sugar
½ tsp. table salt
11 egg whites from large eggs (11 oz./312 g), at room temperature (see p. 371)

1½ tsp. cream of tartar
1 cup (7 oz./198 g) superfine sugar (see p. 589)
2 Tbs. finely grated orange zest (see p. 138)
1½ tsp. pure vanilla extract

Winter Fruit Compote, for serving (recipe on p. 269)
Caramel Sauce, for serving (recipe on p. 269)

1. Position a rack in the center of the oven and heat the oven to 350°F (180°C/gas 4). Have ready an ungreased, metal, not nonstick, 10 x 4-inch (25 x 10 cm) angel food cake pan. If the pan doesn't have feet to support it while cooling the cake, have ready a bottle or funnel to hold the pan in a level, upside down position.

2. Sift together the flour, confectioners' sugar, and salt three times onto a sheet of parchment, waxed paper, or foil and set aside.

3. Start with a very clean bowl for a stand mixer and whisk attachment (or a large bowl if using an electric handheld mixer fitted with wire beaters). I rinse both with a good splash of white vinegar and warm water to rid them of any pesky residue. Put the egg whites in the bowl and beat on medium-low speed until foamy, 1 to 2 minutes. Add the cream

(Big-Time Orange Angel Food Cake continued)

MAKE AHEAD

The cake can be covered and stowed at room temperature for up to 5 days.

TWISTS

Flavor swap

Instead of the orange zest, use one of the following: 2 Tbs. finely grated lemon zest, 2 tsp. pure vanilla extract, or ¹/₂ to ³/₄ tsp. pure almond extract.

of tartar, increasing the speed to medium, and beat until the whites are opaque and climb about halfway up the bowl (the tracks from the whisk will begin to hold their shape), forming very soft peaks. Continue beating while slowly and continuously adding the superfine sugar. Beat until the whites are thick and shiny and form medium-firm peaks. (The peaks should droop over gently.) Don't overbeat or the whites won't expand during baking and the batter won't rise as high. Add the orange zest and vanilla. Beat until just blended, about 10 seconds.

For more about beating egg whites to medium-firm peaks, see p. 212.

4. Sift a quarter of the flour mixture over the beaten whites. Using a large silicone spatula, gently fold the dry ingredients into the whites. Repeat with the remaining flour mixture, one quarter at a time.

For more about folding, see p. 270.

5. Using the spatula to gently coax the batter, pour evenly into the pan. Use a small offset spatula to gently smooth the top. Bake until the cake is light golden brown and springs back when touched with your fingertips, 39 to 42 minutes. Immediately invert the pan onto the counter if the pan has feet or, if it doesn't, invert the pan by sliding the center tube onto the neck of the bottle. Let cool completely.

For more about inverting the cake on a bottle, see p. 243.

6. To remove the cake, place the pan right side up on the counter. Slide a thin knife between the cake and the outside edge of the pan to loosen the cake. Slip the cake from the pan, gently lifting it up as you grasp the center tube of the pan. Slide the knife between the center tube and the cake to loosen the cake. Slide the knife between the cake and the bottom of the pan and run it around while rotating the pan until the cake is released. Gently hold the sides of the cake and lift off the center tube and arrange on a flat serving plate. The cake is best cut with a thin serrated knife. Serve with the Winter Fruit Compote on the side and Caramel Sauce drizzled over the top.

For more about removing the cake from the pan, see p. 243.

Winter Fruit Compote

2 blood oranges
3 ripe passion fruit
1 ripe kiwi, peeled, cut into ½-inch
    (12 mm) thick wedges
½ small mango, diced

¼ fresh pineapple, diced
1 to 2 Tbs. granulated sugar
1 Tbs. finely chopped fresh mint
Pinch of table salt

1. Using a sharp knife, cut away the ends of 1 orange. Stand it on one end and, using long strokes of the blade, cut away the zest and pith. Hold the skinned orange over a large bowl and carefully cut away the orange segments from the white inner pith, allowing the wedges and their juices to drop into the bowl. Once all the segments are removed, squeeze the remaining juice from the membrane into the bowl; discard the membrane. Repeat with the remaining orange. If the segments are large, use a paring knife to cut crosswise in half or thirds.

For more about cutting citrus into segments, see p. 501.

2. Cut the passion fruit in half. Scoop out the pulp and add to the orange segments. Add the remaining fruits, sugar, mint, and salt. Toss gently to combine. Serve immediately.

For more about cutting citrus into segments, see p. 501.

MAKE AHEAD

The compote can be covered and refrigerated for up to 6 hours.

Caramel Sauce

1 cup (240 ml) heavy cream
1 cup (7 oz./198 g) granulated sugar
⅓ cup (80 ml) water

2 Tbs. (1 oz./28 g) unsalted butter
¾ tsp. ground cardamom (optional)
Pinch of table salt

1. Put the heavy cream in a small saucepan or microwave-safe bowl and heat until very warm. Set aside.

2. Put the sugar and water in a medium saucepan. Cook, stirring, over low heat until the sugar is dissolved and the mixture is boiling. Stop stirring and increase the heat to high. When the sugar begins to caramelize, swirl the pan over the heat until the caramel is a deep amber color, 2 to 3 minutes. Swirl the pan over the heat to even out the color. (Test it by putting a drop on a white plate. If the caramel is too light, the sauce will be too sweet.)

For more about gauging caramel doneness, see p. 273.

3. Slide the pan off the heat and slowly and carefully add the warm heavy cream. Be careful—it will sputter and the steam is hot. Whisk until the caramel is completely smooth. If necessary, return the pan to the heat and continue whisking until the caramel is dissolved. Slide the pan off the heat, add the butter, cardamom (if using), and salt, and whisk until blended. Taste and add more salt until the caramel is slightly salty. Use warm or at room temperature. For faster cooling, set the bowl over a larger bowl filled with ice and a little water, stirring and scraping the sides frequently.

For more about gauging caramel doneness, see p. 273.

MAKE AHEAD

Let cool completely, cover, and refrigerate for up to 2 weeks.

(continued)

ESSENTIAL TECHNIQUE

Preparing, baking, and rolling the cake

To ensure the parchment will fit your pan, position a pen or pencil on a sharp angle so that it sits on the inside of the edge—if it's parallel to the edge, the paper will come up the side of the pan. Holding the pencil at this angle, mark around the edge of the pan on the parchment. Using scissors, cut out inside the line—not on the line. If any markings remain, make sure to place the parchment in the pan marked side down.

A

B

After greasing the bottom and sides of the pan and adding the parchment, add flour. I find it easiest to sprinkle flour along one long edge of the pan.

C

Gently tap the opposite long end on the counter while gradually lifting the edge of the pan higher as the flour evenly flows down the parchment to coat.

D

After coating the bottom, be sure all edges and corners of the parchment are floured. Rotate the pan to the left and tap the remaining flour to the edges, tipping, tapping, and rotating the pan to coat the sides, adding more flour if needed. Once the pan is coated, gently tap out and discard any excess flour.

E

Gently spread the batter over the parchment, using a long offset spatula to fill all corners and edges of the pan. Smooth the top, then bake.

F

Once the cake is done baking, it's important to work quickly or the cake will crack when rolling it up. Place the pan on a large rack and run the tip of a paring knife between the cake and pan to release it. Sift a generous amount of confectioners' sugar over the cake, making sure the entire cake is covered.

Again working quickly, cover the top of the cake with two long strips of paper towels and cover with a rack large enough to overhang the edges of the pan. Gripping both racks with towels and the sheet pan sandwiched in between, flip the pan and racks to invert.

Lift off the top rack and the pan. Slide the tip of a paring knife between the cake and parchment in one corner, then grasp the paper in both hands and gently pull it from the cake. It's important to work quickly and do this while the cake is still hot, but don't pull so hard that the cake tears or sticks to the paper. Use the knife to nudge the paper off the cake as needed.

With the cake positioned with a short side facing you, nudge the bottom edge up and over itself and roll up the cake inside the paper towel. Roll as evenly as possible; once rolled, place on the rack seam side down and let cool completely.

Spiced Cupcakes *with* Cinnamon Buttercream

Makes 10 cupcakes

While I love making grand layer cakes swirled with frosting, there are times that a whole cake is just too much. For smaller groups and/or smaller appetites, I turn to these buttercream-topped cupcakes. With only ten in a batch, I can serve a small group and, hopefully, have one or two left over for the next-day nibblers.

Topped with a cinnamon-spiked buttercream, the buttermilk cupcakes have a tender crumb and a well-balanced spiced flavor.

For the cupcakes
Nonstick cooking spray or softened butter, for preparing the pan
1⅓ cups (6 oz./170 g) unbleached all-purpose flour
1¾ tsp. baking powder
¾ tsp. ground cinnamon
¾ tsp. ground ginger
¼ tsp. ground nutmeg
¼ tsp. table salt

6 Tbs. (3 oz./85 g) unsalted butter, softened
1 cup (7 oz./198 g) granulated sugar
2 large eggs, at room temperature
¾ tsp. pure vanilla extract
½ cup (120 ml) buttermilk

For the frosting
5 tsp. unbleached all-purpose flour
½ cup (120 ml) whole milk

⅔ cup (4⅝ oz./131 g) granulated sugar
1¼ tsp. ground cinnamon
14 Tbs. (7 oz./198 g) unsalted butter, softened
2 tsp. vanilla bean paste or pure vanilla extract
⅛ tsp. table salt + more to taste

MAKE AHEAD

The frosted cupcakes can be covered and stowed at room temperature for up to 2 days.

1. Position a rack in the center of the oven and heat the oven to 375°F (190°C/gas 5). Lightly grease the top of a regular-sized muffin tin and line 10 of the muffin cups with paper or foil liners.

2. Put the flour, baking powder, cinnamon, ginger, nutmeg, and salt in a medium bowl and whisk until blended. Put the butter in the bowl of a stand mixer fitted with the paddle attachment (or in a large bowl using an electric handheld mixer fitted with wire beaters) and beat on medium speed until well blended and smooth, about 1 minute. Add the sugar and continue beating on medium-high speed until fluffy and lighter in color, 2 to 3 minutes. Add the eggs one at a time, beating briefly after each addition. Add the vanilla along with the last egg. Add half of the flour mixture and mix on low speed until just blended. Add the buttermilk and mix until just blended. Add the remaining flour and, using a silicone spatula, gently fold until just blended.

For more about folding, see p. 270.

3. Distribute the batter evenly among the prepared muffin cups (about ¼ cup batter will fill each cup about three-quarters full). Bake until a pick inserted in the center comes out clean, 17 to 19 minutes. Move to a rack and let cool for 15 minutes. Carefully remove the cupcakes from the pan, set them on a wire rack, and let cool completely.

Make the frosting

1. While the cupcakes are cooling, make the frosting. Put the flour in a small saucepan. Tipping the pan to one side, add about 2 Tbs. of the milk and whisk until the mixture is a thick, smooth paste. Add another 2 Tbs. and whisk until blended. Set the pan flat on the counter and gradually add the remaining milk, whisking until the mixture is smooth and well blended. Cook, whisking constantly, over medium heat until boiling, then continue to boil, whisking constantly, until thick, 1 minute. Slide the pan off the heat, add the sugar and cinnamon, and whisk until the sugar is dissolved.

2. Pour the mixture through a fine-mesh sieve set over a medium bowl to strain out any small floury bits (do not press down). Scrape the underside of the sieve into the bowl and discard the floury bits. Set aside, stirring occasionally, to cool completely. For faster cooling, set the bowl over a larger bowl filled with ice and a little water, stirring and scraping the sides frequently until chilled to room temperature.

3. Put the butter in the bowl of a stand mixer fitted with the paddle attachment (or in a large bowl using an electric handheld mixer fitted with wire beaters) and beat on medium speed until well blended and smooth, about 1 minute. Add the cooled sugar mixture, vanilla, and salt and beat on medium speed until smooth and well blended, about 2 minutes. If the mixture looks grainy or "broken," keep mixing until the texture is smooth. Taste and add more salt as needed. The flavor should be vibrant.

Assemble the cupcakes
Portion the frosting evenly among the cooled cupcakes (about 2½ Tbs. per cupcake). Using a small metal spatula, mound and swirl the frosting on top of the cupcakes, leaving a border of cake around each one.

(continued)

Flavor swap

Vanilla: Omit the cinnamon from the frosting.

FINISHING TOUCHES

Sprinkle the frosted cupcakes with finely diced toasted nuts or colored sprinkles.

ESSENTIAL TECHNIQUE

Making the frosting

The base of the frosting is milk and flour. Gradually add the milk to the flour in a small saucepan and whisk until smooth. Cook over medium heat until boiling. You'll need to whisk constantly so that the mixture doesn't scorch or form lumps. Once the mixture is boiling—it will bubble vigorously—continue to boil, whisking constantly, until thick, 1 minute (this eliminates the raw flour taste). Slide the pan off the heat, add the sugar and cinnamon, and whisk until well blended and the sugar is dissolved. Pour through a fine-mesh sieve to strain out any small lumps of flour and let cool completely before finishing the frosting.

ESSENTIAL TECHNIQUE

Frosting the cupcakes

A

Use a mini ice cream scoop to portion the frosting evenly between the cupcakes. For a domed top, gently tap the bottom of the cupcake on the counter to settle the frosting slightly. For a casual swirled top, use a small offset spatula to spread the frosting, leaving lots of ridges and peaks.

B

To make a rosette or swirled top, fill a pastry bag fitted with a large, fluted star tip (see p. 205). Position the tip about ½ inch (12 mm) away from the edge of the cupcake at a 90-degree angle and begin pressing out frosting to form a star. Without releasing the pressure, lift the tip slightly, letting the frosting drop and pipe around the edge. Just before closing the circle, lift the tip up toward the center and continue to pipe another small circle to fill in the frosting. Release pressure and lift up for a pointy tip.

C

To make a starred top, fill a pastry bag fitted with a large, fluted star tip. Position the tip on the center of the cupcake at a 90-degree angle and begin pressing out frosting to form a small star. Release pressure and lift up for a pointy tip. Continue piping small stars around the cupcake, keeping them close together and filling in any gaps. Adjust the pastry bag's angle as you reach the edges.

To make a rope or rounded swirl top, fill a pastry bag fitted with a large, plain tip. Position the tip on the center of the cupcake at a 90-degree angle and begin pressing out frosting to form a small mound. Without releasing the pressure, lift the tip slightly, letting the frosting drop and pipe around the center mound. Continue around the cupcake, keeping the frosting "ropes" very close together but not overlapping. Release pressure and let the frosting drop to end the spiral.

> >

Banana–Nut Sour Cream Sheet Cake
with Double Chocolate Velvet Frosting

Serves 16 to 20

In the Dodge family, every birthday is celebrated with a chocolate-frosted banana layer cake. The kids grew up with the recipe I published in *The Weekend Baker*—a classic—so when I mentioned that I was creating a new one for this book, you can imagine the grumbling and complaining that ensued. Thankfully, after a few testing rounds, there were only happy, chocolate-coated smiles in my kitchen as everyone devoured this new, now-favorite version.

Made in a 9 x 13-inch pan, the frosted sheet cake serves 16 to 20, perfect for a larger gathering.

For the cake
Nonstick cooking spray or softened butter + flour, for preparing the pan
2½ cups (11¼ oz./319 g) unbleached all-purpose flour
2 tsp. baking powder
½ tsp. table salt
¼ tsp. baking soda
16 Tbs. (8 oz./227 g) unsalted butter, softened
1 cup (7 oz./198 g) firmly packed light brown sugar
1 cup (7 oz./198 g) granulated sugar
4 large eggs, at room temperature
2 tsp. pure vanilla extract
3 medium very, very ripe bananas (15 to 16 oz./425 to 454 g total weight including peels), peeled and mashed (see p. 114)
½ cup (4 oz./113 g) sour cream
½ cup (2 oz./57 g) finely diced walnuts (optional)

For the frosting
½ cup (3½ oz./99 g) granulated sugar
¼ cup (¾ oz./20 g) unsweetened natural cocoa powder, sifted if lumpy
⅓ cup (80 ml) whole milk
24 Tbs. (12 oz./340 g) unsalted butter, softened
8 oz. (227 g) semisweet or bittersweet chocolate, chopped, melted, and cooled slightly (see p. 302)
1 tsp. pure vanilla extract
¼ tsp. table salt

(continued)

MAKE AHEAD

> The unfrosted cake can be baked, cooled, covered, and stowed at room temperature for 1 day or wrapped tightly and frozen for up to 1 week.

> The frosting can be refrigerated for up to 3 days. Bring to room temperature and stir before frosting the cake.

BAKER'S WISDOM

Be flexible

I've given directions for unmolding the cake before frosting but you can leave it in the pan for an easy, on-the-go dessert. If you, like my family, prefer a layer cake, make this one rectangular with the directions in Re-size it. I've sandwiched the layers with brown butter frosting and coated the sides and top with the velvety, smooth frosting.

Make the cake

1. Position a rack in the center of the oven and heat the oven to 350°F (180°C/gas 4). Lightly grease the sides and bottom of a 9 x 13 x 2-inch (23 x 33 x 5 cm) pan (I prefer the straight-sided kind) and line the bottom with parchment. Lightly flour the sides of the pan.

For more about preparing cake pans, see p. 232.

2. Put the flour, baking powder, salt, and baking soda in a medium bowl and whisk until blended. Put the butter in the bowl of a stand mixer fitted with the paddle attachment (or in a large bowl using an electric handheld mixer fitted with wire beaters) and beat on medium speed until well blended and smooth, about 1 minute. Add the brown and granulated sugars and continue beating on medium-high speed until fluffy and lighter in color, 2 to 3 minutes. Add the eggs one at a time, beating briefly after each addition. Add the vanilla along with the last egg. Stop to scrape down the bowl and the beater as needed (see the Essential Technique on the facing page).

3. Add a third of the flour mixture to the sugar mixture and mix on low speed until just blended. Add the bananas and mix until just blended. Add another third of the flour mixture and, using a silicone spatula, fold until just blended. Add the sour cream and mix until just blended. Add the remaining flour mixture and walnuts, if using, and fold with a silicone spatula until just blended.

For more about folding, see p. 270.

4. Scrape the batter into the prepared pan and, using an offset spatula, spread to an even layer. Bake until the top of the cake springs back when lightly pressed and a pick inserted in the center comes out clean, 42 to 44 minutes.

5. Move the pan to a rack and let cool completely. Leave the cake in the pan or remove. To remove the cake, cool the cake in the pan for 20 minutes. Using a thin-bladed knife, run the blade between the cake and the pan until the cake loosens from the pan. Arrange a large rack upside down on top of the pan and, using pot holders, grip the pan and the rack and invert. Gently lift off the pan and peel away the parchment. Arrange another large rack upside down on top of the cake, grip the racks, and invert so the cake is rounded side up. Set aside until completely cool.

For more about inverting a cake onto a rack, see p. 278.

Make the frosting

1. While the cake is cooling, make the frosting. Put the sugar and cocoa powder in a small saucepan and slowly whisk in the milk until smooth and blended. Cook, whisking constantly, over medium-low heat until the sugar is dissolved. Slide the pan off the heat and set aside, whisking occasionally, to cool completely. For faster cooling, set the bowl over a larger bowl filled with ice and a little water, stirring and scraping the sides frequently.

2. Put the butter in the bowl of a stand mixer fitted with the paddle attachment (or in a large bowl using an electric handheld mixer fitted with wire beaters) and beat on medium speed until smooth, about 1 minute. Add the cooled cocoa mixture, melted chocolate, vanilla, and salt and beat on medium speed until blended, smooth, and still dark in color, about 1 minute. Once you've added the melted chocolate, pop the spatula into the sink and use a clean spatula for the rest of the process; otherwise, small bits of hardened chocolate can get into the smooth frosting. It's not the worst thing if this happens—they'll taste like mini chocolate chips—but they will mar the velvety texture of the frosting.

3. Scrape the frosting onto the top of the cake and use an offset spatula to spread it evenly over the top (and the sides, if unmolded). The cake is best when served at room temperature.

TWISTS

Flavor swap

Orange-scented cake and frosting: For the cake, add 2 tsp. finely grated orange zest along with the vanilla and the last egg. For the frosting, add 2 tsp. finely grated orange zest along with the sugar and cocoa powder before adding the milk.

Re-size it

Make it two layers with brown butter filling and **Double Chocolate Velvet Frosting:**

Prepare and bake the cake as directed, remove from the pan and cool completely. Make the chocolate frosting and the following brown butter filling.

Melt 16 Tbs. (8 oz./227 g) unsalted butter in a medium skillet over medium-low heat. Cook, swirling the pan, until the butter is melted and the milk solids on the bottom of the pan turn deep golden brown (almost dark brown but not black; see p. 162). Pour the butter and solids into a small, heatproof bowl. Refrigerate until the butter is firm (the browned solids will sink to the bottom) or cover and refrigerate for up to 4 days ahead. Bring the cold butter to room temperature before making the frosting.

Put the softened brown butter (not melted) and 1¾ cups (7 oz./198 g) confectioners' sugar, sifted if lumpy, in the bowl of a stand mixer fitted with the paddle attachment (or in a large bowl using an electric handheld mixer fitted with wire beaters) and beat on medium speed until well blended and smooth, about 1 minute. Add 1½ tsp. pure vanilla extract and a scant ¼ tsp. table salt and beat on medium-high speed until light and fluffy, about 2 minutes.

Working on the rack, cut the cake in half crosswise into two 6¼ x 8½-inch (15.75 x 21.5 cm) rectangles. Using your hands, gently brush away any excess crumbs from the layers. Put one cake layer, top side up, on a flat serving plate. To protect the plate from smears during frosting, slip small strips of foil or parchment between the edges of the cake and the plate (see p. 293). Pile the brown butter filling onto the cake and, using a small offset spatula, spread evenly to within ¼ inch (6 mm) of the cake's edge. Place the other layer, top side up, on top of the filling. Be sure the sides are lined up, then press gently on the layer. With an offset spatula, spread a thin layer of the frosting over the top and sides of the cake. Spread the remaining frosting evenly over the entire cake (see p. 293). Refrigerate the cake until the filling and frosting are chilled, about 1 hour.

Making the frosting

Once the butter is beaten smooth in a stand mixer, add the cooled cocoa mixture.

Continue to beat on medium speed until the frosting comes together and is smooth. Use your spatula to scrape down the sides of the bowl and the paddle attachment as needed.

Snow White Layer Cake *with* Strawberry Mascarpone Frosting

Serves 12 to 16   [PHOTO ON P. 253]

Four snow white layers paired with a berry-red whipped mascarpone filling, topped with a crown of white chocolate curls, and served with a strawberry compote make a stunning presentation and an equally impressive decadent yet fresh-flavored dessert worthy of any special occasion. But what you can't see is that this sophisticated stunner is easy enough for a beginning baker to accomplish. The secret to success is to plan ahead (the components can and, in some cases, should be made in advance) and put aside plenty of time for assembly (rushing through this stage will end in disappointment).

The mascarpone cream owes it ruby-red color and very-berry flavor to a strawberry purée that's been reduced to concentrate the flavor. Instead of using a traditional whipped cream frosting, I've paired the cream with some mascarpone. This addition will stabilize the cream so it will hold up in and on the cake, and it adds a slightly tang flavor and added richness to the frosting. The white chocolate curls are optional but they are easy to make and add to the sophisticated appearance of this showstopper.

For the condensed strawberry purée
2 lb. (907 g) strawberries, rinsed, dried, and hulled

For the cake layers
Nonstick cooking spray or softened butter, for preparing the pan
3 cups (12 oz./340 g) cake flour + more for the pan
1 Tbs. + 1 tsp. baking powder
¾ tsp. table salt
16 Tbs. (8 oz./227 g) unsalted butter, softened

1¾ cups (12¼ oz./350 g) granulated sugar, divided
2½ tsp. pure vanilla extract
1 cup whole milk, at room temperature
6 whites (¾ cup) from large eggs

For the frosting
2 cups heavy cream
1½ cups (12 oz./340 g) mascarpone
1½ cups (6 oz./170 g) confectioners' sugar, sifted if lumpy
Pinch of table salt
1½ tsp. pure vanilla extract

For the strawberry compote
16 oz. (454 g) fresh strawberries, rinsed, dried, and hulled + extra for decorating the cake
¼ cup (1 oz./28 g) confectioners' sugar, sifted if lumpy
Pinch of coarse sea salt

For the white chocolate curls
1 thick block white chocolate

Make the purée
Put the berries in a food processor or blender and whiz until completely smooth, 1 to 2 minutes. Pour the purée into a medium saucepan and bring to a boil over medium-high heat, stirring occasionally. Reduce the heat to low and cook, stirring often, until very thick and reduced to 1½ cups (360 ml), 18 to 22 minutes. Slide the pan off the heat and cool completely.

Make the cake
1. Position a rack in the center of the oven and heat the oven to 300°F (150°C/gas 2). Lightly grease the sides and bottoms of two 9-inch (23 cm) round cake pans and line the bottoms with parchment. Lightly flour the sides of the pans.

For more on preparing cake pans, see p. 232.

2. Sift the flour, baking powder, and salt into a medium bowl or onto a large piece of foil or parchment. Put the butter in the bowl of a stand mixer fitted with the paddle attachment (or in a large bowl and using an electric handheld mixer fitted with wire beaters) and beat on medium speed until well blended and smooth, about 1 minute. Add 1½ cups (10½ oz./298 g) of the sugar and the vanilla and beat on medium-high speed until well blended, about 2 minutes. Stop to scrape down the bowl and the beater as needed.

For more on scraping batter off the paddle attachment, see p. 289.

3. Add a third of the flour mixture and mix on low speed until just blended. Add half the milk and mix until just blended. Add another third of the flour mixture and mix briefly until blended. Add the remaining milk and mix until just blended. Add the remaining flour mixture and mix on low until just blended.

4. Put the whites in a very clean, large bowl and beat with an electric handheld mixer fitted with wire beaters on medium-high speed until soft peaks form. Increase the speed to high and gradually add the remaining ¼ cup (1¾ oz./50 g) sugar. Continue beating until the whites form medium-firm peaks. Using a silicone spatula, scoop up about a quarter of the whites and stir gently into the cake batter to lighten the mixture. Add the remaining whites and fold gently until just blended.

For more on beating egg whites to firm peaks, see p. 212.

5. Divide the batter evenly between the prepared pans and, using an offset spatula, spread evenly. Bake until a pick inserted in the center of the cake comes out clean and the edges of the layers are light golden brown, 33 to 35 minutes. Move the pans to a rack and cool for 20 minutes.

For more about weighing batter, see p. 235.

6. To remove the cake layers, working with one pan at a time, rotate the pan, gently tapping the bottom edge of the cake pan on the counter while turning it until the cake loosens. Invert onto a rack and peel away the parchment. Set aside until completely cool.

For more about inverting cake layers, see p. 278.

Make the frosting and assemble the cake

1. Cut the layers in half horizontally to make four layers. Working with one layer at a time, gently place one hand on top of the layer (no need to take it off of the rack) and position a long serrated knife on one side of the cake at the middle mark. Using a sawing motion, begin to cut the cake horizontally toward the center while rotating the cake. Keep your palm on the top and cut and turn the cake until you have cut completely through the cake. If your cut isn't even, cut a small notch into the side of the cake to mark the top and bottom layers and use these marks to position the layers on top of each other so your finished cake isn't listing (see the Essential Technique on p. 293). Repeat with the remaining layer.

2. Put the heavy cream and mascarpone in the bowl of a stand mixer fitted with the whisk attachment (or in a large bowl and using an electric

(continued)

MAKE AHEAD

> The cake layers can be baked, cooled, covered, and stowed at room temperature for 1 day or wrapped tightly and frozen for up to 1 week. To thaw, unwrap the layers, put on cooling racks, and thaw at room temperature for 1 to 2 hours.

> The frosted cake can be refrigerated for up to 2 days.

> The purée can be cooled completely, covered, and refrigerated for up to 2 days or frozen up to 3 months.

TWISTS

Flavor swap

> Blueberry or raspberry frosting:
Instead of using strawberries, substitute the same amount of blueberries or raspberries (strain out the seeds after puréeing, if desired.

> Coconut: Instead of the white chocolate curls, gently press toasted or untoasted, sweetened, shredded coconut around the sides of the cake to cover completely and top with halved strawberries. You can also omit the milk from the cake recipe and substitute an equal amount of coconut milk and add ½ tsp. coconut extract (if desired) along with the vanilla extract. .

Re-size it

Two layers: Omit Step 1 and assemble with the two layers, using half the amount of frosting.

---

handheld mixer fitted with wire beaters) and beat on medium-low speed until well blended and smooth, about 1 minute. Add the confectioners' sugar, salt, and vanilla extract. Beat on medium-high speed until thick enough to hold firm peaks when the beater is lifted, about 2 minutes. Add 1½ cups (360 ml) of the strawberry purée and beat on medium until well blended, 30 to 60 seconds.

For more about beating to firm peaks, see p. 212.

3. Using your hands, gently brush away any excess crumbs from the layers. Put one cake layer, cut side down, on a flat serving plate. To protect the plate from smears during frosting, slide small strips of foil or parchment under the bottom of the cake to cover the plate (see the Essential Technique on the facing page). Using a small offset spatula or the back edge of a table knife, spread about 1⅓ cups (320 ml) of the frosting evenly over the layer. Place the second layer, cut side down, on top of the cream. Be sure the sides are lined up and then press gently on the layer. Using an offset spatula or the back edge of a table knife, spread about 1¼ cups of the frosting evenly over the layer. Place the third layer, cut-side down, on top of the cream. Be sure the sides are lined up and then press gently on the layer. Using an offset spatula or the back edge of a table knife, spread about 1⅓ cups of the frosting evenly over the layer. Top with the remaining layer, cut side down. Be sure the sides are lined up and then press gently on the layer.

4. With an offset spatula, spread a thin layer of frosting over the top and sides of the cake. Refrigerate the remaining frosting and the cake until the frosting on the cake is set, 10 to 15 minutes. Spread the remaining frosting over the top and sides of the cake. Carefully pull away the parchment or foil strips. Refrigerate the cake for 4 hours.

Make the strawberry compote

Coarsely chop the strawberries. Put them in a medium bowl with the confectioners' sugar and salt and toss until well blended. Cover and refrigerate, stirring occasionally, until the juices have released, 4 hours.

Make the chocolate curls and serve the cake

1. Soften the white chocolate block in the microwave using short bursts (10 to 15 seconds) of medium-high power. Holding the block in one hand over a large flat plate, slide a wide vegetable peeler firmly down one side of the block to form thick curls. Repeat the heating and peeling as often as needed. Slide the plate into the fridge until the curls are chilled and firm, about 1 hour.

For more about making chocolate curls, see p. 381.

2. Just before serving, top the cake with the curls and some reserved strawberries. Using a sharp thin knife, cut the cake into slices and serve with some of the strawberry compote.

Cutting cake layers and frosting a cake

A

Cut each layer in half horizontally, working with a long serrated knife and placing your hand on top of the layer to hold it while you slice. Use a sawing motion and rotate the cake as needed until you've cut through the layer.

B

Place the cut layers on top of each other and make a notch through all. These marks will guide you when positioning the layers after frosting to ensure the cake is upright.

C

With strips of parchment positioned under the bottom layer to protect the plate while frosting, spread about 1⅓ cups (320 ml) of frosting evenly over the layer, spreading it to the edge of the layer. Place a cake layer on top, aligning the notches, press gently, then add frosting and spread. Continue adding cake layers, checking for alignment, and frosting, spreading it evenly between all layers and pressing on the layers gently.

D

With a small offset spatula, spread a thin layer of frosting over the top and sides of the cake. This is called a crumb coat and will help the crumbs adhere before spreading the remaining frosting. Refrigerate the cake after crumb coating.

E

Once the crumb coat is set, spread the remaining frosting over the top and sides of the cake, then carefully pull away the parchment strips.

Chapter 6

PIES AND TARTS

> > > >

Crumble-Topped Peach Ginger Pie

Serves 10

To me, a crumb-topped fruit pie is about as good as any dessert can be. For this pie, a flaky crust is filled with peeled peaches that are paired with fresh ginger to bring out their slightly spicy accents. The topping with nutty, crunchy oatmeal crumbles is icing on the cake, or in this case, pie.

For the crumb topping
8 Tbs. (4 oz./113 g) unsalted butter
⅔ cup (2 oz./57 g) rolled or old-fashioned oats
½ cup (2¼ oz./64 g) unbleached all-purpose flour
⅔ cup (4⅝ oz./131 g) firmly packed light or dark brown sugar
1 tsp. ground ginger
Pinch of table salt

½ cup (2½ oz./71 g) chopped walnuts (optional; see p. 304)

For the filling
3 lb. (1.4 kg) ripe peaches (about 6 large)
⅔ cup (4⅝ oz./131 g) granulated sugar
¼ cup (1⅛ oz./32 g) unbleached all-purpose flour
Good pinch of table salt

1 Tbs. finely minced fresh ginger (see p. 312)
2 tsp. freshly squeezed lemon juice

1 prepared and chilled pie crust (not baked) (see p. 313)

Make the crumb topping

1. Cut the butter into ½-inch (12 mm) pieces. Pile onto a plate and slide into the refrigerator until ready to use.

2. Put the oats, flour, brown sugar, ground ginger, and salt in a medium bowl. Whisk until blended, then add the butter pieces. Using your fingers, rub the mixture together until the butter is completely incorporated and the mixture is in medium to large crumbs. Add the walnuts and toss. Refrigerate the topping while the oven heats and the filling is prepared.

For more about making crumb topping, see p. 572.

Make the filling and assemble and bake the pie

1. Position a rack in the center of the oven and set a foil-lined heavy-duty rimmed half sheet pan on the rack. Heat the oven to 375°F (190°C/gas 5).

2. Bring a large pot of water to a boil over high heat and have ready a large bowl of ice-filled water. Using the tip of a small paring knife, cut an X through the skin at the pointed end (opposite the stem end) of the peaches. Using a large slotted spoon, carefully put two peaches in the boiling water and cook for 1 minute. Using the spoon, lift the peaches, one at a time, from the boiling water and into the ice water (this stops the cooking); leave in the water until the peaches are cool enough to handle, about 1 minute. Working with one peach at a time and using the paring knife, carefully peel off the skin, starting at the X where the skin has separated slightly from the flesh and working your way around the peach (see the Essential Technique on p. 296). If the skin resists, repeat the boiling and ice bath for another 30 to 45 seconds. Repeat with the remaining peaches.

MAKE AHEAD

> The topping can be prepared and refrigerated for 2 days or frozen for up to 1 month.

> The baked and cooled pie can be covered and stowed at room temperature for up to 6 hours before serving. Leftovers can be covered and refrigerated for up to 2 days.

(continued)

(Crumble-Topped Peach Ginger Pie continued)

TWISTS

Flavor swap

> **Nectarine:** Instead of peaches, use the same amount of unpeeled nectarines.

> Instead of the crumb topping, use a plain topping (see p. 364) or a lattice topping (see pp. 326–327).

FINISHING TOUCHES

Just before serving, sprinkle the pie with a little sifted confectioners' sugar.

3. Cut each peach in half around the pit, twist to separate, and cut each half into 6 slices; discard the pit. You should have about 8 cups of slices.

4. In a medium bowl, stir together the sugar, flour, and salt until blended. Add about one-quarter of the peach slices, the minced fresh ginger, and the lemon juice and, using a large fork or potato masher, mix and mash until the peaches are mushed and the dry ingredients are blended. Add the remaining peaches and toss until evenly blended.

5. Remove the crust from the fridge, uncover, and scrape the filling into the crust using a silicone spatula. Spread the peaches, keeping them slightly mounded in the center, then scatter the topping (break apart any very large clumps) evenly over the top but don't press down. Leave a small area in the center topping-free so you can check for doneness when the time comes. Put the pie on the heated baking sheet and bake until the filling is bubbling in the center and the crumb topping is deep golden brown, 80 to 90 minutes. If the topping starts to get too brown, cover loosely with foil and continue baking. Let the pie cool to just warm before serving.

ESSENTIAL TECHNIQUE

Peeling peaches

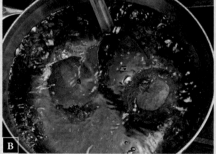

A Cut an X in the pointed end of each peach, using the tip of a small paring knife. Make it ⅛ to ¼ inch (3 to 4 mm) deep.

B Using a large slotted spoon, carefully lower the peaches into boiling water. Boil only two peaches at the same time so you can work quickly and efficiently. After about a minute, transfer the peaches, one at a time, to a large bowl of ice water to stop the cooking.

C Working with one cool peach at a time, rotate the peach in your hand so the pointed end where the X was cut is facing up. With the paring knife, firmly grasp the edge of the skin between your finger and the knife blade and slowly pull the skin down around the peach. The skin shouldn't resist, but if it does, place the peach back in the boiling water for another 30 seconds then try again.

Italian Plum Almond Tart

Serves 8 to 10

Every season has its special fruit—one that's only available in limited quantities and for a very short time period. Fall is no exception. While I love pears, apples, figs, and squashes, my fave fall fruit is Italian plums, also called Empress or prune plums. Known for their tiny, plump, egg-sized shape and purple-bluish skin, they are juicy and delicious eaten out-of-hand, but, in my opinion, they are best when baked, as their natural sugars and flavor intensify.

Here, I've paired these plums with a press-in coconut crust and a ground almond filling that soaks up all the juices as the tart bakes and cools, making each bite an explosion of intoxicating flavor. Adding a thin coating of brandy-spiked glaze adds a touch of shimmering, pastry shop–window glamour.

1 cup (4 oz./113 g) finely ground almonds (see p. 304)
4 Tbs. (2 oz./57 g) unsalted butter, softened
¼ cup (1¾ oz./50 g) granulated sugar
Pinch of table salt
1 large egg, at room temperature

¼ tsp. pure almond extract
1 press-in coconut tart crust, baked and cooled (see p. 317)
8 ripe Italian plums (about 9½ oz./270 g), halved, pitted, and cut into quarters (leave one plum half intact, for the center of the tart) (see p. 587)

For the glaze (optional)
¼ cup (2¾ oz./79 g) apricot jelly
1 Tbs. brandy or water

1. Position a rack in the center of the oven and heat the oven to 350°F (180°C/gas 4).

2. Put the ground almonds, butter, sugar, and salt in a small bowl and mix with a spoon or silicone spatula until well blended. Add the egg and almond extract and mix until blended.

3. Scrape the filling into the prepared tart shell and, using a small offset spatula, spread in an even layer. Arrange the plum quarters, skin side down, around the tart in concentric circles with a half plum in the center and press gently into the almond filling.

4. Bake until the plums are juicy and the filling is puffed and golden brown, 50 to 55 minutes. Move the pan to a rack and let cool completely.

Make the glaze (optional)

1. Put the jelly and brandy in a small saucepan and cook, stirring, over low heat until melted and smooth, 1 to 2 minutes (this can also be done in the microwave). Slide the pan off the heat and let cool slightly before using a pastry brush to thinly coat the top of the baked and cooled tart.

2. To serve, release the tart bottom from the sides by first setting the tart pan on top of a wide can. Use your fingers to press gently on the bottom of the pan while holding on to the sides and allowing the outer ring to drop down. Serve immediately.

For more about removing the bottom from a tart pan, see p. 349.

(continued)

MAKE AHEAD

> The crust can be prepared but not baked, covered, and refrigerated for 2 days or frozen for up to 1 month.

> The crust can be baked, covered, and refrigerated for 1 day or frozen for up to 1 month.

> The almond filling can be prepared, covered, and refrigerated for 2 days before bringing to room temperature and proceeding with the recipe.

> The baked and cooled tart can be covered and stowed at room temperature for up to 6 hours before serving. Leftovers can be covered and refrigerated for up to 2 days and brought to room temperature before serving.

TWISTS

Flavor swap

> Instead of the Italian plums, use about 12 oz. (340 g) ripe apricots, cut into small wedges, or 1 lb. (454 g) whole cherries (red or yellow), pitted.

> Instead of the ground almonds, use the same amount of ground hazelnuts.

FINISHING TOUCHES

Just before serving, sprinkle the tart with 3 Tbs. sliced, toasted almonds and a little sifted confectioners' sugar.

ESSENTIAL TECHNIQUE

Arranging the plums and glazing

With the almond filling in place and starting at the edge of the tart, arrange the plum quarters skin side down in a circle, pressing each one gently into the filling so it sinks in slightly. Work toward the center, forming smaller circles as you go; finish with a plum half in the center.

Once the baked tart has cooled, use a pastry brush to lightly coat the top of the tart (fruit and filling) with the jelly-brandy glaze. This adds a beautiful sheen to the baked plums.

>>

Creamy Orange Ricotta Tart

Serves 12

For those with a big, bad case of pie anxiety—my term for those with a fear of making and rolling pie dough—this tart is the perfect first step for you to ease your way into the world of worry-free pie making. With this crushed cookie crust, you indulge your taste buds but, still impress your friends.

The creamy ricotta filling is reminiscent of an Italian-style cheesecake, and while sumptuous in texture and flavor, it lacks the heaviness and richness of its higher profile relative. I've added orange notes here, but you can easily adapt the filling to a lemon or herb flavor profile.

For the crust

1¼ cups (5 oz./142 g) finely
  ground cookies (choose one from
  the following: gingersnaps,
  chocolate wafers, graham crackers,
  or vanilla wafers) (see p. 330)
2 Tbs. granulated sugar
Pinch of table salt
3 Tbs. (1½ oz./42 g) unsalted
  butter, melted

For the orange ricotta filling

1½ cups (13½ oz./383 g)
  whole-milk ricotta (to make your
  own, see p. 64)
3 oz. (85 g) cream cheese, softened
¾ cup (6 oz./170 g) granulated
  sugar
2 Tbs. unbleached all-purpose flour
¼ tsp. table salt
3 yolks from large eggs (see p. 371)

1 Tbs. finely grated orange zest
  (see p. 138)
1 Tbs. orange-flavored liqueur or
  orange juice

Orange segments, for serving
  (see p. 501)

Make the crust

1. Position a rack in the center of the oven and heat the oven to 350°F (180°C/gas 4). Have ready a 9¼-inch (23.5 cm) fluted tart pan with a removable bottom.

2. Put the cookie crumbs, sugar, and salt in a medium bowl and stir until blended. Pour the melted butter over the crumbs and, using a silicone spatula, mix until well blended and the crumbs are evenly moist. Dump the mixture into the tart pan and lay a large piece of plastic on top. With your fingers directly on the plastic, press the crumbs evenly into the bottom and sides of the pan. (A straight-sided, flat-bottomed coffee mug or a measuring cup works well to ensure the crumbs are tightly packed on the bottom.) Remove the plastic and bake the crust until fragrant, 9 to 11 minutes. Move the pan to a rack and let cool.

For more about making a press-in cookie crust, see p. 300.

Make the filling

1. Put the ricotta and cream cheese in a medium bowl. Using an electric handheld mixer fitted with wire beaters, beat on medium speed until well blended and no cream cheese lumps remain, about 2 minutes. Add the sugar, flour, and salt and continue beating until well blended. Add the yolks, orange zest, and orange liqueur and beat until just incorporated. Scrape the filling into the baked crust and spread evenly.

For more about scraping the bowl and beater, see p. 289.

2. Bake the tart until the center of the filling just barely jiggles when the pan is gently nudged, about 30 minutes. Move to a rack and let cool completely. Refrigerate until chilled and firm, about 4 hours.

3. To serve, release the tart bottom from the sides by first setting the tart pan on top of a wide can. Use your fingers to press gently on the bottom of the pan while holding on to the sides and allowing the outer ring to drop down. Serve with a few orange segments.

For more about removing the bottom from the tart pan, see p. 349.

(continued)

MAKE AHEAD

> The crust can be prepared, cooled completely, covered, and refrigerated for 2 days.

> The filling can be prepared, covered, and refrigerated for 2 days before bringing to room temperature and proceeding with the recipe.

> The baked and cooled tart can be covered and refrigerated for up to 1 day. Leftovers can be covered and refrigerated for up to 2 days.

BAKER'S WISDOM

Pans with a removable bottom

A fluted tart pan with a removable bottom gives a polished, pastry shop finish to a homemade tart, but it's important to remember a few tips for success.

Handle the pan, before and after baking, around the edges and not from underneath. Sliding a hand underneath the pan and lifting will land all those carefully pressed-in crumbs or dough on the floor. If you are new to working with this type of pan, you can place a cookie sheet in the oven while heating and then, using pot holders, carefully slide it under the tart pan. Bake as directed and remove the cookie sheet with the tart pan. Using an unheated cookie sheet might seem easier, but it will throw off the baking time as it will take longer to heat through the cold or room-temperature sheet.

FINISHING TOUCHES

Just before serving, sprinkle the tart with a little sifted confectioners' sugar.

TWISTS

Flavor swap

> Instead of the orange zest, add 1 Tbs. finely chopped mint or lemon basil and omit the liqueur.

> Instead of the orange zest and liqueur, add the same amount of lemon zest and lemon juice or liqueur.

> Instead of the cookie crust, substitute a blind-baked and cooled tart crust (see p. 358).

> Instead of the all-purpose flour, add the same amount of cornstarch.

(see p. 358)

ESSENTIAL TECHNIQUE

Making a press-in cookie crust

A Pour the melted butter over the crumbs and, using a silicone spatula, stir and smear the mixture until well blended and the crumbs are evenly moist.

B Once the crumbs are evenly moistened, dump the mixture into the tart pan and lay a large piece of plastic on top. Using the plastic wrap will keep the crumbs off your fingers.

C With your fingers directly on the plastic, pinch and press some of the crumbs around the inside edge of the pan to cover the sides evenly about ¼ inch thick.

D Using the plastic wrap, scatter the remaining crumbs evenly over the bottom of the pan and, using your palm, press firmly to make a compact layer.

E You can also use a flat-bottomed metal measuring cup or mug to press in the bottom layer.

Double Chocolate Cream Pie

Serves 10 to 12

Chocolate pudding made with a double dose of chocolate power—bold-flavored natural cocoa powder and sweetened chocolate—elevates a simple pudding to silky and decadent. Spoon it into a flaky pie crust and top it with whipped mascarpone and chocolate shards, and you've got a masterful and intriguing showstopper dessert.

A note about my preference for no-skin puddings: I'm in the no-skin camp, preferring my puddings to have a consistent, velvety texture, but I acknowledge that many of you like the layer that forms on top of puddings when it is allowed to cool without being directly covered with plastic wrap.

If you aren't sure which camp—skin or no skin—your heart and palate reside in, cover half of the pudding filling (or any pudding in this book) with plastic directly on the surface, let cool as directed, and taste both sides. Either way, you'll end up with fabulous puddings. I always encourage and applaud everyone's efforts to adjust my recipes to suit their tastes.

For the chocolate pudding filling
½ cup (3½ oz./99 g) granulated sugar
¼ cup (1¼ oz./35 g) cornstarch
¼ cup (¾ oz./20 g) unsweetened natural cocoa powder, sifted if lumpy
¼ tsp. table salt
2⅔ cups (640 ml) whole milk
4 oz. (113 g) semisweet or bittersweet chocolate, chopped (⅔ cup) (see p. 380)

1 tsp. pure vanilla extract
3 Tbs. (1½ oz./42 g) unsalted butter, cut into 2 pieces

1 fully baked and cooled pie crust (see p. 313)

For the whipped mascarpone topping
1½ cups (360 g) heavy cream
1 cup (8 oz./227 g) mascarpone

¼ cup (1¾ oz./50 g) granulated sugar
1½ tsp. pure vanilla extract
Pinch of table salt

Sifted unsweetened cocoa powder, chocolate curls, or chocolate shards, for serving (optional; see p. 250)

Make the filling and bake

1. Put the sugar, cornstarch, cocoa, and salt in a medium saucepan and whisk until well blended. Pour in about ⅔ cup (160 ml) of the milk and whisk until the mixture is smooth. Whisk in the remaining 2 cups (480 ml) milk.

2. Set the pan over medium-high heat and cook, whisking constantly, until the mixture comes to a full boil. Boil for 1 minute, then slide the pan off the heat. Add the chopped chocolate, vanilla, and butter, and whisk until the chocolate is melted and the pudding is smooth.

For more on making pudding, see p. 388.

3. Scrape into the cooled pie crust, spread evenly, and press a piece of plastic wrap directly on the surface to prevent a skin from forming (see the Essential Technique on p. 302). Refrigerate until chilled and firm, about 4 hours.

(continued)

MAKE AHEAD

> The baked crust can be covered and stowed at room temperature for up to 2 days.

> The filling can be prepared, poured into the baked and cooled pie crust, covered, and refrigerated for up to 2 days.

> The assembled pie can be covered and refrigerated for up to 8 hours before serving. Leftovers can be covered and refrigerated for up to 3 days, but the pudding will weep a little.

(Double Chocolate Cream Pie continued)

Melting chocolate

Chopped chocolate can be melted in the microwave or on the stovetop. To melt in the microwave, put the chopped chocolate in a heatproof or microwave-safe bowl. Microwave on full power in short, 30-second bursts to avoid scorching (10-second bursts for white chocolate) until the chocolate is soft and shiny but not completely melted. Stir until smooth.

For stovetop melting, use a traditional double boiler (two nesting saucepans) or a saucepan or skillet and a heatproof bowl. Fill the bottom saucepan with water, set a heatproof bowl on top, and adjust the water level so the bottom of the bowl isn't touching the water. Bring the water to a simmer. Put the chopped chocolate in the bowl and simmer, stirring occasionally, until the chocolate is almost completely melted. Remove from the heat and stir until smooth.

Make the topping

1. Put the heavy cream, mascarpone, sugar, vanilla, and salt in a medium bowl and beat with an electric handheld mixer fitted with wire beaters on low speed until smooth. Increase the speed to medium high and beat until the cream is thick and holds firm peaks.

For more about whipping to firm peaks, see p. 212.

2. Peel off the plastic from the filling. Scrape the whipped topping onto the center of the filling and, using a small offset or silicone spatula, spread it to cover the filling, leaving the center slightly domed along with lots of swirls and peaks. If you'd like, sprinkle with cocoa powder, chocolate curls, or chocolate shards. Serve immediately or cover loosely and refrigerate for up to 8 hours.

For more about making swirls and spikes, see p. 315.

ESSENTIAL TECHNIQUE

Pudding—skin or no skin

If you don't like skin to form on your pudding, press plastic wrap directly on the pudding once you've filled the crust. There's a color as well as texture difference between pudding with and without skin.

Blackberry Pecan Linzer Torte

Serves 8 to 10

Often thought of as a fall or winter dessert, a Linzer torte's spiced flavors partner beautifully with summer berries. This torte is a favorite from my restaurant-baking days. The only change I've made is to shrink the torte to fit in a 9-inch (23 cm) pan instead of the 10-inch (25 cm) size restaurants prefer for larger, more elegant servings.

The soft batter spoons and spreads easily into the springform pan—no piping needed—sandwiching fresh berries between a slightly chewy cake-like crust and topping. Using fresh berries and not the usual jam adds a fresh, bright counterpoint to the warm flavors of the pecans and spices in the mildly spiced cake. Like most spiced cookies, cakes, and tortes, the flavors meld together and improve with time, so I urge you to make this torte up to 1 day ahead of serving.

Nonstick cooking spray or softened butter + flour, for preparing the pan

For the berry filling
12½ oz. (2½ cups/354 g) fresh blackberries, rinsed and dried
1 Tbs. unbleached all-purpose flour
2 tsp. granulated sugar
Pinch of table salt

For the torte
1¼ cups (5 oz./142 g) pecan halves, finely ground (see p. 304)
1⅓ cups (5½ oz./156 g) unbleached all-purpose flour
1 Tbs. unsweetened natural cocoa powder, sifted if lumpy (see p. 158)
½ tsp. ground cinnamon
¼ tsp. baking powder
¼ tsp. ground cloves

¼ tsp. table salt
12 Tbs. (6 oz./170 g) unsalted butter, at room temperature
1 cup (7 oz./198 g) granulated sugar
1 large whole egg, at room temperature
1 yolk from a large egg, at room temperature (see p. 371)
1 tsp. pure vanilla extract

Position a rack in the center of the oven and heat the oven to 350°F (180°C/gas 4). Lightly grease the bottom and side of a 9 x 3-inch (23 x 7.5 cm) springform pan and line the bottom with parchment. Wrap a piece of foil under the pan and about 1 inch (2.5 cm) up the sides to catch any drips.

For more about preparing cake pans, see p. 232.

Make the filling
Put the berries, flour, sugar, and salt in a medium bowl and toss until evenly coated. Set aside.

Make the dough and assemble the torte
1. Put the pecans, flour, cocoa powder, cinnamon, baking powder, cloves, and salt in a medium bowl and whisk until well blended. Put the butter and sugar in the bowl of a stand mixer fitted with the paddle attachment (or in a large bowl using an electric handheld mixer fitted with wire beaters). Beat on medium speed until well blended, about 3 minutes. Add the egg, yolk, and vanilla and beat until just blended. Add the flour mixture to the sugar mixture and mix on low speed until a soft dough forms, about 1 minute.

(continued)

MAKE AHEAD

The baked and cooled torte can be covered and kept at room temperature for up to 1 day before serving or frozen for up to 1 month. Leftovers can be covered and stowed at room temperature for up to 4 days.

TWISTS

Flavor swap

> Instead of the blackberries, use one of the following: 12 oz. (340 g) fresh cherries, pitted and halved; 12 oz. (340 g) figs, trimmed and halved or quartered depending on their size; or 12 oz. (340 g) fresh raspberries.

> Instead of the pecans, use the same amount of blanched hazelnuts or almonds.

BAKER'S WISDOM

Measuring berries

Due to their size differences, even within their own varieties, raspberries, blueberries, and blackberries are difficult to measure by volume. In general, 1 cup of average-size berries will weigh 5 oz. (142 g). That said, it's easy to find some fruit, blackberries in particular, that are double the size of the average raspberry or blueberry. Be sure to weigh your ingredients for consistent results.

FINISHING TOUCHES

> Just before serving, lightly dust the top of the torte with confectioners' sugar.

> The torte is also delicious with lightly sweetened whipped cream (p. 367).

2. Scoop out about two-thirds (17⅜ oz./493 g) of the dough into the prepared pan; using an offset spatula, spread evenly, leaving a slightly raised edge around the pan. To prevent the parchment liner from slipping while spreading, use a finger or two to hold it down. Scatter the berry mixture over the dough in an even layer. Using a 1-Tbs. mini scoop, drop the remaining dough over the berries in a random pattern. It will not completely cover the berries. (Alternatively, use two small spoons to drop tablespoonfuls of the reserved dough over the berries, spacing them evenly.)

3. Bake until the crust is puffed and light brown and a pick inserted in the center of the dough comes out almost clean (it should still have a few moist crumbs clinging to it), 50 to 55 minutes. Move the pan to a rack and let cool completely, about 3 hours.

To serve

Unlock the springform pan's outer ring and carefully remove it. Set a flat plate on top of the torte, grip the edge of the pan and plate, and invert the torte. Peel away the parchment and place a second flat serving plate on the torte and invert so the torte is right side up.

For more about removing a springform pan, see p. 249.

ESSENTIAL TECHNIQUE

Processing nuts

Process the nuts (in this instance, pecans) until fine and powdery, like the ones on the left. If over processed, the nuts will release their oils and become pasty, like the ones on the right.

Plum Galette

Serves 8

Also known as a "croustade," a galette is a freeform, open-faced tart or pie. Because the shape varies and is casual, a galette can be less intimidating to make than a pie, so it's a great starter recipe for beginning bakers or for those who harbor fears of working with pie dough. A batch of galette dough is slightly larger than a single pie crust, but it is just as easy to work with and manage.

Fruit for the fillings can—and should—vary based on what's in season and ripe at your market. I developed this recipe at the height of plum season here in Connecticut, so I took advantage of the varieties available, including pluots and plumcots, to create a sensational and gorgeous galette.

That said, if it's peach, apple, or pear season where you are, don't hesitate to sub those in for the plums. Adjust the sweetness level in the filling to balance with the fruit, and feel free to add in other complementary flavors like citrus zest, ground spices, candied or dried fruits, or nuts. It's all good.

For the dough
10 Tbs. (5 oz./142 g) unsalted butter
¼ cup (60 ml) very cold water
2 cups (9 oz./255 g) unbleached
  all-purpose flour
2 Tbs. granulated sugar
1 tsp. finely grated lemon zest
  (see p. 138)
½ tsp. table salt

For the plum filling
2¼ lb. (1 kg) firm, ripe plums,
  cut into ¾-inch (2 cm) wedges
  (see p. 587)
½ cup (3½ oz./99 g) granulated
  sugar
3 Tbs. unbleached all-purpose flour
Good pinch of table salt
1 tsp. freshly squeezed lemon juice
  (optional)

2 Tbs. heavy cream or milk
¼ cup (1⅜ oz./39 g) small sugar
  cubes (about 12), crushed
  (see p. 307)

Make the dough

1. Cut the butter in half lengthwise and then cut each strip into 6 pieces. Pile onto a plate and slide into the freezer until ready to use. Measure the water and refrigerate until ready to use.

2. Whisk the flour, sugar, lemon zest, and salt in a large bowl until well blended. Add the cold butter pieces and, using a pastry blender or two knives, cut the butter into the flour mixture until the pieces are no bigger than pea-sized, about 3 minutes. (You can also do this in a food processor using short pulses, scraping the blended mixture into the large bowl before proceeding.)

For more about mixing butter and flour together until the butter is pea-sized, see p. 80.

3. Pour the water over the flour and, using a silicone spatula, stir and fold until it forms a shaggy, moist dough with some floury bits remaining (I like to use one hand to help mix while keeping the other working the spatula). Scrape the dough and any remaining floury bits onto the counter and gather into a mound. Starting with the top of the mound and using

ESSENTIAL TECHNIQUE

Working with fresh ginger

A

When using fresh ginger, choose a piece with skin that is smooth and unblemished. When you break off a piece, the interior should be firm and crisp and smell vibrant and citrusy.

B

To peel fresh ginger, slide the edge of a metal spoon over the ginger to scrape off the paper-thin skin. Using a knife or peeler will pull away more than just the skin, and a spoon lets you maneuver better around the knobs.

C

Use a sharp paring knife to slice the ginger, holding the knob by your fingertips.

D

Stack several of the slices, then hold with your fingertips tucked inward and carefully slice into matchsticks. Pushing out your knuckles slightly will help keep the blade away from your fingertips as you slice. Turn the pile and finely chop the ginger.

E

To grate ginger, hold the peeled piece of ginger against a zester and slide it over the rasps in short strokes to form gratings.

F

Left to right: slices, matchsticks, finely chopped ginger, grated ginger.

Spicy Lemon Meringue Pie

Serves 10 [PHOTO ON P. 254]

I've taken a few liberties with this summertime classic and, after just one bite, I know this version will become your go-to recipe year-round. Steeping (or infusing) the lemon juice and water with grated lemon zest gives the custardy filling extra pucker-worthy flavor, and the dash of ground cayenne pepper adds a subtle kick that's sure to intrigue. I haven't veered too far from the classic topping except to add poppy seeds for a touch of crunch and pizzazz to the silky-smooth, mile-high meringue.

For the dough
6 Tbs. (3 oz./85 g) unsalted butter
2 Tbs. (1 oz./28 g) vegetable
  shortening
2 Tbs. very cold water
1 Tbs. freshly squeezed lemon juice
1⅓ cups (6 oz./170 g) unbleached
  all-purpose flour
1 Tbs. granulated sugar
½ tsp. table salt

For the filling
⅔ cup (160 ml) freshly squeezed
  lemon juice
⅔ cup (160 ml) water
1 Tbs. finely grated lemon zest
  (see p. 138)
1 cup (7 oz./198 g) granulated sugar
¼ cup (1⅝ oz./46 g) cornstarch
Pinch of table salt
Pinch of ground cayenne pepper
½ cup (120 ml) heavy cream
6 yolks from large eggs (see p. 371)

For the topping
¾ cup (5¼ oz./149 g) superfine
  sugar (see p. 589)
½ tsp. cream of tartar
Pinch of table salt
6 whites (6 oz./170 g) from large
  eggs
1 Tbs. poppy seeds
1 tsp. pure vanilla extract

Make the dough

1. Cut the butter in half lengthwise and then cut each strip into 6 pieces. Pile the shortening and the butter onto a plate and slide into the freezer until ready to use. Measure the water, add the lemon juice, and refrigerate until ready to use.

2. Whisk the flour, sugar, and salt in a large bowl until well blended. Add the cold butter and shortening pieces and, using a pastry blender or two knives, cut them into the flour mixture until the pieces are pea-sized, about 3 minutes. (You can also do this in a food processor using short pulses, scraping the blended mixture into the large bowl before proceeding.)

For more about mixing butter and flour together until the butter is pea-sized, see p. 80.

3. Pour the water over the flour and, using a silicone spatula, stir and fold until it forms a shaggy, moist dough with some floury bits remaining (I like to use one hand to help mix while keeping the other working the spatula). Scrape the dough and any remaining floury bits onto the counter and gather into a mound. Starting with the top of the mound and using the heel of your hand, smear a section of the dough down the side and along the work surface away from you to blend the butter pieces into the dough. Repeat with the remaining dough in sections. Using a bench scraper, fold the dough together (the mixture will be rough and crumbly).

(Spicy Lemon Meringue Pie continued)

TWISTS

Flavor swap

Classic: Omit the cayenne from the filling and the poppy seeds from the topping.

strainer over the bowl, pressing on the solids to release all the juices; discard the solids. Add the heavy cream and yolks and whisk until well blended. Pour and scrape the mixture back into the saucepan. Cook, whisking constantly, over medium heat until it comes to a full boil. Boil, whisking constantly, for 45 seconds. Pour and scrape the filling into the crust and, using a small offset spatula, spread in an even layer. Cover the surface directly with plastic wrap and refrigerate until well chilled and very firm, about 6 hours.

For more about making a lemon curd/custard, see p. 65.

Make the topping and finish the pie

1. Position a rack in the center of the oven and heat the oven to 375°F (190°C/gas 5).

2. Put the sugar, cream of tartar, and salt in a large heatproof bowl and stir until well blended. Add the whites and arrange on top of a pot of simmering water over medium-low heat (the water shouldn't touch the bottom of the bowl). Whisk until the sugar is dissolved and the mixture is foamy and warm, 2 to 3 minutes. Remove the bowl from the heat and set on a towel (this keeps the bowl from dancing around on the counter while mixing). Beat with a handheld mixer on medium high until the mixture holds firm peaks (the tip will bend slightly at the top) when the beater is lifted, 4 to 5 minutes (see the Essential Technique on p. 315). The meringue will still feel warm. Add the poppy seeds and vanilla and beat briefly until blended.

3. Uncover the chilled pie and scrape some of the meringue onto the center of the filling. Using a small offset or silicone spatula, spread to completely cover the filling up to the edges of the crust. Scrape the remaining meringue onto the pie and spread, mounding slightly in the center. Using a silicone spatula or the back of a spoon, swirl the meringue or pull up into spiky points (see the Essential Technique on p. 315).

4. Bake until the meringue peaks are deep golden brown, 12 to 15 minutes (you'll have a few dark brown spots as well). Move to a rack and let cool for about 30 minutes before refrigerating until well chilled, 2 to 3 hours. To serve, cut with a well-greased knife (re-greasing in between slices).

Tropical Fruit Tart

Serves 10 [PHOTO ON P. 255]

When I was studying in Paris, one of the first tarts I mastered was a classic pastry cream–filled tart topped with summer's finest berries. While stunning and sensational, it seemed a shame to me that this beauty was only a summertime star—it deserves a year-round place in everyone's dessert repertoire. Here, I've tinkered with the classic flavors to include tropical notes of coconut in the crust and coconut milk in the pastry cream custard. The smooth, mellow flavors pair beautifully with a host of tropical fruits that are plentiful in the late winter and early spring months.

When it comes time to arrange the fruit, don't fuss! A jumble of mixed fruit on top is more beautiful than a formal, precision-placed fruit tart. It's a good reminder that perfection is not the goal and that a casual, relaxed approach creates a most stunning result.

Nonstick cooking spray or softened butter, for greasing the pan

For the coconut crust
1 cup (4½ oz./128 g) unbleached all-purpose flour
⅓ cup (1⅜ oz./39 g) confectioners' sugar
¼ tsp. table salt
8 Tbs. (4 oz./113 g) unsalted butter, cut into 8 pieces and chilled

3 Tbs. unsweetened flaked coconut (see p. 13)
1 Tbs. cold water

For the coconut cream filling
¼ cup (1¾ oz./50 g) granulated sugar
3 Tbs. unbleached all-purpose flour
Pinch of table salt
4 yolks from large eggs (see p. 371)
1⅔ cups (395 ml) unsweetened coconut milk (see p. 318)

1 Tbs. unsalted butter, cut into 4 pieces
2 tsp. dark rum or 1 tsp. pure vanilla extract

For the topping
3 cups (15 oz./425 g) assorted sliced tropical fruit, such as pineapple, mango, kiwi, star fruit, papaya, and grapes
Toasted coconut chips, for garnish

Make the crust

1. Lightly grease the bottom of a fluted 9¼-inch (23.5 cm) tart pan with a removable bottom.

2. Put the flour, sugar, and salt in a food processor. Process until blended, about 2 seconds. Scatter the chilled butter pieces over the flour mixture and pulse until the mixture forms coarse crumbs. Add the coconut, sprinkle the water over the flour mixture, then pulse just until the dough forms moist crumbs, about 10 seconds.

3. Scoop up some of the dough and, using your hands, roll it back and forth on the counter to form a rope about ½ inch (12 mm) thick. Arrange the rope in the prepared pan against the side of the pan and press until the dough covers the side up to the top. It will be about ¼ inch (6 mm) thick. Repeat rolling and pressing the dough until the sides are completely covered. Scatter the remaining dough in the bottom of the pan and, using lightly floured fingertips, pat the dough to make an even layer (or as close to even as you can get) on the bottom and into the corners of the pan. Refrigerate the pan while the oven heats.

For more about making a press-in crust, see p. 360.

(continued)

(Tropical Fruit Tart continued)

MAKE AHEAD

> The crust can be prepared, covered, and refrigerated for up to 2 days or frozen for up to 1 month.

> The baked crust can be covered and stowed at room temperature for up to 2 days.

> The filling can be prepared, covered, and refrigerated for up to 2 days.

> The assembled tart can be covered and refrigerated for up to 6 hours before serving.

> Leftovers can be covered and refrigerated for up to 2 days.

TWISTS

Flavor swap

> Instead of the coconut milk, use the same amount of whole milk.

> Instead of tropical fruit, use the same amount of any combination of fresh fruit.

> Instead of the toasted coconut chips garnish, use the same amount of chopped pistachios or pomegranate seeds.

> For a vanilla- or almond-flavored crust, omit the flaked coconut and stir in ¼ tsp. pure vanilla or almond extract into the water and proceed as directed.

4. Position a rack in the center of the oven and heat the oven to 350°F (180°C/gas 4).

5. Line the tart pan with foil and pie weights and bake for 20 minutes, until the edges are light brown (a technique called blind-baking). Remove the foil and pie weights and continue baking until the crust is pale golden, another 12 to 14 minutes. Move the pan to a rack and let cool completely. Keep the oven set to 350°F (180°C/gas 4).

For more about blind-baking, see p. 51.

Make the coconut cream filling

Put the sugar, flour, and salt in a medium saucepan and whisk until well blended. Add the yolks and whisk until well blended and lighter in color. Slowly add the coconut milk, whisking, until well blended. Cook over medium heat, whisking constantly, until the mixture boils. Continue cooking, whisking constantly, for 60 seconds. Slide the pan off the heat, add the butter and rum, and whisk until well blended. Scrape into a small bowl and press a piece of plastic wrap directly on the surface to prevent a skin from forming (see the Essential Technique on the facing page). Refrigerate until cold, about 3 hours.

Assemble the tart

Scrape the chilled cream into the prepared tart shell and, using a small offset spatula, spread in an even layer. Arrange the fruit in a decorative, whimsical way. Just before serving, scatter the toasted coconut chips over the fruit. Use a serrated knife to cut the tart into wedges.

For more about removing the bottom from a tart pan, see p. 349.

BAKER'S WISDOM

Unsweetened coconut milk

In my recipes, I use canned unsweetened coconut milk (preferably from Thailand). Made from steeping coconut meat in hot water (sometimes milk or cream is used), the liquid is strained and squeezed to produce a thick and creamy texture with a fresh, rich taste. Reduced-fat or "lite" coconut milk is diluted with water and should not be used as a substitute. Unless otherwise directed, vigorously shake the can of coconut milk before opening it. This will blend the thick cream layer on top (sometimes called coconut cream) and the more watery liquid below. Once opened, the coconut milk is perishable, so it should be used immediately or covered and stowed in the fridge for a day or two (don't forget to stir well before using).

Don't confuse cream of coconut (like Coco Lopez®) for coconut milk. It is intensely sweetened and best used in blender cocktails. Coconut water is also popular but, like cream of coconut, it isn't a substitute for coconut milk.

Making pastry cream

A

B

C

Constant whisking is important in making smooth pastry cream. Blend the dry ingredients, then add the yolks and liquid, whisking until blended. Cook over medium heat, whisking constantly, until the mixture comes to a full boil.

After whisking and boiling the cream for 1 minute, the cream will peel away from the bottom when the pot is tipped toward you.

Scrape the pastry cream into a bowl and cover with plastic wrap; press the wrap directly on top of the cream so that a skin doesn't form. Chill.

Cutting tropical fruit

A

B

Peel the furry skin from kiwi with a vegetable peeler, then slice in half lengthwise from stem to blossom end. Working with the cut side down, cut lengthwise into wedges (left) or crosswise into slices (right).

When working with star fruit, first trim off the stem end, then slice until you reach the other end. Star-shaped slices can be used whole or cut in half or quarters.

Triple Cherry Galette

Serves 8 [PHOTO ON P. 256]

Summertime is sweet cherry time—my idea of heaven. I take advantage of this fruit's short season by using cherries in all ways: eaten out of hand, puréed and frozen into ice creams and sorbets, and baked into pies, tarts, and galettes. I call for both Rainier and dark cherries in this dessert because their contrasting colors are gorgeous, but Rainiers can be a bit hard to come by. If that's the case in your area, feel free to use all dark cherries here. The flavors will still be wonderful.

On the other end of the cherry spectrum, tart cherries are harder to come by, especially in Connecticut. But that doesn't mean I forgo adding their deep, wonderfully tart flavor to as many desserts as I can. In this rustic, full-flavored galette, I use dried tart cherries and fresh sweet cherries to get the best of both flavors. Mixing together simmered and puréed dried cherries and fresh, sweet cherries means that each bite of this tart is packed with big-time cherry flavor.

For the dough
10 Tbs. (5 oz./142 g) unsalted butter
¼ cup (60 ml) very cold water
1 cup (4½ oz./128 g) unbleached all-purpose flour
½ cup (2¼ oz./64 g) whole-wheat flour
3 Tbs. granulated sugar
½ tsp. table salt

For the almond filling
½ cup (2 oz./57 g) finely ground almonds (see p. 304)

2 Tbs. (1 oz./28 g) unsalted butter, very soft
2 Tbs. granulated sugar
Pinch of table salt
1 yolk from a large egg, at room temperature (see p. 371)
⅛ tsp. pure almond extract

For the cherry filling
½ cup (3 oz./85 g) lightly packed dried tart cherries
½ cup (3½ oz./99 g) granulated sugar

¼ cup (60 ml) water
1 lb. (454 g) firm, ripe sweet cherries (a mix of dark and Rainier), stemmed, rinsed, and dried
1 tsp. freshly squeezed lemon juice
1 Tbs. cornstarch
Good pinch of table salt

For assembly
2 Tbs. heavy cream or milk
2 Tbs. coarse sanding sugar (see p. 6)
2 Tbs. slivered almonds, toasted

Make the dough

1. Cut the butter in half lengthwise and then cut each strip into 6 pieces. Pile onto a plate and slide into the freezer until ready to use. Measure the water and refrigerate until ready to use.

2. Whisk the flour, whole-wheat flour, sugar, and salt in a large bowl until well blended. Add the cold butter pieces and, using a pastry blender or two knives, cut the butter into the flour mixture until the pieces are no bigger than pea-sized, about 3 minutes. (You can also do this in a food processor using short pulses, scraping the blended mixture into a large bowl before proceeding.)

For more about mixing butter and flour together until the butter is pea-sized, see p. 80.

3. Pour the water over the flour and, using a silicone spatula, stir and fold until it forms a shaggy, moist dough with some floury bits remaining (I like to use one hand to help mix while keeping the other working the spatula). Scrape the dough and any remaining floury bits onto the counter and gather into a mound. Starting with the top of the mound and using the heel of your hand, smear a section of the dough down the side and along the work surface away from you to blend the butter pieces into the dough. Repeat with the remaining dough in sections. Using a bench scraper, fold the dough together (the mixture will be rough and crumbly). Turn the pile about 90 degrees and repeat the smearing process until the mixture just comes together into a cohesive dough (this is a technique called *fraisage*). Be careful not to overwork the dough because that will make the crust dense. Shape the dough into a 7-inch (17 cm) disk. Wrap in plastic and refrigerate until well chilled, about 2 hours.

For more about using your hand to help mix, see p. 85.

For more about *fraisage*, see p. 549.

Make the almond filling

Put the almonds, butter, sugar, and salt in a small bowl and mix with a spoon or spatula until well blended. Add the egg yolk and almond extract and mix until blended.

Make the cherry filling

1. Put the dried cherries, sugar, and water in a small pan. Bring to a boil over medium-high heat, reduce the heat to medium low, and simmer, stirring occasionally, until the cherries are plump and the liquid is reduced and syrupy but not dry, 5 to 8 minutes. Slide the pan off the heat and let cool until just warm to the touch.

2. Pit the sweet cherries, cut in half, and pile into a medium bowl with the lemon juice (see the Essential Technique on p. 322). Sprinkle the cornstarch and salt evenly over the cherries and, using a spatula, toss and stir until the cherries are evenly coated with the cornstarch.

3. Scrape the cooled tart cherries into a food processor and process until puréed, about 15 pulses. The mixture won't be completely smooth. (You can also use a food mill or a mini chopper.) Scrape the purée into the sweet cherry mixture and stir until well blended.

Assemble and bake

1. Line a 13 x 18 x 1-inch (33 x 46 x 2.5 cm) half sheet pan with parchment or nonstick liner. Put the heavy cream in a small ramekin.

2. Pull the dough disk from the fridge and, if it's very cold, set it out at room temperature until it's just pliable enough to roll, 10 to 20 minutes. Arrange a large piece of parchment on the work surface, put the unwrapped dough in the center, and cover with another piece of parchment. Using a rolling pin, roll the dough between the parchment to a round slightly larger than 14 inches (35.5 cm), turning, lifting, and repositioning the parchment and lightly flouring throughout the rolling.

For more about rolling dough between parchment, see p. 133.

TWISTS

Flavor swap

> Peach–almond: Substitute 4 large fresh peaches, peeled and cut into wedges, for the fresh cherries. Add 2 to 3 Tbs. granulated sugar to the fruit along with the cornstarch and lemon juice. Let stand, stirring occasionally, until the sugar and cornstarch are dissolved, about 15 minutes. Omit the dried cherry purée.

> Mixed berry: Substitute a mixture of fresh blueberries, blackberries, and raspberries for the fresh cherries. Add 2 to 3 Tbs. granulated sugar to the fruit along with the cornstarch and lemon juice. Let stand, gently stirring occasionally, until the sugar and cornstarch are dissolved, about 15 minutes. Omit the dried cherry purée and the slivered almonds. Instead of the coarse sanding sugar, use crushed sugar cubes (see p. 307).

Re-size it

Mini: Follow the recipes for making the dough, then portion the dough into four equal pieces and shape into flat 3-inch (7.5 cm) disks. Wrap and chill as directed. Make the filling and cherries. To assemble, roll the dough as directed into 8-inch rounds, chilling if they get too soft. Portion the almond filling among the rounds (about 1 oz. each) and spread as directed. Portion the cherries evenly and proceed as directed, baking for 25 to 30 minutes.

Making a lattice top and placing on the pie

A

Working on parchment, roll out the dough until it's just slightly larger than 14½ x 9½ inches (37 x 24 cm), then trim the dough to the exact size with a fluted pastry wheel. Using a ruler and a sharp knife, score the two short sides of the rectangle into twelve ¾-inch (2 cm) wide strips. Following the length of the ruler, cut strips using the fluted pastry wheel.

B

Pick up 6 strips, one at a time, and place them on the parchment-lined cookie sheet, measuring to ensure they are ¾ inch (2 cm) apart. These are the "bottom" strips. The remaining strips will be the "top" strips.

C

Without pulling or tearing the dough, fold back every other "bottom" strip so that the fold is slightly right of the center of the strip. Be sure the dough for each strip is lined up on top of each other.

D

Now lay down one of the "top" strips vertically and right next to the fold. Unfold the folded strips over the "top" strip and fold back the other three "bottom" strips.

E

Place another "top" strip ¾ inch (2 cm) to the left of the first "top" strip (measure for accuracy), then unfold the "bottom" strips. Repeat with one more strip on the left side.

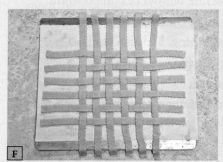

F Working to the right side of the center strip, repeat the process of folding alternating "bottom" strips and arranging "top" strips until all strips are used. You'll end up with a dough checkerboard.

G Once all strips are in place, dab a bit of water between the strips where they overlap. Press gently to seal. Cover and refrigerate the lattice top.

H When ready to place the lattice top over the berry-filled bottom crust, uncover it and slide your palm under the parchment, centering it under the lattice. Working in one fluid motion, flip the lattice onto the filling using your other hand to help center it. It takes a leap of faith, but have confidence that it is easier than it looks.

I Once the lattice is in place, dab a bit of water between the strips and the bottom crust and press gently to seal. With scissors, trim the lattice dough, leaving about a ³/₄-inch (2 cm) overhang, then roll the top and bottom crusts under and rest the excess on the rim of the pie plate. Working around the plate, use your fingers to crimp the edge.

3. To serve, remove the pie from the refrigerator. Dip a small knife in hot tap water, wipe dry, and cut the pie into 8 to 10 wedges, dipping and wiping the knife after each cut. Serve immediately with the compote and a few white chocolate shards (optional).

ESSENTIAL TECHNIQUE

Crushing cookie crumbs two ways

To crush cookie crumbs with a rolling pin, first put the cookies in a large zip-top bag, press to remove the air, then seal. Using a rolling pin, pound the cookies to break them into large pieces, then roll over the cookies, pressing hard and pounding as needed until no pieces of cookie remain.

If you have one, use a food processor to whiz cookies into crumbs. Put the cookies in the food processor, cover with plastic wrap (this makes cleanup easier), then place the top on the processor and power it on. Continue to process until you're left with uniform crumbs, not cookie pieces.

Lemon Ginger Mousse Soufflés

[PAGE 382]

Pink Berry Summer Mousse

[PAGE 391]

332

**Salted Caramel–Toffee
Icebox Cake**

[PAGE 396]

Rustic Country Bread

[PAGE 427]

334

Braided Challah Round

[PAGE 429]

335

Sweet Potato Bread

[PAGE 434]

336

Grossie's Stöllen

[PAGE 437]

337

338

Honey–Raisin Whole-Wheat English Muffins

[PAGE 472]

Double Tomato–Basil
Open-Faced Tart

[PAGE 481]

Goat Cheese Olive Spirals

[PAGE 485]

Plum Frangipane
Turnovers

[PAGE 487]

342

Pistachio Phyllo Cups *with*
Honeyed Peaches *and* **Ricotta**

[PAGE 490]

343

Baked Fig-Stuffed Brie

[PAGE 493]

344

Glazed Napoleons *with*
White Chocolate–Blood
Orange Mousse

[PAGE 499]

345

Minty Asparagus Phyllo
Triangles

[PAGE 504]

346

Banana Rum Truffle Tart

Serves 12 to 16   [PHOTO ON P. 258]

Chocolate is one of my favorite treats, and holiday occasions are the perfect excuse to indulge. The no-bake chocolate filling for this tart is based on my favorite truffle recipe. For a rich and sophisticated flavor, I like to use a bittersweet chocolate with a high percentage (68% to 70%) of cocoa solids (Scharffen Berger has a lovely one), but any bittersweet variety will work well. I've topped it with a sophisticated whipped mascarpone and paired it with a killer sweet-and-salty pretzel press-in crust. The combination is intriguing and divinely addictive.

Don't be fooled by this tart's appearance. While it looks like a simple chocolate cream tart, a thin wedge of this rich, fudgy confection is all that's needed to satisfy one's chocolate passion.

For the crust
1 cup (3⅝ oz./103 g) finely crushed salted pretzel crumbs
2 Tbs. granulated sugar
Good pinch of table salt
5 Tbs. (2½ oz./71 g) unsalted butter, melted

For the filling
5 Tbs. (2½ oz./71 g) unsalted butter, divided

14 oz. (397 g) bittersweet chocolate, finely chopped (see p. 380)
1 cup (240 ml) whole milk
1¼ tsp. table salt
2 medium (5 oz./142 g each) ripe bananas (see p. 114)
2 Tbs. firmly packed light or dark brown sugar
2 Tbs. dark rum

For the topping
1 cup (240 ml) heavy cream
1 cup (8 oz./227 g) mascarpone
⅓ cup (2⅜ oz./67 g) firmly packed brown sugar
2 Tbs. dark rum
Pinch of table salt

Pretzel sticks, for garnish

Make the crust

1. Position a rack in the center of the oven and heat the oven to 350°F (180°C/gas 4). Have ready a 9¼-inch (23.5 cm) fluted tart pan with a removable bottom.

2. Put the pretzel crumbs, sugar, and salt in a medium bowl and stir until blended. Pour the melted butter over the crumbs and, using a silicone spatula, mix until well blended and the crumbs are evenly moist. Taste and add more salt if needed—the flavor should be both sweet and salty. Dump the mixture into the tart pan and lay a large piece of plastic on top of the crumbs. With your fingers directly on the plastic, press the crumbs evenly into the bottom and sides of the pan. (A straight-sided, flat-bottomed coffee mug or a measuring cup works well at the end to ensure the crumbs are tightly packed on the bottom.) Remove the plastic and bake the crust until fragrant, 9 to 11 minutes. Move the pan to a rack and set aside to cool.

For more about making a press-in cookie crust, see p. 300.

Make the filling

1. Cut 4 Tbs. (2 oz./57 g) of the butter into pieces, then add it with the chocolate and milk to a medium, heatproof bowl and melt in a microwave

TWISTS

Flavor swap

Change the fruit: Instead of the bananas, omit the cooking, butter, sugar, and rum and use 6 oz. (170 g) raspberries or 8 oz. (227 g) cherries (Bing or Rainier), pitted and halved (see p. 322).

FINISHING TOUCHES

Just before serving, lightly dust with unsweetened Dutch-processed cocoa powder.

or in a medium bowl set over simmering water. Remove from the heat, add the salt, and whisk until well blended and smooth. Set aside.

2. Peel the bananas, slice into ½-inch (12 mm) pieces, and cut each piece in half. Put the remaining 1 Tbs. butter in a medium skillet and cook over medium heat until melted and bubbling. Add the banana pieces and sprinkle with the brown sugar and rum. Cook, using a silicone spatula to turn and gently stir, until the bananas are slightly softened and the juices are reduced and very thick, 2 to 3 minutes (see the Essential Technique on the facing page). Slide the pan off the heat.

3. Pour about one-third of the chocolate mixture into the crust and spread evenly to form a thin layer. Scatter the bananas in an even layer over the top and pour the remaining chocolate on top to cover the bananas and form an even layer. Refrigerate until the filling is chilled, about 3 hours. Cover and continue chilling until the filling is set, about another 4 hours, or up to 2 days, before proceeding with the recipe.

Make and add the topping

1. Put the heavy cream, mascarpone, brown sugar, rum, and salt in a medium bowl and beat with an electric handheld mixer fitted with wire beaters on low speed until smooth. Increase the speed to medium high and beat until the cream is thick and holds firm peaks.

For more about whipping cream to firm peaks, see p. 368.

2. Scrape the topping onto the center of the filling and, using a small offset or silicone spatula, spread to cover the filling, leaving the center slightly domed along with lots of swirls and peaks. Cover loosely and refrigerate until chilled, about 2 hours or up to 8 hours.

For more about making swirls and spikes, see p. 315.

To serve

Set the tart pan on top of a wide can and allow the outer ring to drop down (see the Essential Technique on the facing page). Move the tart to the counter and run a long, thin metal spatula between the bottom crust and the bottom of the pan. Using two long, wide spatulas, carefully lift and slide the tart onto a flat serving plate. Run a thin knife under hot water, wipe it dry, and cut the tart into slices, heating and wiping the knife after every slice. Serve the slices topped with the pretzel sticks.

Making the filling and assembling the tart

A Cook the banana mixture until it's thick and browned. Gently stir and fold the bananas so you don't mash them.

B Pour about a third of the chocolate mixture into the tart shell, nudging it into the edges with an offset spatula, then spoon the bananas evenly over the top. Pour the remaining chocolate over the bananas, covering them.

C Once chilled, release the tart bottom from the sides by first setting the tart pan on top of a wide can. Use your fingers to press gently on the bottom of the pan while holding on to the sides and allowing the outer ring to drop down.

> >

Maple Pear Slab Pie

Serves 12 [PHOTO ON P. 259]

An intensely flavored, ginger-studded pear filling paired with a tender, flaky cream cheese crust laced with poppy seeds and cornmeal is a partnership made in culinary heaven. The pie's braided top makes this a visual masterpiece. "The eye is the first to feast," one of my favorite expressions, rings true with this fall dessert.

The secret to the filling's deep, rich flavor begins with cooking half of the pears with maple syrup until they are caramelized and reduced to a thick purée. This step concentrates both flavors to maximize their boldness and gives a buttery richness to the filling's base. Folding in lemon, ginger, and more pears injects bright, fresh notes that balance out the richness. The buttery cream cheese dough is laced with cornmeal and poppy seeds, giving it a subtle, nubby texture and making it a perfect complement to the filling.

Don't be intimidated by the braided design—it's easier than it looks. The step-by-step photos (p. 352) will guide even less-experienced bakers to sweet success. For those time-pressed, the components—filling and dough—can be made in advance, making this a perfect recipe for holiday gatherings.

(continued)

For the dough

8 Tbs. (4 oz./113 g) unsalted butter

2 oz. (57 g) cream cheese,

3 Tbs. ice cold water

1 Tbs. freshly squeezed lemon juice

1 cup + 2 Tbs. (5 oz./142 g) unbleached all-purpose flour + more for rolling the dough

⅓ cup (1½ oz./42 g) finely ground yellow cornmeal

2 Tbs. granulated sugar

1½ tsp. poppy seeds

¼ tsp. table salt

For the filling

2¼ lb. (1 kg.) ripe pears (about 5 medium)

2 Tbs. (1 oz./28 g) unsalted butter

½ cup (120 ml) pure maple syrup (grade B) (see p. 8)

1 Tbs. freshly squeezed lemon juice

2 tsp. minced fresh ginger (see p. 312)

Pinch or two of table salt

2 Tbs. unbleached all-purpose flour

2 Tbs. chopped crystallized ginger (see p. 218)

For assembly

1 large egg

1 tsp. water

MAKE AHEAD

> The dough can be made and refrigerated for up to 2 days or frozen for up to 1 month. Thaw overnight in the refrigerator before rolling.

> The filling can be made, covered, and refrigerated for up to 2 days.

Make the dough

1. Cut the butter in half lengthwise and then cut each strip into 6 pieces. Cut the cream cheese into 1-inch (2.5 cm) pieces. Pile the butter and cream cheese on a plate and slide into the freezer until ready to use. Measure the water, add the lemon juice, and refrigerate until ready to use.

2. Whisk the flour, cornmeal, sugar, poppy seeds, and salt in a large bowl until well blended. Add the cold butter and cream cheese pieces and, using a pastry blender or two knives, cut the butter and cream cheese into the flour mixture until the pieces are pea-sized, about 3 minutes. (You can also do this in a food processor, omitting the cornmeal and poppy seeds, using short pulses; scrape the blended mixture into a large bowl before adding the cornmeal and poppy seeds and proceeding.)

For more about mixing butter and flour together until the butter is pea-sized, see p. 80.

3. Pour the water mixture over the flour mixture and, using a silicone spatula, stir and fold until it forms a shaggy, moist dough with some floury bits remaining (I like to use one hand to help mix while keeping the other working the spatula). Scrape the dough and any remaining floury bits into a pile on the counter. Starting with the top of the mound and using the heel of your hand, smear a section of the dough down the side and along the work surface away from you to blend the butter pieces into the dough. Repeat with the remaining dough in sections. Using a bench scraper, fold the dough together (the mixture will be rough and crumbly). Turn the pile about 90 degrees and repeat the smearing process until the mixture just comes together into a cohesive dough (this is a technique called *fraisage*). Be careful not to overwork the dough because that will make the crust dense. Shape the dough into a 6 x 8-inch (15 x 20 cm) rectangle, wrap in plastic, and refrigerate until well chilled, about 2 hours.

For more about using your hand to help mix, see p. 85.

For more about *fraisage*, see p. 549.

Make the filling

1. Peel and core the pears, chop into ½-inch (12 mm) pieces, and divide into two equal piles. Melt the butter in a large skillet over medium heat. Add one pile of pears and the maple syrup to the butter. Bring to a boil and cook over medium, stirring frequently and pressing on the pears to smash them as they cook, until the mixture is a deep amber color, very thick, and no longer juicy, 14 to 16 minutes. Slide the pan off the heat and add the lemon juice, fresh ginger, and salt; stir until well blended.

For more about coring pears, see p. 122.

2. Put the remaining pears in a medium bowl, sprinkle with the flour, and toss with a spatula until blended. Scrape the pears and any remaining flour or juices into the skillet and stir until blended. Cook over medium heat, stirring frequently, until the pears are tender and the mixture is very thick, 7 to 9 minutes. Slide the pan off the heat, taste and adjust the seasoning, and set aside, stirring occasionally, until completely cool. If using immediately, stir in the crystallized ginger. Or cover and refrigerate for up to 2 days and add the crystallized ginger just before using.

Assemble and bake

1. Have ready a large cookie sheet. Mix the egg and water with a fork in a small bowl until well blended.

2. Roll the dough between floured parchment, lightly flouring between rolling and flipping, to a rectangle slightly larger than 12 x 14 inches (30.5 x 35.5 cm). Peel away the top piece of parchment and, using a sharp paring knife and a ruler, trim the edges to get a neat 12 x 14-inch (30.5 x 35.5 cm) rectangle. Arrange the parchment so one short end of the dough is facing you. Using the ruler and the dull side of the knife, mark the dough lengthwise into three 4-inch (10 cm) wide panels, being careful not to push through the dough. Starting at the top, cut 1-inch (2.5 cm) wide strips at a 45-degree angle down the length of the two outer panels, discarding the 2 triangles at both the top and bottom.

For more about rolling dough between parchment, see p. 133.

3. Spoon the cooled filling down the center panel and spread evenly, leaving a ½-inch (12 mm) border of dough on the top and bottom. Fold these borders of dough over the filling, pinching the corners to seal. Starting at the top and alternating sides, fold the strips of dough at a 45-degree angle over the filling, pressing the edges firmly into the dough before continuing with the next strip (see the Essential Technique on p. 352). Be careful not to pull or stretch the dough. Tuck the end of the last strip under the pile. Slide the cookie sheet under the pie and parchment and transfer to the fridge. Position a rack in the center of the oven and heat the oven to 375°F (190°C/gas 5).

4. Brush the top of the slab pie generously with the egg wash. Bake, rotating the cookie sheet halfway through, until the pie is deep golden brown, 40 to 45 minutes. Move the sheet to a rack and let cool for 20 minutes. Using a long offset spatula, carefully remove the pie from the sheet, set on a rack, and let cool completely. The slab pie is best when served the same day and can be warmed slightly in a 300°F (150°C/gas 2) oven, if desired.

(continued)

Flavor swap

> Orange-cranberry pear: Instead of the minced fresh ginger, use 1 tsp. finely grated orange zest; substitute ¼ cup (1⅛ oz./32 g) dried cranberries for the crystallized ginger.

> Cinnamon-pecan pear: Instead of the minced fresh ginger, use ½ tsp. pure vanilla extract and ½ tsp. ground cinnamon; substitute ¼ cup (1 oz./ 28 g) toasted, chopped pecans for the crystallized ginger.

FINISHING TOUCHES

> Sprinkle the top with confectioners' sugar.

> Serve with vanilla, cinnamon, or maple ice cream.

ESSENTIAL TECHNIQUE

Assembling the slab pie

A

Once you've rolled out your dough, trim the edges to get a neat 12 x 14-inch (30.5 x 35.5 cm) rectangle. Position the rectangle so that a short end is facing you.

B

Using a ruler and the dull side of a knife, mark the dough lengthwise into three 4-inch (10 cm) wide panels. Be careful not to cut through the dough.

C

Starting at the top of one outer panel, cut 1-inch (2.5 cm) wide strips at a 45-degree angle down the length of the panel. Repeat for the other outer panel.

D

Remove and discard the two corner triangles at the top and bottom of the outer panels.

E

Spoon the cooled filling down the middle of the uncut center panel, then spread it evenly with an offset spatula. Leave a ½-inch (12 mm) border of dough on the top and bottom.

F

Fold the top and bottom borders of dough over the filling, pressing down on the corners to seal.

G

Starting at the top, fold a strip of dough over the filling at a 45-degree angle, pressing the edge firmly into the dough before continuing with the next strip. Repeat with the strip on the opposite side.

H

Continue folding strips down the slab, alternating sides. Be careful not to pull or stretch the dough. Instead, lift the strip up and over the filling with one hand while you gently press it up against the filling with the finger of your other hand.

I

When you get to the last strip, tuck the end under the bottom of the slab. Slide a cookie sheet under the slab pie and its parchment, and brush the top generously with egg wash.

Sugar-Coated Strawberry Mini Turnovers

Makes 14 turnovers [PHOTO ON P. 260]

I love these homey, fried turnovers. They are bursting with summer strawberries and, because of their small size, they make a perfect grab-and-go dessert for a potluck picnic or backyard barbecue. If strawberries aren't available or aren't your thing, take advantage of what's ripe at your market or farmstand. Not everyone is into frying turnovers, so I've given directions on how to bake them in the oven (see Twists on p. 354). The turnovers will leak some of their filling but still be delicious.

I think of this dough as a hybrid of my favorite crusts. Adding cream cheese and a touch of vanilla to my traditional pie dough recipe makes the fried crust tender, flaky, and sweet. The cream cheese makes the dough a bit softer and, therefore, a bit more challenging to work with, so I urge you to do as I do and roll it between sheets of parchment.

For the dough
8 Tbs. (4 oz./113 g) unsalted butter
2 oz. (57 g) cream cheese,
¼ cup (60 ml) ice cold water
½ tsp. pure vanilla extract
1½ cups (6 oz./170 g) unbleached
   all-purpose flour
2 Tbs. granulated sugar
¼ tsp. table salt

For the strawberry filling
10 oz. (283 g) fresh strawberries,
   rinsed, dried, and hulled
2 Tbs. granulated sugar
¾ tsp. unbleached all-purpose flour
Pinch of table salt

For finishing and frying
¾ cup (5¼ oz./149 g) granulated
   sugar
¼ cup (1 oz./28 g) very finely
   chopped walnuts or pecans
   (see p. 304)
About 4 cups (2 lb./907 g) Crisco
   (or about 4 cups /950 ml canola
   oil), for frying

Make the dough

1. Cut the butter in half lengthwise, then cut each strip into 6 pieces. Cut the cream cheese into ¾-inch (2 cm) pieces. Pile the butter and cream cheese onto a plate and slide into the freezer until ready to use. Measure the water, add the vanilla, and refrigerate until ready to use.

2. Whisk the flour, sugar, and salt in a large bowl until well blended. Add the cold butter and cream cheese pieces and, using a pastry blender or two knives, cut the butter and cream cheese into the flour mixture until the pieces are pea-sized, about 3 minutes. (You can also do this in a food processor using short pulses, scraping the blended mixture into the large bowl before proceeding.)

For more about mixing butter and flour together until the butter is pea-sized, see p. 80.

3. Pour the water mixture over the flour and, using a silicone spatula, stir and fold until it forms a shaggy, moist dough with some floury bits remaining (I like to use one hand to help mix while keeping the other working the spatula). Scrape the dough and any remaining floury bits onto the counter and gather into a mound. Starting with the top of the mound and using the heel of your hand, smear a section of the dough down the side and along the work surface away from you to blend the butter pieces into the dough. Repeat with the remaining dough in sections. Using a

MAKE AHEAD

> The dough can be made and refrigerated for up to 2 days before using or frozen for up to 1 month. Thaw overnight in the refrigerator before rolling.

> The turnovers can be assembled, covered in plastic, and stowed in the refrigerator for up to 1 day before frying.

TWISTS

Flavor swap

> Instead of strawberries, use the same amount of blueberries or raspberries.

> Instead of this crust, use a single crust (see p. 313).

> **TO BAKE THE TURNOVERS:**
1. Position a rack in the center of the oven and heat the oven to 400°F (200°C/gas 6). Line a cookie sheet with parchment or nonstick liner.

2. Arrange the turnovers about 1½ inches apart on the prepared cookie sheet. Lightly brush the top of each turnover with a little milk and sprinkle evenly with 2 scant tsp. of the sugar-nut mixture. Using the tip of a small, sharp knife, cut 2 small slits in the top of each turnover to let steam escape.

3. Bake until the turnovers are deep golden brown, 22 to 24 minutes. Move the sheet to a rack and cool 10 minutes. Carefully remove the turnovers from the sheet and set them on a cooling rack until cool enough to eat.

bench scraper, fold the dough together (the mixture will be rough and crumbly). Turn the pile about 90 degrees and repeat the smearing process until the mixture just comes together into a cohesive dough (this is a technique called *fraisage*). Be careful not to overwork the dough because that will make the crust dense. Shape the dough into an 8-inch (20 cm) disk, wrap in plastic, and refrigerate until well chilled, about 2 hours.

For more about using your hand to help mix, see p. 85.

For more about *fraisage*, see p. 549.

Make the filling

Cut the strawberries into ½-inch (12 mm) pieces (1¾ cups). Put them in a small skillet with the sugar, flour, and salt and toss until combined. Cook over medium heat, stirring, until the strawberries are tender and the juices have released and thickened, 3 to 4 minutes. Slide the pan off the heat and set aside, stirring frequently, to cool completely.

Assemble and cook the mini turnovers

1. Pull the dough disk from the fridge and, if it's very cold, set it out at room temperature until it's just pliable enough to roll, 10 to 20 minutes. Arrange a large piece of parchment on the work surface, put the unwrapped dough in the center, and cover with another piece of parchment. Using a rolling pin, roll the dough between the parchment to ⅛-inch (3 mm) thickness, turning, lifting, and repositioning the parchment and lightly flouring throughout the rolling. Peel away the top parchment.

For more about rolling dough between parchment, see p. 133.

2. Using a 4-inch (10 cm) round cookie cutter, cut out as many rounds as possible. Gather up the scraps, reroll to a ⅛-inch (3 mm) thickness, and cut more rounds. You can reroll the scraps twice, if necessary, until you have 14 rounds.

3. Arrange the rounds on the work surface. Spoon an even amount of the cooled strawberry mixture (1 Tbs.) onto the center of each round. Don't be tempted to overfill the turnovers or the filling will ooze out during cooking. Using a pastry brush or a fingertip, brush the edges of each round with water. Fold the dough over the filling to form half-moons. Using the tines of a fork, gently press the pastry edges to seal. Arrange them on a cookie sheet lined with parchment or a nonstick liner, cover, and refrigerate until the dough is firm, about 20 minutes.

4. Put the sugar and nuts in a shallow bowl and stir until blended. Have ready a large rimmed baking sheet lined with several layers of paper towels and a Chinese-style skimmer or slotted spoon. Put enough Crisco (or enough oil) in a large pot (I use a 3-quart/3 l Dutch oven) to fill it to a 1-inch (2.5 cm) depth and clip a candy thermometer to the side of the pan, making sure it doesn't touch the bottom. Heat the oil to 365°F (185°C) over high heat.

5. Carefully slip a few turnovers (if you fry too many at one time, the temperature of the oil will drop and the turnovers will be greasy) into the oil and cook, turning once with the skimmer, until deep golden brown, 90 seconds per side. Keep an eye on the oil temperature and adjust the heat up or down accordingly, making sure to bring the temperature back up to 365°F (185°C) before cooking the subsequent batches. With a skimmer or slotted spoon, remove the turnovers from the pan and drain on the paper towel–lined baking sheet. When just barely cool enough to handle, roll the turnovers in the sugar–nut mixture. Serve warm or at room temperature.

For more about deep frying, see p. 62.

For more about deep frying, see p. 62.

Filling and folding the turnovers

A

With the dough rounds on the work surface, spoon about 1 Tbs. of the strawberry mixture into the center of each. Too much and the mixture will ooze out during frying or baking.

B

Dab a little water around the outside edge of the round, then fold the dough over the filling.

C

Press the edges of the half-moon with your fingertips to seal, then use the tines of a fork to crimp the edges.

Roasted Butternut Squash Pie *with* Pecan Praline

Serves 10   [PHOTO ON P. 261]

Over my baking years, I've made hundreds of pumpkin pies. In fact, it was the very first pie I made. My mom and I baked together often, and she eagerly passed on her knowledge about rolling pie dough and baking custard pies like this one. Little did I know that pie was the beginning of my career as a pastry chef, baker, instructor, author, and devoted dessert lover.

While I've made a few tweaks along the way, the essence of my pumpkin pie remains very similar to that first one I made with Mom, but with one major exception: I now use butternut squash instead of pumpkin. The change came when I was running the bakery for a large farm market. One fall there was a bumper crop of butternut squash and the produce manager begged me to put them to use. After roasting the squash and baking off the first batch of pies, we all agreed that the butternut flavor was outstanding; our customers agreed and I know you will, too.

My pie dough is soft and supple, making it remarkably easy to handle—perfect for newbie bakers. For a stress-free rolling experience, I like to roll the dough between two sheets of parchment. This facilitates the process, prevents sticking, and makes maneuvering the dough much easier. The dough bakes up into a tender, slightly flaky crust with a rich, buttery flavor that is a perfect complement to the satin-smooth custard filling.

For the purée
Nonstick cooking spray or softened
  butter, for preparing the pan
3 lb. (1.4 kg.) whole butternut
  squash

For the filling
1¼ cups (11 oz./312 g) butternut
  squash purée

½ cup (3½ oz./99 g) granulated
  sugar
1¼ tsp. ground cinnamon
½ tsp. ground ginger
¼ tsp. ground nutmeg
Good pinch of table salt
1¼ cups (300 ml) half-and-half
5 tsp. (25 ml) brandy or 1¼ tsp.
  pure vanilla extract

2 large eggs, at room temperature

1 partially baked and cooled pie
  crust (see p. 313)
Slightly sweetened whipped cream
  (see p. 367) and Pecan Praline
  (recipe on the facing page), for
  serving

Make the purée

1. Position a rack in the center of the oven and heat the oven to 400°F (200°C/gas 6). Line a rimmed baking sheet with parchment or foil and lightly grease.

2. Using a large knife, cut the squash in half lengthwise. Scoop out and discard the seeds and fibers from the cavity and put the halves on the baking sheet, cut side down (see the Essential Technique on p. 358). Roast until the long neck end is very tender when pierced with a paring knife, 50 to 60 minutes. Move the sheet to a rack until the squash is cool enough to handle.

3. Scoop the flesh into a food processor and process until smooth. Alternately, scoop the flesh into a medium bowl and mash with a fork or potato masher until smooth. Let cool completely. Divide the purée in half, about 1¼ cups (11 oz./312 g) each; there will be enough for two pies.

Make the filling and bake the pie

1. Position a rack in the center of the oven and heat the oven to 325°F (165°C/gas 3).

2. Put the squash purée, sugar, cinnamon, ginger, nutmeg, and salt in a medium bowl and whisk until well blended. Add the half-and-half and brandy or vanilla and whisk until well blended. Add the eggs and whisk until blended. Pour and scrape the filling into the crust.

3. Bake until the filling jiggles like Jell-O when the pie plate is nudged, 50 to 54 minutes. Move the pie to a rack and let cool to room temperature. Cover loosely and refrigerate until ready to serve. The pie is best served within 1 day and can be warmed slightly in a 300°F (150°C/gas 2) oven, if desired. Serve slices with a dollop of whipped cream and sprinkled with some Pecan Praline.

Pecan Praline

Makes 1½ cups (6½ oz./184 g)

⅔ cup (4⅝ oz./131 g) granulated sugar

¼ cup (60 ml) water

¾ cup (3 oz./85 g) chopped, toasted pecans (see p. 33)

1. Lightly grease the underside of a wide offset spatula and line a cookie sheet with a nonstick liner.

2. Put the sugar and water in a medium, heavy saucepan. Cook, stirring, over medium-low heat until the sugar dissolves, about 5 minutes. Increase the heat to high and bring to a boil. Boil, without stirring, until the sugar begins to color around the edges of the pan, about 5 minutes. Swirl the pan over the heat until the caramel is an even deep amber, another 1 to 2 minutes.

For more about making caramel, see p. 273.

3. Slide the pan off the heat and immediately add the pecans. Swirl the pan to coat the nuts, pour onto the cookie sheet, and, using the spatula, quickly spread into an even layer. Move to a rack and let cool completely.

4. Chop the praline into very small, bite-sized pieces and serve immediately or stow in an airtight container at room temperature for up to 1 month.

(continued)

MAKE AHEAD

> The filling can be prepared, covered, and refrigerated for up to 1 day; bring to room temperature before proceeding.

> The squash purée makes enough for two pies. Use immediately or refrigerate in heavy-duty freezer bags for up to 2 days or freeze for up to 3 months.

TWISTS

Flavor swap

Instead of the roasted butternut squash purée, substitute 1 can (13½ oz.) canned pumpkin purée.

ESSENTIAL TECHNIQUE

Roasting squash

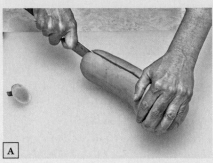  

A	**B**	**C**
Hold a large knife tightly in one hand and brace the squash on one end with your other hand. Using firm pressure, cut down the length of the squash. Flip the squash if needed to cut all the way through.	Use a tablespoon to scoop out the squash fibers and seeds. Scrape the cavity as you do a pumpkin before carving it.	A potato masher is the best tool for mashing the roasted squash flesh until smooth, but a fork will work too.

> >

Almond Caramel Tart

Serves 10   [PHOTO ON P. 262]

This tart crust is a no-roll marvel! It starts with a soft, butter–cocoa dough that whizzes up in the food processor and easily presses into a tart pan. No rolling—no kidding.

The caramel filling is one of my all-time favorites for two reasons. First, the silky, not-too-sticky texture is the perfect foil for the chocolate crust; second, the buttery, creamy, bittersweet caramel flavor pairs perfectly with the meaty, toasted almonds. This might sound like a candy bar commercial, but don't be misled. This sophisticated dessert will thrill every palate.

For the crust
1 cup (4½ oz./128 g) unbleached
  all-purpose flour
⅓ cup (1⅜ oz./39 g) confectioners'
  sugar
3 Tbs. unsweetened natural cocoa
  powder, sifted if lumpy
¼ tsp. table salt
8 Tbs. (4 oz./113 g) unsalted butter,
  cut into 8 pieces and chilled
1 Tbs. cold water

For the filling
2 cups (10 oz./283 g) whole
  blanched almonds, toasted and
  very coarsely chopped (see p. 304)
½ cup (120 ml) heavy cream
1¼ cups (8¾ oz./248 g)
  granulated sugar
½ cup (120 ml) water
4 Tbs. (2 oz./57 g) unsalted butter,
  cut into 5 pieces and softened

1 tsp. pure vanilla extract
½ tsp. table salt + more to taste
Orange-Scented White Chocolate
  Ganache, for serving (recipe on
  p. 360)

Make the crust

1. Have ready a fluted 9¼-inch (23.5 cm) tart pan with a removable bottom.

2. Put the flour, sugar, cocoa, and salt in a food processor. Process until blended, about 2 seconds. Scatter the chilled butter pieces over the flour mixture and pulse until the mixture forms coarse crumbs. Sprinkle the water over the flour mixture, then pulse just until the dough forms moist crumbs, about 10 seconds.

3. Scoop up some of the dough and, using your hands, roll back and forth on the counter to form a rope about ½ inch (12 mm) thick. Arrange the rope in the tart pan against the side of the pan and press until the dough covers the side up to the top. It will be about ¼ inch (6 mm) thick. Repeat rolling and pressing the dough until the sides are completely covered. Scatter the remaining dough in the bottom of the pan and, using lightly floured fingertips, pat the dough to make an even layer (or as close to even you can get) on the bottom and into the corners of the pan. Refrigerate the pan while the oven heats.

4. Position a rack in the center of the oven and heat the oven to 350°F (180°C/gas 4).

5. Line the tart pan with foil and pie weights, then bake for 20 minutes (a technique called blind-baking). Remove the foil and pie weights and continue baking until the crust looks dry, another 10 to 12 minutes. Move the pan to a rack and set aside while you make the filling.

For more about lining a pie with pie weights, see p. 51.

Make the filling and finish the tart

1. Sprinkle the toasted, very coarsely chopped nuts evenly in the baked and cooled tart shell.

2. Put the heavy cream in a small saucepan or microwave-safe bowl and heat until very warm. Set aside.

3. Put the sugar and water in a 4- or 5-quart (4 or 5 liter) heavy saucepan. Cook, stirring, over low heat until the sugar is dissolved and the mixture is boiling. Once the sugar is dissolved and the mixture is boiling, stop stirring and increase the heat to high. When the sugar begins to caramelize, swirl the pan over the heat until the caramel is deep amber in color, 2 to 3 minutes. Gently swirl the pan over the heat to even out the caramel color. (I like to test the color by putting a drop or two on a white plate. If the caramel is too light in color, the sauce will be too sweet.) Slide the pan off the heat and slowly and carefully add the warm heavy cream. Be careful, as it will sputter and the steam is very hot. Whisk until the caramel is completely smooth. If necessary, return the pan to the heat and continue whisking until the caramel is dissolved. Slide the pan off the heat, add the butter, vanilla, and salt, and whisk until blended. Taste and add more salt, little by little, until the caramel is slightly salty.

(continued)

MAKE AHEAD

> The crust can be prepared and baked, then covered and stowed at room temperature for up to 1 day.

> The tart can be prepared, cooled, covered, and refrigerated for up to 3 days before serving.

BAKER'S WISDOM

Cleaning sticky pans and utensils

Pots and utensils used to make caramel can be a real drag to clean because of the sticky remnants. The easiest cleanup is simply to fill the pot with water, set in on the stove, and bring to a boil over high heat. Once boiling, add the utensils and boil until the caramel is dissolved, about 5 minutes. Keep an eye on any utensils with wooden handles as they can scorch. Drain the water and clean the pot and utensils with soapy water.

FINISHING TOUCHES

Just before serving, sprinkle the slices with fleur de sel.

For more about making caramel, see p. 273.

4. Pour the caramel evenly over the nuts to cover completely. Gently jiggle the tart pan to settle the caramel. Set aside to cool completely, about 3 hours, then refrigerate until well chilled and ready to serve, about 4 hours.

5. Remove the tart from the refrigerator 15 minutes before serving. Carefully release the outer ring and slide onto a flat serving plate. Just before serving, drizzle some of the ganache over each plate and arrange a chilled tart slice on top.

For more about releasing the tart pan, see p. 349.

Orange-Scented White Chocolate Ganache

Makes ¾ cup (180 ml)

4 oz. (113 g) white chocolate
  (not chips)

¼ cup (60 ml) heavy cream
1 Tbs. orange-flavored liqueur

Melt the chocolate and cream in a small heatproof bowl. (I use the microwave but an improvised double boiler works just fine.) Add the orange liqueur and whisk until well blended and smooth.

ESSENTIAL TECHNIQUE

Making a press-in tart crust

A Once the dough is processed, scoop up a little and shape it into a rope, rolling as you would if making a snake from Play-Doh®.

B Position the rope along the side of the tart pan, then press it into the edges and up the side of the fluted pan. Continue until the entire side of the pan is covered with ¼-inch (6 mm) thick dough.

C Scrape in the rest of the dough, scatter evenly, and then use both hands to smooth it out and cover the bottom of the pan evenly. Dip your fingers in flour if the dough starts to stick.

Caramel Velvet Apple Pie

Serves 10 [PHOTO ON P. 263]

Combining caramel and apple in a dessert is reminiscent of a childhood favorite, but trust me, there's nothing childlike about this pie. The filling's caramel flavor is sophisticated and elegant, and the baked apple texture is downright velvety. Put them together and you have a filling that's a far cry from its stick-to-your-teeth candy-apple cousin. There's nothing complicated about the filling—just peel and cut some apples, make a caramel, fold them together, and cool.

The dough for this double-crusted pie is not your standard ho-hum crust. It's rich in butter, which gives it great flavor, heightened by a little sugar, fresh lemon juice, and just a touch of salt. A small amount of shortening gives the dough its supple texture, which makes it easy to handle and roll (even for novice bakers), so it bakes up into a tender, flaky crust.

For the dough
12 Tbs. (6 oz./170 g) unsalted butter
4 Tbs. (2 oz./57 g) vegetable shortening
5 Tbs. (75 ml) very cold water
1 Tbs. freshly squeezed lemon juice
2⅔ cups (12 oz./340 g) unbleached all-purpose flour
2 Tbs. granulated sugar
1 tsp. table salt

For the filling
3½ lb. (1.6 kg.) crisp, firm apples (such as Honey Crisp or Golden Delicious)
⅓ cup (1½ oz./42 g) unbleached all-purpose flour
¼ cup (60 ml) heavy cream
1 cup (7 oz./198 g) granulated sugar
⅓ cup (80 ml) water

2 Tbs. (1 oz./28 g) unsalted butter, softened
Good pinch of table salt or fleur de sel

For assembly
1 large egg
1 tsp. water

Make the dough

1. Cut the butter in half lengthwise and then cut each strip into 6 pieces; cut the shortening into 2 pieces. Pile the shortening and butter on a plate and slide into the freezer until ready to use. Measure the water, add the lemon juice, and refrigerate until ready to use.

2. Whisk the flour, sugar, and salt in a large bowl until well blended. Add the cold butter and shortening pieces and, using a pastry blender or two knives, cut them into the flour mixture until the pieces are pea-sized, about 3 minutes. (You can also do this in a food processor using short pulses, scraping the blended mixture into the large bowl before proceeding.)

For more about mixing butter and flour together until the butter is pea-sized, see p. 80.

3. Pour the water and lemon juice over the flour and, using a silicone spatula, stir and fold until it forms a shaggy, moist dough with some floury bits remaining (I like to use one hand to help mix while keeping the other working the spatula). Scrape the dough and any remaining floury bits into a pile on the counter. Starting with the top of the mound and using the heel of your hand, smear a section of the dough down the side and along the work surface away from you to blend the butter pieces into the dough. Repeat with the remaining dough in sections. Using a bench scraper, fold

MAKE AHEAD

The pie dough can be prepared and refrigerated for 2 days or wrapped in plastic and frozen for up to 1 month. If frozen, thaw in the refrigerator overnight.

TWISTS

Flavor swap

> **Pear or pear-apple caramel:**
Substitute all or half of the apples with the same amount of firm-ripe pears.
> **Apple-raisin or apple-cranberry:**
Reduce the apple amount to 3¼ lb. (1.5 kg) and add ¾ cup (3¾ oz./106 g) dark raisins or dried cranberries to the caramel along with the apple mixture.
> **Caramel apple bourbon:** Instead of using cream in the caramel, use 3 Tbs. bourbon.

Re-size it

Instead of cutouts for the top crust, make a prefab lattice crust (see pp. 326–327).

the dough together (the mixture will be rough and crumbly). Turn the pile about 90 degrees and repeat the smearing process until the mixture just comes together into a cohesive dough (this is a technique called *fraisage*). Be careful not to overwork the dough because that will make the crust dense. Divide the dough in half (12 oz./340 g each) and shape into two 6-inch (15 cm) disks. Wrap in plastic wrap and refrigerate until firm, about 2 hours, or up to 2 days.

For more about using your hand to help mix, see p. 85.

For more about *fraisage*, see p. 549.

Make the filling

1. Peel and core the apples and cut into ½- to ¾-inch (12 mm to 2 cm) thick slices. Put the slices in a large bowl and sprinkle the flour over the top. Using a silicone spatula, toss and stir until the slices are evenly coated with the flour.

For more about coring apples, see p. 122.

2. Put the heavy cream in a small saucepan or microwave-safe bowl and heat until very warm. Set aside.

3. Put the sugar and water in a 4- or 5-quart (4 or 5 liters) heavy saucepan. Cook, stirring, over low heat until the sugar is dissolved and the mixture is boiling. Once the sugar is dissolved and the mixture is boiling, stop stirring and increase the heat to high. When the sugar begins to caramelize, swirl the pan over the heat until the caramel is deep amber in color, 2 to 3 minutes. Gently swirl the pan over the heat to even out the caramel color. (I like to test the color by putting a drop or two on a white plate. If the caramel is too light in color, the sauce will be too sweet.) Slide the pan off the heat and slowly and carefully add the warm heavy cream. Be careful, as it will sputter and the steam is very hot. Whisk until the caramel is completely smooth. If necessary, return the pan to the heat and continue whisking until the caramel is dissolved. Slide the pan off the heat, add the butter and salt, and whisk until blended. Taste and add more salt, little by little, until the caramel is slightly salty.

For more about making caramel, see p. 273.

4. Scrape the apples and any remaining flour into the pan and toss and stir until blended. The mixture will be sticky and very thick. Cook over medium heat, stirring frequently and scraping the bottom of the pan with a spatula, until the caramel is liquid, boiling, and thick enough to coat the apples, 5 to 7 minutes. If the mixture boils too vigorously, reduce the heat to medium low. Slide the pan off the heat and set aside, stirring occasionally, until cooled to room temperature (no longer than 1 hour).

Make the top crust

1. Remove one of the dough disks from the fridge and, if it's very cold, set it out at room temperature until it's just pliable enough to roll, 10 to 20 minutes. Arrange a large piece of parchment on a work surface, put the unwrapped dough in the center, and cover with another piece of parchment. Using a rolling pin, roll the dough between the parchment to a 13½-inch (34 cm) round, lifting, turning, and repositioning the parchment and lightly flouring throughout the rolling.

For more about rolling dough between parchment, see p. 133.

2. Slide a large cookie sheet under the parchment and dough. Remove the top sheet of parchment, and using a small 2-inch (5 cm) leaf-shaped cookie cutter, stamp out 6 or 7 shapes about 3 inches (7.5 cm) apart, starting in the center of the round. Cover the dough with parchment or plastic, and slide into the fridge.

Make the bottom crust and line the pan

Following the directions in Step 1 for making the top crust, roll the second disk to a 13½-inch (34 cm) round and peel away the top parchment. Carefully roll the dough around the pin, leaving the bottom parchment behind, and position over a 9-inch (23 cm) pie plate (I prefer Pyrex). Unroll the dough onto the plate and gently nudge it into the bottom and sides of the plate. Gently but firmly press the dough against the sides and bottom, being careful not to stretch or tear the dough, allowing the excess dough to hang over the edges (see the Essential Technique on p. 364).

Assemble and bake the pie

1. Position a rack in the center of the oven and set a foil-lined rimmed baking sheet on the rack. Heat the oven to 425°F (220°C/gas 7).

2. Scrape the cooled filling into the bottom crust and spread evenly. Remove the top crust from the fridge, uncover, and, using the tip of a small knife, lift the cut-out leaves and set on the counter or a piece of plastic wrap. (The dough should be cold but not firm. If it's too cold, the dough will break.) Slide your palm under the parchment and center it under the top crust. Lift the paper and invert the dough onto the filling, using your palm as a guide to center it.

3. Press the top and bottom edges together and trim both crusts so there's about ¾ inch (2 cm) hanging over the edge of the plate. Roll the overhang under itself to shape a high-edge crust that rests on top of the rim. Crimp the edge. Roll out the dough scraps and cut out another 4 or 5 leaf shapes.

4. In a small bowl, mix the egg and water with a fork until well blended. Brush the top generously with the egg wash, randomly arrange the leaf cutouts on the crust, and brush the leaves with the egg wash.

5. Put the pie on the heated baking sheet and reduce the oven temperature to 375°F (190°C/gas 5). Bake until the filling is bubbling and thickened and the pastry is deep golden brown, 68 to 75 minutes. If the pastry starts to get too brown, cover loosely with foil and continue baking. Move the sheet to a rack and let cool until warm (or cool completely) before serving. The pie is best when served within 1 day and can be warmed slightly in a 300°F (150°C/gas 2) oven, if desired.

(continued)

BAKER'S WISDOM

Apples

Apples range in taste from just plain sweet to spicy-sweet to tart; in texture, from downright hard to crisp and juicy to dry to mealy; and in color, from blackish red to palest yellow. Some are tender-skinned, others have thick, waxy coats, and still others have tougher, leathery skins. With endless varieties available, picking just one can be tricky because each variety has a unique flavor and behaves a little differently when cooked.

For this pie, I like Honey Crisp or Golden Delicious, but any apple with a sweet-tart flavor and a crisp bite that bakes up to a soft texture will be yummy. A couple to avoid when baking are Red Delicious and Fuji. Of course, regional and heirloom varieties are worth experimenting with as well. Ask the vendors at your local farmers' market for suggestions.

FINISHING TOUCHES

Serve with vanilla or cinnamon ice cream or slightly sweetened whipped cream (see p. 367).

ESSENTIAL TECHNIQUE

Making a double-crust pie with cutouts

A

Position a disk of dough on a large piece of parchment, cover with a second piece, and roll out the dough, turning and flipping after each roll. Peel back the parchment and lightly flour the dough frequently to prevent sticking.

B

Apply gentle but firm pressure on the rolling pin as you roll from the center outward, rotating the paper after each pass and flipping occasionally. Continue to roll the dough to a 13½-inch (34 cm) round that's about ⅛ inch (3 mm) thick.

C

Remove the top sheet of parchment from the chilled top crust dough and cut out shapes around the center of the round with a 2-inch (5 cm) cookie cutter.

D

Roll the dough for the bottom crust the same way you did the top crust. To transfer the crust to the pie plate, use the parchment to help and roll the bottom crust dough around the rolling pin. Leave the parchment behind.

E

Gently unroll the dough onto the pie plate. Gently but firmly press the dough into the bottom and sides of the pie plate, being careful not to stretch or tear it. Fill the crust with the apple mixture.

F

Center your palm under the parchment under the middle of the top crust. In one motion, flip the dough onto the filling, using your palm as a guide to center it.

G

Trim the top and bottom crusts with
kitchen shears, leaving a ¾-inch (2 cm)
overhang.

H

Pinch together the two crusts and then roll
the excess under itself to shape a high-edge
crust that rests on the rim of the plate.

I

Crimp the edge of the dough using the
thumb and index finger of one hand and
the index finger of the other hand to pinch
the dough into deep V shapes.

J

Brush egg wash evenly all over the top
crust, arrange the leaf cutouts on the crust,
and brush them with egg wash as well

Chapter 7

PUDDINGS AND CUSTARDS

> > > >

Classic Berry Trifle

Serves 8 to 10

I've always been fascinated by this summer classic. As a kid, the juicy berries, vanilla cream, and tender cake layered and suspended in a glass bowl were mesmerizing. I wondered how it was made—did it bake in the glass bowl and separate or was it a berry-filled layer cake that someone put in a bowl? Thankfully, my mom indulged my curiosity and helped me solve these riddles of my early baking years. I was also lucky enough to have three older brothers who were happy recipients (maybe I should call them guinea pigs) of my baking explorations.

Assembling this trifle isn't complicated as long as you have all the recipe elements ready to go. The cream should be chilled and the berries freshly tossed. For the dramatic and classic presentation, trim the cake so it will fit snugly in your glass vessel and then cut in half crosswise to make two layers to sandwich the berries and cream. I've also used sliced vanilla pound cake (see p. 274) instead of the cake layers and, while the presentation is less organized, the flavors are just as wonderful.

1 hot-milk sponge cake, baked and cooled (recipe on p. 246)

For the vanilla custard
⅓ cup (2⅜ oz./67 g) granulated sugar
2 tsp. unbleached all-purpose flour or cornstarch
Pinch of table salt
4 yolks from large eggs (see p. 371)
2 cups (475 ml) half-and-half

1 tsp. pure vanilla extract or vanilla bean paste (see p. 10)

For the fruit
6 cups (30 oz./850 g) mixed fresh berries, rinsed and well drained
2 Tbs. light rum or berry-flavored vodka
3 Tbs. granulated sugar
Pinch of table salt

For the sweetened whipped cream
¾ cup (180 ml) heavy cream, chilled
2 to 3 Tbs. granulated sugar
½ tsp. pure vanilla extract

⅓ cup (1⅝ oz./46 g) chopped pistachios, lightly toasted, for serving

Make the vanilla custard

Put the sugar, flour or cornstarch, and salt in a medium saucepan and whisk until well blended. Add the yolks and whisk until well blended and lighter in color. Pour in the half-and-half, whisking until well blended, and cook over medium heat, whisking constantly, until the mixture just begins to boil and is thick, 2 to 4 minutes. Slide the pan off the heat, add the vanilla, and whisk until well blended. Scrape into a small bowl and press a piece of plastic wrap directly on the surface to prevent a skin from forming. Refrigerate until cold, 3 to 4 hours.

Assemble the trifle

1. Trim the cake so it is the same circumference as a 2- to 2½-quart (2 to 2.5 liter) trifle bowl or soufflé dish (preferably glass so you can see the layers), then cut in half horizontally.

For more about cutting the cake, see p. 594.

(continued)

MAKE AHEAD

The custard can be prepared, covered, and refrigerated for 2 days.

(Tom Cat's Chocolate Mousse continued)

Flavor swap

> **Coffee:** Instead of the brandy or rum, use the same amount of coffee liqueur and add 1 tsp. instant espresso or coffee powder to the yolk mixture.

> Instead of the brandy or rum, use the same amount of water.

> Instead of the chocolate shards garnish, use the same amount of toasted sliced almonds or pomegranate seeds.

> Instead of the homemade pound cake, use the same amount of store-bought pound cake or soft ladyfingers or 1 layer of hot milk sponge cake (baked, cooled, and cut in half crosswise; see p. 293).

the chopped chocolate, butter, and vanilla, and stir until smooth. Set aside until the mixture is room temperature, about 5 minutes.

For more about making your own double-boiler, see p. 376.

3. Put the egg whites in the bowl of a stand mixer fitted with the whisk attachment (or in a medium bowl and using an electric handheld mixer and wire beaters) and beat on medium speed until the whites are frothy, 30 to 45 seconds. Increase the speed to medium high and beat until the whites form soft peaks, 1 to 2 minutes. Continue beating while gradually adding the remaining 3 Tbs. sugar, stopping occasionally to scrape down the sides of the bowl. Beat until the whites form medium-firm, glossy peaks when the beater is lifted. Scoop about one-quarter of the whites into the chocolate mixture and, using a silicone spatula, gently stir until blended. Add the remaining whites and gently fold in until just blended.

For more about beating egg whites, see p. 212.

For more about folding, see p. 270.

4. Pour about half of the mousse into a 6-cup (1.4 liters) serving bowl. Arrange the cake slices snugly next to each other to cover and gently press into the mousse. Pour and scrape the remaining mousse over the cake and spread evenly. Cover and refrigerate until well chilled, about 6 hours or up to 1 day.

Make the whipped cream and serve

1. Put the heavy cream, sugar, and vanilla in a medium bowl. Beat with an electric handheld mixer fitted with wire beaters on medium speed until medium-firm peaks form when the beater is lifted.

For more about whipping cream, see p. 368.

2. Drop dollops of the cream on top of the mousse cake. If desired, cover with chocolate shards just before serving.

Separating eggs

A

Holding an egg firmly, tap the shell on the edge of a glass bowl. It is best to make a solid crack with the first hit against the bowl; otherwise, a bunch of gentle hits will result in a splintered shell and less chance of making a clean break, resulting in more tiny shell bits in the whites.

B

Holding the cracked egg in both hands, use your thumbs to separate the halves at the crack. Apply gentle pressure as you push in and release the halves from each other. Some of the egg white will drop into the bowl, but keep the yolk intact in one half of the shell.

C

Let the white drop into a small bowl as you move the yolk from one half of the egg shell to the other.

D

Continue sliding the yolk between the two egg shell halves, letting the white drip out, until no white remains in the shell. Use the edge of one finger if needed to help coax the last of the white from the yolk.

E

If there is any yolk in the white (left), discard the white, clean the bowl, and begin again. If the white is clean (right), pour it into a larger bowl, pop the yolk into a separate bowl, and continue as directed. This way you avoid contaminating all the whites with yolk as you work. Scoop up any rogue shell bits in the whites with a yolk-free shell half—you'll never get 'em with your fingers.

Chocolate–Bourbon Croissant Pudding

Serves 8 to 10   [PHOTO ON P. 264]

For me, just saying "bread pudding" is comforting. With its softened pudding-like consistency, it was originally considered nursery or toddler food. But make no mistake about it—this dangerously delicious version will have adults swooning. The bread in this case—leftover croissant—is soaked in a sweetened vanilla custard, topped with bittersweet chocolate, and baked in a water bath; topping it off is a boozy bourbon sauce that elevates this dessert from everyday to extra-special.

6 medium-sized croissants,
   preferably stale
3 oz. (85 g) bittersweet or semisweet
   chocolate, coarsely chopped
   (see p. 380)

3 large whole eggs
2 yolks from large eggs (see p. 371)
$\frac{2}{3}$ cup ($4\frac{5}{8}$ oz./131 g) firmly
   packed light brown sugar
Pinch of table salt

3 cups (700 ml) half-and-half
2 Tbs. bourbon
Bourbon Sauce, for serving
   (recipe on the facing page)

MAKE AHEAD

> The pudding can be assembled, covered as directed, and refrigerated for up to 8 hours. Press down on the croissants occasionally to cover with the custard.

> The pudding can be baked, cooled, covered, and refrigerated for up to 3 days. Serve at room temperature or warm slightly in the oven or microwave.

TWISTS

Flavor swap

> **Dried fruit:** Instead of the chocolate, use $\frac{2}{3}$ cup ($3\frac{3}{8}$ oz./96 g) lightly packed dried fruit (chopped if large) and proceed as directed.

> **Almond:** Instead of the plain croissants, use the same amount of almond croissants. Instead of the bourbon, add $\frac{1}{2}$ tsp. pure almond extract to the custard. Just before baking, sprinkle the top of the pudding with sliced almonds.

> Instead of using croissants, use 6 to 7 cups (1.4 to 1.7 liters) $\frac{3}{4}$-inch (2 cm) cubed challah, brioche, or French bread. The bread's crust can be trimmed before cubing, if desired. Put the bread in the prepared pan and spread evenly. The pan will be almost completely full. Proceed with the recipe.

Make the pudding

1. Lightly grease an 8-inch (20 cm) square baking dish (I like Pyrex) and have ready a larger baking pan that can comfortably hold the small baking dish (a 9 x 13 x 2-inch/23 x 33 x 5 cm or roasting pan works well).

2. Using a serrated knife, cut the croissants in half horizontally. Arrange the bottoms in the prepared pan to form an even, slightly overlapping layer. Scatter half of the chopped chocolate on top of the croissants (see the Essential Technique on the facing page). Arrange the croissant tops in the pan so they form an even, slightly overlapping layer and scatter the remaining chocolate on top. The pan will be almost completely filled.

3. Put the eggs, yolks, brown sugar, and salt in a medium bowl and whisk until well blended. Add the half-and-half and bourbon and whisk until well blended. Pour the egg mixture over the croissants. Cover the surface of the pudding directly with plastic wrap and let it sit at room temperature, pressing down on the croissants occasionally to cover with the custard, until the croissants are evenly soaked, 45 to 60 minutes.

Bake and serve

1. Position a rack in the center of the oven and heat the oven to 350°F (180°C/gas 4). If the pudding was refrigerated, let it sit at room temperature while the oven heats. Remove the plastic wrap and arrange the baking dish with the pudding in the larger baking pan. Pull out the oven rack slightly and put the baking pan on the rack. Carefully pour very hot tap water into the pan to reach halfway up the sides of the baking dish.

For more about baking in a water bath, see p. 390.

2. Bake until the custard is set (a knife inserted in the center comes out clean) and the center of the pudding springs back when gently pressed with a finger, 44 to 46 minutes. Move the larger baking pan to a rack and let cool for about 15 minutes. Carefully lift the pudding out of the water and move to a rack to cool. Serve warm or at room temperature with the bourbon sauce.

Bourbon Sauce

Makes 1½ cups (360 ml)

1½ cups (360 ml) heavy cream
⅔ cup (4⅝ oz./131 g) firmly
   packed light brown sugar

3 to 4 Tbs. bourbon

Put the heavy cream and brown sugar in a medium saucepan. Bring to a boil over medium-high heat and cook, stirring frequently, until the cream is thick enough to coat the back of a spoon and hold a line drawn through it with your finger, 6 to 8 minutes. Slide the pan off the heat, stir in 3 Tbs. of the bourbon, taste, and add the additional 1 Tbs., if desired. Set aside to cool. Serve the sauce warm or at room temperature.

FINISHING TOUCHES

Instead of serving with the bourbon sauce, sprinkle each serving with confectioners' sugar, chocolate shavings, or both just before serving.

MAKE AHEAD

The bourbon sauce be prepared, cooled, covered, and refrigerated for up to 2 weeks. Serve at room temperature or heat gently in the microwave or on top of the stove.

ESSENTIAL TECHNIQUE

Assembling the bread pudding

A

With the palm of one hand resting on top of a croissant and fingers extended upward, use a serrated knife to slice through the croissant horizontally, using a sawing motion to make the cut.

B

Arrange the bottoms of the croissants in the pan, overlapping them but keeping them in an even layer, then scatter half of the chopped chocolate on top of the croissants.

C

Once the croissant tops have been placed, cut side down, on top of the chocolate-topped bottoms, scatter the remaining chocolate on top. It's fine if some chocolate slides between the croissants.

Individual Tiramisu

Serves 6 [PHOTO ON P. 265]

This classic, coffee-flavored Italian dessert is one of my favorite go-to party desserts. Pairing rich and decadent mascarpone custard with layers of a Kahlúa-spiked, syrup-soaked homemade ladyfinger cake is a perfect finale for a holiday or celebratory meal. What's even better is that it can—and should be—made ahead of time.

Instead of using store-bought crunchy ladyfingers, I use an easy-to-make génoise cake—a porous, drier cake that readily absorbs liquid and takes on the flavor of the liquid. Baking it in a quarter sheet pan means it bakes quickly, and the flat layer is easy to cut into equal portions for assembly. Make sure you soak the cake in enough of the coffee syrup; otherwise, the mouth-feel of the finished dish will be dry.

For the cake
Nonstick cooking spray or softened unsalted butter + flour, for preparing the pan
½ cup (2¼ oz./64 g) unbleached all-purpose flour
¼ tsp. baking powder
¼ tsp. table salt
2 large eggs, at room temperature
⅓ cup (2⅜ oz./67 g) firmly packed light brown sugar
½ tsp. pure vanilla extract

For the coffee syrup
½ cup (120 ml) water
⅓ cup (2⅜ oz./67 g) firmly packed light brown sugar
¼ cup (60 ml) Kahlúa or other coffee liqueur
2 tsp. instant coffee granules or instant espresso powder

For the mascarpone filling
2 large whole eggs
1 yolk from a large egg (see p. 371)
¼ cup (1¾ oz./50 g) firmly packed light brown sugar

3 Tbs. Kahlúa or other coffee liqueur
1½ tsp. instant coffee granules or instant espresso powder
Pinch of table salt
1 cup (8 oz./227 g) mascarpone (see p. 11)
¾ cup (180 ml) heavy cream
1 tsp. pure vanilla extract

½ cup (2 oz./57 g) finely grated bittersweet or semisweet chocolate (see p. 380)

MAKE AHEAD

> The cake can be prepared, wrapped in plastic, and stowed at room temperature for up to 2 days or frozen for up to 1 month.

> The coffee syrup can be prepared, covered, and refrigerated for up to 4 days.

> The tiramisu can be assembled, covered with plastic, and refrigerated for up to 2 days.

Make the cake

1. Position a rack in the center of the oven and heat the oven to 350°F (180°C/gas 4). Lightly grease the bottom and sides of a 9-inch (23 cm) square pan (I prefer a straight-sided one). Line the bottom with parchment and lightly flour the sides, tapping out any excess.

For more about preparing cake pans, see p. 232.

2. Whisk the flour, baking powder, and salt in a small bowl until well blended. Put the eggs in a large bowl. Beat with an electric handheld mixer fitted with wire beaters on medium speed until well blended, about 1 minute. Add the brown sugar and vanilla and beat on medium-high speed until pale and tripled in volume and a thick ribbon forms when the beater is lifted, about 5 minutes. Sprinkle the flour mixture over the beaten egg mixture and fold with a silicone spatula until just blended. Pour into the prepared pan and use an offset spatula to gently spread the batter evenly. Bake until the cake springs bake when lightly touched (the cake is too thin to use a cake tester or pick to test), 14 to 16 minutes.

For more about folding, see p. 270.

3. Move the pan to a rack and let cool for 15 minutes. Run a knife between the cake and the pan to loosen the cake. Invert onto a rack, lift off the pan, and gently peel away the parchment. Let cool completely.

4. Using a serrated knife, cut the cake into 6 equal rectangles. Cut each rectangle into eight cubes, keeping each set of cubes in a separate pile.

Make the syrup

Put the water and sugar in a small pan and cook over medium heat until the sugar is dissolved. Bring to a boil and remove from the heat. (This can also be done in the microwave using a heatproof bowl.) Add the coffee liqueur and the instant coffee and stir until dissolved. Set aside to cool to room temperature. For faster cooling, set the bowl over a larger bowl filled with ice and a little water, stirring and scraping the sides frequently.

Make the filling and assemble

1. Arrange a large, heatproof bowl on top of a pot of barely simmering water over medium-low heat (the water shouldn't touch the bottom of the bowl). Put the eggs, yolk, brown sugar, coffee liqueur, instant coffee, and salt in the bowl and whisk (I use an electric handheld mixer) until the mixture is thick enough to coat a spatula and hold a line drawn through it with your finger (170°F/77°C on an instant-read thermometer), 5 to 7 minutes (see the Essential Technique on p. 376). Remove from the heat and, using an electric handheld mixer fitted with wire beaters, beat on medium-low speed until the mixture has cooled to room temperature, 5 to 7 minutes. For faster cooling, set the bowl over a larger bowl filled with ice and a little water, stirring and scraping the sides frequently.

2. Put the mascarpone, heavy cream, and vanilla in a medium bowl and beat with an electric handheld mixer until firm peaks form. Scrape the mascarpone mixture into the cooled egg mixture and gently fold in with a large silicone spatula until just blended.

For more about folding, see p. 270.

3. Have ready six 10- to 12-oz. (300 to 350 ml) glasses, the cake cubes, cooled syrup, and chocolate shavings. Working with one pile of cake cubes at a time, dip the bottom half of the cubes in the syrup and drop into the bottoms of each glass. Spoon about ⅓ cup (80 ml) (I use a mini scoop) of the filling over the cake, spreading to cover. Sprinkle with about 1 tsp. of the grated chocolate. Repeat with another layer of syrup-soaked cake, filling, and grated chocolate, ending with chocolate. There should be two layers of cake, cream, and grated chocolate. (You'll use about ⅔ cup/ 160 ml filling and 2 tsp. grated chocolate per glass.)

4. Cover each glass with plastic and refrigerate for at least 2 hours. Serve the tiramisu slightly chilled.

(continued)

TWISTS

Flavor swap

Use 1½ packages (4½ oz./128 g total) store-bought ladyfingers instead of the from-scratch cake. Unwrap and set aside for 1 to 2 hours before assembling to let them dry out a bit.

FINISHING TOUCHES

Instead of the final layer of grated chocolate, top with a dollop of whipped cream and white and bittersweet chocolate curls (see p. 381) or shards (see p. 250).

Making the filling

A Make a water bath by placing a large heatproof bowl on top of a pot of barely simmering water and make sure the water doesn't touch the bottom of the bowl.

B Beat with an electric hand mixer until the mixture is thick enough to coat a spatula and hold a line drawn through it with your finger (170°F/77°C on an instant-read thermometer).

> >

Ricotta Panna Cotta *with* Raspberry "Brezza Fresca" Sauce

Serves 6   [PHOTO ON P. 266]

Lunching with my dear friend and colleague Gail Dosik on a warm summer day is a celebratory event, and that means we start with a cocktail. On one such afternoon, we were dining at Barbuto in New York City and Gail's tall, ruby-red drink, a "Brezza Fresca," arrived at the table—and it had me at hello. Ice-cold, bursting with big berry flavor and a touch of lime, a splash of sparkling water, and gin, this was one of the most beautiful and delicious drinks I had tasted in a long while. It was so good that I immediately thought it should be on the dessert menu.

Re-creating Gail's cocktail as a dessert sauce was just the beginning. While it was to be the star of the dessert, it still needed a strong supporting player; that's where my Ricotta Panna Cotta enters stage left. The ricotta is creamy smooth, thanks to a whiz in the blender, and lends just the right rich, velvety texture to this classic dessert. I've flavored this version with vanilla bean paste; the visual of millions of tiny seeds suspended in the lightly thickened custard is magical but will taste just as delicious with pure vanilla extract. As a nod to the sauce's origin, I like to serve this dessert in cocktail glasses—martini, wine, or mini parfait.

For the panna cotta
¼ cup (60 ml) water
1½ tsp. unflavored powdered
  gelatin
1½ cups (13⅛ oz./372 g) whole-
  milk ricotta (see p. 64 for
  homemade)
½ cup (3½ oz./99 g) granulated
  sugar

1 tsp. vanilla bean paste or pure
  vanilla extract
Pinch of table salt

For the raspberry sauce
1 cup (5 oz./142 g) raspberries,
  rinsed and dried (or frozen and
  thawed)
⅓ cup (1⅜ oz./39 g) confectioners'
  sugar + more to taste

2 Tbs. gin + more to taste
1 Tbs. fresh lime juice
Pinch of table salt
1 tsp. finely grated lime zest
  (see p. 138)

San Pellegrino® or other sparkling
  water (optional)
Lime slices or wedges, for garnish
  (optional)

Make the panna cotta

1. Have ready 6 small dessert glasses or bowls and make room in the fridge. For the asymmetrical look, arrange your empty glasses in the fridge so they are resting against something so that they are on a slight angle and balanced securely (I use a loaf of bread). To gauge how high to fill the glasses, put water in one of the glasses, leaving some room at the top and position in the fridge. Adjust the water amount and the glasses' position accordingly, making sure they are positioned so you can fill them. Empty the water-filled glass, wipe dry, and reposition. (For a traditional layered look, leave the glasses or bowls upright.)

2. Put the water in a 1-cup (8 oz./240 ml) Pyrex measure or a small, heatproof ramekin and sprinkle the gelatin evenly over the top (see the Essential Technique on p. 378). Set aside to soften. Once the gelatin has absorbed the liquid and is plump (about 3 minutes), microwave briefly until it is completely melted and crystal clear, 1 to 2 minutes. This can also be done in a small saucepan (instead of the ramekin) over low heat.

3. Put the melted gelatin, ricotta, sugar, vanilla bean paste, and salt in a blender or food processor and pulse until smooth and well blended. Pour the mixture evenly among the glasses or bowls and chill until set, about 4 hours. Cover the tops with plastic and refrigerate until ready to serve.

Make the raspberry sauce

Put the raspberries, confectioners' sugar, gin, lime juice, and salt in a blender or food processor and pulse until smooth and well blended. Taste and add more confectioners' sugar or gin accordingly. Pour the mixture through a fine-mesh sieve over a small bowl or 2-cup (16 oz./ 480 ml) measure, pressing firmly on the seeds. Scrape the underside of the sieve into the bowl and discard the seeds. Stir in the lime zest, cover, and refrigerate until ready to serve.

For more about straining and scraping, see p. 395.

To serve

Add a splash or two of San Pellegrino, if using, to the raspberry mixture and stir until blended. Remove the panna cotta–filled glasses or bowls from the fridge and pour a little sauce over the panna cotta; serve the rest of the sauce on the side.

(continued)

(Ricotta Panna Cotta continued)

MAKE AHEAD

> The panna cotta can be covered and refrigerated for up 2 days.

> The raspberry sauce can be prepared, covered, and refrigerated for up to 1 week or frozen for up to 1 month. If frozen, thaw completely before stirring in the sparkling water and serving.

TWISTS

Flavor swap

> **Almond:** Instead of the vanilla bean paste, add ¼ tsp. pure almond extract to the mixture and mold in small ramekins. Instead of the raspberry sauce, sprinkle the top of the panna cottas with toasted sliced almonds just before serving.

> **Other berry:** Instead of raspberries, use the same amount of strawberries, blueberries, or blackberries, rinsed and dried.

ESSENTIAL TECHNIQUE

Softening gelatin

A

B

To soften powdered gelatin, sprinkle it over the tap water. Use the amount of powdered gelatin and water called for in your recipe, but, regardless of the amounts, be sure to sprinkle the gelatin evenly over top of the water. Notice the white color and granular texture of the dry gelatin.

As the gelatin absorbs water, it will plump up and no longer look white and granular. Microwave briefly until it is completely melted and crystal clear, 1 to 2 minutes. This can also be done in a small saucepan (instead of the ramekin) over low heat.

No-Bake Double Chocolate Pots de Crème

Serves 6

More than a simple pudding, this rich, creamy, deeply satisfying pot de crème need not bake "low 'n' slow"—the traditional method of baking these desserts at a low temperature for a long time. In fact, my take on the classic doesn't see a minute in the oven, making it easy and very accessible for even novice bakers.

The secret to the pots' velvety texture lies in the ratio of cream, butter, and chocolate. To increase the flavor profile of the crèmes, I like to use a fine-quality bittersweet (62% to 70%) chocolate like Valrhona or Lindt and pair it with a dose of Dutch-processed cocoa powder to create a smooth yet intense double hit of the "good stuff." More adventurous palates will enjoy boutique chocolate flavors and higher cocoa percentages, so experiment to develop your own repertoire of pots de crème.

Remember, the vessels don't need to be ovenproof since this recipe is no-bake, so use your prettiest—even demitasse or small teacups!

2 cups (480 ml) heavy cream
2 Tbs. unsweetened cocoa powder, preferably Dutch-processed, sifted if lumpy

2 Tbs. granulated sugar
8 oz. (227 g) bittersweet chocolate, finely chopped (see p. 380)
8 Tbs. (4 oz./113 g) unsalted butter, cut into 6 pieces

1½ tsp. pure vanilla extract
Pinch of table salt

1. Have ready six 6-oz. (180 ml) ramekins (3½ inches wide and 1⅔ inches high/9 cm wide and 4.25 cm high) or other cups and make room in the fridge.

2. Put the heavy cream in a small saucepan (or microwave in a 4-cup/960 ml heatproof bowl) and heat until just boiling. Once boiling, slide off the heat and whisk in the cocoa powder until smooth. Add the sugar, chopped chocolate, butter, vanilla, and salt and whisk until the chocolate and butter are melted and the mixture is smooth. Set aside to cool until warm and no longer hot.

3. Pour the chocolate cream evenly into the ramekins or cups. Depending on what size cups you are using, they will be filled two-thirds to three-quarters of the way. Set aside until cooled to room temperature. Cover the tops (not the custard surface) with plastic and refrigerate until chilled and firm, about 4 hours.

(continued)

MAKE AHEAD

The crèmes can be prepared and refrigerated for up to 4 days before serving.

FINISHING TOUCHES

Serve with a dollop of lightly sweetened whipped cream (see p. 367), and a few chocolate shavings (see p. 381), if desired.

TWISTS

Flavor swap

> Mocha: Add 1 tsp. instant espresso powder or instant coffee granules along with the cocoa powder. Add 1 Tbs. dark rum or coffee-flavored liqueur along with the vanilla.

> Orange: Add 2 tsp. finely grated orange zest with the cocoa powder. Add 1 Tbs. orange-flavored liqueur along with the vanilla. For a smooth texture, set a fine-mesh sieve over a bowl or 4-cup (960 ml) measure and strain the liquid, pressing on the zest before mixing with the chocolate (see p. 395 for more about straining). For stronger flavor, heat the zest and cream, cover, and let the mixture sit for about 15 minutes before reheating and proceeding with the recipe.

> Mint: Add 5 hearty sprigs of mint to the heavy cream before heating. Set a fine-mesh sieve over a bowl or 4-cup (960 ml) measure and strain the mixture, pressing on the leaves before mixing the cream with the chocolate. For stronger flavor, heat the mint and cream, cover, and let the mixture sit for about 15 minutes before reheating and proceeding with the recipe.

ESSENTIAL TECHNIQUE

Working with block chocolate

A

Block chocolate is hard, so be sure to use a large, sharp chef's knife. Hold the handle tightly and position your other hand on top of the knife's blade as you press down. Make sure to keep your fingers well away from the blade.

B

To chop chocolate, remove larger chunks from the block, then use the knife to chop it to the size called for in your recipe.

.C

For grating chocolate, hold the block in one hand as you move it over the grater, keeping your fingers away from the rasps. The chocolate block will get warm and a little sticky, so you can wrap part of the block in a paper towel if needed as you continue to work with it.

D

E

To make smaller pieces or shavings, hold the chocolate firmly in one hand, using a paper towel to help you grip it, and rub the opposite palm over one narrow flat side to warm the chocolate slightly. Drag a Y-shaped peeler down the edge of the chocolate block, letting the shavings fall on the paper. Repeat the rubbing before peeling as needed.

To make large chocolate curls, use a similar technique to the shavings but the chocolate must be a bit warmer. Microwave the block in short, 5-second bursts (white and milk chocolate will need much less time) until it feels just warm. Hold the chocolate firmly, using a paper towel to hold it in one hand as you drag the Y-peeler down the flat length of the narrow side of the chocolate block using one firm motion. If the chocolate still makes shards or won't make big curls, it isn't warm enough, so heat again for another 5 seconds (or more, if needed) until large, even curls fall on the paper.

F

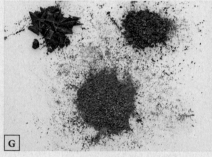
G

To make smaller but longer ribbons, warm the chocolate and hold with a paper towel as for shavings and curls and drag the peeler down the edge of the block to form a curl.

Photo left: roughly chopped chocolate (top left), grated chocolate (top right), finely chopped chocolate (bottom); photo right (left to right): large chocolate curls, chocolate ribbons, chocolate shavings.

Lemon Ginger Mousse Soufflés

Serves 6   [PHOTO ON P. 331]

These light, billowy individual soufflé-like mousses are a variation on a pie filling in my book, *The Weekend Baker.* Instead of adding heavy cream to the mousse, I use puréed ricotta (for a smooth texture) to add richness without heaviness. The lemon and fresh ginger make for a refreshing flavor profile, but it's the ginger cookies hidden inside that are the surprise ingredient. Softened by the mousse, they bring texture and a burst of ginger flavor.

Adding a collar of parchment adds additional height to the ramekins. This way you can mimic the impressive height of a baked soufflé without the need for any last-minute fussing.

Neutral oil (safflower, canola, vegetable, or corn), for the ramekins

For the mousse
¾ cup (180 ml) freshly squeezed lemon juice
1 envelope (¼ oz./7 g) unflavored powdered gelatin
1¼ cups (11¼ oz./319 g) ricotta (part skim is fine) (for homemade, see p. 64)

¾ cup (5½ oz./156 g) granulated sugar
1 Tbs. finely grated lemon zest (see p. 138)
2 tsp. finely grated fresh ginger (see p. 312)
Pinch of table salt
4 whites from large eggs (4 oz./ 113 g), at room temperature (see p. 371)
½ tsp. cream of tartar

½ cup (2 oz./57 g) confectioners' sugar, sifted if lumpy

12 gingersnap cookies + more for the crushed cookie topping (I use Nabisco or homemade molasses cookies, see p. 195)
Blackberry Compote (recipe on the facing page; optional)

MAKE AHEAD

The soufflés can be prepared, covered, and refrigerated for up to 2 days before serving.

Have ready six 6-oz. (180 ml) ramekins (3½ inches wide and 1⅔ inches high/9 cm wide and 4.25 cm high) arranged on a flat plate or quarter sheet pan. Cut parchment into six strips 2½ inches (6 cm) wide and 12 inches (30.5 cm) long. Wrap one strip around each ramekin so that the paper covers the ramekin and stands 1 inch (2.5 cm) above the rim; secure with tape (see the Essential Technique on p. 384). Lightly grease the inside of the paper rim (I use a paper towel dipped in a bit of neutral oil).

Make the mousse

1. Pour the lemon juice into a small heatproof ramekin (or keep it in the measuring cup) and sprinkle the gelatin evenly over the top. Set aside to soften. Once the gelatin has absorbed the liquid and is plump (about 3 minutes), microwave briefly until it is completely melted and crystal clear, 1 to 2 minutes. This can also be done in a small saucepan (instead of the ramekin) over low heat.

For more about softening gelatin, see p. 378.

2. Put the ricotta, granulated sugar, lemon zest, ginger, and salt in a blender. Scrape the lemon–gelatin mixture into the blender, cover, and process until the ricotta is smooth and the mixture is well blended, about 1½ minutes, scraping down the sides once or twice. Pour into a medium bowl and refrigerate, stirring frequently, until the mixture is cooled and thickened, 20 to 30 minutes. It should be as thick as unbeaten egg whites. For faster cooling, set the bowl over a larger bowl filled with ice, stirring and scraping the sides frequently until cooled.

For more about beating to the proper thickness, see p. 407.

3. Put the egg whites and cream of tartar in the bowl of a stand mixer fitted with the whisk attachment (or in a medium bowl and using an electric handheld mixer fitted with wire beaters) and beat on medium speed until the whites are frothy, 30 to 45 seconds. Increase the speed to medium high and beat until the whites form soft peaks, 1 to 2 minutes. Continue beating while gradually adding the confectioners' sugar, stopping occasionally to scrape down the sides of the bowl. Beat until the whites form firm and glossy peaks when the beater is lifted.

For more about beating egg whites, see p. 212.

4. Scoop about one-quarter of the whites into the thickened lemon mixture and, using a silicone spatula, gently stir until blended. Add the remaining whites and gently fold in until just blended.

For more about folding, see p. 270.

Assemble the mousses

Arrange one cookie in the bottom of each ramekin. Using a large spoon, fill the ramekins halfway with the mousse. Arrange a cookie on top of the mousse and evenly portion the remaining mousse on top of the cookies. Using a small offset spatula, smooth the tops. Cover loosely with plastic wrap and refrigerate until firm, at least 6 hours or up to 1 day.

To serve

Using a sharp paring knife, carefully peel away the parchment from the ramekins (up to 3 hours ahead). Just before serving, place each ramekin on a small plate and top with some of the crushed ginger cookie or a little of the blackberry compote, passing the remainder at the table.

Blackberry Compote

2 cups (10 oz./283 g) blackberries, rinsed and well dried

2 to 3 Tbs. limoncello liqueur

2 Tbs. granulated sugar

1 tsp. finely grated lemon zest (see p. 138)

Put the blackberries, limoncello, sugar, and lemon zest in a medium bowl. Toss with a silicone spatula, lightly crushing the berries to release some of their juices. Cover and refrigerate until ready to use or for up to 6 hours.

(continued)

FINISHING TOUCHES

Instead of serving with Blackberry Compote, serve with Double Raspberry Sauce (recipe on p. 215), Crushed Blueberry Sauce (recipe on p. 279), or Ruby Red Cranberry Sauce (recipe on p. 403).

ESSENTIAL TECHNIQUE

Assembling the soufflés

A

B

To mimic the height of a baked soufflé, wrap each ramekin with a strip of parchment, making sure it stands about an inch over the top edge of the ramekin, and tape it together. This paper rim will hold the mousse in place as it chills and sets.

Use a paper towel dipped in a bit of oil to lightly grease the inside of the parchment rim. Hold your fingers against the outside of the paper as you brush on the oil to help keep the paper in place.

C

D

Place a cookie in the bottom of each ramekin, then fill each halfway with mousse. Use a small ladle, large spoon, or measure to fill.

Position another cookie in each ramekin, pressing down gently to help secure it in the mousse, then fill each with the remaining mousse. Smooth the tops with an offset spatula, then loosely cover and chill.

E

Just before serving, gently remove the parchment wrap from the chilled soufflés. Use a paring knife to help loosen the tape, then hold one side of the ramekin as you gently peel away the parchment.

Brûléed Pots de Crème

Serves 4

I like to call these gems little pots of heaven. With a gentle tap of your spoon onto the caramelized sugar, the topping shatters into gorgeous shards of bittersweet crunch and uncovers the silky, barely sweetened vanilla-infused filling. A heavenly combination not to be missed.

1¾ cups (420 ml) half-and-half
1 vanilla bean
5 yolks from large eggs (see p. 371)

¼ cup (1¾ oz./50 g) granulated
    sugar + 4 tsp. for brûléeing
⅛ tsp. table salt

1. Pour the half-and-half into a small saucepan. Position the vanilla bean on a cutting board and, using the tip of a sharp knife, split the bean lengthwise down the middle. Slide the edge of the knife down the cut side of each piece of the bean to release the seeds. Add the seeds and vanilla bean pieces to the half-and-half. Over medium heat, bring the mixture to a simmer. Slide the pan off the heat, cover, and let the mixture steep for 30 minutes or up to 2 hours. The longer the half-and-half and the vanilla bean and seeds steep, the more pronounced the vanilla flavor will be.

For more about scraping a vanilla bean, see p. 275.

2. Position a rack in the center of the oven and heat the oven to 325°F (165°C/gas 3). Arrange four 6-oz. (180 ml) ramekins (3½ inches wide and 1⅔ inches high/9 cm wide and 4.25 cm high) in a baking pan with 2-inch (5 cm) high sides (I use an 8-inch/20 cm square baking pan).

3. Put the yolks, sugar, and salt in a small bowl and whisk until thick and pale. Uncover the half-and-half and, whisking constantly, slowly pour it (with the vanilla bean pieces) into the yolk mixture. Whisk until well blended. Return the liquid to the pan. Cook over medium-low heat, stirring constantly, until the mixture is thick enough to coat the back of a spoon and hold a line drawn through it with your finger (170°F/77°C on an instant-read or candy thermometer), 4 to 5 minutes.

For more about custard doneness, see p. 388.

4. Slide the pan off the heat and fish out the vanilla bean; scrape any custard from the pod back into the pan. Pour the custard into the ramekins. (For a super-clean pot filling, I like to pour the custard into a clean 2-cup/480 ml measure and then pour it from there into the ramekins—the pour spout makes it so easy.) Pull out the oven rack slightly and put the baking pan with the ramekins on the rack. Carefully pour very hot tap water into the pan to reach halfway up the sides of the ramekins and cover the pan loosely with foil.

For more about baking in a water bath, see p. 390.

5. Bake until the pots de crème wiggle like Jell-O when nudged, 35 to 45 minutes depending on the thickness of the ramekin walls. Move the

---

MAKE AHEAD

The pot de crèmes can be prepared, covered, and refrigerated for up to 2 days before brûléeing and serving.

TWISTS

Flavor swap

> Instead of using the vanilla bean, use 1½ tsp. pure vanilla extract or pure vanilla bean paste. Skip Step 1 and add the vanilla extract or paste at the end of Step 3.

> Instead of brûléeing the tops, serve with **Double Strawberry Sauce:**

1 package (10 oz./283 g) frozen
    strawberries (not in syrup), thawed
¼ cup (2¾ oz./79 g) seedless
    strawberry jam
¼ to ½ cup (1 to 2 oz./28 to 57 g)
    confectioners' sugar
Pinch of table salt

Combine the thawed strawberries, jam, ¼ cup (1 oz./28 g) of the confectioners' sugar, and the salt in a food processor or blender. Whiz until puréed and well blended. Taste and add more confectioners' sugar, if desired.

pan to a rack and, using wide rubber band–wrapped tongs, carefully transfer the ramekins to another rack. Cover with plastic wrap and refrigerate for at least 4 hours before serving.

For more about using tongs to transfer ramekins, see p. 400.

6. Just before serving, arrange the ramekins on the work surface and uncover. Working with one at a time, evenly sprinkle 1 tsp. of the remaining sugar over the surface of the custard. Position a handheld kitchen torch about 2 inches (5 cm) above the sugar and slowly move the flame over the top until the sugar melts and is deep amber in color (expect some small black spots). Repeat with the remaining pots and serve immediately.

ESSENTIAL TECHNIQUE

Brûléeing

For first-time torch users, it's prudent to set the ramekins on a metal surface (not plastic or wooden). To brûlée sugar-crusted custard, sprinkle the tops of the chilled custards with sugar, hold a kitchen torch about 2 inches (5 cm) above the dish, and slowly move the flame across the top of the custard. It takes just a couple of minutes for the sugar to change from light colored to deep golden brown. If you see very dark brown spots (right photo), shift the flame to another area.

The sugar should form a crisp shell on top of the creamy custard.

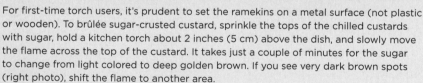

Butterscotch Stovetop Pudding

Makes about 2 cups (480 ml)

Homemade pudding is one of the easiest and fastest desserts around. With just a few on-hand ingredients, a saucepan, a whisk, and less than 10 minutes, you can whip up this creamy, rich pudding. If you are in a rush, spoon it warm from the pot into bowls with a few crisp cookies crushed and sprinkled on top. If time is less pressing, spoon the pudding into ramekins and cover the surface directly with plastic to prevent a skin from forming; for those who live for the skin, just loosely cover and chill.

I've added a hint of scotch to the pudding—not so much that it's boozy and unappealing, but just enough to elevate the flavor for a more sophisticated taste. Served with a dollop of whipped cream lightly sweetened with brown sugar and a Brown Butter–Almond Lace Cookie (see p. 161), this dessert is a showstopper.

4 yolks from large eggs (see p. 371)
½ cup (3½ oz./99 g) firmly packed dark brown sugar
2 Tbs. + 1 tsp. cornstarch

Good pinch of table salt
1¾ cups (420 ml) whole milk or half-and-half
1½ to 2 tsp. Scotch whiskey or brandy

2½ Tbs. (1½ oz./42 g) unsalted butter, cut into 4 pieces, softened
¾ tsp. pure vanilla extract

1. In a medium bowl, whisk the egg yolks until well blended; set aside.

2. Whisk the brown sugar, cornstarch, and salt in a medium saucepan until well blended. Slowly pour in the milk, whisking constantly, until well blended. Whisk in the Scotch or brandy. Make sure to scrape the bottom edges of the pan to incorporate all the sugar and cornstarch. (Tip the pan in several directions so the edges are exposed and whisk more, if necessary.)

3. Set the pan over medium heat and cook, whisking constantly, until simmering, about 3 minutes. Once the milk mixture is thickened and just boiling, slowly pour it into the egg yolks, whisking constantly. Adding the hot milk too quickly can curdle or cook the yolks. Using a silicone spatula, pour and scrape the mixture back into the saucepan. Cook over medium heat, whisking constantly, until the mixture comes back to a boil (the foam will dissipate and the liquid will thicken as it cooks). Boil, whisking constantly, for 1 minute. Slide the pan off the heat, add the butter and vanilla, and whisk until just blended.

4. Pour and scrape the hot pudding into a clean medium bowl (or portion evenly among 4 small cups or ramekins). Press a piece of plastic wrap directly on the pudding's surface to prevent a skin from forming. (If you like the skin, cover only the top of the bowl or ramekins with plastic and not the surface of the pudding.) Set aside to cool until warm and then refrigerate until chilled, about 4 hours.

(continued)

(Butterscotch Stovetop Pudding continued)

FINISHING TOUCHES

Sprinkle the tops with Pecan Praline (recipe on p. 357).

TWISTS

Flavor swap

> **Espresso:** Omit the Scotch or brandy and use the same amount of coffee liqueur. Add 2 tsp. instant espresso powder along with the brown sugar, cornstarch, and salt.

> **Vanilla:** Instead of the dark brown sugar, use ⅓ cup (2⅜ oz./67 g) granulated sugar. Omit the Scotch or brandy and use 1 vanilla bean, split and scraped, or 1 tsp. pure vanilla extract or vanilla bean paste. Add the vanilla seeds and bean along with the milk. If using extract or paste, wait until the end of cooking to add it along with the butter.

> **Banana:** Omit the Scotch or brandy and use the same amount of rum. Make the vanilla pudding as directed. Add ½ cup (2½ oz./71 g) chopped ripe banana along with the butter and vanilla and stir gently until the butter is melted and the bananas are coated with pudding.

ESSENTIAL TECHNIQUE

Making the pudding

A

Gradually add the milk to the pan and whisk until well blended. Tip the pan to expose the eggs and whisk more if needed.

B

Cook the mixture until it's just beginning to boil and has thickened, then slowly pour it into the bowl of beaten yolks, whisking constantly.

C

Pour the pudding back into the saucepan and cook until boiling for 1 minute. Stir in the butter and vanilla and pour into one large bowl or four individual serving cups.

Coconut Lemon Pudding Cakes

Serves 6

I am fond of concentrating flavors to maximize their boldness, and the coconut flavor in these pudding cakes is testament to that. Boiling the coconut milk not only intensifies the flavor but also thickens it. Plus it adds a silky, creamy texture to the pudding layer of these mini treats. If you don't have time to reduce the coconut milk, you can use regular coconut milk, adding some coconut oil or extract to help make up for the lack of deeper coconut flavor.

1 can (13½ oz./383 g) unsweetened coconut milk (see p. 318)

¾ cup (5¼ oz./149 g) granulated sugar
2 Tbs. unbleached all-purpose flour

½ tsp. ground cardamom (see p. 147)
¼ tsp. table salt
2 Tbs. (1 oz./28 g) unsalted butter, melted
3 large eggs, separated, at room temperature (see p. 371)

½ tsp. pure vanilla extract
⅓ cup (80 ml) freshly squeezed lemon juice

1. Give the can of coconut milk a shake before opening, pour into a medium saucepan, and bring to a boil over medium heat. Boil, stirring occasionally, until reduced to 1 cup (240 ml), 10 to 15 minutes. Set aside to cool completely. For faster chilling, pour the reduced coconut milk into a bowl, set the bowl over a larger bowl filled with ice, and stir until cooled to room temperature.

2. Position a rack in the center of the oven and heat the oven to 350°F (180°C/gas 4). Arrange six 6-oz. (180 ml) ramekins (3½ inches wide and 1⅔ inches high/9 cm wide and 4.25 cm high) in a 9 x 13 x 2-inch (23 x 33 x 5 cm) baking pan.

3. Whisk the sugar, flour, cardamom, and salt in a medium bowl until blended. Add the butter, egg yolks, and vanilla and whisk until well blended. Slowly pour in the 1 cup (240 ml) reduced coconut milk and the lemon juice, whisking constantly until blended and smooth.

4. Put the egg whites in the bowl of a stand mixer fitted with the whisk attachment (or in a medium bowl and using an electric handheld mixer fitted with wire beaters) and beat on medium speed until the whites are frothy, 30 to 45 seconds. Increase the speed to medium high and beat until the whites form medium-firm peaks when the beater is lifted, 1 to 2 minutes. The tip of the peaks should droop over just slightly. Do not overbeat. Scoop about one-quarter of the whites into the coconut milk–egg yolk mixture and, using a silicone spatula, gently stir until blended. Add the remaining whites and gently fold in until just blended.

For more about beating egg whites, see p. 212.

For more about folding, see p. 270.

5. Using a large ladle or a 1-cup (240 ml) metal measuring cup, scoop the batter from the bottom (the mixture may have begun separating and

MAKE AHEAD

> The reduced coconut milk can be made, cooled, covered, and refrigerated for up to 3 days.

> The pudding cakes can be made, cooled, covered, and refrigerated for up to 2 days before serving.

TWISTS

Flavor swap

> Instead of using the reduced coconut milk, use the same amount of coconut milk or half-and-half and add ½ tsp. coconut extract or oil.

> Instead of using cardamom, add 1 Tbs. finely grated fresh ginger to the coconut milk before reducing and strain it out before proceeding as directed.

Re-size it

Instead of using ramekins, pour the batter into an 8-inch (20 cm) square pan and bake as directed for 29 to 31 minutes.

MAKE AHEAD

The custards can be prepared, covered, and refrigerated for up to 3 days before serving.

drop or two on a white plate. If the caramel is too light in color, the sauce will be too sweet.) Working quickly and carefully (the caramel is very hot), immediately pour the caramel evenly into each ramekin. Give each ramekin a swirl to spread the caramel evenly over the bottom.

For more about making caramel, see p. 273.

Finish the custards

1. Arrange a fine-mesh sieve over a medium bowl or 4-cup (960 ml) measure and pour the popcorn–milk mixture into the sieve. Using a silicone spatula, firmly press on the popcorn to squeeze out all the milk. Scrape the underside of the sieve and add to the milk (see the Essential Technique on the facing page); discard the solids.

2. Put the eggs, yolks, sugar, and salt in a small bowl and whisk until thick and pale. Whisking constantly, slowly pour the infused milk into the yolk mixture. Add the vanilla and whisk until well blended. Pour the custard into the ramekins. (For a super-clean ramekin filling, I like to pour the custard into the 4-cup/960 ml measure and then pour it from there into the ramekins—the pour spout makes it so easy.)

3. Pull out the oven rack slightly and put the baking pan with the ramekins on the rack. Carefully pour very hot tap water into the pan to reach halfway up the sides of the ramekins and cover the pan loosely with foil. Bake until the custard jiggles like Jell-O when one ramekin is nudged, 53 to 57 minutes. Move the pan to a rack, using wide rubber band–wrapped tongs, and carefully transfer the ramekins to another rack. Let cool completely, cover with plastic (not touching the custards), and refrigerate for at least 6 hours. The longer the ramekins sit, the more caramel will dissolve to form the sauce.

For more about baking in a water bath, see p. 390.

For more about using tongs to transfer ramekins, see p. 400.

4. To serve, run a small sharp knife around the inside rim of each ramekin and invert onto a small serving dish with a rim to hold the caramel sauce.

For more about inverting a ramekin, see p. 215.

TWISTS

Flavor swap

> **Vanilla:** Omit the popcorn and vanilla extract and use 1 large vanilla bean, split; steep in the milk and heavy cream (see p. 275).

> **Ginger:** Omit the popcorn and use 1/2 oz. (15 g) fresh ginger (about 2 inches/ 5 cm long), peeled and thinly cut; steep in the milk and heavy cream (see p. 312).

> **Basil:** Omit the popcorn and use 1 cup (2 oz./57 g) packed fresh basil leaves; and steep in the milk and heavy cream.

Tilghmans' Popcorn

Makes about 5 cups popcorn

3 Tbs. olive oil (or a neutral oil, like safflower, canola, or vegetable)

⅓ cup (2½ oz./71 g) organic corn kernels

½ tsp. fine-grain sea salt or to taste

Heat the oil in a 6-quart (6 liter) heavy-duty pot over medium-high heat. Add 2 or 3 kernels and cover the pan tightly. When the kernels pop, add the remaining kernels and cover with the lid. Vigorously shake and slide the pot over the heat. When the corn is popping, reduce the heat to low and crack the top slightly away from you to let steam escape. Once the popping action has slowed to one pop every 3 or 4 seconds (this will take about 5 to 9 minutes), slide the pan from the heat, dump the popcorn onto a half sheet pan, and pick out any burnt or unpopped kernels. Salt to taste.

ESSENTIAL TECHNIQUE

Making the popcorn milk

A

B

Once the milk, cream, and popcorn have come to a simmer (A), turn off the heat, cover, and let the mixture steep for up to 2 hours. This will infuse the liquid with popcorn flavor and soften and shrink the popcorn as well (B). The longer it steeps, the more pronounced the popcorn flavor will be.

C

D

E

Set a sieve over a medium bowl or 4-cup (960 ml) measure and pour in the popcorn–milk mixture. Scrape all the popcorn from the pan into the sieve.

Using the back of a spoon or spatula, press firmly on the popcorn, squeezing out all the milk, along with some of the pulp from the popcorn.

Be sure to scrape any popcorn pulp from the underside of the sieve into the milk. Discard the solids in the sieve.

TWISTS

Flavor swap

> Instead of the pumpkin purée, use a total of 2 cups (480 ml) milk or half-and-half.

> Instead of the pumpkin purée, use the same amount of roasted butternut squash purée (see p. 356).

Re-size it

Instead of using ramekins, pour the batter into an 8-inch (20 cm) square pan (I like Pyrex) and bake as directed for 30 to 32 minutes.

Mixing in cornmeal

To avoid lumps, be sure to add the cornmeal slowly to the milk–pumpkin mixture as you whisk constantly.

As it cooks, the mixture will thicken. This takes only a couple of minutes. Continue to whisk, scraping around the sides of the pan and from the bottom.

Toasted Coconut Soufflés *with* Ruby Red Cranberry Sauce

Serves 10; makes 1¼ cups (300 ml) sauce

A classic soufflé is nothing short of spectacular and a true example of those "baking miracles" I often mention. Coating the sides of the ramekins with toasted coconut creates a crunchy counterpart to the airy coconut soufflé. The recipe serves ten and, when accompanied by the cranberry sauce, it's one of the most elegant and festive desserts in my repertoire.

The fresh, tart cranberry flavor of the sauce is a nice contrast to the sweet soufflé, but it is strong, so use only a spoonful per serving so as not to overwhelm. To add sauce to a soufflé without completely and immediately deflating it: Using a tablespoon filled with sauce, cut into the center of the soufflé with the side of the spoon, adding more sauce as desired.

Softened butter, for preparing the
  ramekins

For the Ruby Red Cranberry Sauce
1 cup (4½ oz/128 g) cranberries
  (fresh or frozen), rinsed and dried
¾ cup (180 ml) cranberry juice
  cocktail

¾ cup (5½ oz./156 g) granulated
  sugar

For the soufflés
1 cup (2½ oz./71 g) sweetened
  shredded coconut, toasted and
  cooled (see p. 235)
1 can (13½ oz. /383 g)
  unsweetened coconut milk

2 Tbs. (1 oz./28 g) unsalted butter
2 Tbs unbleached all-purpose flour
½ cup (3½ oz./99 g) granulated
  sugar, divided
1½ tsp. coconut extract
Pinch of table salt
5 whites from large eggs (5 oz./
  142 g) (see p. 371)

Make the Ruby Red Cranberry Sauce

1. In a small saucepan, combine the cranberries, cranberry juice, and sugar. Bring to a boil, stirring occasionally, over medium-high heat. Reduce the heat to medium low and cook, stirring occasionally, until the berries are very soft, about 6 minutes.

2. Strain the mixture through a fine-mesh sieve into a small bowl, firmly pressing on the solids. Scrape the underside of the sieve and add to the sauce; discard the solids. Serve immediately or let cool, cover, and refrigerate for up to 4 days. Reheat to warm (not hot) before serving.

Make the soufflés

1. Brush the softened butter generously all over the inside and rim of ten 6-oz. (180 ml) ramekins (3½ inches wide and 1⅔ inches high/9 cm wide and 4.25 cm high).

2. Using your hands, crush the toasted coconut until it resembles small flakes and set aside ¼ cup (¾ oz./20 g). Sprinkle the remainder over the buttered ramekins, tilting to coat completely. Gently tip out any excess (see the Essential Technique on p. 405). Arrange the ramekins on a half sheet pan or cookie sheet and set in the refrigerator.

3. Put the coconut milk in a medium saucepan and bring to a boil over medium heat. Boil, stirring occasionally, until reduced to 1¼ cups (300 ml), 7 to 10 minutes.

(continued)

TWISTS

Flavor swap

Orange: Instead of the toasted coconut, line the buttered ramekins with granulated sugar. Instead of the coconut milk and extract, use 1 cup (240 ml) milk or half-and-half along with ¼ cup (60 ml) Grand Marnier and 1 Tbs. finely grated orange zest.

FINISHING TOUCHES

Instead of the sauce, sprinkle with additional toasted coconut just before serving.

4. Put the butter in a medium saucepan and cook over medium heat, stirring, until melted. Add the flour and cook, whisking constantly, for 2 minutes until bubbling but not brown. Slowly pour in the reduced coconut milk, whisking constantly until well blended. Cook over medium-high heat, whisking constantly, until the mixture boils. Boil, whisking constantly, until thick, about 1 minute. Slide the pan off the heat and whisk in about half of the sugar, the coconut extract, and salt until well blended.

For more about making a pastry cream, see p. 523.

5. Scrape the custard into a medium bowl and place a piece of plastic wrap directly on the surface; let cool to room temperature.

Bake the soufflés

1. If refrigerated, set the custard on the counter and allow to come to room temperature. Position a rack in the center of the oven and heat the oven to 375°F (190°C/gas 5).

2. Whisk the custard until smooth. Put the egg whites in the bowl of a stand mixer fitted with the whisk attachment (or in a large bowl using an electric handheld mixer fitted with wire beaters) and beat on medium-high speed until they form soft peaks. Increase the speed to high and gradually add the remaining sugar. Continue beating until medium-firm peaks form, about 1 minute. Add about a quarter of the whites to the custard and whisk until just blended and lightened. Add the remaining whites and fold in gently with a large silicone spatula. Add the reserved crushed toasted coconut toward the end of folding. Pour into the prepared ramekins and gently smooth the tops.

For more about beating egg whites to medium-firm peaks, see p. 212.

For more about folding, see p. 270.

3. Bake the soufflés until puffed and risen about 1½ to 2 inches (4 to 5 cm) above the ramekin rims, about 13 minutes. Move the pan to a rack and, using wide rubber band–covered tongs, immediately move the soufflés to dessert plates. Serve immediately with warm Ruby Red Cranberry Sauce.

For more about using tongs to transfer ramekins, see p. 400.

BAKER'S WISDOM

Cranberries

As fresh cranberries are only available in the winter months, I always stow some in my freezer so they are ready to use at a moment's notice any time of the year. Rinsed, dried, and tucked into heavy-duty freezer containers or bags, they freeze well for 6 to 8 months. They can be used directly from the freezer—discard any shriveled ones first. Use whole or coarsely chop before adding them to a recipe.

Coating the ramekins with coconut

A Sprinkle some of the crushed toasted coconut into a buttered ramekin then tip the dish so the excess coats the sides. Put an uncoated buttered ramekin below the one you're working with to catch the extra coconut as it spills out.

B Continue to tip the ramekin to thoroughly coat all sides with coconut. If needed, add another pinch or two in empty spots, then tip to adhere the coconut to the butter. Gently tap out any extra coconut.

> >

Classic Strawberry Mousse

Makes 6 cups (1.4 liters) mousse; serves 8

I'm a big fan of professional tennis. I love watching all the major tournaments, but the British classic Wimbledon is my favorite. I'm captivated by the charming traditions of the fortnight tourney. Between the royal box and those seated within, the grass courts, the all-white attire, the British accents, and, of course, the all-star athletes, there's nothing that I don't love about these two weeks of tennis.

Required for the early morning broadcasts (my East Coast time is 5 hours behind London) is a serving of the classic Wimbledon fare of strawberries and clotted cream. Being a bit of a sweets and treats rebel, I have been known to take the traditional combo a step further and serve this full-flavored, ruby red mousse alongside June's best and ripest strawberries. The tennis fans in my house never object! While a morning extravagance, this mousse's true destiny is to cap off a warm summer night's meal. Served alone, it is gorgeous, luxuriant, and deceptively light. I've also paired it with sliced berries and pound cake (see the recipe on p. 274) or shortcakes (see Double Chocolate–Cherry Shortcakes on p. 577) or have layered it with crushed cookies and berries parfait-style (see p. 560). During the height of strawberry season, consider tucking some puréed berries into the freezer so you can have this mousse at the ready any time of the year.

(continued)

3 Tbs. water
1 Tbs. freshly squeezed lemon juice
1 envelope (¼ oz./7 g) unflavored
    powdered gelatin
1 lb. (454 g) strawberries, rinsed,
    dried, and hulled (about 4 cups)

½ cup (3½ oz./99 g) granulated
    sugar, divided
1 tsp. finely grated lemon zest
    (see p. 138)
Pinch of table salt
3 whites from large eggs (3 oz./85 g),
    at room temperature (see p. 371)

¼ tsp. cream of tartar
½ cup (120 ml) heavy cream,
    chilled
8 small strawberries, rinsed, dried,
    hulled, and halved, for garnish
Fresh mint sprigs, for garnish

MAKE AHEAD

The mousse can be prepared, covered, and refrigerated for up to 2 days before serving.

TWISTS

Flavor swap

> **Other berries, peaches, nectarines, apricots, or cherries:** Instead of the strawberry purée, use 1¾ cups (420 ml) of another berry, a combination of berries, or peaches, nectarines, apricots, or cherries. Process with the sugar and lemon zest in a blender and continue with the recipe as directed.

> **Super strawberry:** Concentrate the strawberry flavor by puréeing 2 lb. (907 g) of strawberries and cooking until reduced to 1¾ cups (420 ml). See the Strawberry Mascarpone Frosting on p. 290.

1. Have ready eight 8- to 10-oz. (240 to 300 ml) glasses and make room in the fridge.

2. Pour the water and lemon juice into a small heatproof ramekin (or keep it in the measuring cup) and sprinkle the gelatin evenly over the top. Set aside to soften. Once the gelatin has absorbed the liquid and is plump (about 3 minutes), microwave briefly until it is completely melted and crystal clear, 1 to 2 minutes. This can also be done in a small saucepan (instead of the ramekin) over low heat.

For more about softening gelatin, see p. 378.

3. Put the strawberries, ⅓ cup (2⅜ oz./67 g) of the granulated sugar, the lemon zest, and salt in a blender; cover and process until the strawberries are smooth and the mixture is well blended, about 1 minute, scraping down the sides once or twice. Scrape the gelatin mixture into the blender, cover, and process until well blended, about 1½ minutes, scraping down the sides once or twice. Pour into a large bowl and refrigerate, stirring frequently, until the mixture is cooled and thickened, 10 to 30 minutes. It should be as thick as unbeaten egg whites. For faster cooling, set the bowl over a larger bowl filled with ice and a little water, stirring and scraping the sides frequently.

4. Put the egg whites and cream of tartar in the bowl of a stand mixer fitted with the whisk attachment (or in a medium bowl and using an electric handheld mixer fitted with wire beaters) and beat on medium speed until the whites are frothy, 30 to 45 seconds. Increase the speed to medium high and beat until the whites form soft peaks, 1 to 2 minutes. Continue beating while gradually adding the remaining sugar, stopping occasionally to scrape down the sides of the bowl. Beat until the whites form firm and glossy peaks when the beaters are lifted.

For more about beating egg whites to firm peaks, see p. 212.

5. Put the heavy cream in a medium bowl and beat with an electric handheld mixer fitted with wire beaters (you can use the same beaters as you used for beating the whites—no need to clean) on medium speed until firm peaks form when the beaters are lifted, 2 to 3 minutes.

For more about beating cream, see p. 368.

6. Scrape the whipped cream into the chilled strawberry mixture and fold until blended. Scoop about one-quarter of the whites into the strawberry–

cream mixture and, using a silicone spatula, gently stir until blended. Add the remaining whites and gently fold in until just blended.

For more about folding, see p. 270.

7. Pour or spoon the mousse evenly into the glasses. Cover the tops with plastic wrap and refrigerate until firm, at least 6 hours.

8. When ready to serve, top each of the chilled mousses with the halved strawberries and a mint sprig.

FINISHING TOUCHES

Serve with Double Strawberry Sauce (recipe on p. 385) or Blackberry Compote (recipe on p. 383).

ESSENTIAL TECHNIQUE

Making the mousse

Pour the gelatin-strawberry mixture into a large bowl and refrigerate, stirring frequently, until the mixture is chilled and thickened. It should fall from the spatula like gelatinous, unbeaten egg whites and mound slightly (left). Too loose (on the right), and the finished mousse will lack volume.

If the mixture is overchilled and too thick, the cream and whites won't incorporate easily and you'll end up with a lumpy mousse. Before adding the beaten cream and whites, heat it gently over a double boiler (see p. 376) until it becomes more liquidy, then repeat the chilling process.

Scrape the whipped cream into the chilled strawberry mixture and fold until incorporated (left), then add about a quarter of the beaten egg whites and gently stir until just blended. Add the remaining whites and gently fold in until just blended.

Chapter 8

YEAST BREADS

> > > >

Whole-Wheat Peasant Boule

Makes 1 loaf (1¾ lb./794 g)

This is one of my favorite all-purpose breads. It makes excellent toast and delicious, soft sandwich bread that pleases even the most finicky eaters. The combination of whole-wheat flour, all-purpose flour, and a touch of wheat germ gives the bread a lovely chewy texture that is unusual for a soft bread.

Baking the bread in a springform pan on a hot baking sheet produces a well-browned loaf with a rounded top and straight sides, perfect for even slices.

2 cups (9 oz./255 g) whole-wheat flour
1⅓ cups (6 oz./170 g) unbleached all-purpose flour + more for dusting
2 Tbs. wheat germ

1 Tbs. granulated sugar
2¼ tsp. quick-rise (instant) yeast
1½ tsp. table salt
1⅓ cups water, warmed to between 115° and 125°F (45° to 52°C)

3 Tbs. (1½ oz./42 g) unsalted butter, melted
Nonstick cooking spray or neutral oil (safflower, canola, vegetable, or corn), for greasing the bowl

Make the dough

1. Put the flours, wheat germ, sugar, yeast, and salt in the bowl of a stand mixer, whisk until well blended, and fit the mixer with the dough hook. Mix on medium speed while pouring the warm water into the flour mixture. Increase the speed to medium high and beat until the dough is smooth and elastic, 4 to 6 minutes. If the dough climbs up the hook, stop the mixer and scrape the dough into the bowl as necessary. The dough will be soft and slightly sticky to the touch.

For more about scraping dough from a dough hook, see p. 449.

2. Remove the dough hook, scrape the dough onto the counter, knead once or twice, until it no longer sticks to the counter and passes the "windowpane" test, and shape into a ball. Lightly grease the sides of the bowl and put the dough, rounded side up, back in (see the Essential Technique on p. 410). Cover the bowl with a plate or plastic wrap. Let rise in a warm spot until doubled in size, about 1 hour.

For more about hand kneading, see p. 449.

For more about the windowpane test, see p. 470.

Shape the dough

Generously brush an 8-inch (20 cm) springform pan with some of the melted butter. Scrape the dough onto an unfloured work surface and press down on the dough to deflate it. Shape the dough into a round ball about 6 inches wide, making sure the top is smooth and there is no seam on the bottom. Arrange in the center of the prepared pan and cover with a domed cake keeper or a large overturned bowl. Let rise until puffed and almost doubled in size, 1 to 1½ hours (it will fill the pan and the center will rise about 2 inches/5 cm above the rim).

(continued)

TWISTS

Flavor swap

Add ⅓ cup (1⅜ oz./39 g) sunflower seeds or ⅓ cup (1⅜ oz./39 g) chopped walnuts toward the end of kneading.

(Whole-Wheat Peasant Boule continued)

Bake the bread

1. Position a rack in the center of the oven and place a half sheet pan on the rack. Heat the oven to 375°F (190°C/gas 5). Re-melt the remaining butter.

2. Brush the top of the risen bread with the butter. Bake until the top is well browned and an instant-read thermometer inserted in the center of the loaf reads 190° to 200°F (88° to 95°C), 34 to 36 minutes. Move the pan to a rack and carefully invert the pan to release the bread. Set the bread right side up and let cool for at least 1½ hours before slicing with a serrated knife. Serve warm or let cool completely, cover, and stow at room temperature for up to 3 days.

For more about checking temperature, see p. 471.

Shaping the dough

A Use a bench scraper to scrape the dough onto an unfloured work surface, then shape into a 6-inch (15 cm) ball, rotating the dough between your hands and pulling the underside of the dough with one hand while smoothing the top with the other.

B The dough will be sticky as you work. Lightly flour your fingers and hands as needed to shape the ball so it's smooth on top.

C Put the shaped round of dough in the prepared pan and cover with an overturned large bowl (I use stainless) or a domed cake keeper top (left). The dough will have doubled in size after sitting for 1 to 1½ hours (right).

Danish Pecan Ring

[PAGE 512]

112

Naan

[PAGE 527]

413

Summer Veggie Pizza

[PAGE 530]

414

Roasted Red Pepper–
Goat Cheese Whole-Wheat
Focaccia

[PAGE 545]

415

Spicy Pine Nut Kalamata Parmesan Sablés

[PAGE 548]

"Everything" Flatbread
Crackers

[PAGE 550]

417

Spicy Cheese Grissini

[PAGE 553]

418

**Brown Sugar Hazelnut Fig
Clafoutis**

[PAGE 576]

419

Double Chocolate–Cherry
Shortcakes

[PAGE 577]

420

Skillet Ginger Plum Cobbler *with* **Poppy Seed Dumplings**

[PAGE 580]

421

Sparkling Mixed Berry
Terrine

[PAGE 582]

422

Boozy Mango Brûlée

[PAGE 584]

423

Peaches *and* Cream Pavlova

[PAGE 588]

424

Melon Compote

[PAGE 591]

Mixed Berry Summer Pudding

[PAGE 592]

426

Rustic Country Bread

Makes 1 loaf (1¼ lb./567 g)   [PHOTO ON P. 334]

This bread is one of the most straightforward recipes in the book, and I would argue that it is also one of the most satisfying and delicious. All you need is five ingredients, tap water, a bit of time, and a pizza stone like my Baking Steel. Started in the morning, this bread will be ready by dinnertime, providing you with a crusty, baked round of goodness ready to dunk into stew, soup, and gravy. Don't forget to slice and toast any leftovers and spread with butter and jam for breakfast or use for sandwiches or panini.

2 cups (9 oz./255 g) bread flour
1 cup (4½ oz/128. g) unbleached all-purpose flour + more for dusting
1½ tsp. quick-rise (instant) yeast

1 tsp. granulated sugar
1½ tsp. table salt
1 cup + 2 Tbs. (270 ml) water, warmed to between 115° and 125°F (45° and 52°C)

Nonstick cooking spray or neutral oil (safflower, canola, vegetable, or corn), for greasing the bowl
Fine or coarse cornmeal, for dusting

Make the dough

1. Put the flours, yeast, sugar, and salt in the bowl of a stand mixer, whisk until well blended, and fit the mixer with a dough hook. Mix on medium speed while pouring the warm water into the flour mixture. Increase the speed to medium high and beat until the dough is smooth and elastic, 4 to 6 minutes. If the dough climbs up the hook, stop the mixer and scrape the dough into the bowl. The dough will be soft and sticky to the touch.

For more about scraping dough from a dough hook, see p. 449.

2. Remove the dough hook, scrape the dough onto the counter, knead once or twice until it no longer sticks to the counter and passes the "windowpane" test, and shape into a ball. Lightly grease the sides of the bowl and put the dough, rounded side up, back in. Cover the bowl with a plate or plastic wrap. Let rise in a warm spot until doubled in size, 2 to 3 hours.

For more about hand kneading, see p. 449.

For more about the windowpane test, see p. 470.

Shape the dough

Generously dust a pizza peel or cookie sheet with cornmeal. Scrape the dough onto an unfloured work surface and press down on the dough to deflate it. Shape the dough into a round ball about 6 inches (15 cm) wide, making sure the top is smooth and there is no seam on the bottom (see the Essential Technique on p. 428). Arrange on the peel and cover with a large overturned bowl or cake cover. Let the dough rise until puffed and almost doubled in size, 2 to 2½ hours.

Bake the bread

1. Position a rack in the bottom third of the oven and set a pizza stone on the rack. Heat the oven to 450°F (230°C/gas 8) for at least 20 minutes. Fill a spray bottle with water.

(continued)

BAKER'S WISDOM

Pay attention during bread making

Two things I'd like you to pay close attention to when making this bread: First, the water (1 cup + 2 Tbs./270 ml) is the exact amount to pair with the flour. Any less and the dough will be on the dry side and difficult to shape. Any more and you'll end up with a sticky dough.

Second, one of my favorite parts of baking this type of crusty loaf is paying attention to it when it's fresh from the oven. Sitting on the rack, the crust begins to crackle as it cools; I like to think the bread is "singing." Listen for it next time—I hope it makes you smile.

2. Dust the top of the loaf with 2 or 3 Tbs. flour and, using a razor or long, very sharp knife, cut 4 slits across the top of the dough, about ½ inch (12 mm) deep, in a tic-tac-toe design. Slide the bread from the peel onto the stone and, using the spray bottle, spritz the inside of the oven several times.

3. Bake until the loaf is deep golden brown and an instant-read thermometer inserted in the center reads 190° to 200°F (88° to 95°C), 32 to 35 minutes. Slide the bread onto the peel or cookie sheet and move to a rack. Let cool for at least 1 hour before slicing with a serrated knife.

For more about checking temperature, see p. 471.

ESSENTIAL TECHNIQUE

Shaping the dough

A

Use a bench scraper to scrape the dough onto an unfloured work surface. Cup your hands slightly around the dough with the bottom edges of your palms, pressing gently but firmly inward toward the bottom of the dough. Keeping pressure on the bottom edge of your palms, slide your right hand from the front to the back. This will rotate the dough while keeping the top side up. Repeat until you've formed a smooth-skinned ball with a sealed bottom.

B

Here are two close-up, slightly exaggerated looks at the motion of the edges of hands pressing inward then rotating to close the seam on the bottom while creating a tight-skinned top.

C

Arrange the dough on the prepared peel toward the front (for easier sliding off the peel), then cover with a large overturned bowl or a cake cover. Be sure the bowl is large enough to accommodate the dough's rising. Let stand until the dough is almost doubled in size.

Braided Challah Round

Makes 1 loaf (1¾ lb./794 g)   [PHOTO ON P. 335]

Much like French brioche, Jewish challah bread is noted for its stunning appearance along with its velvety, soft texture. While traditionally made for holiday gatherings like Rosh Hashanah or the Shabbat, this bread is so scrumptious that you'll make baking it a weekly habit. Honey lends a mellow sweetness to this soft, egg-rich bread.

The intricately woven braid looks impossible to create but it's easier than it looks. The step-by-step photos on pp. 432–433 will guide even less experienced bakers to success. The secret is to plan ahead and put aside plenty of time for braiding (rushing through this stage will end in disappointment) and rising.

For a different shape, try the turban-shaped challah in Twists on p. 431 (the recipe makes two loaves in this shape). This style is traditionally served at Rosh Hashanah. These smaller loaves are also perfect for serving a small group, with one to freeze for later. I use two round cake pans for baking the turbans. They don't affect the shape of the finished bread but simply allow the loaves to bake together on the same oven rack.

3¾ cups (16⅞ oz./479 g) unbleached all-purpose flour
2¼ tsp. quick-rise (instant) yeast
1¾ tsp. table salt
½ cup (120 ml) water, warmed to between 115° and 125°F (45° to 52°C)

¼ cup (60 ml) neutral oil (safflower, canola, vegetable, or corn)
⅓ cup (80 ml) honey
2 whole large eggs, at room temperature

3 yolks from large eggs, at room temperature (see p. 371)
Nonstick cooking spray or neutral oil (safflower, canola, vegetable, or corn), for greasing the bowl
1 egg, lightly beaten, for the egg wash

Make the dough

1. Put the flour, yeast, and salt in the bowl of a stand mixer, whisk until well blended, and fit the mixer with a dough hook. With the mixer on medium-low speed, add the warm water, oil, and honey along with the eggs and yolks. Mix on medium speed, scraping down the bowl as necessary, until the flour is completely incorporated, about 2 minutes. Increase the speed to medium high and beat until the dough is smooth and slightly sticky (some dough will still be stuck to the bottom and sides of the bowl), 9 to 11 minutes. If the dough climbs up the hook or sticks to the side of the bowl, stop the mixer and scrape the dough into the bowl as necessary.

For more about scraping dough from a dough hook, see p. 449.

2. Using a plastic, rounded bench scraper, scrape the dough onto an unfloured surface. With the bench scraper in one hand, work the dough by lifting it up and over itself several times until it is smooth, supple, and no longer sticking to the surface and shape it into a ball. Lightly grease the sides of the bowl and put the dough, rounded side up, back in. Cover the bowl with a plate or plastic wrap and let rise in a warm spot until doubled in size, 1½ to 2 hours.

(continued)

(Braided Challah Round continued)

Shape the braid

1. Have ready a cookie sheet lined with parchment or a nonstick liner. Scrape the dough onto an unfloured work surface and press down on the dough to deflate it. Using a bench scraper or knife, portion the dough into four equal pieces. Working with one piece of dough at a time, gently stretch the dough and roll back and forth on the surface until you've formed a rope that is 14 inches (35.5 cm) long (see the Essential Technique on pp. 432–433). Repeat with the remaining pieces of dough.

For more about deflating risen dough, see p. 477.

2. Arrange the ropes like a tic-tac-toe board, spacing them 1 inch (2.5 cm) apart, with two ends pointing toward you (A1 and A2—starting with the right one), two pointing to the left (B1 and B2), two pointing away from you (C1 and C2), and the remaining two pointing to the right (D1 and D2). Lift D2 and arrange A1 underneath and reposition D2. Lift B2 and arrange C1 underneath and reposition B2. Leave about 1 inch (2.5 cm) in the center open.

3. Moving clockwise and keeping the ropes close together, weave the ropes together as follows: Lift A1 over A2, B1 over B2, C1 over C2, and D1 over D2. This completes one rotation. Beginning with A2 (the end that is facing you), reverse direction (counter clockwise) and repeat the pattern of lifting the rope that is underneath over the one to its right. Reverse direction and repeat one more time. Pinch the rope ends together and gather them over the center of the braid and pinch well to seal (see pp. 432–433). Using your palms, lift the braided dough, turn upside down, and arrange on the prepared cookie sheet.

Rise and bake the bread

1. Cover the dough with an overturned large bowl or domed cake keeper and let it rise in a warm spot until doubled, 60 to 90 minutes. After about 1 hour, position a rack in the center of the oven and heat the oven to 350°F (180°C/gas 4); continue to let the dough rise.

For more about covering dough, see p. 428.

2. When the oven is heated and the dough is doubled, uncover and brush the top with some of the egg wash. Bake until the bread is browned and an instant-read thermometer inserted into the side and reaching the center reads 190° to 200°F (88° to 95°C), 37 to 40 minutes. Cover the bread loosely with foil during baking if it browns too much before it is cooked through. Move the sheet to a rack and let cool for about 10 minutes, then use a spatula to lift the loaf from the sheet and onto a rack until completely cooled.

For more about checking temperature, see p. 471.

Flavor swap

> Add sesame or poppy seeds: Just after applying the egg wash, evenly sprinkle 2 Tbs. of sesame or poppy seeds over the top.

> Add raisins (turban): After the first rise, scrape the dough onto an unfloured work surface, gently press down to deflate the dough, and divide the dough in half. Working with one piece of dough at a time, use a rolling pin to roll the dough into a 1/2-inch (12 mm) thick rectangle about 6 inches (15 cm) long. With one long side facing you, evenly scatter 1/2 cup (2 1/2 oz./71 g) golden (or dark) raisins lengthwise down the middle of the rectangle. Beginning with the long side closest to you, tightly roll the dough jellyroll style, pinching the edge to seal. Repeat with the remaining dough and more raisins. Proceed with the directions for shaping and baking two challah turbans.

Re-size it

> Make two turban-shaped challahs:

1. Lightly grease two 9-inch springform or 9 x 2-inch (23 x 5 cm) round cake pans. Scrape the risen dough onto an unfloured work surface and press down on the dough to deflate it. Using a bench scraper or knife, cut the dough in half. Working with one piece of dough at a time, gently stretch the dough and roll back and forth on the surface until you've formed a 20-inch (50 cm) long rope with one tapered end. The thicker end should be about 1 1/2 inches (4 cm) and the tapered end about 3/4 inch (2 cm).

2. Turn the nontapered end inward to begin making the spiral snail-shell shape. Holding the tapered end, coil the rope around the center and tuck the end under the spiral, turn the dough over in your hand, and pinch to seal. Put the spiral in the center of one of the pans and lightly grease the surface. Lightly flour your index finger and press down into the middle of the spiral to seal the center seam. Repeat with the remaining dough. Let the dough rise as directed. It will double in size but it won't fill the pans.

3. Brush the loaves with egg wash and bake at 350°F (180°C/gas 4) until deep golden brown and an instant-read thermometer inserted into the side and reaching the center reads 190° to 200°F (88° to 95°C), 30 to 35 minutes. Move the pans to a rack and let cool for about 10 minutes, then use a spatula to lift the loaves from the pans and onto a rack until completely cooled.

For a matte finish: Instead of using an egg wash, substitute 3 Tbs. neutral oil (safflower, canola, vegetable, or corn) and brush over the surface of the dough as directed.

Time and temperature for rising

As a yeast dough rises, the gluten stretches and strengthens to help create the finished structure of this bread. Most doughs rise at least twice before baking—once after mixing and once after shaping. Usually the rise is until the dough doubles in size; sometimes, as in the case of croissants, the dough only partially rises before baking.

Judging how much time that will take depends on your kitchen's temperature. Ideal rising temperature is between 75° and 80°F (24° to 27°C) with little or no breeze passing through but, if your kitchen is like mine, the temperature is never close. In wintertime, it tends to be colder and in summertime, it tends to be much warmer, so your timing will change accordingly. In hopes of controlling the temperature, I close off my office and turn on the lights, but a closet or cabinet with a light will also work as a makeshift proofing box.

(continued)

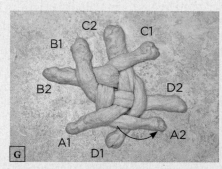

ESSENTIAL TECHNIQUE

Shaping the braid

A

Working on an unfloured surface, roll out the four pieces of dough into 14-inch (35.5 cm) long ropes.

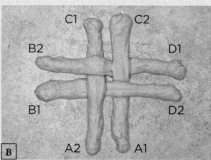

B

Space the ropes 1 inch (2.5 cm) apart and arrange like a tic-tac-toe board, positioning the ropes over and under each other and leaving just 1 inch of empty space in the center.

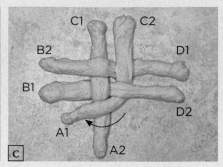

C

Keep the ropes together as you work, weaving A1 over A2.

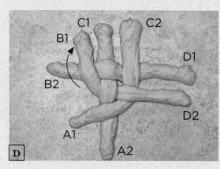

D

Position B1 over B2.

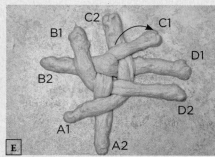

E

Position C1 over C2.

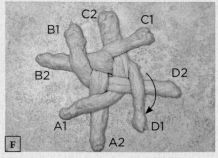

F

Position D1 over D2, which completes one rotation.

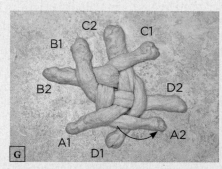

G

Reverse direction and position A2 over D1.

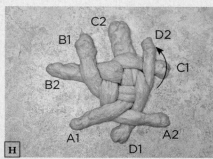

H

Position D2 over C1.

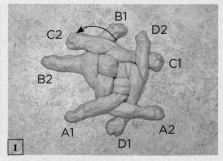

I

Position C2 over B1.

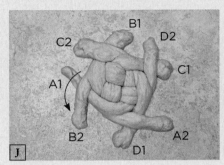

J

Position B2 over A1.

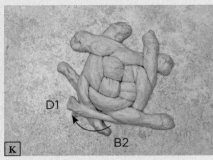

K

Reversing direction one more time, repeat the sequence, positioning D1 over B2.

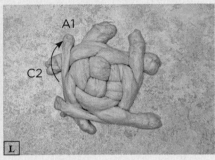

L

Position A1 over C2.

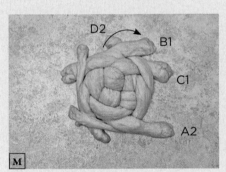

M

Position B1 over D2.

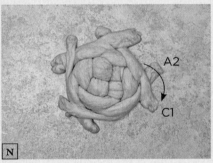

N

Position C1 over A2.

O

With the braiding complete, pinch the ends of the ropes together, pulling them toward the center in a bundle. Pinch to seal.

P

Turn the braided dough upside down, with the braid facing up, and place on the prepared baking sheet.

Sweet Potato Bread

Makes 1 loaf (1¾ lb./794 g)   [PHOTO ON P. 336]

I have a weakness for soft, rich breads, and this one is no exception. In fact, this sweet potato bread takes me beyond "weakness" and straight into "wildly obsessed." Its deep yellow–orange color is swoon-worthy, and one bite of this honey-sweetened, pumpkin seed–studded loaf and you will be hooked. It's a perfect pairing for chilis or stews, and leftovers are delicious toasted and slathered with butter and honey.

The interior color of the bread depends entirely on the color of the sweet potato you use. For this reason, I prefer to use Garnet sweet potatoes, with their deep orange flesh. However, the flavors of the different types of sweet potato aren't incredibly distinct, so if you can't find the Garnet variety, use whatever type is available.

Shaping this loaf is a snap. Simply press the risen dough into a rectangle, roll it up like a jellyroll, pinch the seams, and pop it into the pan. You'll need to use a large, 10 x 5-inch (25 x 12 cm) loaf pan that has a capacity of 8 cups (2 liters). (Standard Pyrex loaf pans hold 6 cups, so they are too small.) Squeezing the dough into a smaller pan will cause it to burst up and out of the pan during baking. The bread will still taste the same but it won't look nearly as pretty.

1 large (1½ lb./680 g) sweet
   potato (preferably Garnet),
   scrubbed and dried
6 Tbs. (3 oz./85 g) unsalted butter,
   divided
2 Tbs. honey

4 cups (18 oz./511 g) unbleached
   all-purpose flour
1¾ tsp. quick-rise (instant) yeast
1½ tsp. table salt
⅓ cup (80 ml) sour cream
1 large egg, at room temperature

½ cup (2 oz./57 g) unsalted
   pumpkin seeds
Nonstick cooking spray or neutral
   oil (safflower, canola, vegetable, or
   corn), for greasing the bowl

MAKE AHEAD

> The bread can be baked, cooled, covered, and stowed at room temperature for up to 5 days or wrapped tightly and frozen for up to 1 week. To freeze, wrap the bread in plastic and put in a large zip-top freezer bag. To thaw, unwrap the bread and set on a rack at room temperature for 1 to 2 hours.

> The sweet potato purée can be cooled completely, covered, and refrigerated for up to 2 days or frozen for up to 3 months before proceeding with the recipe.

Make the sweet potato purée

1. Position a rack in the center of the oven and heat the oven to 425°F (220°C/gas 7). Using the tines of a fork, prick the skin of the sweet potato several times. Put it on a small foil-lined cookie sheet and bake until very tender when pierced with a small knife, 55 to 60 minutes. Move the cookie sheet to a rack and let cool until the potato is just cool enough to handle, 10 to 15 minutes.

2. Make a long cut down the top of the potato and push the ends toward the middle to open it up. Using a spoon, scoop the flesh into a medium bowl and mash until almost smooth.

Make the dough

1. Scoop out 1⅓ cups (10⅝ oz./301 g) packed sweet potato purée and put it in a small saucepan over medium-low heat with 4 Tbs. (2 oz./ 57 g) of the butter, cut into pieces, and the honey. Cook, stirring constantly, until the butter melts and the mixture is about 115°F (45°C). (This can also be done in the microwave.) Put the flour, yeast, and salt in the bowl of a stand mixer, whisk until well blended, and fit the mixer with a dough hook. With the mixer on medium-low speed, pour the warm sweet potato mixture into the flour along with the sour cream and egg and beat until completely incorporated. Add the pumpkin seeds, increase the speed to medium high, and beat until the dough is smooth and shiny, 5 to 8 minutes. If the dough climbs up the hook, stop the mixer and scrape the dough into the bowl as necessary. The dough will pull away completely from the sides and bottom of the bowl and it will be soft and slightly sticky to the touch.

2. Remove the dough hook, scrape the dough onto the counter, knead once or twice until it no longer sticks to the counter and passes the windowpane test, and shape into a ball. Lightly grease the sides of the bowl and put the dough, rounded side up, back in. Cover the bowl with a plate or plastic wrap. Let rise in a warm spot until doubled in size, about 1 hour.

For more about hand kneading, see p. 449.

For more about the windowpane test, see p. 470.

3. Lightly grease a 10 x 5-inch (25 x 12 cm) loaf pan (8 cups/2 liters). Scrape the dough onto an unfloured work surface and press down on the dough to deflate it. Gently press and shape the dough into a 5 x 10-inch (12 x 25 cm) rectangle, about 1¾ inches (4.5 cm) thick. Starting at one of the short sides, roll up like a jellyroll and pinch the ends closed to form a smooth, rounded top. Place it seam side down in the prepared pan. Press on the dough to flatten and fill the pan in an even layer.

For more about deflating risen dough, see p. 477.

4. Cover the pan loosely (to allow for rising) but completely with plastic and let the dough rise in a warm spot until the top of the loaf reaches the rim of the pan, 30 to 45 minutes. Position a rack in the center of the oven and heat the oven to 350°F (180°C/gas 4); continue to let the dough rise.

For more about working with plastic wrap, see p. 546.

5. When the oven is heated and the dough is risen to about 1 inch above the pan in the center, remove the plastic. Melt the remaining 2 Tbs. (1 oz./28 g) butter and brush it on the top of the bread. Using a razor (lame) or long, very sharp knife, cut a long slit, about ½ inch (12 mm) deep, down the center length of the loaf. Bake until the loaf is browned and an instant-read thermometer inserted in the center of the loaf reads 195° to 200°F (91° to 95°C), 40 to 45 minutes. Move the pan to a rack and let cool for about 20 minutes, then tip the loaf onto a rack, lift off the pan, and set the loaf on its side until completely cooled.

For more about checking temperature, see p. 471.

(continued)

TWISTS

Flavor swap

> Herb-flavored: Add ¾ cup (1 oz./ 28 g) lightly packed, chopped fresh herbs (I like a combination of chives, parsley, basil, and dill) to the dough just as it is beginning to pull up from the bottom of the bowl. Continue kneading until the herbs are well blended and the dough is smooth.

> Nutty: Instead of the pumpkin seeds, add the same amount of sunflower seeds or medium-fine chopped walnuts and proceed as directed.

> Potato bread: Instead of using sweet potato purée, use the same amount of mashed baked potato. Use 3½ cups (15¾ oz./446 g) unbleached all-purpose flour, ¾ cup (180 ml) sour cream, and keep the remaining ingredients the same. Proceed as directed.

(Sweet Potato Bread continued)

Sweet potatoes

Sweet, moist, and typically orange, this root vegetable is often and incorrectly called a yam. True yams are starchy and dry with white flesh and thick, dark skin; they are not available in most grocery stores. Sweet potatoes have thin, edible skins and come in many shapes and colors, from the more common orange-fleshed varieties to yellow- and even purple-fleshed ones. Rich in beta carotene, vitamin C, and good carbohydrates, sweet potatoes come into season in late summer and are available right through spring, but they're at their best in the fall and early winter. Choose firm, unblemished sweet potatoes and store in a cool, dark place for up to 3 or 4 months.

ESSENTIAL TECHNIQUE

Shaping the loaf

A

Once the dough has doubled in size, scrape it onto an unfloured work surface.

B

Gently press on the dough to deflate it while gently shaping it into a 5 x 10-inch (12 x 25 cm) rectangle that's about 1¾ inches (4.5 cm) thick.

C

Starting at one of the short sides of the dough rectangle, roll it up like a jellyroll.

D

Pinch the ends of the dough to seal.

E

Put the dough, seam side down, into the prepared pan, pressing down on the dough to flatten it and fill the pan in an even layer. To allow for rising, cover the pan loosely (but completely) with plastic wrap.

F

After rising, brush the top with the remaining melted butter and then, using a long, very sharp knife, cut a long slit, about ½ inch (12 mm) deep, down the center length of the loaf.

Grossie's Stöllen

Makes 1 loaf (2½ lb./1.2 kg) [PHOTO ON P. 337]

When I decided to include a traditional stöllen in this book, I reached out to my dear friend Jennifer Smith and her mother, Juli Towell, with hope that they would share their long-held family recipe. I am grateful they were not only willing to share their family treasure but also to abide some changes I made to reduce and modernize the recipe.

A note from Juli: "My mother always said it was pronounced by shaping your mouth as if you were going to say 'O' and then say 'E.' So it isn't stolen, like a thief. This recipe for stöllen comes from my great grandmother, Elizabeth Ruhr Lueke, known in the family as Grossie. She brought it with her from Germany in the 1870s 'in her apron pocket' when she came to Cleveland, Ohio, with her doctor husband. Before you could buy almonds already peeled and chopped, my small children and I would soak the almonds until the skin loosened and then pop them at each other, a hilarious and messy process. Citron only came in hunks and I would find a German delicatessen and have it weighed out. I hope you have fun making it and enjoy the results."

For the dried fruit
⅔ cup (3⅜ oz./96 g) golden raisins
½ cup (3 oz./85 g) candied citron
⅔ cup (2⅝ oz./74 g) slivered almonds
2 Tbs. dark rum
1 tsp. finely grated lemon zest (see p. 138)
1 tsp. finely grated orange zest
½ tsp. ground cinnamon
⅛ tsp. ground nutmeg

For the sponge
¼ cup (1⅛ oz./32 g) unbleached all-purpose flour
2¼ tsp. active dry yeast
¾ tsp. granulated sugar
¼ cup (60 ml) whole milk, at room temperature or slightly warm (not cold)

For the dough
½ cup (120 ml) whole milk
6 Tbs. (3 oz./85 g) unsalted butter, cut into 8 pieces

3¼ cups (14⅝ oz./415 g) unbleached all-purpose flour
½ cup (3½ oz./99 g) granulated sugar
1 Tbs. quick-rise (instant) yeast
¾ tsp. table salt
1 yolk from a large egg (see p. 371)

Nonstick cooking spray or neutral oil (safflower, canola, vegetable, or corn), for greasing the bowl
3 Tbs. (1½ oz./42 g) unsalted butter, melted, for brushing after baking

Mix the fruit
Put the raisins, citron, almonds, rum, lemon and orange zests, cinnamon, and nutmeg in a medium bowl and stir until well blended.

Make the sponge
Put the flour, active dry yeast, and sugar in the bowl of a stand mixer and stir with a silicone spatula until well blended. Add the milk and mix until blended. The dough will be very thick and pasty. Cover with plastic wrap and set aside until bubbly, 15 to 20 minutes.

For more about making the sponge, see p. 470.

Make the dough
1. Heat the milk until very hot but not boiling. (I do this in a Pyrex measure in the microwave, but a small pan on the stovetop will also work.)

(continued)

(Grossie's Stöllen continued)

MAKE AHEAD

> The bread can be baked, cooled, covered, and stowed at room temperature for up to 7 days or wrapped tightly and frozen for up to 1 month. To freeze, wrap the bread in plastic and put in a large zip-top freezer bag. To thaw, unwrap the bread and set on a rack at room temperature for 1 to 2 hours.

> The dried fruit mixture can be mixed, covered, and stowed at room temperature for up to 24 hours.

TWISTS

Flavor swap

> Instead of the golden raisins, use the same amount of dried cranberries or cherries.

> Instead of the almonds, use the same amount of walnuts or pistachios.

> Instead of the citron, use the same amount of candied lemon or orange peel or a combination of both.

Add the butter and stir until melted. Check the temperature using an instant-read thermometer. For the yeast to activate, the liquid needs to be between 115° and 125°F (45° and 52°C).

2. Uncover the sponge and add the flour, sugar, yeast, and salt along with the milk–butter mixture and egg yolk. Fit the mixer with the dough hook and mix on medium speed until well blended. Add the fruit and mix until incorporated. Increase the speed to medium and beat until the dough is smooth and slightly sticky, 9 to 11 minutes. It will be stiff at first but will loosen as it is kneaded. If the dough climbs up the hook or sticks to the side of the bowl, stop the mixer and scrape the dough into the bowl as necessary.

For more about scraping dough from a dough hook, see p. 449.

3. Remove the dough hook, scrape the dough onto the counter, knead once or twice until it no longer sticks to the counter and passes the windowpane test, and shape into a ball. Lightly grease the sides of the bowl and put the dough, rounded side up, back in. Cover the bowl with a plate or plastic wrap. Let rise in a warm spot until doubled in size, 2 to 3 hours (see the Essential Technique on the facing page).

For more about hand kneading, see p. 449.

For more about the windowpane test, see p. 470.

Shape, proof, and bake the dough

1. Have ready a cookie sheet lined with parchment or a nonstick liner. Scrape the dough onto the center of the cookie sheet and press down on the dough to deflate it. Press and gently shape the dough into a 7 x 10-inch (17 x 25 cm) oval. Lift one long side up and over the dough, leaving about ¾ inch (2 cm) of the bottom dough showing. Reshape the dough as needed to form a half-moon shape.

2. Cover the dough loosely (to allow for rising) but completely with plastic and let the dough rise in a warm spot until lightened and slightly risen, 2 to 3 hours. After about 1¾ hours, position a rack in the center of the oven and heat the oven to 350°F (180°C/gas 4); continue to let the dough rise.

For more about working with plastic wrap, see p. 546.

3. When the oven is heated and the dough is risen to about 11½ inches (29 cm) long, 5½ inches (14 cm) at its widest point, and about 2½ inches (6 cm) tall, remove the plastic and bake until the bread is deep golden brown and an instant-read thermometer inserted in the side and reaching the center reads 190°F/88°C, 38 to 42 minutes. Move the sheet to a rack, brush liberally with the melted butter, and let cool for 10 minutes. Using a large metal spatula, move the loaf to a rack and let cool completely.

For more about checking temperature, see p. 471.

Shaping the dough

A

B

After the first kneading, the dough needs to rise in a warm spot for 2 to 3 hours. The dough has risen completely and is ready for the second knead when it has doubled in size. Use your eyes as the guide rather than the clock.

Scrape the dough onto a nonstick liner and press gently to deflate it.

C

D

Continue to press the dough gently with your fingertips until it's shaped into a 7 x 10-inch (17 x 25 cm) oval. Use a ruler to check the size.

Gently lift one long side up and over the dough, forming what looks like a clamshell and leaving about ¾ inch (2 cm) of the bottom dough uncovered. If needed, reshape gently to form a half-moon.

Pretzels

Makes 12 pretzels   [PHOTO ON P. 338]

The city street smelling of warm pretzels and roasted chestnuts is synonymous with my Brooklyn childhood. One whiff of a passing pretzel truck takes me back to simpler days filled with walks with my mom and our basset hound, Dutch, to the grocery store on Montague Street and roller skating (me, not Mom) or hopscotching on the promenade with my childhood pals. Dusted with coarse salt, cinnamon-sugar, or "everything," these soft, flavorful pretzels harken back to those sweet days. I hope they conjure up happy childhood memories for you and create new ones for the youngsters in your life.

I include a touch of rye flour in the dough to add just the right amount of earthy flavor to the boiled and baked pretzels. The yield is on the smaller side (12) as I think these pretzels are best eaten the same day they are made. And while mustard is the classic pairing, I like to swipe them through a bowl of freshly made guacamole or hummus.

For the dough
2½ cups (11¼ oz./319 g) unbleached all-purpose flour
1 cup (4½ oz./128 g) whole-wheat flour
¼ cup (1⅛ oz./32 g) medium rye flour
2¼ tsp. quick-rise (instant) yeast
1 Tbs. firmly packed dark or light brown sugar
1½ tsp. table salt
1⅓ cups (320 ml) water, warmed to between 115° and 125°F (45° and 52°C)
3 Tbs. (1½ oz./42 g) unsalted butter, melted

Nonstick cooking spray or neutral oil (safflower, canola, vegetable, or corn), for greasing the bowl

For the boiling and topping
1 large egg
1 Tbs. water
¼ cup (1¾ oz./50 g) baking soda
Pretzel salt or very coarse salt

Make the dough

1. Put the flours, yeast, brown sugar, and salt in the bowl of a stand mixer, whisk until well blended, and fit the mixer with the dough hook. Mix on medium speed while pouring the warm water into the flour mixture. Add the melted butter and mix on medium speed until the flour is completely incorporated. Increase the speed to medium high and beat until the dough is smooth and pulls away from the sides and bottom of the bowl, 4 to 6 minutes. If the dough climbs up the hook, stop the mixer and scrape the dough into the bowl as necessary. The dough will be soft and sticky to the touch.

For more about scraping dough from a dough hook, see p. 449.

2. Remove the dough hook, scrape the dough onto the counter, knead once or twice until it no longer sticks to the counter and passes the windowpane test, and shape into a ball. Lightly grease the sides of the bowl and put the dough, rounded side up, back in. Cover the bowl with a plate or plastic wrap and let rise in a warm spot until doubled in size, about 45 minutes.

For more about hand kneading, see p. 449.

For more about the windowpane test, see p. 470.

Shape the dough

1. Line two cookie sheets with nonstick liners (parchment won't work here). Scrape the dough onto an unfloured work surface and press down on the dough to deflate it. Using a bench scraper or knife, portion the dough into 12 equal pieces (about 2⅜ oz./67 g each). Working with one piece of dough at a time and keeping the remaining pieces loosely covered with plastic wrap, gently stretch the dough and roll it back and forth on the unfloured work surface, starting in the middle and working outward until it forms a 25-inch (63.5 cm) long rope.

For more about deflating risen dough, see p. 477.

For more about rolling dough into a rope, see p. 432.

2. To make the pretzel shape, pull the ends of the rope toward you, forming a wide U shape at the top. Cross the ends over each other twice then pull the ends up and over the pretzel, laying each about 1½ inches (4 cm) apart and slightly over the U (see the Essential Technique on p. 442). Arrange on a prepared sheet, about 2 inches (5 cm) apart, and reshape as needed. Cover loosely but completely with plastic wrap while you shape the remaining dough. Arrange the pretzels on the cookie sheet 2 inches (5 cm) from one another. Let the pretzels rise until puffed and almost double in size, about 45 minutes.

For more about working with plastic wrap, see p. 546.

Cook the pretzels

1. While the dough is rising, pour enough water into a large pot (I use a 4-quart/4 liter Dutch oven) to fill it to a 3½-inch (9 cm) depth and bring to a boil over high heat. (If the water boils before the pretzels have risen, cover the pot and reduce the heat to low.) Position a rack in the center of the oven and heat the oven to 425°F (220°C/gas 7). Put the egg and water in a small bowl and, using a fork, mix until well blended.

2. When the first sheet of pretzel dough is ready, return the water to a boil, if necessary, and slowly add the baking soda. Be careful—it will bubble and splatter. Carefully (don't pinch or the dough will collapse) slip two pretzels into the boiling water and cook, turning once with a skimmer or spider until puffed and slightly darker looking, 45 seconds per side. With a skimmer, spider, or slotted spoon, remove the pretzels from the water and return to the cookie sheet (they will be much closer together after boiling). Brush the surface generously with the egg wash and sprinkle with some of the pretzel salt. Repeat with the remaining pretzels on the sheet.

3. Once all of the pretzels have been boiled, bake the first sheet until they are deep golden brown, 15 to 18 minutes. Move the sheet to a rack. While the first sheet is baking, repeat the boiling and baking with the remaining pretzels. Serve warm or let cool completely, cover, and stow at room temperature for up to 2 days.

(continued)

TWISTS

Flavor swap

> **Cinnamon-sugar:** Make and shape the dough as directed. After boiling, do not brush the pretzels with the egg wash. Bake as directed and let cool slightly, then lightly brush the tops with some melted butter and dip into cinnamon-sugar (recipe on p. 197).

> **"Everything":** Make and shape the dough as directed. After boiling, brush the pretzels with the egg wash and sprinkle with some of the everything mix (see Everything Flatbread Crackers on p. 550). Bake as directed and cool.

Re-size it

Small: Make the dough as directed. Portion the risen dough into 24 equal pieces (about 1⅛ oz./32 g each) and shape into 15-inch (38 cm) long ropes. Continue as directed for shaping and rising. Boil for 30 seconds per side, then top and bake as directed.

Shaping the pretzels

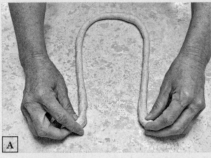

A

With the dough shaped into a 25-inch (63.5 cm) long rope, form it into a U shape, positioning it so the rounded side is facing you.

B

Cross the ends over each other twice, making sure they are at the same length after crossing.

C

Pull the ends up and lay them slightly over the outside of the U shape. Keep the ends about 1½ inches (4 cm) apart at the top of the U. Carefully pick up the pretzel and move it to the prepared baking sheet; reshape if needed and cover loosely with plastic while you shape the remaining dough pieces.

D

Once the shaped pretzels have risen, cook two at a time in a large pot of boiling water. Place in the water one at a time, gently slipping it in without pinching the dough and ruining the shape.

E

Boil the pretzels on the first side until puffed and the underside is slightly darker looking, about 45 seconds, then use a skimmer or slotted spoon to carefully flip them to the other side. Boil for another 45 seconds.

F

Lift the pretzels one at a time from the water and transfer to the cookie sheet. Continue boiling the rest of the pretzels before finishing in the oven.

Ciabatta

Makes 1 loaf (1½ lb./680 g)

If you've never had ciabatta, then you are in for a treat. The open-holed, chewy texture is stunning and, thanks to the slow-rising process, the flavor is earthy and rich.

Most bread dough is kneaded by hand or in a stand mixer until it pulls away from the bowl or counter and passes the telltale windowpane test. But ciabatta (and my baguette recipe on p. 458) has such a high percentage of water to flour, it's impossible to follow the same rules. While the very sticky, wet dough begins in the stand mixer, the similarities end there, as the majority of kneading takes place throughout the rising process. Instead of traditional kneading, which would be impossible, the wet dough is pulled and folded over onto itself to develop and lengthen the gluten. This stretching and folding is done twice over the course of the dough rising to about double its size.

For the sponge
⅔ cup (3 oz./85 g) unbleached all-purpose flour
¼ tsp. active dry yeast
½ cup (120 ml) whole milk, room temperature or slightly warm (not cold)

For the dough
1 cup (240 ml) warm (not hot) water
¼ tsp. quick-rise (instant) yeast
1½ cups (6¾ oz./191 g) unbleached all-purpose flour + more for the pan
1½ cups (6¾ oz./191 g) unbleached bread flour

1¾ tsp. table salt
1 tsp. granulated sugar
Nonstick cooking spray or neutral oil (safflower, canola, vegetable, or corn), for greasing the bowl

Make the sponge

Put the flour and active dry yeast in the bowl of a stand mixer and stir with a silicone spatula until well blended. Add the milk and stir until blended; scrape down the sides. The sponge will be very thick and pasty. Cover and set aside until bubbly, 60 to 75 minutes, or refrigerate overnight.

For more about making the sponge, see p. 470.

Make the dough

1. Uncover the sponge and add the water, followed by the quick-rise yeast, both of the flours, the salt, and sugar. Fit the mixer with the dough hook and mix on medium speed until the dough comes together. Continue mixing on medium speed until the dough is smooth and shiny, 5 to 7 minutes. The dough will not pull away from the sides and bottom of the bowl and it will be very sticky.

2. Remove the dough hook and, using wet hands, scrape the dough off the hook and back into the bowl. Lightly grease the sides of the bowl (the dough is too sticky to pull from the bowl) and cover with a plate or plastic wrap. Let rise in a warm spot until it has risen about 50%, about 1 hour. It won't be doubled in size. Using one wet hand, pull one part of the dough away from the bowl and lift it up and over the dough, tucking it into the center. Turn the bowl about a quarter of the way around, rewet your hand, and pull the dough away from the edge and over the dough, and tuck it

(Ciabatta continued)

MAKE AHEAD

The bread can be baked, cooled, covered, and stowed at room temperature for 2 days or wrapped tightly and frozen for up to 1 month. To freeze, wrap the bread in plastic and put in a large zip-top freezer bag. To thaw, unwrap the bread, set it on a rack, and thaw at room temperature for 1 to 2 hours.

into the center. Repeat this process all the way around the bowl, rewetting your hand as you work (see the Essential Technique on the facing page).

3. Cover the bowl with a plate or plastic wrap and let the dough rise in a warm spot until it has risen about 50%, about 1 hour. Repeat the lift and tuck process, cover, and let the dough rise until it is doubled in size from its original height, about 1 to 1½ hours.

Shape, rise, and bake the dough

1. Line a cookie sheet with parchment and coat it generously with flour. Using wet fingers, release the dough from the edge of the bowl, rewetting as needed. Wet both hands and slide them under the dough down to the bottom of the bowl. Scoop and lift up the dough from the bottom—it's slippery so work quickly—and hold it over the center of the prepared cookie sheet. Spreading your hands—and therefore the dough—apart, allow the dough to fall to the parchment into a long oval that's 13 inches (33 cm) long and 5 inches (12 cm) wide.

2. Generously sprinkle the dough with flour, cover loosely (to allow for rising) but completely with plastic, and let the dough rise in a warm spot until lightened and slightly risen, 1 to 1½ hours. After about 45 minutes, position a rack in the bottom third of the oven and set a pizza stone on the rack. Heat the oven to 450°F (230°C/gas 8) and continue to let the dough rise.

For more about working with plastic wrap, see p. 546.

3. When the oven is heated and the dough is risen, remove the plastic. Using the cookie sheet as a peel, slide the loaf, parchment and all, onto the baking stone and bake until the bread is deep brown and an instant-read thermometer inserted in the side and reaching the center reads 190°F (88°C), 33 to 35 minutes. Use a peel or cookie sheet to move the bread to a rack and let cool for about 10 minutes. When cool enough to handle, peel away the parchment (it will crumble a bit) and continue to let the bread cool.

For more about checking temperature, see p. 471.

BAKER'S WISDOM

What is a sponge?

Also called a "poolish" or "starter," sponge is a batter-consistency mixture of flour, water (though sometimes I use milk), and a commercial yeast (active or instant) and is usually made the same day or up to 1 day before making the bread. Because a sponge is made and used within 2 to 24 hours, I make it in the same bowl as I plan on making the bread dough.

Other types of starters include a biga and a mother (sometimes called a "chef"). Made from commercial yeast, a biga tends to have a stiffer consistency than a sponge. A mother is made with wild or natural yeasts and, if fed regularly with flour and water, it can be kept for months, if not years.

Folding and shaping the dough

A

After the first rise, the dough will be very sticky. With wet hands, scoop down the side of the bowl, pick up some of the dough, and fold it over, pressing into the center of the dough.

B

Continue all the way around the bowl, lifting and tucking the dough into the center. Keep your hands wet. Cover, let rise for 1 hour, and repeat the lifting and pressing. Cover and let rise for another hour until it has almost doubled its original size.

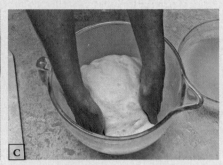

C

After the dough has gone through its second rise, wet your hands and scoop the dough away from the sides of the bowl, rewetting your hands as needed. Using both hands, reach under the dough down to the bottom of the bowl and lift from the bowl.

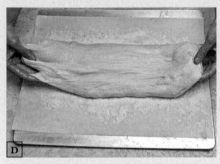

D

The dough is slippery when wet, so move quickly after you lift it out of the bowl; hold the dough over the prepared cookie sheet, then stretch it to about 13 inches (33 cm) long and lay it flat.

E

Sprinkle the dough generously with flour, cover loosely but completely with plastic wrap, then set aside to rise before baking.

F

Using a serrated knife, cut into the baked bread to see the large, airy pockets.

Rich *and* Delicious Dinner Rolls

Makes 16 rolls

I make these dinner rolls throughout the year. They are as delicious paired with marinated and grilled chicken as they are with Thanksgiving dinner. They have a buttery, egg-rich taste and a soft, airy texture. I love them warm and smeared with butter, but they are also an excellent vehicle for mopping up juices, sauces, and soups. And don't forget about any leftovers. My family likes to split and toast leftovers and use them for their morning egg and cheese sandwiches.

Making the dough is straightforward but shaping the rolls might take a little practice. I've given you several shapes to choose from—you can even make four of each variety in one batch if you like. You'll catch on to the shaping as you make them and even the less-than-perfect ones will still be yummy.

3¾ cups (16⅞ oz./479 g)
    unbleached all-purpose flour
¼ cup (1¾ oz./50 g) granulated
    sugar
2¼ tsp. quick-rise (instant) yeast
1½ tsp. table salt

1 cup (240 ml) whole milk
8 Tbs. (4 oz./113 g) unsalted butter,
    cut into 6 pieces
4 yolks from large eggs (see p. 371)
1 whole large egg
1 Tbs. water

Nonstick cooking spray or neutral
    oil (safflower, canola, vegetable,
    or corn), for greasing the dough
    and bowl

1. Put the flour, sugar, yeast, and salt in the bowl of a stand mixer and whisk until well blended. Heat the milk until very hot but not boiling. (I do this in a Pyrex measure in the microwave, but a small pan on the stovetop will also work.) Add the butter and stir until melted. Check the temperature using an instant-read thermometer. For the yeast to activate, the liquid needs to be between 115° and 125°F (45° and 52°C). Fit the mixer with the dough hook, turn the mixer on medium-low speed, and pour the warm milk mixture into the flour mixture along with the egg yolks, mixing until the flour is completely incorporated. Increase the speed to medium and beat until the dough is smooth and shiny, 8 to 10 minutes. If the dough climbs up the hook, stop the mixer and scrape the dough into the bowl as necessary. The dough will not pull away completely from the sides and bottom of the bowl, and it will be soft and slightly sticky to the touch.

For more about scraping dough from a dough hook, see p. 449.

2. Remove the dough hook, scrape the dough onto the counter, and knead once or twice until it no longer sticks to the counter and passes the windowpane test, about 1 minute. Shape the dough into a ball. Lightly grease the sides of the bowl and put the dough, rounded side up, back in. Cover the bowl with a plate or plastic wrap. Let rise in a warm spot until doubled in size, about 60 minutes.

For more about hand kneading, see p. 449.

For more about the windowpane test, see p. 470.

For round rolls

1. Lightly grease a 9 x 13 x 2-inch (23 x 33 x 5 cm) baking dish (metal or Pyrex). Scrape the dough onto an unfloured work surface and press down on the dough to deflate it. Using a bench scraper or knife, portion the dough into 16 equal pieces, about 2 oz. (57 g) each. To ensure even rolls, use a scale to weigh the portions. Working with one piece at a time and keeping the others covered, arrange the dough toward the back of your flattened palm near the thumb joint. With the edge of your other palm (curved slightly), press gently but firmly on the bottom of the dough, moving your top hand from the front to the back. This will rotate or spin the dough while keeping the top side up. Repeat until it forms a smooth-skinned ball with a sealed bottom (see the Essential Technique on p. 451). The goal is to stretch the top of the dough ball while simultaneously sealing the bottom. This will keep the dough from opening up as it expands during baking.

For more about deflating risen dough, see p. 477.

For another method of shaping rolls, see p. 477.

2. Put the ball, rounded side up, in the prepared baking dish, cover loosely with plastic wrap, and repeat with the remaining dough. (The dough balls can be arranged in four rows of four or just randomly yet evenly placed.) Lightly spray the tops of the dough and cover loosely but completely with plastic. Let the dough rise in a warm spot until doubled in size, 25 to 40 minutes.

For single-knot rolls

1. Line two cookie sheets with parchment or nonstick liners. Scrape the dough onto an unfloured work surface and press down on the dough to deflate it. Using a bench scraper or knife, portion the dough into 16 equal pieces, about 2 oz. (57 g) each. To ensure even rolls, use a scale to weigh the portions. Work with one piece at a time and keep the others loosely but completely covered. Gently stretch the dough and roll it back and forth, starting in the middle and working outward on the unfloured surface, until an 8-inch (20 cm) rope is formed; tie into a loose knot (see the Essential Technique on p. 450).

2. Place the knot on the prepared sheet, cover loosely with plastic wrap, and repeat with the remaining dough, arranging the knots about 1½ inches (4 cm) apart on the sheets. Lightly spray the tops of the dough and cover loosely but completely with plastic. Let the dough rise in a warm spot until doubled in size, 25 to 40 minutes.

For twist rolls

1. Line two cookie sheets with parchment or nonstick lines. Scrape the dough onto an unfloured work surface and press down on the dough to deflate it. Using a bench scraper or knife, portion the dough into 16 equal pieces, about 2 oz. (57 g) each. To ensure even rolls, use a scale to weigh the portions. Work with one piece at a time and keep the others loosely but completely covered. Gently stretch the dough and roll it back and forth, starting in the middle and working outward on the unfloured surface, until a 16-inch (40.5 cm) rope is formed.

2. Pull the ends of the rope toward you, forming a wide U shape at the top. Cross the ends over each other to form a circle, leaving tails about 3 inches (7.5 cm) long. Lift and wrap the tails up and over the circle twice on each side, then tuck the ends under the circle (see the Essential Technique on p. 450).

3. Place the twist on the prepared sheet, cover loosely with plastic wrap, and repeat with the remaining dough, arranging the twists about 2 inches (5 cm) apart on the sheets. Lightly spray the tops of the dough and cover loosely but completely with plastic. Let the dough rise in a warm spot until doubled in size, 25 to 40 minutes.

For cloverleaf rolls

1. Lightly grease 16 regular muffin cups. Scrape the dough onto an unfloured work surface and press down on the dough to deflate it. Using a bench scraper or knife, portion the dough into 16 equal pieces, about 2 oz. (57 g) each, and divide each into 3 equal pieces. To ensure even rolls, use a scale to weigh the portions. Working with one piece at a time and keeping the others loosely but completely covered, shape into a round ball. With the edge of your other palm (curved slightly), press gently but firmly on the bottom of the dough, moving your top hand from the front to the back. This will rotate or spin the dough while keeping the top side up. Repeat until it forms a smooth-skinned ball with a sealed bottom (see the Essential Technique on p. 451). The goal is to stretch the top of the dough ball while simultaneously sealing the bottom. This will keep the dough from opening up as it expands during baking.

2. Put three balls, rounded side up, in each of the prepared muffin tins (see the Essential Technique on p. 451). Lightly spray the tops of the dough and cover loosely but completely with plastic. Let the dough rise in a warm spot until doubled in size, 25 to 40 minutes.

Bake the rolls

Position a rack in the center of the oven and heat the oven to 375°F (190°C/gas 5). Put the egg and water in a small bowl and mix with a fork until well blended. When the rolls have risen to about ½ inch (12 mm) above the pan, remove the plastic and brush with the egg wash. Bake until the rolls are puffed and deep golden brown, 17 to 21 minutes. For the knots and twists, bake the sheets one at a time, starting with the first ones shaped and risen until doubled. Move the pans to a rack. Serve warm or let cool completely, cover, and stow at room temperature for up to 2 days.

Kneading yeast dough

A

Measure your ingredients and add to the mixing bowl, keeping the sugar, yeast, and salt separate until whisking together with the flour. Placed together, salt can kill off the yeast. This method also helps you keep track of your ingredient additions.

B

When using the dough hook on a stand mixer, it's common for dough to walk up the hook.

C

Stop the machine and use a bench scraper to ease the dough from the hook and back into the bowl.

D

Once the dough is well mixed and shiny, scrape it onto an unfloured work surface. It will be sticky. For **French-style kneading:** Using one hand, lift the dough and slap it back onto the surface, folding the dough over on top of itself.

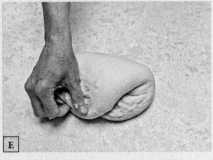

E

Repeat the lifting, slapping, and folding process until the dough is soft and supple and no longer sticks to the surface.

F

For **traditional American-style kneading:** Using the heel of one hand, push the top part of the dough away from you and fold that piece over the dough nearest to you. Give the dough a quarter turn and repeat, using the bench scraper as needed. Keep kneading and turning until the dough is soft and supple and no longer sticks to the surface.

(continued)

Shaping the rolls

A

Using a bench scraper, cut the dough into pieces. Use a scale to ensure the pieces are all the same size, and cover the pieces with plastic wrap as you work to prevent them from drying out.

B

To make a **single-knot roll**, form an 8-inch (20 cm) rope with a piece of dough.

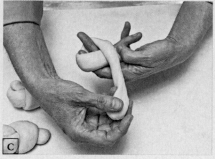

C

Use one hand to hold an end of the rope while the other gently pulls the tail through a loose knot. Two fingers placed in the center of the loose knot will help when weaving through the tail.

D

Grab the tail as it comes through the knot, gently pulling it so the tail sticks out the other side. Place on the prepared baking sheet.

E

To form a **twist roll**, shape a 16-inch (40.5 cm) rope, then place on the unfloured work surface in a large U shape. Form a circle by crossing the rope ends over each other, leaving the tails about 3 inches (7.5 cm) long.

F

Lift one tail up and over the circle . . .

G

. . . then pull the tail through the circle, as if you were tying a knot.

H

Continue lifting and wrapping the first tail two more times, then follow the same method with the other tail until you've formed a dough wreath with both ends tucked underneath.

To form **round balls**, work with one piece of dough in the palm of one hand near the thumb joint. Slightly curve the other palm and gently but firmly press the outside edge of your palm toward

the bottom of the ball. Move your top hand from front to back, turning the dough clockwise (for righties like me) and keeping the rounded top facing up.

The goal is to seal the bottom (shown) while stretching the top of the dough into a smooth round.

Create **butterfly or fan rolls** by filling lightly greased muffin tin cups with the balls. Using scissors, cut the center of the ball almost through to the bottom. Repeat the cuts, evenly spaced, twice more on each side.

Form **cloverleaf rolls** by dividing into 16 equal pieces. Shape the pieces into small, smooth balls, then place seam side down in the bottom of the muffin tin cups, pressing them gently but snugly.

Bagels

Makes 8 bagels

Splitting, toasting, and smearing a bagel is a weekend tradition in my house. Sometimes, Chris will sneak out early to collect a few from our local spot, but more often I plan ahead and stow a batch of shaped and rising bagels in the fridge overnight. All that's left to do is boil, bake, and devour—easily done, especially when I set it up before turning in for the night.

Cracking into a freshly baked bagel is a sensory delight worth savoring. The crispy, hard crust covered with seeds contrasts superbly with the chewy, slightly sour inside with airy pockets to hold melting butter (for me) or scallion cream cheese (for Chris). When the kids are home, we power through this batch of eight, but extras stow well in the freezer to toast up midweek for breakfast or lunch.

Don't shy away from making bagels at home. With a little planning, they are surprisingly easy. The dough is soft and supple, and shaping is fun and doesn't call for extreme precision. Moving through the boiling and baking process is seamless, especially if you set up your equipment ahead of time.

For the dough
2¾ cups (12⅜ oz./351 g)
   unbleached all-purpose flour +
   more as needed
1 cup (4½ oz./113 g) bread flour
1 Tbs. granulated sugar
1 Tbs. buttermilk powder
   (see p. 459)

2½ tsp. quick-rise (instant) yeast
1½ tsp. table salt
1⅓ cups water, warmed to between
   115° and 125°F (45° to 52°C)
Nonstick cooking spray or neutral
   oil (safflower, canola, vegetable,
   or corn), for greasing the dough
   and bowl

For the boiling and topping
2 Tbs. baking soda
Poppy seeds, sesame seeds, or
   "everything" mix (see p. 550)
Cornmeal, for dusting (optional)

MAKE AHEAD

> Prepare the dough and let the bagels rise for 30 minutes. Lightly spray with oil, cover loosely but completely with plastic, and refrigerate for up to 10 hours. When ready to continue, set the cookie sheets on the counter while heating the oven and boiling the water.

> The baked bagels can be covered and stowed at room temperature for up to 2 days.

Make the dough

1. Put the flours, sugar, buttermilk powder, yeast, and salt in the bowl of a stand mixer, whisk until well blended, and fit the mixer with the dough hook. Mix on medium speed while pouring the warm water into the flour mixture until the flour is completely incorporated. Increase the speed to medium high and beat until the dough is smooth and pulls away from the sides and bottom of the bowl, 4 to 6 minutes. If the dough climbs up the hook, stop the mixer and scrape the dough into the bowl as necessary. The dough will be soft and slightly sticky to the touch and will have a webbed texture when a piece is pulled (see p. 470).

For more about scraping dough from a dough hook, see p. 449.

2. Remove the dough hook, scrape the dough onto the counter, knead once or twice until it no longer sticks to the counter and passes the windowpane test, and shape into a ball. Lightly grease the sides of the bowl and put the dough, rounded side up, back in. Cover the bowl with a plate or plastic wrap. Let rise in a warm spot until doubled in size, about 45 minutes.

For more about hand kneading, see p. 449.

For more about the windowpane test, see p. 470.

Shape the dough

1. Line two cookie sheets with silicone liners or parchment and lightly grease. Scrape the dough onto an unfloured work surface and press down on the dough to deflate it. Using a bench scraper or knife, portion the dough into 8 equal pieces (about 3½ oz./99 g each). Working with one piece of dough at a time and keeping the remaining pieces loosely covered with plastic wrap, shape each piece into a round ball. Very lightly flour your hands if needed.

For more about weighing dough, see p. 450.

For more about deflating risen dough, see p. 477.

For more about shaping dough into balls, see p. 451.

2. To make the bagel shape, push your thumb through the center of one dough ball to make a hole. Using both hands, gently stretch the dough by circling and rolling between your fingers until the inside opening is about 2 inches (5 cm) and the outside measures 4 inches (10 cm) across (see the Essential Technique on p. 454). Place on the prepared sheet and reshape as needed. Cover loosely but completely with plastic wrap while you shape the remaining dough, arranging the bagels about 3 inches (7.5 cm) apart on the sheet. Cover the cookie sheets with plastic and let the bagels rise in a warm spot until puffed and almost doubled in size, about 45 minutes.

For more about working with plastic wrap, see p. 546.

Cook the bagels

1. While the dough is rising, fill a large pot (I use a 4-quart/4-liter Dutch oven) with water to a 3-inch (7.5 cm) depth and bring to a boil over high heat. (If the water boils before the bagels have risen, cover the pot and reduce the heat to low.) Position a rack in the lower third of the oven and heat the oven to 450°F (230°C/gas 8). Fill a spray bottle with water.

2. When the first sheet of bagels is ready, return the water to a boil, if necessary, and slowly add the baking soda. Be careful—the water will bubble up and splatter. Have ready two cookie sheets lined with parchment and scattered with some of the topping ingredients or cornmeal. Lightly spray the tops of the bagels with water (this will prevent the dough from sticking to your fingers) and, working with one bagel at a time, carefully (don't pinch or the dough will collapse) lift a bagel and slip it into the boiling water. Depending on the size of your pot, you can cook two or three bagels at a time; just be sure they have plenty of room to expand. Cook, turning once with a skimmer or slotted spoon, until puffed and slightly darker looking, 1½ minutes per side.

For more about boiling dough, see p. 442.

3. With a skimmer or slotted spoon, lift the bagels, one at a time, from the water and arrange on one of the lined cookie sheets top side up (they can be placed much closer together after boiling). Sprinkle with more toppings. Repeat with the remaining bagels on the first sheet.

(continued)

TWISTS

Flavor swap

Cinnamon-sugar: Make and shape the dough as directed. After boiling, generously sprinkle with cinnamon-sugar (see p. 197), then bake as directed.

FINISHING TOUCHES

Serve with cream cheese, flavored if you prefer, or butter.

4. Once the sheet is full, bake until the bagel tops are deep golden brown, 16 to 18 minutes. Move the sheet to a rack, use a spatula to flip the bagels, then return the sheet to the oven and continue to bake until the bottoms of the bagels are golden brown, 4 to 6 minutes. Move the sheet to a rack. While the first sheet is baking, boil the remaining bagels and bake them when the oven is free. The bagels are best when served warm or cooled on the day they are made.

ESSENTIAL TECHNIQUE

Shaping bagels

To shape a bagel, center your thumb in one dough ball and push in, making a hole. Using both thumbs, gently stretch the dough until the hole is about 2 inches (5 cm).

Reposition the bagel on two fingers of one hand and one or two fingers of your other hand as if the dough were a wheel and your fingers were the axle. Gently circling, rolling, and stretching the dough between your fingers, increase the opening in the center while still maintaining the round shape. Smooth and round the outside of the bagel by rolling between your hands before placing on the prepared cookie sheet.

Hazelnut Sticky Buns

Makes 12

Cinnamon buns are served for breakfast at all major holidays (at least the ones we celebrate), and the Dodge family members take them seriously. Long before he could drive a car, Alex took over the honors of making and baking our family's version of Cinnabons®; even now when he prepares them, we deem them "the best ever."

Naturally, when it came to including a new recipe in this book, I consulted with the head 'bon baker and the rest of the fam. There was much grumbling (some of us aren't good with change) and discussion on what could be changed as well as what parts of the recipe were sacred. After many tests, we reached balance and compromise. These buns are soft, eggy, and filled with a thick layer of cinnamon with the added goodness of a slightly sticky, glistening layer of honey-butter and toasted nuts coating the tops.

For the dough
3¾ cups (16⅞ oz./479 g) unbleached all-purpose flour
¼ cup (1¾ oz./50 g) granulated sugar
2 tsp. quick-rise (instant) yeast
1 tsp. table salt
1 cup (240 ml) whole milk
8 Tbs. (4 oz./113 g) unsalted butter, cut into 6 pieces
1 large egg

Nonstick cooking spray or neutral oil (safflower, canola, vegetable, or corn), for greasing the bowl

For the sticky topping
8 Tbs. (4 oz./113 g) unsalted butter, softened
1½ cups (10½ oz./298 g) firmly packed dark brown sugar
⅓ cup (80 ml) honey
¼ cup (60 ml) heavy cream
Pinch of table salt

1¾ cups (7 oz./198 g) chopped hazelnuts, toasted and skinned, divided (see p. 457)

For the filling
¾ cup (4⅝ oz./131 g) granulated sugar
2 Tbs. unbleached all-purpose flour
5 tsp. ground cinnamon
3 Tbs. (1½ oz./42 g) unsalted butter, melted

Make the dough

1. Put the flour, sugar, yeast, and salt in the bowl of a stand mixer and whisk until well blended. Heat the milk until very hot but not boiling. (I do this in a Pyrex measure in the microwave, but a small pan on the stovetop will also work.) Add the butter and stir until melted. Check the temperature using an instant-read thermometer. For the yeast to activate, the liquid needs to be between 115° and 125°F (45° and 52°C). Fit the mixer with the dough hook, turn the mixer on medium-low speed, and pour the warm milk mixture into the flour mixture along with the egg, mixing until the flour is completely incorporated. Increase the speed to medium and beat until the dough is smooth and shiny, 8 to 10 minutes. If the dough climbs up the hook, stop the mixer and scrape the dough into the bowl as necessary. The dough will not pull away completely from the sides and bottom of the bowl, and it will be soft and slightly sticky to the touch.

For more about scraping dough from a dough hook, see p. 449.

2. Remove the dough hook, scrape the dough onto the counter, knead once or twice until it no longer sticks to the counter and passes the windowpane test, and shape into a ball. Lightly grease the sides of

MAKE AHEAD

> The sticky buns can be made through Step 3, covered, and refrigerated overnight. To bake, set the covered pan on the counter for 30 to 60 minutes while the oven heats before baking as directed.

> The sticky buns can be made, cooled completely, covered, and stowed at room temperature for up to 2 days. Serve warm or at room temperature.

TWISTS

Flavor swap

Instead of the hazelnuts, use the same amount of slivered almonds or coarsely chopped pecans or walnuts.

the bowl and put the dough, rounded side up, back in. Cover the bowl with a plate or plastic wrap. Let the covered dough rise in a warm spot until doubled in size, about 60 minutes.

For more about hand kneading, see p. 449.

For more about the windowpane test, see p. 470.

Make the topping

Lightly grease a 9 x 13 x 2-inch (23 x 33 x 5 cm) baking dish (metal or Pyrex). Put the butter, brown sugar, honey, heavy cream, and salt in a medium saucepan and cook over medium-low heat, stirring constantly, until the sugar is melted and the mixture is well blended. Scrape into the pan and spread evenly. Scatter 1¼ cups (5 oz./142 g) of the hazelnuts evenly over the sugar mixture.

Make the filling and rolls

1. Whisk the sugar, flour, and cinnamon in a small bowl until well blended.

2. Scrape the dough onto an unfloured work surface and press down on the dough to deflate it. Using your hands, shape the dough into a 12 x 15-inch (30.5 x 38 cm) rectangle and arrange it so one short side is closest to you. Pour the melted butter into the center of the dough rectangle and spread evenly with a small offset spatula. Sprinkle the sugar mixture over the butter and spread evenly with your hands. Scatter the remaining ½ cup (2 oz./57 g) hazelnuts on top.

For more about deflating risen dough, see p. 477.

3. Roll up the dough jellyroll style and pinch to seal the seam. Position the roll, seam side down, on the work surface and, using a lightly floured serrated knife, cut into twelve 1-inch (2.5 cm) thick slices. Using the flat part of the blade, arrange the slices in the pan on top of the sugar and nuts.

For more about filling, rolling, and cutting, see p. 55.

For more about arranging in the pan, see p. 477.

4. Loosely but completely cover the baking dish with plastic and let rise in a warm spot until doubled in size, 45 to 60 minutes. About 30 minutes into rising, position a rack in the center of the oven and heat the oven to 350°F (180°C/gas 4); continue to let the dough rise.

For more about working with plastic wrap, see p. 546.

5. Bake until the rolls are puffed and deep golden brown, 40 to 42 minutes. Move the pan to a rack and let cool for 5 minutes. Cover with a sheet of parchment and set a half sheet pan or serving tray (top side down) on top of the parchment. Using pot holders, grip the pan, parchment, and plate and invert. Let the inverted pan rest for a few minutes to let the topping settle on the rolls. Gently remove the pan, slide out the parchment, and cool to warm, then serve.

Skinning hazelnuts

A

B

C

To toast and skin hazelnuts, spread in a single layer on a baking sheet and toast in a 375°F (190°C/gas 5) oven for about 10 minutes, or until the nuts are fragrant and the skins are split. Transfer the hot nuts to a clean kitchen towel.

Wrap the hot nuts in the towel for a few minutes, then vigorously rub them between the towel and against themselves to release the skin. Open the towel to check on the progress and continue the process as needed to remove the skins.

Although you want most of the nuts to be skinless before chopping, it's fine if a few have some skin still clinging to them like the ones in the front. The nuts in the back still need some work.

Baguettes

Makes 2 loaves (1¾ lb./794 g each)

While living in Paris as a culinary student, I was on a daily quest for the best pastries and breads, but no treasure was held higher than the perfect baguette. I savored my samples as I eagerly took note of the tastes, textures, and nuances that made each unique, ultimately guiding me to my own version of Paris's finest. With time, I have tweaked and honed my version. Crispy-crackly on the outside and chewy and webby on the inside, with a hearty, yeasty taste, French bread (baguette) is not out of reach for the average home baker. What's more, jaw-dropping results don't require years of culinary training.

The dough is wet and sticky, so I use a kneading and rising technique that's similar to the one I use for ciabatta (see p. 443) to create the bread's texture. I let the dough rise slowly, unattended, in the fridge to develop its unique flavor. If you are in a hurry, you can skip this step, but once you taste it made with the retarded rising time, you will want to plan a day ahead.

2⅔ cups (12 oz./340 g) bread flour
1 Tbs. buttermilk powder
1 tsp. quick-rise (instant) yeast

1½ tsp. table salt
1 cup (240 ml) water, at room
temperature

Nonstick cooking spray or neutral
oil (safflower, canola, vegetable, or
corn), for greasing the bowl

MAKE AHEAD

The bread can be cooled completely, covered, and stowed at room temperature for up to 1 day before reheating or slicing and toasting.

Make the dough

1. Put the flour, buttermilk powder, yeast, and salt in the bowl of a stand mixer, whisk until well blended, and fit the mixer with the dough hook. Mix on medium speed while pouring the water into the flour mixture. Increase the speed to medium high and beat until the dough is smooth and elastic, 4 to 6 minutes. If the dough climbs up the hook, stop the mixer and scrape the dough into the bowl as necessary. The dough will be soft and slightly sticky to the touch.

For more about scraping dough from a dough hook, see p. 449.

2. Remove the dough hook and, using wet hands, scrape the dough off the hook and back into the bowl. Lightly grease the sides of the bowl (the dough might be too sticky to pull from the bowl) and cover with a plate or plastic wrap. Let the dough rise in a warm spot for about 1 hour. It won't be doubled in size. Using one wet hand, pull one part of the dough away from the bowl and lift it up and over the dough, tucking it into the center. Turn the bowl about a quarter of the way around, rewet your hand, and pull the dough away from the edge of that section of the bowl and tuck into the center. Repeat this process all the way around the bowl, rewetting your hand as you work.

For more about shaping after the first rise, see p. 445.

3. Cover the bowl with a plate or plastic wrap and refrigerate for at least 12 hours or up to 36 hours. It will rise about one and a half times its original size.

Shape, rise, and bake the dough

1. Fold two pieces of parchment lengthwise into fourths to form a deep V in the center, with the two outside edges measuring 2½ inches (6 cm) wide. Arrange the parchment pieces side by side on a cookie sheet.

2. Scrape the dough onto an unfloured work surface and press down on the dough to deflate it. Using a bench scraper or knife, portion the dough in half (about 10 oz./283 g each). Working with one piece at a time, use your hands to shape the dough into a rectangle about 6 inches (15 cm) long and 5 inches (12 cm) wide. With the shorter side facing you, fold the top third over the dough and, using your fingers, firmly press down on the edge, very lightly flouring as needed. Fold the bottom third over the dough and use your fingers to press and seal the edge (see the Essential Technique on pp. 460–461).

3. Very lightly dust the surface with flour and roll the dough into a log so that the seam is on top. Using lightly floured fingers, press down the center of the dough log through the seam but not all the way to the bottom. Fold the log in half lengthwise and use your fingers to press and seal. The dough should be about 10 inches (25 cm) long. Repeat. Using your hands, gently roll the dough on the work surface, seam side up and very lightly flouring as needed (the dough needs to be slightly tacky to stretch), to shape into a 16-inch (40.5 cm) long cylinder with tapered ends.

4. Generously dust the dough with flour, roll so that the seam side is down, and generously dust the rounded side with flour. Carefully lift the dough and arrange on the cookie sheet in one of the parchment Vs. Repeat with the remaining dough. Cover the cookie sheet loosely but completely with plastic wrap. (Arrange cups or jars along the outside edges of the parchment to hold up the sides, if necessary.) Let the dough rise in a warm spot until puffy and doubled, 2 to 2½ hours.

For more about working with plastic wrap, see p. 546.

Bake the bread

1. Position a rack in the bottom third of the oven and set a baking steel or stone on the rack. Heat the oven to 500°F (260°C/gas 10) for at least 20 minutes. Fill a spray bottle with water.

2. Dust the tops of the loaves with flour; using a razor or very sharp knife, cut 4 or 5 slits diagonally across the tops, about ⅓ inch (8 mm) deep. Using scissors, cut away the excess parchment so that the loaves will brown evenly. Using a long spatula, slide the bread, parchment and all, onto the stone. Immediately after sliding the loaves onto the stone, use the spray bottle to spritz the loaves with water several times. Reduce the oven temperature to 450°F (230°C/gas 8) and bake for 15 minutes, spritzing once or twice. Using the cookie sheet and a mitted hand, carefully and quickly slide the parchment out from under the loaves, then continue baking the bread until the crust is deep brown, 13 to 15 minutes more. Use the cookie sheet or a peel to move the loaves to a rack. Let cool for at least 1 hour before slicing.

(continued)

BAKER'S WISDOM

Powdered buttermilk

Not meant to be reconstituted and drinkable, dried buttermilk powder is a substitute for liquid buttermilk (4 Tbs. powder to 1 cup/240 ml water = 1 cup/240 ml buttermilk). Once opened, it can be stored in your fridge for up to a year. As in this bread, it's meant to be added to the dry ingredients to add a slightly acidic tang to baked goods. I have used the powder and water substitution for liquid buttermilk in many baked goods with success but I find the batter to be thinner. For recipes calling for buttermilk when I'm all out, I measure out 1 cup (240 ml) whole milk, spoon out 2 Tbs., and stir in 2 Tbs. freshly squeezed lemon juice.

For this recipe, I add some buttermilk powder to give the bread a slightly sour or acidic taste that I really like. Not to be mistaken for a sourdough replacement or shortcut, partnered with the yeast, the powder is simply my secret ingredient for full-bodied flavor.

Shaping baguettes

A Working with one large sheet of parchment (12 x 16¼ inches/30.5 x 41 cm), fold it lengthwise into fourths accordion style, forming a deep V in the center. The two outside edges should be about 2½ inches (6 cm) wide. Repeat with another sheet of parchment, then place them side by side on a cookie sheet. These parchment slings will hold the baguette dough as it rises.

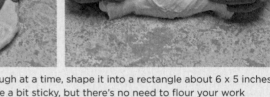

B Working with one half of the dough at a time, shape it into a rectangle about 6 x 5 inches (15 x 12 cm). The dough might be a bit sticky, but there's no need to flour your work surface. Fold the top third of the dough over . . .

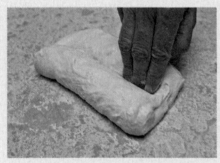

. . . then press down at the seam with your fingers. If needed, lightly flour your fingers.

C Fold over the bottom third of the dough, forming a bulky log, and use your fingers to press and seal the edge.

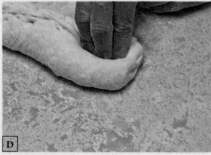

D With your work surface very lightly dusted with flour, roll the log and position the seam on top. Lightly flour your fingers then press down into the seam, about three-quarters of the way to the bottom.

E Fold the dough in half, with the press-in seam acting as the center point, to form a 10-inch (25 cm) long log. Use your fingers to press and seal the edge, lightly flouring them if needed. Repeat this step one more time.

Using both hands, roll the dough, seam side up, on the work surface (very lightly flour if it sticks) to shape and lengthen the log to 16 inches (40.5 cm) with tapered ends. Roll so the seam side is down and generously dust the dough with flour.

Lift the cylinder, seam side down, from both ends and carefully position it in the parchment sling so that it's in the center V. Position ramekins or small cups along the edge of the parchment to hold up the sides if necessary. Cover with plastic wrap and let the dough rise.

Once the dough is risen, dust the tops with more flour, cut 4 or 5 slits diagonally in the top of each loaf, and trim away the excess parchment so that the baguettes will brown evenly as they bake.

Working at the oven, transfer the loaves on their parchment onto the hot baking stone (or steel), using a long offset spatula to slide them off the cookie sheet. Immediately spritz the loaves generously with water, then bake, spritzing with water another one or two times over the course of baking.

Cinnamon Swirl Bread

Makes 1 loaf

A toasted slice of this bread loaded with sweet cinnamon goodness leaves me weak in the knees. Add a smear of butter on top and I'm swooning, so much so that I will admit to testing this recipe many, many times. Was it to be 150% sure the directions are as good as they could be, or was it because the loaf was so damn good? Once you've tried a slice, let me know what you think!

My two pet peeves with most cinnamon swirl bread recipes are a swirled filling that isn't cinnamony enough to carry the flavor throughout the bread and a filling that separates while baking, leaving a gaping divide between the rolls of bread. Solving both issues was easy enough. First off, I've added a whopping 2 Tbs. ground cinnamon (for the biggest flavor, use a high-quality cinnamon) to the filling along with some flour to bind it so it doesn't melt away. A double layer of egg wash sandwiching the filling solved the gaping problem by creating a protein barrier for the dough to stick to. The extra egg wash makes the dough a bit sloppy, especially when working through the double swirl variation, so work quickly and with confidence to help keep the loaf intact.

For the dough
3 cups (13½ oz./383 g) unbleached all-purpose flour
3 Tbs. granulated sugar
2¼ tsp. quick-rise (instant) yeast
1¼ tsp. table salt
1 cup (240 ml) whole milk

4 Tbs. (2 oz./57 g) unsalted butter, cut into 2 pieces
1½ tsp. pure vanilla extract
½ cup (2½ oz./71 g) dark raisins, chopped (optional)
Nonstick cooking spray or neutral oil (safflower, canola, vegetable, or corn), for greasing the dough, bowl, and pan

For the egg wash
1 large egg
1 Tbs. water

For the filling
⅓ cup (2⅜ oz./67 g) firmly packed dark brown sugar
2 Tbs. unbleached all-purpose flour
2 Tbs. ground cinnamon

MAKE AHEAD

The bread can be baked, cooled, covered, and stowed at room temperature for up to 5 days or wrapped tightly in plastic, placed in a large zip-top freezer bag, and frozen for up to 1 week. To thaw, unwrap the bread, set on a rack, and thaw at room temperature for 1 to 2 hours.

Make the dough

1. Put the flour, sugar, yeast, and salt in the bowl of a stand mixer and whisk until well blended. Heat the milk until very hot but not boiling. (I do this in a Pyrex measure in the microwave, but a small pan on the stovetop will also work.) Add the butter and stir until melted. Check the temperature using an instant-read thermometer. For the yeast to activate, the liquid needs to be between 115° and 125°F (45° and 52°C). Fit the mixer with the dough hook, turn the mixer on medium-low speed, pour the warm mixture and the vanilla into the flour mixture, and mix until the flour is almost incorporated. Add the raisins, increase the speed to medium high, and beat until the dough is smooth and shiny, 5 to 8 minutes. If the dough climbs up the hook or sticks to the side of the bowl, stop the mixer and scrape the dough into the bowl as necessary. The dough will pull away completely from the sides and bottom of the bowl and will be soft and slightly sticky to the touch.

For more about scraping dough from a dough hook, see p. 449.

2. Remove the dough hook, scrape the dough onto the counter, knead once or twice until it no longer sticks to the counter and passes the windowpane test, and shape into a ball. Lightly grease the sides of the bowl and put the dough, rounded side up, back in. Cover the bowl with a plate or plastic wrap. Let rise in a warm spot until doubled in size, about 60 minutes.

For more about hand kneading, see p. 449.

For more about the windowpane test, see p. 470.

Make the egg wash and filling

1. In a small bowl or ramekin, make the egg wash by mixing the egg and water with a fork until well blended.

2. Put the sugar, flour, and cinnamon in a ramekin and stir until blended.

Shape and bake the bread

1. Lightly grease an 8½ x 3½-inch (21.5 x 9 cm) loaf pan (6 cups/1.4 liters).

2. Scrape the dough onto an unfloured work surface and press down on the dough to deflate it. Gently press and shape the dough into a 6 x 18-inch (15 x 46 cm) rectangle. Using a pastry brush, brush some of the egg wash evenly over the dough to coat completely. Scatter the filling evenly over the rectangle, using your fingers to smooth and spread it to the edges of the dough. Using the pastry bush, drizzle the filling evenly with more of the egg wash to cover completely.

For more about deflating risen dough, see p. 477.

3. Starting at one of the short sides, roll up the dough like a jellyroll. Pinch the bottom seam and the ends closed and place seam side down in the prepared pan. Press on the dough to flatten and fill the pan in an even layer (see the Essential Technique on p. 464).

4. Cover the pan loosely (to allow for rising) but completely with plastic and let the dough rise in a warm spot until the top reaches the rim of the pan, about 60 minutes. Position a rack in the center of the oven and heat the oven to 350°F (180°C/gas 4); continue to let the dough rise.

For more about working with plastic wrap, see p. 546.

5. When the oven is hot and the dough is risen to about 1 inch above the pan in the center, remove the plastic and brush the top of the loaf with some of the egg wash. Bake until the loaf is browned and an instant-read thermometer inserted in the center of the loaf reads 190° to 200°F (88° to 95°C), 43 to 45 minutes. Move the pan to a rack and let cool for 20 minutes. Tip the loaf onto the rack, lift off the pan, and set the loaf on its side to cool completely.

For more about checking temperature, see p. 471.

(continued)

Flavor swap

Nutty: Instead of the raisins, add the same amount of sunflower seeds or chopped walnuts.

Re-size it

Double swirl: Make the dough, egg wash, and filling. Shape, fill, and roll the dough as directed, pinching the seam and ends closed. Arrange the dough, seam side down, with one short side facing you. Using a sharp knife, cut the dough lengthwise down the center, leaving the top 1 inch (2.5 cm) intact (see the Essential Technique on pp. 464–465). Turn both sides cut side up and, working quickly (each side will open up and look a bit messy), lift one side up and over the other twice; pinch the ends together. Position your hands under both ends of the loaf, lift up, and arrange, seam side down, in the prepared pan. Press gently on the dough to flatten and fill the pan. The top will not be even. Proceed as directed.

Cinnamon

Cinnamon is the dried bark of the Asian cinnamon or cassia trees. Each type has a unique color and flavor and subtle nuances. I develop and test all my recipes with store-bought brands like McCormick® Gourmet and Spice Islands® (both made with the dark red-brown and strong, sweet taste of cassia) with great results, but I encourage you to explore the different types of cinnamon. A great resource is Penzeys.com.

ESSENTIAL TECHNIQUE

Shaping the dough two ways

After shaping the dough into a 6 x 18-inch (15 x 46 cm) rectangle, position it so one short side is facing you. Brush some of the egg wash over the top. Scatter the filling over the rectangle, then use your fingers to spread it evenly to the edges. Drizzle more egg wash over the top of the filling.

Roll up jellyroll style. Try to roll evenly and tightly without pinching or squeezing, and don't worry if a little of the filling falls out as you roll.

Pinch the lengthwise seam closed tightly by squeezing the dough between your fingers. Pinch the ends closed in the same way, squeezing the dough between your fingers to seal completely. Place in the prepared pan, flattening the dough to fit, or braid, as shown below.

To create a braided double swirl, arrange the dough, seam side down, with one short side facing you. Using a sharp knife, cut the dough lengthwise down the center, leaving the top 1 inch (2.5 cm) intact. Gently pull both sides apart and turn so the cut side is facing up.

E Working quickly, lift the left side (facing you) up and over the right side; repeat, beginning with the left side to form two twists.

F Pinch the bottom ends together to seal, then lift up the loaf using both hands and place in the prepared pan, cut side up. Press the dough into the sides of the pan to fit.

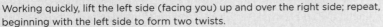

Herbed Monkey Bread

Serves 10

Breaking with tradition, I've chosen to make this monkey bread (also known as bubble or pull-apart bread) a savory lunch or dinner accompaniment instead of the more traditional sweet breakfast treat. This bread is beautiful to look at, delectable to eat, and fun for the whole family to make.

I've doubled down on the savory flavorings by adding ground Parmigiano Reggiano to the milky egg dough before rolling in melted butter and dipping in an abundance of fresh herbs. You won't use all of the butter, but you'll need the large amount to coat the pieces, leaving some of the watery whey behind. Remember to keep your dough portions on the small size, as they grow into larger, one- or two-bite pieces during rising and baking. If the dough is cut into larger portions, the flavor balance between the butter and herbs and cheesy bread will be compromised.

Freshly baked, the bread is easily pulled apart and savored piece by piece. I've served it alongside soup and stew, but it's a refreshing substitute for traditional starches usually teamed with a roast or even my husband's famous Sunday night meatloaf. Leftovers can be reheated or cut into thick slices and toasted. The slices may break apart but they are still crazy delicious.

(continued)

For the dough

3¾ cups (16⅞ oz./479 g)
  unbleached all-purpose flour
2 Tbs. granulated sugar
2¼ tsp. quick-rise (instant) yeast
1½ tsp. table salt
1 cup (240 ml) whole milk
8 Tbs. (4 oz./113 g) unsalted butter,
  cut into 6 pieces

½ cup (2 oz./57 g) ground
  Parmigiano Reggiano cheese
  (see p. 38)
1 large egg
Nonstick cooking spray or neutral
  oil (safflower, canola, vegetable, or
  corn), for greasing the bowl

For the butter and herbs

16 Tbs. (8 oz./227 g) unsalted
  butter, cut into 6 pieces
1 large garlic clove, crushed, peel
  removed
2 cups (about 2 oz./57 g) finely
  chopped mixed fresh herbs (basil,
  chives, thyme, parsley, tarragon)

MAKE AHEAD

The bread can be cooled completely, covered, and stowed at room temperature for up to 1 day.

Make the dough

1. Put the flour, sugar, yeast, and salt in the bowl of a stand mixer and whisk until well blended. Heat the milk until very hot but not boiling. (I do this in a Pyrex measure in the microwave, but a small pan on the stovetop will also work.) Add the butter and stir until melted. Check the temperature using an instant-read thermometer. For the yeast to activate, the liquid needs to be between 115° and 125°F (45° and 52°C). (This can also be done in the microwave.) Fit the mixer with the dough hook, turn the mixer on medium-low speed, and pour the warm milk mixture into the flour mixture along with the cheese and egg, mixing until the flour is completely incorporated. Increase the speed to medium and beat until the dough is smooth and shiny, 8 to 10 minutes. If the dough climbs up the hook, stop the mixer and scrape the dough into the bowl as necessary. The dough will not pull away completely from the sides and bottom of the bowl, and it will be soft and slightly sticky to the touch.

For more about scraping dough from a dough hook, see p. 449.

2. Remove the dough hook, scrape the dough onto the counter, knead once or twice until it no longer sticks to the counter and passes the windowpane test, and shape into a ball. Lightly grease the sides of the bowl and put the dough, rounded side up, back in. Cover the bowl with a plate or plastic wrap. Let rise in a warm spot until doubled in size, about 60 minutes.

For more about hand kneading, see p. 449.

For more about the windowpane test, see p. 470.

Assemble and bake the bread

1. Put the butter and garlic in a small saucepan. Cook, stirring frequently, over medium-low heat until the butter is melted, 2 to 4 minutes. Slide the pan off the heat and let the butter cool until barely warm.

2. Brush some of the melted butter generously over the bottom, sides, and center tube of a 12-cup (2.8 liters) bundt pan. Put the chopped herbs in a small bowl and have the rest of the melted butter ready.

3. Scrape the dough onto an unfloured work surface and press down on the dough to deflate it. Using a bench scraper or knife, portion the dough into ½- to ¾-inch (12 mm to 2 cm) pieces (no need to weigh). Working with one piece at a time, dip into the butter to coat, dip one side of the dough into the herbs, and then put the piece in the prepared pan (see the Essential Technique below). Repeat with remaining dough pieces, arranging them randomly next to each other and in several layers (the pan will be about half full). Cover loosely but completely with plastic. Let the dough rise in a warm spot until doubled in size, 45 to 60 minutes.

For more about deflating risen dough, see p. 477.

4. Position a rack in the center of the oven and heat the oven to 350°F (180°C/gas 4). Bake until the bread is browned and an instant-read thermometer inserted into the center reads 190° to 200°F (88° to 95°C), 33 to 36 minutes. Move the pan to a rack and let cool for about 5 minutes. To remove the bread, rotate the pan, gently tapping the bottom edge on the counter as you turn it, until the bread loosens from the pan. Put a large flat plate on top of the pan; using pot holders, hold the plate and the pan and invert; lift off the pan. Let the bread cool for 5 to 10 minutes, then serve warm.

For more about checking temperature, see p. 471.

Re-size it

> 2 minis: Instead of using one 12-cup (2.8 liters) bundt pan, use two 6-cup (1.4 liters) bundt pans, equally dividing the dipped dough between the two pans. Rise and bake as directed. When completely cool, one (or both) can be frozen in a heavy-duty zip-top bag for up to 3 months.

> 1 plain loaf: Make the dough as directed and omit the herbs and butter. Instead, shape, rise, and bake the dough as directed in Sweet Potato Bread (see p. 434).

ESSENTIAL TECHNIQUE

Preparing the bread

A   Cut the dough into small pieces using a bench scraper. The pieces don't need to be the same size but they should be small (between ½ and ¾ inch/12 mm and 2 cm), since they will grow as they rise.

B   With bowls of melted butter and herbs close by, dip a piece of dough into the butter, coating completely, then dip one end into the herbs to generously coat. Place randomly in the prepared bundt pan.

C   Part of the fun of this bread is its shape once it's done baking. Continue to dip dough pieces into the butter and herbs and place randomly in the bundt pan until it's about half full.

ESSENTIAL TECHNIQUE

Grinding caraway and rye flakes

While caraway seeds and rye flakes add texture and flavor to rye bread, I prefer to add them finely ground. Put the rye flakes and caraway seeds (on the left) in a small bowl of a food processor, blender, or spice grinder and process until the flakes are coarsely chopped with some fine powder (on the right).

Making the sponge

Also called a "poolish" or "starter," a sponge is a batter-consistency mixture of flour, water (though sometimes I use milk), and a commercial yeast (active dry or quick-rise) and is usually made the same day or up to one day before making the bread. The bowl on the left shows the ingredients just mixed. The bowl on the right shows the sponge after it has sat for an hour.

Making and shaping the dough

A

To test if the dough has been kneaded enough, pull off a piece of the dough and, holding it between the fingers on both hands, gently pull in opposite directions. If the dough breaks apart (on the left), continue kneading and retest after a minute or so. If the dough stretches evenly and thinly until it holds an opaque film or "windowpane" (on the right), it's ready to shape into a ball.

B

Working with the dough on an unfloured work surface, press to deflate, then form into a rectangle roughly 10 inches (25 cm) long and 6 inches (15 cm) wide. With one short side facing you, fold over the top third of the dough, then use the heel of your hand to press down firmly on the edge all the way across.

For more about kneading by hand, see p. 449.

For more about the windowpane test, see p. 470.

5. Line a cookie sheet with parchment or a nonstick liner and sprinkle evenly with the cornmeal. Scrape the dough onto a very lightly floured work surface (the dough is sticky but use the least amount of flour possible) and press down on the dough to deflate it. Using a bench scraper or knife, portion the dough into 8 equal pieces (about 3⅜ oz./96 g each). Shape into round balls, making sure the top is smooth and there is no seam on the bottom. Again, use very little flour. Working with one piece at a time and keeping the others covered, arrange the dough toward the back of your flattened palm near the thumb joint. With the edge of your other palm (curved slightly), press gently but firmly on the bottom of the dough, moving your top hand from the front to the back. This will rotate or spin the dough while keeping the top side up. Repeat until it forms a smooth-skinned ball with a sealed bottom (see the Essential Technique on p. 474). The goal is to stretch the top of the dough ball while simultaneously sealing the bottom. This will keep the dough from opening up as it expands during baking.

For more about deflating risen dough, see p. 477.

6. Arrange the dough balls about 2 inches (5 cm) apart on the prepared cookie sheet and gently press down on each, lightly flouring your hands as needed, until they are about 3 inches (7.5 cm) in diameter and about ¾ inch (2 cm) thick. Lightly grease the tops, then cover loosely but completely with plastic. Let the dough rise in a warm spot until doubled in size, 25 to 40 minutes.

Cook the muffins

1. Arrange a large, flat griddle pan on the stovetop (I use a double-sized one set over two burners). Heat over medium heat. Brush or spread the butter evenly over the griddle (it will sizzle). Carefully lift the muffins, one at a time, and place gently, cornmeal side down, on the hot griddle about 2 inches (5 cm) apart; be careful that you don't deflate the dough. Reduce the heat to medium low and cook until the bottom is well browned (reduce the heat if the muffins are browning too quickly) and the sides look dull and a bit dry, about 10 minutes. Using a wide spatula, carefully turn the muffins over, reduce the heat to low, and continue to cook, without pressing down on the muffins, until the bottom is browned and the muffins sound hollow when gently tapped, 10 to 15 minutes (see the Essential Technique on p. 474).

2. Using a wide spatula, lift the muffins from the griddle, move to a rack, and let cool until warm. The muffins are best when served toasted. Using a fork (you can use a serrated knife but your muffin will lose its crumble-topped texture), split the muffins in half and toast until golden.

(continued)

MAKE AHEAD

The muffins can be prepared, cooled completely, covered, and stowed at room temperature for up to 4 days or frozen for up to 1 week. To freeze, put in a zip-top freezer bag. To thaw, unwrap, set on a rack, and let sit at room temperature before splitting and toasting.

FINISHING TOUCHES

Serve immediately with butter, jam, honey, or nut butter.

ESSENTIAL TECHNIQUE

Shaping and grilling

A

With the dough portioned into 8 pieces, shape one at a time into a round ball, as shown on p. 428. The goal is to stretch the top of the dough ball while simultaneously sealing the bottom. This will keep the dough from opening up as it expands during baking. After a couple of rotations, turn the dough ball over and check the bottom. If it's still open (as shown on the left and center), turn over and repeat the process until the bottom is closed (as shown on the right). Place the shaped ball on the cornmeal-sprinkled baking sheet.

B

C

Arrange the balls about 2 inches (5 cm) apart on the prepared cookie sheet and press down on each, lightly flouring your hands as needed. The muffins should be about 3 inches (7.5 cm) in diameter and ¾ inch (2 cm) thick.

When ready to cook, lift each muffin with both hands and place gently, cornmeal side down, on the hot griddle.

D

Cook until the bottom is well browned—lift an edge with a wide spatula to check—then carefully flip the muffin over and cook the other side, with a total cooking time of 20 to 25 minutes.

Citrus-Spiced Hot Cross Buns

Makes 12 buns

Growing up as part of a large and extended Irish Catholic family, hot cross buns were an Easter tradition but, honestly, not one of my favorite treats. The store-bought ones were dry with an unpleasant artificial taste, and I didn't enjoy them even when toasted and slathered with butter.

Easter week of 2013, I was working on the recipe for buttery dinner rolls (see p. 446) and I had a bit of a hot cross bun epiphany. As I was tasting one of the rolls, it occurred to me that this buttery, tender, and egg-rich roll was the perfect base for my take on the holiday favorite. For a fresh burst of flavor, I added ground ginger and lemon zest to the dough—just delicious. For the dried fruit, I wanted more than just individual bites here and there. Adding the currants at the beginning of kneading breaks them down a bit so they lend more flavor and sweetness throughout the whole dough. If you prefer your currants intact, add them toward the end of kneading.

For the dough
1 cup (240 ml) whole milk
8 Tbs. (4 oz./113 g) unsalted butter, cut into 6 pieces
1 tsp. pure vanilla extract
3¾ cups (16¾ oz./474 g) unbleached all-purpose flour
⅓ cup (2⅜ oz./67 g) granulated sugar
2¼ tsp. quick-rise (instant) yeast

2 tsp. finely grated lemon zest (see p. 138)
¾ tsp. ground ginger
1 tsp. table salt
1 large egg
½ cup (2½ oz./71 g) dried currants
Nonstick cooking spray or neutral oil (safflower, canola, vegetable, or corn), for greasing the bowl and pan

For the egg wash
1 large egg
1 Tbs. water

For the vanilla icing
1 cup (4 oz./113 g) confectioners' sugar
3 Tbs. heavy cream
⅛ tsp. pure vanilla extract
Colored sugars (optional)

1. Heat the milk until very hot but not boiling. (I do this in a Pyrex measure in the microwave, but a small pan on the stovetop will also work.) Add the butter and stir until melted. Check the temperature using an instant-read thermometer. For the yeast to activate, the liquid needs to be between 115° and 125°F (45° and 52°C). Add the vanilla.

2. Put the flour, sugar, yeast, lemon zest, ginger, and salt in the bowl of a stand mixer and whisk until well blended. Check that the milk–butter temperature registers about 120°F (48°C) and if not, warm gently until it does. Fit the mixer with the dough hook and begin mixing on medium-low speed as you slowly pour in the liquid. Add the egg and mix on medium low until the flour is completely incorporated, 1 to 2 minutes. Add the currants. Increase the speed to medium high and knead until the dough is very smooth and elastic and pulls away from the bottom of the bowl, 8 to 10 minutes. If the dough climbs up the hook, stop the mixer and scrape the dough into the bowl as necessary. The mixer might dance around on the counter, so don't venture too far away when the dough is mixing.

For more about scraping dough from a dough hook, see p. 449.

(continued)

TWISTS

Flavor swap

> Instead of the grated lemon zest, switch in one of the following: 1 Tbs. finely grated orange zest or 1 tsp. ground cardamom.

> Instead of the currants, switch in one of the following: ½ cup (4½ oz./ 128 g) lightly packed finely chopped dried apricots, ½ cup (2¼ oz./64 g) finely chopped crystallized ginger, ½ cup (3 oz./85 g) lightly packed, finely chopped dried cherries, or ½ cup (approximately 4½ oz./ 128 g) combination of any dried finely chopped dried fruit.

> Instead of the vanilla extract in the icing, switch in one of the following: 1½ tsp. finely grated lemon zest, 2 tsp. finely grated orange zest, or the seeds from ¼ vanilla bean pod.

Re-size it

Portion the dough into 16 pieces (2 to 2¼ oz./57 to 64 g each) and proceed as directed.

3. Remove the dough hook, scrape the dough onto the counter, knead once or twice until it no longer sticks to the counter and passes the windowpane test, and shape into a ball. Lightly grease the sides of the bowl and put the dough, rounded side up, back in. Cover the bowl with a plate or plastic wrap. Let rise in a warm spot until nearly doubled in size, 45 to 60 minutes.

For more about kneading by hand, see p. 449.

For more about the windowpane test, see p. 470.

4. Lightly grease a 9 x 13 x 2-inch (23 x 33 x 5 cm) baking dish (I use Pyrex). Scrape the dough onto an unfloured work surface and press down on the dough to deflate it. Using a bench scraper or knife, portion it into 12 equal pieces (about 2⅞ oz./82 g each).

For more about weighing dough, see p. 450.

5. Working with one piece at a time and keeping the others covered, arrange the dough toward the back of your flattened palm near the thumb joint. With the edge of your other palm (curved slightly), press gently but firmly on the bottom of the dough, moving your top hand from the front to the back. This will rotate or spin the dough while keeping the top side up. Repeat until it forms a smooth-skinned ball with a sealed bottom (see the Essential Technique on the facing page). The goal is to stretch the top of the dough ball while simultaneously sealing the bottom. This will keep the dough from opening up as it expands during baking. Put the ball, rounded side up, in the prepared baking dish, cover loosely with plastic, and repeat with the remaining dough. (The dough balls can be arranged in rows or placed randomly; just be sure they're evenly spaced.) Cover the baking dish with plastic and let the balls rise in a warm spot until they're about double their original size and the tops of the dough balls have risen to the top of the baking dish (they won't yet fill the dish), 45 to 60 minutes.

6. When the buns are almost risen, position a rack in the center of the oven and heat the oven to 375°F (190°C/gas 5). In a small bowl or ramekin, make the egg wash by mixing the egg and water with a fork until well blended. When the buns have risen, remove the plastic wrap and, using a pastry brush, evenly coat the tops of the buns with the egg wash. Bake the buns until they're puffed and well browned (an instant-read thermometer will read about 190°F/88°C), 24 to 26 minutes. Move the sheet to a rack. Serve warm or, to serve with icing, let cool completely and frost, or cover and stow at room temperature for up to 1 day and frost just before serving.

For more about checking temperature, see p. 471.

7. To serve with icing, mix the confectioners' sugar, cream, and vanilla in a small bowl until smooth and thick. Spoon the icing over each bun to form a wide cross. Sprinkle with colored sugar, if desired, and serve.

ESSENTIAL TECHNIQUE

Shaping the dough

A

After the dough has risen, scrape it onto the work surface and gently press to deflate. The dough isn't sticky, so there's no need to flour your hands or the work surface.

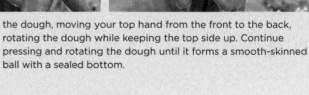

B

Working with one piece at a time (keep the others covered so they don't dry out), arrange the dough toward the back of your flattened palm near the thumb joint. With the edge of your other palm (curved slightly), press gently but firmly on the bottom of the dough, moving your top hand from the front to the back, rotating the dough while keeping the top side up. Continue pressing and rotating the dough until it forms a smooth-skinned ball with a sealed bottom.

C

Put each ball, seam side down, in the prepared baking dish. You can arrange the balls in rows or randomly, but it's important that they're spaced evenly to give them ample room to rise evenly.

Chapter 9

PASTRY

> > > >

Bourbon Maple Pecan Baklava

Makes 24 pieces

When I was in high school, my friend Harriet and I had a small catering business we called Four Hands. In the beginning, we were hostess helpers—passing, serving, and cleaning up. As our clients got to know us, we were asked to help with the food prep, sometimes using our moms' recipes (Tom Cat's Chocolate Mousse on p. 369 is one example) and other times, cooking and baking their recipes. It was on one of these occasions that I made and tasted my first baklava. Working alongside the client, I was awed by the methodical process of layering the phyllo and nut mixture, the meticulous precision of cutting the pastry, and, finally, watching, in disbelief, as the thick honey syrup was magically absorbed. But nothing matched my wonder and delight as when I took my first bite. At once crispy, crunchy, sticky, gooey, sweet, rich, and nutty—that baklava changed my perception of desserts.

Throughout my baking years, the qualities of that first baklava have stayed with me while the flavor profiles of my variations have evolved. Here, maple syrup and bourbon—not honey—take the lead flavor roles with pecans and coconut—not pistachios—for the filling. It still takes time—no short-cuts for a classic like this one—but your taste buds will be rewarded.

For the nut mixture
2½ cups (10 oz./283 g) coarsely chopped pecans
⅓ cup (2⅜ oz./67 g) granulated sugar
2 tsp. ground cinnamon
Pinch of table salt
1 cup (2½ oz./71 g) shredded sweetened coconut

For assembly
16 Tbs. (8 oz./227 g) unsalted butter, melted and cooled slightly
½ package (8 oz./227 g) frozen phyllo dough (one roll from a twin pack), thawed

For the syrup
1½ cups (360 ml) pure maple syrup (preferably grade B) (see p. 8)
1 cup (7 oz./198 g) firmly packed dark brown sugar
½ cup (120 ml) bourbon
½ cup (120 ml) water
1 Tbs. freshly squeezed lemon juice

Make the nut mixture

Put the pecans, sugar, cinnamon, and salt in a food processor. Pulse until the nuts are finely chopped but not ground. Scrape into a medium bowl, add the coconut, and stir until well blended.

For more about chopping nuts, see p. 304.

Assemble and bake the baklava

1. Position a rack in the center of the oven and heat the oven to 350°F (180°C/gas 4). Lightly brush the bottoms and sides of a 9 x 13 x 2-inch (23 x 33 x 5 cm) pan (preferably straight-sided) with some of the melted butter.

2. Unroll the phyllo sheets and lay flat on a clean, dry surface. Using a sharp knife, trim one short side so the phyllo measures 9 x 13 inches (23 x 33 cm). Cover completely with plastic wrap or a damp (not wet) dishtowel. Working with one sheet of phyllo at a time and keeping the rest covered so they don't dry out, place a sheet in the prepared pan. Lightly but completely brush with some of the melted butter and cover

MAKE AHEAD

> The syrup can be made, cooled completely, and refrigerated for up to 3 days before reheating.

> The baklava can be assembled, covered, and refrigerated for up to 1 day before baking. Cut the baklava while the oven heats.

> The syrup-coated baklava can be baked, cooled, covered, and refrigerated for up to 5 days.

Pistachio Phyllo Cups *with* Honeyed Peaches *and* Ricotta

Serves 6   [PHOTO ON P. 343]

The paper-thin phyllo dough layers can be a bit finicky to work with, so it's important to be organized and get your ingredients and work space set up before you begin. I've included a few extra sheets so don't panic if you tear a sheet or if a few are too stuck together to work with. Once you've handled the dough a few times, you'll be a pro.

The phyllo cups are the perfect vehicle for just about any dessert. You can assemble them, as I've suggested here, with fresh ricotta along with the compote or with ice cream or sorbet along with any type of fruit mixture. I like making my own ricotta (it's very easy to do), but if you aren't feeling adventurous, fresh ricotta can be found in gourmet and Italian markets.

There isn't a lot of honey in the recipe but don't underestimate its importance. Honey not only sweetens this dessert but it also adds a distinct floral nuance to the overall flavor. I like lavender or orange blossom honey for this recipe, but I encourage you to seek out your local honey sources and sample the many varietals available.

Nonstick cooking spray or softened butter, for preparing the pan

For the phyllo cups
3 Tbs. (1½ oz./42 g) unsalted butter
1 Tbs. honey (preferably local)
Pinch of table salt
½ package (8 oz./227 g) frozen phyllo dough (one roll from a twin pack), thawed (you'll use 4 to 8 sheets) (see p. 480)
3 Tbs. very finely chopped pistachios (see p. 304)

For the compote
3 Tbs. honey (preferably local)
1 Tbs. freshly squeezed lime juice
¾ tsp. finely grated lime zest (see p. 138)
Pinch of table salt
3 to 4 ripe peaches (16 oz./454 g), rinsed and dried

For serving
Fresh ricotta cheese (for homemade, see p. 64)
½ cup (120 ml) pomegranate seeds
¼ cup (1¼ oz./35 g) chopped pistachios, or more to taste

Position a rack in the center of the oven and heat the oven to 325°F (165°C/gas 3). Lightly grease six large (10 oz./300 ml each) ramekins (I use Pyrex) and set on a baking sheet.

Make the phyllo cups

1. Put the butter, honey, and salt in a small saucepan. Cook over medium heat, stirring often, until the butter is melted and the mixture is syrupy, about 2 minutes.

2. Clean off one large work surface and have ready a large cutting board, long ruler, sharp knife, and pastry brush, along with the butter mixture and pistachios.

3. Unwrap the phyllo sheets, peel off 8 sheets, lay them flat, and cover with plastic or a damp towel. (If they are left uncovered, they will dry out and become too brittle to work with.) Reroll, wrap, and refrigerate or freeze the remaining phyllo. Lift one sheet and lay it flat on the cutting board and re-cover the remaining sheets. It's all right if the sheet tears a bit, but if it rips severely or sticks to itself, use another sheet. Using the pastry brush, carefully brush some of the butter–honey mixture over the entire sheet. Sprinkle with 1 Tbs. of the pistachios. Place a second sheet of dough directly on top of the first and press down gently. Brush the sheet with some of the butter–honey mixture and sprinkle another 1 Tbs. of the pistachios evenly over the phyllo. Top with a third sheet of phyllo and press gently. Brush with the butter–honey mixture and sprinkle with the remaining pistachios. Top with a fourth and final layer of phyllo and press gently (see the Essential Technique on p. 492).

4. Using the knife, cut the phyllo lengthwise into two 5½-inch (14 cm) wide strips. Cut each strip into three 5½-inch (14 cm) squares. Working with one square at a time, gently ease the square into a ramekin so the bottom fits snugly and the sides form a cup shape. The sides will be a bit ruffled. Bake until the bottoms are golden brown, 15 to 18 minutes. Move the sheet to a rack and let cool completely.

Make the peach compote

1. In a small saucepan, combine the honey, lime juice, zest, and salt. Set over medium heat, stirring frequently, until the mixture is smooth and syrupy. Set aside to cool slightly.

2. Cut the peaches in half and remove the pits. Cut into ½-inch (12 mm) thick slices. Put the slices in a large bowl. Drizzle some of the warm honey mixture over the fruit and gently toss to coat the fruit.

For more about pitting and cutting peaches, see p. 108.

To assemble

Carefully lift the phyllo shells from the ramekins and set on small dessert plates. Spoon some ricotta into each shell. Stir the compote and spoon some fruit and juices on top and sprinkle with the pomegranate seeds and pistachio nuts along with a final drizzle of the honey mixture. Serve immediately.

MAKE AHEAD

> The phyllo cups can be prepared, cooled completely, covered, and stowed at room temperature for up to 1 day before serving.

> The compote can be made and stowed in the refrigerator for up to 6 hours.

TWISTS

Flavor swap

> Instead of the lime juice and zest in the peach compote, choose one of the following: 2 Tbs. finely chopped crystallized ginger (see p. 218); ¾ tsp. finely grated lemon or orange zest (see p. 138) and 1 Tbs. lemon or orange juice; or ½ tsp. pure vanilla extract.

> Instead of peaches, use the same amount of strawberries, raspberries, blueberries, blackberries, pitted cherries, or a combination.

(continued)

ESSENTIAL TECHNIQUE

Making rough puff pastry

A pastry blender is a great tool for cutting butter into flour. Hold it with one or both hands, as you'll need to chop the butter into the flour until it's in ½- to ¾-inch (12 mm to 2 cm) pieces. A towel under your bowl will hold it steady so it won't slide around on the surface as you work.

B

C

Add the water and continue the chopping and cutting until the dough comes together, is shaggy, and barely hangs together. Scrape it onto a lightly floured work surface and shape into a rough rectangle.

Roll the dough into a 6 x 18-inch (15 x 46 cm) rectangle, with one short end facing you. The dough will be ragged and piece-meal at first.

D

With the help of a bench scraper, fold both short ends toward each other so they meet in the middle. Fold the short end closest to you, then lift and fold over the other half to make a 4 x 6-inch (10 x 15 cm) rectangle, aligning the edges. This completes one double turn (or fold). Turn the dough rectangle so that the seam is on the right. Repeat the rolling and folding as directed one more time. Wrap and refrigerate for 20 minutes.

Working with chilled dough, turn it so the seam is on your right, then repeat the rolling and folding process one final time. You'll notice that the dough will become smoother and the butter forms long streaks in the dough (this creates the layers and puff in the baked dough). Lightly flour as needed to prevent sticking.

Finishing the Napoleon pastry

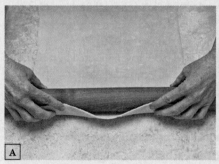

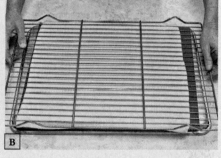

Once the dough is rolled out, transfer it to the upside-down sheet pan by rolling it over the rolling pin. Use your fingers to ease one short edge of the dough on the pin, then loosely roll the dough around the pin. Position the pin near one edge of the liner-covered pan, then unroll the dough over the top of the liner. It's okay if the dough hangs off the pan slightly.

Position the cooling rack—lightly greased side down—on top of the dough. Be sure it covers the dough completely. The rack prevents the pastry from puffing and gives it nice indentations, which not only look pretty but will hold the filling and chocolate drizzle nicely.

The pastry is done baking when it's deep golden brown. Be sure to use pot holders to lift off the rack. If it sticks to the pastry, insert a small offset spatula between the rack and the pastry to ease the rack off.

ESSENTIAL TECHNIQUE

Folding the triangles

A

Make a tick mark on both short ends of the phyllo layers at 4½ inches (11 cm), line up a ruler, and then use a pizza wheel to make two strips. You can use a sharp knife to cut as well.

B

Spoon ¼ cup (60 ml) filling into one short end of the strip, pushing it to one outside corner, and hold it in place with your fingers as you fold it over on the diagonal to form a triangle.

C

Continue to hold the wrapped filling as you fold the strip like a flag, alternating the direction of the fold. If a bit of filling falls out, push it back in with your finger, then continue folding.

D

Once you've reached the end of the strip, place the triangle on the prepared cookie sheet with the phyllo edge on the bottom. Repeat to form a total of 6 triangles, brush the tops with melted butter, and bake.

Croissants

Makes 14 [PHOTO ON P. 411]

In my baking apprentice days in Paris and New York, I learned many different ways to make croissants. As I worked with each new chef, they would teach me their own unique take on making this French classic. I kept a mental list of the different tips and tricks that I liked from each version, knowing that one day I would combine many of them into my own version. The result is an easy-to-work-with dough that bakes into wonderfully buttery, flaky pastries that are stand-alone divine but even better served warm with a touch of homemade jam.

Don't be intimidated by the length of the recipe. It's long but only because I wanted to be sure to add enough step-by-step directions to make the process easy for you to achieve success.

For the dough
3½ cups (16 oz./454 g) unbleached all-purpose flour + more for dusting
¼ cup (1¾ oz./50 g) granulated sugar
1 Tbs. active dry yeast
2¼ tsp. table salt
1 cup (240 ml) whole milk, at room temperature

¼ cup (60 ml) water
1 Tbs. distilled white vinegar
3 Tbs. (1½ oz./42 g) unsalted butter, cut into 4 pieces, very soft
Nonstick cooking spray or oil

For the butter layer
24 Tbs. (12 oz./340 g) unsalted butter, softened

¼ cup (1⅛ oz./32 g) unbleached all-purpose flour

For the egg wash
2 large eggs
1 Tbs. water

Make the dough

1. Put the flour, sugar, yeast, and salt in a large bowl of a stand mixer and whisk until well blended. Fit the mixer with the dough hook. Add the milk, water, and vinegar and beat on medium speed until the dough comes together, 1 to 2 minutes.

2. With the mixer on medium speed, add the butter pieces, one at a time, waiting until the butter is completely incorporated before adding the next piece. Continue beating until the dough is smooth and shiny, about 2 minutes. It will not pull away completely from the sides of the bowl and it will be soft and sticky to the touch. Remove the dough hook, scrape down the sides of the bowl, and lightly grease the top of the dough with a little oil or spray (I use spray). Cover the bowl and refrigerate while you make the butter layer.

Make the butter layer

1. On a small piece of parchment, draw a 7-inch (17 cm) square. Invert the paper onto a cookie sheet and make room in the freezer.

2. Put the butter and flour in a medium bowl and beat with an electric handheld mixer fitted with wire beaters until well blended and very smooth. (This step can also be done in an extra stand mixer bowl using the paddle attachment.)

MAKE AHEAD

While at their very best when first baked, the croissants can be covered and stowed at room temperature for up to 2 days and warmed in a 325°F (165°C/gas 3) oven or toaster oven.

(continued)

TWISTS

Flavor swap

> **Almond:** Make the dough as directed. In a medium bowl, stir in 1 cup (4 oz./113 g) finely ground almonds, 4 Tbs. (2 oz./57 g) unsalted butter, softened, ¼ cup (1¾ oz./50 g) granulated sugar, a pinch of table salt, 1 large egg, and ½ tsp. pure almond extract until well blended.

Roll and cut the dough as directed for the croissants, without the notches. Spread 1 rounded Tbs. of the almond filling over the triangles. Roll as directed for the croissants, leaving the ends straight (not bent) and continue as directed for rising, glazing, and baking the croissants.

> **Chocolate:** Make the dough as directed. Roll half of the dough to a 5 x 24-inch (12 x 61 cm) rectangle and cut into six 4-inch (10 cm) wide strips. Arrange ½ oz. (1½ Tbs.) chopped chocolate in a strip on the bottom edge of each rectangle. Roll each strip jellyroll style around the chocolate and pinch the edges to seal. Continue as directed for rising, glazing, and baking the croissants.

3. Scrape the butter–flour mixture onto the parchment in the center of the 7-inch (17 cm) square. Using a small offset spatula, spread the butter in an even layer just to the lines. Slide the cookie sheet into the freezer and chill until firm enough to hold its shape but not cold, about 20 minutes. The goal is to have both the dough and the butter layer at the same temperature and consistency.

Laminate the dough

1. Scrape the dough onto a lightly floured surface and gently stretch and shape it into a 10-inch (25 cm) square, with one corner pointing toward you. Invert the butter layer onto the center of the dough with one flat edge facing you and peel away the parchment (see the Essential Technique on p. 510). The butter layer should be centered on the dough with the dough corners pointing above, below, and to both sides of the butter. Lift the top dough flap over the butter, stretching slightly if necessary, with the point in the center of the butter square. Repeat with the remaining dough flaps and pinch the edges together, sealing the butter inside.

2. Lightly flour the top of the dough and arrange in the center of the work surface with one straight edge facing you. Using a rolling pin, gently but firmly press down on the dough at the top and bottom edge and at several spots in between. This will ensure that the butter is soft enough to roll and help the dough relax. Roll the dough to an 8 x 20-inch (20 x 50 cm) rectangle, lifting and loosening the dough and lightly dusting the top and bottom as you roll to prevent sticking. Use the side of the rolling pin (or the flat edge of a long ruler) to straighten the sides as needed.

3. Use your hands and the rolling pin to square off the top and bottom edge and brush off any excess flour. With a short side facing you, fold the top one-third of the dough toward the middle, brushing off any excess flour, and fold the bottom third over the two layers to make a rectangular dough package (this is similar to folding a letter). Using the rolling pin, press down on the short open edges of the dough. This will help the dough maintain its shape. Turn the dough so the long open edge is to the right and repeat the pressing, rolling, and folding process one more time. Wrap in plastic and refrigerate for 1 to 2 hours.

4. Unwrap the dough and arrange on a lightly floured surface with the long open edge to the right. Using the rolling pin, repeat the process of pressing, rolling, and folding (Steps 2 and 3 above) two more times. Wrap the dough in plastic and refrigerate for 4 to 12 hours.

Shape and bake the croissants

1. Line two cookie sheets with nonstick liners or parchment.

2. Unwrap the dough, cut in half crosswise, and rewrap one half and keep refrigerated. Arrange the other half on a lightly floured surface with the cut edge to the left. Using a rolling pin, gently but firmly press down on the dough at the top and bottom edge and at several spots in between.

This will ensure that the butter is soft enough to roll and help the dough relax. Roll the dough to slightly larger than a 7 x 20-inch (17 x 50 cm) rectangle, lifting and loosening the dough and lightly dusting the top and bottom as you roll to prevent sticking. Using a sharp chef's knife and a ruler, trim the edges to get a neat 7 x 20-inch (17 x 50 cm) rectangle.

3. Turn the rectangle so that one long edge is facing you, measure the rectangle, and re-roll, if necessary, lifting and loosening to make sure the dough isn't sticking on the bottom. (This will ensure that the dough doesn't overshrink when it's cut into triangles.) Using the ruler and a small paring knife, mark the bottom long edge of the dough at 5-inch (12 cm) intervals (see the Essential Technique on p. 511). Working from left to right, mark the top edge of the dough at 2½ inches (6 cm) and then at subsequent 5-inch (12 cm) intervals. These marks will fall halfway between the bottom edge marks. Using a large chef's knife, make diagonal cuts from the bottom to the top and then from top to bottom across the length of the dough to make seven triangles. Discard the two end pieces.

4. Using the small knife, make a ½- to ¾-inch (12 mm to 2 cm) long notch in the center of each short edge of the triangles. (This will help shape the curve of the croissants.) Working with one triangle at a time, pick up the triangle and dangle it while very gently stretching it until it's 7 inches (17 cm) long. Arrange the triangle on the work surface with the notched edge toward you and, using your fingers, gently pull the corners of the notch in opposite directions toward the outer edges while rolling toward the point. As you roll, pull gently on the outside corners to keep them long. Stop rolling when the point is directly underneath the roll.

5. Gently pull the outer corners outward and bend them in front of the roll until they overlap to make a classic crescent shape, pressing to seal them together. Arrange on one of the prepared cookie sheets. Repeat rolling and shaping with the remaining triangles, spacing them about 2 to 3 inches apart on the sheet. Cover loosely but completely with plastic and set aside to rise at room temperature (this is called proofing) for 45 minutes. Do not let the croissants double in size; overproofing will result in flattened, dense croissants. Meanwhile, repeat the process with the remaining dough and cookie sheet.

Make the egg wash and bake the croissants

1. Position a rack in the center of the oven and heat the oven to 400°F (200°C/gas 6). Put the egg and water in a small bowl and, using a fork, mix until well blended.

2. After the first sheet of croissants has rested for 45 minutes, unwrap and brush the surface generously with the egg wash. Bake until the croissants are puffed and deep brown, 22 to 26 minutes. Move the sheet to a rack, then glaze and bake the second sheet as directed.

3. Serve immediately or let cool completely, cover, and stow at room temperature for up to 2 days.

(continued)

BAKER'S WISDOM

Save time

Once you get the hang of making the croissants, consider using the double-turn technique described for the Glazed Napoleons with White Chocolate–Blood Orange Mousse (recipe on p. 499), which will save you a little time.

FINISHING TOUCHES

Serve with Honey or Maple Butter (recipe on p. 85).

ESSENTIAL TECHNIQUE

Laminating the dough

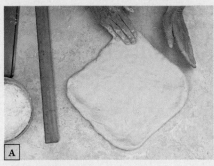

A

Gently stretch and shape the dough into a 10-inch (25 cm) square, with one corner pointing toward you. Place the butter layer at the center of the dough with one flat edge facing you and peel away the parchment.

B

Lift the top dough flap over the butter, stretching slightly if necessary and bringing the point to the center of the butter square.

C

Repeat with the remaining dough flaps. Pinch the edges together, sealing the butter inside like an envelope.

D

Using a rolling pin, gently but firmly press down on the dough at the top and bottom edge and at several spots in between to help soften the butter and relax the dough.

E

Roll the dough to an 8 x 20-inch (20 x 50 cm) rectangle, using the rolling pin to square off and straighten the sides.

F

Fold the top third of the dough toward the middle, and fold the bottom third over the two layers—just like folding a letter. You should have an 8 x 6-inch (20 x 15 cm) rectangle.

G

Turn the dough so the long open edge is to the right and repeat the process: Roll to an 8 x 20-inch (20 x 50 cm) rectangle, square off the edges, and do the letter fold. Each time you do this is called giving the dough a turn. Wrap the dough in plastic and refrigerate for 1 to 2 hours before giving it another two turns.

Shaping the croissants

A

Roll half of the dough into a rectangle slightly larger than 7 x 20 inches (17 x 50 cm), lifting and loosening the dough and lightly dusting the top and bottom as you roll to prevent sticking. Turn so the long edge faces you, then trim to exactly 7 x 20 inches (17 x 50 cm).

B

Using a small paring knife, mark the bottom edge of the dough every 5 inches (12 cm). Next mark the top edge of the dough at 2½ inches (6 cm) and then at 5-inch (12 cm) intervals beyond that, so the top marks fall halfway between the bottom edge marks.

C

With a large chef's knife, make diagonal cuts connecting the top and bottom marks across the length of the dough. Discard the two end pieces. You will have 7 large triangles.

D

Use the paring knife to make a ½- to ¾-inch (12 mm to 2 cm) long notch in the center of the edge of the triangles opposite the point.

E

Working with one triangle at a time, gently dangle and stretch the triangle until it's 7 inches (17 cm) long.

F

Put the triangle on the surface with the notched edge toward you and, using your fingers, gently pull the corners of the notched end outward while rolling it up toward the point.

G

When the point is directly underneath the roll, gently pull the outer corners around to the front of the roll so they overlap, and press the ends to seal them together.

FINISHING TOUCHES

Just before serving, dust with confectioners' sugar or drizzle with Honey Glaze (p. 55) or confectioners' sugar glaze (p. 77).

Shape the Danish

1. Line a 13 x 18 x 1-inch (33 x 46 x 2.5 cm) half sheet pan with parchment. (A nonstick liner won't work for this recipe because you'll be cutting the dough on the paper. The baking sheet will hold in the little bit of liquid that releases from the Danish filling when it bakes.) Put the egg and water in a small bowl and, using a fork, mix until well blended.

2. Arrange the dough on a lightly floured surface with the open edge to the left. Once again, using a rolling pin, gently but firmly press down on the dough at the top and bottom edge and several spots in between. This will ensure that the butter is soft enough to roll and help the dough relax. Roll the dough into a 10 x 16-inch (25 x 40.5 cm) rectangle, lifting and loosening the dough and lightly dusting the top and bottom as you roll to prevent sticking.

3. Scatter the chocolate–pecan filling evenly over the dough to within ¹⁄₂ inch (12 mm) of one long edge. Cover with a large piece of plastic wrap and, using your hands and the rolling pin, press to compact the filling. Brush the exposed edge with some of the egg wash and, starting on the long edge closest to you, roll up jellyroll style (see the Essential Technique on the facing page). Pinch the seam to seal and arrange the roll, seam side down, on the parchment-lined sheet pan.

4. Brush the ends of the roll with a little egg wash, then join them together to make a circle and pinch to seal. Using a sharp knife, cut the ring into 16 slices (about 1 inch/2.5 cm apart), leaving the center ¹⁄₂ inch (12 mm) attached. Lift up and turn each piece slightly. Cover loosely but completely with plastic wrap, then set aside to rise until light and airy to the touch and risen about 1¹⁄₂ times, about 1 hour.

Let rise and bake

1. After the Danish has rested for 45 minutes, position a rack in the center of the oven and heat the oven to 350°F (180°C/gas 4). The dough will continue to rise while the oven heats.

2. When the Danish is light and airy to the touch and has risen about 1¹⁄₂ times, about 1 hour, brush the dough with the remaining egg wash. Bake until puffed and deep golden brown, 35 to 38 minutes. Move the sheet to a rack and let cool for 15 minutes before serving.

Filling and shaping the ring

A

B

C

Once the dough is rolled out to a 10 x 16-inch (25 x 40.5 cm) rectangle, position one long edge in front of you and sprinkle with the chocolate–pecan filling. Cover with plastic and use your hands to press down on the filling, then use a rolling pin, pressing to form a compact layer of filling. You aren't rolling the dough any larger, so you don't need to be aggressive in rolling out. This will keep the filling intact.

Brush the outer exposed edge with a little egg wash, then roll up the dough jellyroll style, beginning with the long edge closest to you. Nudge the dough up with your fingers and keep rolling evenly as you reach the end. Don't worry if a little bit of filling falls out.

Using your thumb and index finger, pinch the seam to seal the dough. Be sure to pinch all along the seam so that the roll doesn't break open when shaped. Place the rolled dough, seam side down, on the parchment-lined sheet, then brush the ends with egg wash. Don't be stingy with the egg wash, which will help seal the ends.

D

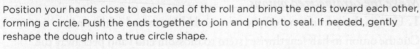

E

Position your hands close to each end of the roll and bring the ends toward each other, forming a circle. Push the ends together to join and pinch to seal. If needed, gently reshape the dough into a true circle shape.

Hold the ring with one hand while you use the other to cut 16 slices evenly spaced around the ring. You can eyeball it or make tick marks with the knife blade before cutting. As you cut, leave about 1/2 inch (12 mm) attached at the center of the ring.

F

Being gentle so you don't rip the dough, lift up and turn each slice slightly, laying the slices against each other so they fan out in the circle. Cover the Danish loosely but completely with plastic and let rise before baking.

ESSENTIAL TECHNIQUE

Making caramelized onions

A

Using a sharp knife, cut off the stem and blossom end of the onion.

B

Cut the onion in half lengthwise (stem to blossom end) and use your fingers to peel away the outer skin; discard.

C

Working with one half at a time, arrange flat side down on the cutting board and cut into thin, even slices.

D

Cook the onions, stirring frequently until they're beginning to brown, 10 to 15 minutes. Reduce the heat to medium low and continue cooking and stirring (more toward the end of cooking) until the onions are deep brown and reduced down, another 5 to 8 minutes.

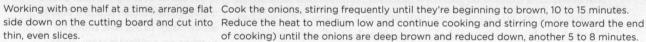

Roasted Veggie Galette

Serves 4 to 6

Wrapping a savory, flaky crust around your favorite combination of cooked veggies and crumbled cheeses not only breathes new life into leftovers but also elevates them to main-dish material. Whether for lunch, brunch, or dinner, all that's needed is a nice tossed salad and a glass of something chilled. Of course, a wedge of this rustic tart is just as tasty served alongside grilled chicken or fish.

When I need to extend my veggie combo to equal the 3 cups (720 ml) of filling or want to add protein to the meal, I simply mix in some chopped ham, prosciutto, turkey, or cooked beans.

For the dough
8 Tbs. (4 oz./113 g) unsalted butter
3 Tbs. cold water
1⅓ cups (6 oz./170 g) unbleached all-purpose flour
¼ cup (1 oz./28 g) ground Parmigiano Reggiano cheese (see p. 38)
¾ tsp. table salt
½ tsp. freshly ground black pepper

For the roasted veggies
2 cups (5 oz./142 g) packed coarsely chopped broccoli
2 cups (8 oz./227 g) packed coarsely chopped cauliflower
1½ cups (7 oz./198 g) diced carrots
3 Tbs. olive oil
Table salt and freshly ground black pepper

5 scallions, coarsely chopped
1 medium garlic clove, minced
1½ tsp. finely chopped fresh rosemary

For assembly
1 large egg
1 tsp. water
¾ cup (3⅜ oz./96 g) crumbled goat cheese

Make the dough

1. Cut the butter in half lengthwise and cut each strip into 6 pieces. Pile the butter onto a plate and slide into the freezer until ready to use. Measure the water and keep in the fridge until ready to use.

2. Whisk the flour, cheese, salt, and pepper in a large bowl until well blended. Add the cold butter and, using a pastry blender or two knives, cut them into the flour mixture until the butter pieces are pea-sized, about 3 minutes. (You can also do this in a food processor using short pulses, scraping the blended mixture into a large bowl before proceeding.)

For more about mixing butter and flour together until the butter is pea-sized, see p. 80.

3. Pour the water over the flour mixture and, using a silicone spatula, stir and fold until it forms a shaggy, moist dough with some floury bits remaining (I like to use one hand to help mix while keeping the other working the spatula). Scrape the dough and any remaining floury bits onto the counter and gather into a mound. Starting with the top of the mound and using the heel of your hand, smear a section of the dough down the side and along the work surface away from you to blend the butter pieces into the dough. Repeat with the remaining dough in sections. Using a bench scraper, fold the dough together (the mixture will be rough and crumbly). Turn the pile about 90 degrees and repeat the smearing process until the mixture just comes together into a cohesive dough (this is a technique called *fraisage*). Be careful not to overwork the dough because

(Roasted Veggie Galette continued)

ESSENTIAL TECHNIQUE

Cutting ingredients to size

When cooking different veggies at the same time, it's important to size them according to how fast they cook so they cook evenly in the same amount of time. Carrots are more dense so they need to be in small cubes; cauliflower is broken into florets and sliced into thin wedges; broccoli is broken into small florets.

TWISTS

Flavor swap

> Substitute any combination of a generous 3 to 3½ cups (I measure in a 4-cup/480 ml Pyrex, as the weight will vary depending on the ingredients) of loosely packed chopped, roasted veggies for the filling.

> Instead of the goat cheese, use the same amount of feta, herb–garlic cheese spread, or softened cream cheese, using a small offset spatula to spread in an even layer.

FINISHING TOUCHES

Scatter 3 Tbs. toasted pine nuts over the filling before serving.

that will make the crust dense. Shape the dough into a 6-inch (15 cm) disk. Wrap in plastic and refrigerate until firm, about 2 hours.

For more about using your hand to help mix, see p. 85.

For more about *fraisage*, see p. 549.

Make the filling

Position a rack in the center of the oven and heat the oven to 400°F (200°C/gas 6). Put the broccoli, cauliflower, and carrots in a medium bowl, drizzle with the oil, and generously sprinkle with salt and pepper; toss until blended. Scrape into a 9 x 13 x 2-inch (12 x 33 x 5 cm) pan and spread evenly. Bake until just tender, stirring and flipping once halfway through baking, about 25 minutes. Move the pan to a rack; add the scallions, garlic, and rosemary and stir until blended. Return the pan to the oven and continue to bake until the herbs and garlic are fragrant, about 5 minutes. Move to a rack and set aside to cool completely. Leave the oven on.

Assemble and bake the galette

1. Line a 13 x 18 x 1-inch (33 x 46 x 2.5 cm) half sheet pan with parchment, nonstick liner, or foil. Taste the cooled filling and adjust the seasonings as necessary.

2. Pull the dough disk from the fridge and, if it's very cold, set it out at room temperature until it's just pliable enough to roll, 10 to 20 minutes. Roll the dough between sheets of parchment, lightly flouring between rolling and flipping, to a round slightly larger than 13½ inches (34 cm) (a little bit of the dough round will peek out the sides of the parchment). Peel away the top piece of parchment. Trim off some of the jagged edges to make a clean 13½-inch (34 cm) round, if desired. Carefully and loosely roll the dough around the pin, leaving the bottom parchment behind, and transfer it to the prepared sheet pan. The dough will hang over the edges of the pan for now.

For more about rolling dough between parchment, see p. 133.

3. In a ramekin or small bowl, mix the egg and water with a fork until blended. Scatter the goat cheese on top of the dough in an even layer, leaving a 2½-inch (6 cm) border. Spoon and scrape the filling over the cheese and spread evenly. Using your fingers, fold the dough edge up and over the filling, pleating the dough as you go. Press the pleats to seal. Be careful not to pull or stretch the dough. It will not cover the filling completely.

For more about pleating dough, see p. 308.

4. Using a small pastry brush, spread the egg wash evenly over the pleated edge of the dough. Bake until the crust is deep golden brown, 35 to 38 minutes. Move the sheet to a rack and let cool for 15 to 20 minutes. Using two wide, long offset spatulas, carefully remove the galette from the sheet, set on a serving plate or cutting board, and cut into serving pieces. The galette is best when served hot, warm, or room temperature and can be warmed slightly in a 300°F (150°C/gas 2) oven, if desired.

Curried Parmesan Twists

Makes 48 twists

Savory, flaky, and crispy, these curry-spiced twists are the perfect nibbler to serve alongside a full-bodied red wine. They are ridiculously easy to make with either thawed homemade rough puff or store-bought puff pastry. Like most recipes with few ingredients, the ultimate flavor and success of these twist relies on the quality of the ingredients you use. Here, you can choose either mild or spicy curry powder but, for a big flavor punch, make sure it's no older than 3 to 6 months or the taste will fall flat.

¾ cup (3 oz./85 g) ground
   Parmigiano Reggiano cheese
   (see p. 38)
1 to 1½ tsp. mild or hot curry
   powder
1 large egg, at room temperature

1 tsp. water
½ recipe rough puff pastry
   (see p. 499) or 1 sheet (about
   9 oz./255 g) store-bought puff
   pastry, thawed if frozen
   (see p. 486)

Table salt and freshly ground
   black pepper

1. Put the cheese and curry powder in a small bowl and mix until well blended.

2. Position a rack in the center of the oven and heat the oven to 400°F (200°C/gas 6). Line two cookie sheets with parchment or nonstick liners. Put the egg and water in a small bowl and, using a fork, mix until well blended.

3. If you are using store-bought puff, unfold the puff pastry, if necessary. Roll out the dough between two pieces of parchment into a square slightly larger than 12 inches (30.5 cm), lightly flouring and flipping the dough as you work. Using a sharp chef's knife and a ruler, trim the edges, using short, crisp cuts (dragging the blade will pinch the pastry layers together) to get a neat 12-inch (30.5 cm) square. Cut the square in half to make two 6 x 12-inch (15 x 30.5 cm) rectangles.

For more about rolling dough between parchment, see p. 133.

4. Brush the egg wash over the pastry to coat evenly and completely. Scatter the curry–cheese filling over the pastry, then use your fingers to spread it evenly and to the edges of the pastry. Sprinkle with salt and pepper. Cover with plastic and, using the rolling pin, gently roll to press the cheese onto the pastry. Lift off the plastic and discard. With the tip of a knife, mark the dough at ½-inch (12 mm) intervals, then, using a sharp chef's knife or pastry wheel and a ruler, cut crosswise into ½-inch (12 mm) strips (see the Essential Technique on p. 522).

5. Working with one strip at a time, hold the strip ends in each hand and twist two or three times, ending with the cheese side up at the ends.

(continued)

TWISTS

Flavor swap

Instead of the curry powder, use ¼ tsp. smoked paprika or ⅛ to ¼ tsp. ground cayenne pepper.

Arrange on the prepared cookie sheets about 1 inch (2.5 cm) apart, pressing the strip ends onto the liner. Bake, one sheet at a time, until the pastry is puffed and deep golden brown, 11 to 13 minutes. Move the sheet to a rack and let cool for 10 minutes. The twists are best when served the same day and can be warmed slightly in a 300°F (150°C/gas 2), if desired.

ESSENTIAL TECHNIQUE

Making the twists

A

With the pastry cut into two 6 x 12-inch (15 x 30.5 cm) rectangles, sprinkle the cheese mixture over top, then use your hands to spread it to the edges, covering the dough completely.

B

Cover with plastic and use a rolling pin to press the cheese mixture into the dough. You aren't rolling the dough any larger, so you don't need to be aggressive in rolling out. The goal is to help the cheese adhere to the dough. Remove the plastic wrap, being careful to remove little or no cheese.

C

With the tip of a knife, mark the dough at 1/2-inch (12 mm) intervals, then, using a sharp chef's knife or pastry wheel and a ruler, cut crosswise into 1/2-inch (12 mm) strips.

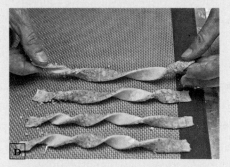

D

Hold both ends of one strip with your hands and make two or three twists. Place the strip on the nonstick liner, gently pressing the end into the liner to adhere so that the twist remains. Follow the same process to twist all of the strips.

Classic Pastry Cream Éclairs

Makes twelve 6-inch (15 cm) éclairs

Like gougères (see p. 495), the base of this charming and delectable classic is an easy-to-make dough that the French refer to as pâte à choux. The pastry base cooks up quickly on the stovetop into a shiny, pasty-thick dough. For this sweet version, the dough is then piped into logs—short or long—and baked until puffed and crispy on the outside with a moist, web-like interior. In my mind, it's the ideal vessel to hold creamy, vanilla-scented pastry cream and to top with a bittersweet chocolate glaze worthy of pastry shops around the world.

For the pâte à choux
¾ cup (180 ml) water
6 Tbs. (3 oz./85 g) unsalted butter,
  cut into 6 pieces
2 Tbs. granulated sugar
¼ tsp. table salt
¾ cup (3½ oz./99 g) unbleached
  all-purpose flour
3 large eggs, at room temperature

For the pastry cream filling
4 yolks from large eggs (see p. 371)
½ cup (3½ oz./99 g) granulated
  sugar
2 Tbs. + 2 tsp. unbleached all-
  purpose flour
Pinch of table salt
1⅔ cups (400 ml) whole milk
1½ tsp. pure vanilla extract

For the chocolate glaze
4 oz. (113 g) bittersweet chocolate,
  finely chopped (see p. 380)
⅓ cup (80 ml) heavy cream

Make the pastry shells

1. Position racks in the center of the oven and heat the oven to 425°F (220°C/gas 7). Line a cookie sheet with parchment or a nonstick liner.

2. Put the water, butter, sugar, and salt in a 3-quart saucepan. Cook over medium heat, stirring occasionally, until the butter is melted, about 2 minutes. Increase the heat to high and bring to a boil. As soon as the mixture is boiling, slide the pan off the heat and immediately add all of the flour. Using a wooden spatula, stir quickly until the dough is smooth and thick. Cook over low heat, stirring constantly, until the dough is shiny, about 1 minute.

3. Slide the pan off the heat and add the eggs, one at a time, beating with the wooden spatula until the egg is completely incorporated and the dough is smooth before adding the next egg. The pâte à choux will be soft and should fall from the spatula by the count of three.

4. Fit a 1-inch (2.5 cm) plain or fluted pastry tip into a pastry bag and fill with the dough. Evenly pipe the dough into twelve 1 x 5-inch (2.5 x 12 cm) strips, flicking the tip backward to end the strips without tails, spaced about 2½ inches (6 cm) apart onto the prepared baking sheet. Using a lightly dampened fingertip, gently tamp down any tips or pointy parts of the dough (see the Essential Technique on p. 525).

5. Bake for 15 minutes, then reduce the oven temperature to 375°F (190°C/gas 5) and bake until deep golden brown and crisp, about another 15 minutes. Move to a rack and, using the tip of a chopstick or

TWISTS

Flavor swap

Peanut butter: Use the same amount of brown sugar in place of the granulated sugar in the pastry cream filling and add ¼ tsp. salt. Whisk in ½ cup (4½ oz./128 g) creamy peanut butter along with the vanilla extract. Sprinkle the tops of the glazed éclairs with chopped, lightly salted peanuts before chilling.

Re-size it

Small (makes forty 2-inch [5 cm] éclairs):

Fit a ½-inch (12 mm) plain pastry tip into a pastry bag and fill with the dough. Evenly pipe the dough into 2-inch (5 cm) long strips, flicking the tip backwards to end the strips without tails, spaced about 1½ inches (4 cm) apart onto one of the prepared cookie sheets. Bake until the pastry is an even, deep golden brown, 20 to 25 minutes. Pipe the remaining batter onto a second sheet while the first one is baking.

To fill, fit a ¼-inch (6 mm) plain or fluted pastry tip into a pastry bag and fill with the cream. Working with one éclair at a time, gently push the tip into the vent hole and pipe in the filling. (Alternatively, assemble as directed at right.)

Working with one éclair at a time, dip the top half of the pastry into the warm chocolate and tap it gently on the side of the bowl to eliminate any excess chocolate. Arrange the éclairs, glazed side up, on a cookie sheet or tray and refrigerate until the glaze is set, about 30 minutes. Serve chilled.

wide skewer, pierce one end of each shell to let the steam escape (see the Essential Technique on the facing page). Let cool completely.

Make the filling

Put the egg yolks, sugar, flour, and salt in a medium saucepan and whisk until well blended and lighter in color. Add the milk, whisking constantly. Cook, whisking constantly, over medium-low heat until the pastry cream comes to a boil. Cook, whisking constantly, for 1 minute. Slide the pan off the heat, whisk in the vanilla, and scrape into a medium bowl. Press a piece of plastic wrap directly onto the surface of the pastry cream to prevent a skin from forming and refrigerate until cold, at least 2 hours.

For more about making a pudding, see p. 388.

For more about pressing plastic directly on custard or cream, see p. 302.

Make the glaze

Put the chocolate and heavy cream in a small microwave-safe bowl and microwave for 30-second bursts, whisking between bursts, until the chocolate is melted and the mixture is smooth. (Alternatively, use a metal bowl set over a pan of barely simmering water.) Set aside until slightly cooled.

Assemble the éclairs

1. Using a small serrated knife, cut off the top one-quarter of each éclair. Spoon or pipe the pastry cream into the bottom pastries.

For more about using a pastry bag or zip-top bag for piping, see p. 205.

2. Working with one pastry top at a time and using both hands, dip the top into the chocolate and gently shake to remove excess chocolate. You can also graze the top along the side of the bowl to eliminate any excess chocolate. Re-dip as needed to cover the top completely. Arrange the tops, glazed side up, on the filled bottoms, set on a cookie sheet or flat plate, and refrigerate until the glaze is set, about 20 minutes. Serve chilled.

BAKER'S WISDOM

Sizing the shells

For easy and consistent piping, working with a pencil and a piece of parchment, mark 2 rows of six 5-inch (12 cm) lines about 2½ inches (6 cm) apart. Flip the parchment onto a cookie sheet, marked side down, and use the lines as a guide when piping the pastry.

Making the pâte à choux

A

B

Once the water–butter mixture has come to a boil, add the flour all at once. Stir quickly to form a smooth dough. Keep cooking over low heat, stirring constantly with a wooden spatula, until the dough is shiny. The dough is thick, so you'll need to put some muscle behind stirring.

Slide the pan off the heat before adding the eggs, one at a time, beating with the wooden spatula until the egg is completely incorporated and the dough is smooth before adding the next egg. When you first add an egg, the dough will break up, but it will come together in a smooth dough after mixing. Using an angled wooden spatula will scrape the bottom and edges of the pan to help in making sure you completely incorporate the eggs into the dough.

Filling the pastry bag and piping shells

A

B

Roll down the top of the pastry bag to form a cuff, then use a bench scraper to transfer the fluid, soft dough from the pot to the bag. Because the dough is thick, you'll need to scrape it against the side of the bag to release it from the bench scraper.

Holding the top of the filled bag at the twisted area with one hand and using your other to guide the tip, pipe the dough onto the prepared baking sheet. Be sure the top of the bag remains closed as you apply pressure from the top.

C

D

Before baking, dab a little water onto the top of each piped strip to smooth any tips or pointy ends of the dough. (The strips shown are minis.)

A chopstick is the perfect tool for piercing the cooled shells. Insert just the tip, allowing steam to escape.

Chapter 10

FLATBREAD

> > > >

Naan

Serves 6 [PHOTO ON P. 413]

I think of naan as the ultimate culinary cross-over bread. While traditionally an Indian staple, I happily serve naan alongside a steamy bowl of soup, stew, or pasta; grilled steak or chicken; or even a supper-sized salad. Any way it's served, naan is always at the ready to swab up dinner's savory juices.

Serving a warm, fragrant bread with every dinner is my dream, and naan's short prep time and small yield make this dream come true for any meal—especially on weeknights. I make the dough at the beginning of dinner prep, let it rise as I cobble together our meal, and then cook up the naan while the meal is resting. Traditionally made in a clay tandoor oven, I use my cast iron skillet, which works beautifully and produces a soft-textured bread with a slightly smoky flavor.

For the dough
2¼ cups (10⅛ oz./287 g) unbleached all-purpose flour
1¼ tsp. quick-rise (instant) yeast
1 tsp. granulated sugar
¾ tsp. table salt
½ cup (120 ml) water, warmed to between 115° and 125°F (45° and 52°C)

½ cup (4 oz./113 g) plain yogurt, at room temperature
⅓ cup (scant ½ oz./15 g) chopped fresh herbs (any combination of chives, basil, parsley, thyme, and rosemary)
2 Tbs. ghee, clarified or melted butter, or vegetable oil + more for greasing the dough and bowl (see p. 528)

For serving
6 Tbs. (3 oz./85 g) ghee or clarified butter, melted (optional)
⅓ cup (scant ½ oz./15 g) chopped fresh herbs (any combination of chives, basil, parsley, thyme, and rosemary)

Make the dough

1. Put the flour, yeast, sugar, and salt in the bowl of a stand mixer and whisk until well blended. With the mixer fitted with the dough hook, beat on medium speed while pouring the warm water, yogurt, herbs, and butter or oil into the flour mixture. Mix on medium speed until the flour is completely incorporated, scraping the sides of the bowl as needed. Increase the speed to medium high and beat until the dough is smooth, 5 to 7 minutes. If the dough climbs up the hook, stop the mixer and scrape the dough back down into the bowl. The dough will be soft and slightly damp to the touch.

For more about scraping dough from a dough hook, see p. 449.

2. Remove the dough hook, scrape the dough onto the counter, knead once or twice until it no longer sticks to the counter and passes the windowpane test, and shape into a ball. Lightly grease the sides of the bowl and put the dough, rounded side up, back in. Cover the bowl with a plate or plastic wrap. Let rise in a warm spot until doubled in size, about 45 minutes.

For more about hand kneading, see p. 449.

For more about the windowpane test, see p. 470.

(continued)

(*Naan continued*)

MAKE AHEAD

Naan can be cooked, cooled completely, wrapped in plastic, and stowed at room temperature for up to 2 days. Reheat in a warm oven or toaster oven before garnishing and serving.

TWISTS

Flavor swap

> **Classic:** Eliminate the herbs in the dough and proceed as directed. Instead of garnishing with fresh herbs, sprinkle the buttered naan with some poppy seeds or sesame seeds.

> **Sour cream:** Substitute the same amount of sour cream for the yogurt.

Shape and cook

1. Scrape the dough onto an unfloured work surface and press down on the dough to deflate it. Using a bench scraper or knife, divide the dough into 6 equal pieces (about 3 oz./85 g each), shape each into a ball, and cover loosely with plastic or a towel.

For more about deflating risen dough, see p. 477.

For more on weighing dough, see p. 450.

2. Working with one dough ball at a time, use your hands to press and deflate the dough and shape into a round. The dough should be tacky on the unfloured work surface; otherwise it will be impossible to shape. Using a rolling pin, roll the dough into an oval about 9 inches (23 cm) long, 3 to 4 inches (7.5 to 10 cm) wide at the top, and about ⅛ to ¼ inch (3 to 6 mm) thick, lifting and loosening the dough as you roll to prevent sticking. Using two hands, lift the oval from one end and gently stretch to square off the top to form an upside down triangle or tear shape (see the Essential Technique on the facing page). The shape is less important than an even thickness. With practice, you'll become a pro, but for now, don't worry about the shape. Repeat with another dough ball and then continue shaping while cooking.

3. Set a large (10½- to 14-inch/26.5 to 35.5 cm) cast iron skillet over medium heat and heat until very, very hot. To test, sprinkle a few drops of water into the skillet. They should sizzle and evaporate immediately. Lifting one of the dough triangles from two corners at the short side, lay it flat in the skillet. Cover and cook until the top of the dough is bubbly and looks dry around the edges, 60 to 90 seconds. (If the dough doesn't bubble, the pan isn't hot enough. Continue cooking but let the pan heat a bit more before adding the next one.) Using tongs or a wide spatula, flip the naan. Cover and cook until the underside is dark brown in spots and the naan smells a bit smoky, 30 to 45 seconds more. Adjust the heat as needed. Wrap the naan in a clean towel or foil and repeat with the remaining dough.

For more about testing a pan for heat, see p. 65.

4. To serve, brush one side of the warm naan with ghee or butter and sprinkle with some of the herbs.

BAKER'S WISDOM

The difference between clarified butter and ghee

Clarified butter and ghee are very similar. For both, the butterfat is separated from the water and milk solids, allowing it to keep longer and cook to a higher temperature without burning. They are prepared in a similar fashion by slowly melting butter over low heat until the milk solids drop to the bottom, leaving only the golden liquid on top. For ghee, the butter is brought to just below simmering and cooked longer than for clarified butter. As long as no flavorings or spices have been added, they can be used interchangeably.

Shaping and cooking

Working directly on the counter, press the dough with your hands to deflate, then roll into an oval about 9 inches (23 cm) long and 3 to 4 inches (7.5 to 10 cm) wide at the top.

Using two hands, lift the oval from one end and gently stretch to square off the top to form an upside down triangle or tear shape. Don't worry too much about the shape—it's more important that the thickness be an even ⅛ to ¼ inch (3 to 6 mm).

Once the skillet is hot, arrange one dough triangle flat in the skillet. The naan will be ready to turn when the top of the dough is bubbly and looks dry around the edges and the underside is dark brown in spots.

Summer Veggie Pizza

Makes three 13-inch (33 cm) pizzas   [PHOTO ON P. 414]

If you are new to breadmaking, pizza dough is a great one to start with. The dough comes together so quickly and easily that it is all but foolproof. Once again, for the most consistent results (between your batches and as compared to my results), I urge you to weigh your flour, as even small changes in the volume can upset the flour-to-water ratio of this dough. (See p. 5 for more information on weighing flour.)

For the dough (enough for 3 pizzas)
2 cups (9 oz./255 g) unbleached all-purpose flour
2 cups (9 oz./255 g) whole-wheat flour
2¼ tsp. quick-rise (instant) yeast
1½ tsp. table salt
2 tsp. granulated sugar
1½ cups (360 ml) water, warmed to between 115° and 125°F (45° and 52°C)

3 Tbs. olive oil + more for greasing the dough and bowl

For the topping (enough for 1 pizza)
¼ cup (2¼ oz./64 g) Basil Pesto (recipe on p. 532)
¾ cup (3 oz./85 g) loosely packed halved and very thinly sliced yellow or green summer squash, or a mix
½ cup (2½ oz./71 g) ripe cherry tomatoes, halved or quartered if larger

½ cup (1½ oz./42 g) loosely packed very thinly sliced red onion
1 cup (4 oz./113 g) mozzarella cheese, cut into ¾-inch (2 cm) pieces (if using bocconcini, cut in half)
2 Tbs. olive oil
Coarse sea salt and freshly ground black pepper

Cornmeal or unbleached all-purpose flour, for dusting

MAKE AHEAD

The dough can be prepared, risen, and refrigerated (as directed) for up to 1 day or frozen up to 1 month before shaping and baking. If frozen, thaw for 6 to 8 hours in the fridge or 1½ to 2 hours on the counter.

Make the dough

1. Put the flours, yeast, salt, and sugar in the bowl of a stand mixer and whisk until well blended. With the mixer fitted with the dough hook, mix on medium speed while pouring the warm water and oil into the flour mixture. Mix on medium speed until the flour is completely incorporated, scraping the sides of the bowl as needed. Increase the speed to medium high and beat until the dough is smooth, 5 to 7 minutes. If the dough climbs up the hook, stop the mixer and scrape the dough back down into the bowl. The dough will be soft and slightly sticky to the touch.

For more about scraping dough from a dough hook, see p. 449.

2. Remove the dough hook, scrape the dough onto the counter, knead once or twice until it no longer sticks to the counter and passes the windowpane test, and shape into a ball. Lightly grease the sides of the bowl with olive oil and put the dough, rounded side up, back in. Cover the bowl with a plate or plastic wrap. Let rise in a warm spot until doubled in size, about 45 minutes.

For more about hand kneading, see p. 449.

For more about the windowpane test, see p. 470.

3. Scrape the dough onto an unfloured work surface and press down on the dough to deflate it. Using a bench scraper or knife, portion the dough into 3 equal pieces (about 10 oz./283 g each) and shape each into a smooth, round ball. Drizzle a little olive oil into 3 heavy-duty, quart-sized zip-top bags and rub each bag together to completely coat the inside. Put a dough ball into each bag, press out the air, and close. Refrigerate the dough for 1 hour or up to 24 hours before making the pizza.

For more about deflating risen dough, see p. 477.

For more about weighing dough, see p. 450.

Shape and bake the pizza

1. Position a rack in the bottom third of the oven and set a pizza stone on the rack. Heat the oven to 500°F (260°C/gas 10) for at least 20 minutes. Have ready the pesto, squash, tomatoes, onions, and cheese. Have ready a wooden peel or cookie sheet.

2. Put one dough ball on an unfloured work surface. Using your hands, press and deflate the dough and shape into a round. Continue using your hands or switch to a rolling pin, working from the center outward, and firmly shape the dough into a 12- to 13-inch (30.5 to 33 cm) round about ⅛ to 3⁄16 inches (3 to 4.5 mm) thick, lifting and loosening the dough as you roll to prevent sticking (see the Essential Technique on p. 532). The dough will shrink back as you lift but just keep rolling. The shape is less important than an even thickness. With practice, you'll become a pro, but for now, don't worry about the shape. The dough should be tacky or it will be impossible to shape; dust with just a little flour if necessary.

3. Lightly but thoroughly coat a peel or cookie sheet with cornmeal and arrange the dough near the edge. This will make it easier to slide the dough onto the pizza stone. Reshape or roll if necessary to make the round 12 to 13 inches (30.5 to 33 cm). Using a small offset spatula, spread the pesto in an even layer over the dough, leaving about a ½-inch (12 mm) border. Scatter layers of the squash slices, onions, and tomatoes over the dough, and top with the cheese. Drizzle with some of the olive oil and sprinkle with salt and pepper.

4. Open the oven door and, working quickly so the oven maintains its temperature, gently and quickly jerk the peel forward and back to slide the beginning of the pizza onto the hot stone. Slip the peel from under the pizza until it rests on the stone. If the pizza sticks to the peel, slide a long metal spatula under the bottom third of the dough and slightly lift and slide the dough. Bake until the crust is golden brown and the cheese is bubbling, 13 to 16 minutes (the thicker the dough, the longer the baking time). Open the oven door and use the peel or cookie sheet to move the pizza from the stone to a cutting board. Let cool for 3 to 4 minutes, then cut with a large knife or pizza wheel.

FINISHING TOUCHES

Sprinkle some freshly grated Parmigiano Reggiano or Romano cheese over the freshly baked pizza.

(continued)

TWISTS

Flavor swap

> Classic (enough for 1 pizza): Omit the squash topping and basil pesto. Spread the pizza dough with ⅓ cup (80 ml) tomato sauce (home-made or store bought) to within ½ inch (12 mm) of the edge and top with 4 oz. (113 g) mozzarella cheese, cut into ¾-inch (2 cm) pieces (if using bocconcini, cut in half), and ½ cup (2½ oz./71 g) ripe cherry tomatoes, halved or quartered if large. Drizzle with 2 Tbs. olive oil and sprinkle with ½ tsp. dried oregano, coarse sea salt, and freshly ground black pepper. Bake as directed and sprinkle with ¼ cup (⅜ oz./10 g) thinly sliced fresh basil before serving.

> Red pepper–onion–meatball–ricotta (enough for 1 pizza): Omit the squash topping and basil pesto. Spread the pizza dough with ⅓ cup (80 ml) tomato sauce to within ½ inch (12 mm) of the edge and top with 2 oz. (57 g) mozzarella cheese, cut into ¾-inch (2 cm) pieces (if using bocconcini, cut in half), ⅓ cup (2 oz./57 g) coarsely chopped roasted red pepper (well drained), ¼ cup (1 oz./28 g) very thinly sliced red or yellow onion, and 2 medium-sized (4 oz./113 g) cooked meatballs, thickly sliced. Drop small dollops of ⅓ cup (3 oz./85 g) ricotta cheese evenly over the pizza, drizzle with 2 Tbs. olive oil, and sprinkle with coarse sea salt and freshly ground black pepper. Bake as directed.

Basil Pesto

3 cups (2½ oz./71 g) loosely packed
  fresh basil leaves
½ cup (4 oz./113 g) neutral oil
  (safflower, canola, vegetable,
  or corn)
2 medium garlic cloves

¼ tsp. table salt
Freshly ground black pepper
¼ cup (1 oz./28 g) ground
  Parmigiano Reggiano cheese
  (see p. 38)

Put the basil, oil, garlic, salt, and a few grinds of black pepper in a food processor and process until well blended. Add the cheese and process briefly until blended. Taste and adjust the seasonings as needed. Use immediately or cover and refrigerate for up to 1 week or freeze for up to 1 month.

ESSENTIAL TECHNIQUE

Shaping the dough, topping the pizza, and baking

A

Working with one dough ball at a time on an unfloured surface, use your fingers to press out the air and begin to flatten the dough.

B

Switch to a rolling pin, if desired, or continue shaping with your fingers (or a combination of both) until you have a round that's about 12 to 13 inches (30.5 to 33 cm). Lift and rotate the dough as you shape to prevent sticking and to help ensure the thickness is even, ⅛ to 3/16 inch (3 to 4.5 mm).

C

Sprinkle a pizza peel or cookie sheet generously with cornmeal and arrange the dough round toward the front edge. Scatter the toppings evenly across the top. It's important for toppings to be about the same size and thickness to ensure even cooking.

D

Working in the oven, gently and quickly jerk the peel forward and back to slide the beginning of the pizza onto the hot stone. Slip the peel from under the pizza until it rests on the stone. If the pizza sticks to the peel, slide a long metal spatula under the bottom third of the dough and slightly lift and slide the dough.

Cheesy Bacon Focaccia Rolls

Makes 9 rolls

What's better than a grilled bacon, tomato, and cheese? This focaccia is. Legendary for its chewy texture, focaccia is delicious alone or with toppings (see Roasted Red Pepper–Goat Cheese Whole Wheat Focaccia on p. 545). I've taken it a step further by loading it with this homey and classic flavor combo and turning it into rolls. A hearty addition to any meal, these rolls also make for a warm and savory breakfast, though I'll admit that I'm partial to serving them alongside a Caesar salad (hold the croutons) for a deeply satisfying lunch.

If you want to use these for a sandwich or panini, make the rolls without the tomato. This way, they bake up a bit higher, making them perfect when sliced horizontally and piled with whatever suits your mood.

For the dough
3⅓ cups (15 oz./425 g) unbleached bread flour
2 tsp. quick-rise (instant) yeast
2 tsp. granulated sugar
2 tsp. table salt
1⅓ cups (320 ml) water, warmed to between 115° and 125°F (45° and 52°C)

1 cup (4 oz./113 g) loosely packed coarsely shredded sharp Cheddar cheese
5 slices (5 oz./142 g) bacon, cooked, cooled, and coarsely chopped (see p. 534)
¼ cup (¼ oz./7 g) thinly sliced chives, divided
5 Tbs. olive oil, divided

Cornmeal, for dusting

For the topping
⅓ cup (1½ oz./42 g) ground Parmigiano Reggiano cheese (see p. 38)
1 Tbs. chopped fresh oregano
1 or 2 medium, ripe tomatoes
Coarse sea salt and freshly ground black pepper

Make the dough

1. Put the flour, yeast, sugar, and salt in the bowl of a stand mixer and whisk until well blended. With the mixer fitted with the dough hook, pour the warm water into the flour mixture and mix on medium speed until the flour is completely incorporated. Increase the speed to medium high and beat until the dough is smooth and pulls away from the sides and bottom of the bowl, 9 to 11 minutes. If the dough climbs up the hook, stop the mixer and scrap the dough back down into the bowl as necessary. The dough will be soft and sticky to the touch.

For more about scraping dough from a dough hook, see p. 449.

2. Add the cheese, bacon, and half of the chives and knead until blended. Remove the dough hook, scrape the dough onto the counter, knead once or twice until it no longer sticks to the counter and passes the windowpane test, and shape into a ball. Lightly grease the sides of the bowl with about 1 Tbs. olive oil and put the dough, rounded side up, back in. Cover the bowl with a plate or plastic wrap. Let rise in a warm spot until doubled in size, about 45 minutes.

For more about hand kneading, see p. 449.

For more about the windowpane test, see p. 470.

(continued)

MAKE AHEAD

The rolls can be baked, cooled, covered, and stowed at room temperature for up to 2 days.

TWISTS

Flavor swap

Omit the tomatoes.

Shape and bake the dough

1. Generously sprinkle the bottom of a 13 x 18 x 1-inch (33 x 46 x 2.5 cm) half sheet pan with cornmeal. Scrape the dough onto a work surface. Using your hands and working from the center outward toward the edges, gently press out the gas while shaping the dough into a 13-inch (33 cm) square about ½-inch (12 mm) thick. Using a bench scraper, cut the dough into 9 squares. Working with one piece at a time, reshape, as necessary, into randomly shaped squares (don't worry about perfection here) and arrange about ½ inch (12 mm) apart on the prepared baking sheet.

2. Drizzle about 2 Tbs. of the olive oil evenly over the tops, then smear it around with your fingers to spread it evenly. Cover the dough loosely (to allow for rising) but completely with plastic and let the dough rise in a warm spot. After about 15 minutes, position a rack in the center of the oven and heat the oven to 400°F (200°C/gas 6); continue to let the dough rise.

3. Put the cheese and oregano in a small bowl and mix until blended. Thinly slice the tomatoes and arrange on a paper towel–lined plate to drain.

4. When the oven is heated and the dough is puffy and about 1 inch (2.5 cm) thick, carefully peel away the plastic and scatter the oregano–cheese mixture evenly over the top. Using your three middle fingers, press into the dough down to the bottom of each square (see the Essential Technique on the facing page). Repeat the dimpling two or three times in each square. Arrange a tomato slice on top of each square, pressing gently into the dough. Sprinkle with salt (about 1 tsp.), pepper, and the remaining chives.

5. Bake until the bread is golden brown on top, 28 to 30 minutes. Move the pan to a rack, drizzle with the remaining 2 Tbs. olive oil, and let cool for 5 minutes. Using a large metal spatula, move the squares to a rack and let cool completely. The rolls are best served warm the day they're made.

BAKER'S WISDOM

Cooking bacon

Arrange bacon strips in an even layer in a large skillet. Cook over medium heat, turning the slices two or three times, until the fat has rendered and the bacon is brown. Slide the pan from the heat and, using tongs or a fork, move the strips to a paper towel–lined plate and serve warm or let cool completely. The bacon will become firm as it cools.

Shaping, cutting, and dimpling the dough

A

Once the dough is shaped into a 13-inch (33 cm) square, use a bench scraper to cut it into 9 equal squares. While there's no need to measure with a ruler, try to make them all about the same size.

B

Lift and move the squares onto a half sheet pan generously sprinkled with cornmeal. The cornmeal will prevent sticking as the rolls bake and also add a nice bit of texture to the finished roll. Drizzle with oil, then smear with your fingers to ensure the entire top is covered. Cover loosely but completely with plastic wrap and set aside to rise.

C

When the dough is puffy and about 1 inch (2.5 cm) thick, peel away the plastic, scatter the cheese mixture over the top, and then dimple the dough—use your three middle fingers to press all the way to the bottom of the dough. Dimple each square two or three times.

D

Arrange one slice of tomato on top of each square, sprinkle with chives, and bake. Heirloom tomatoes in different colors look really pretty.

Black Pepper Cream Crackers

Makes about sixty 2-inch (5 cm) crackers

My cookbook author confession: Recipes that end up in the final version of a book aren't always the same ones that appear in the original proposal. This recipe is a case in point. I had wanted to include a recipe for homemade oyster crackers, but a funny thing happened during recipe testing. My favorite appliance guy—Burt from All American Appliance—was tending to my freezer and calibrating my ovens (a frequent occurrence in my kitchen) and, as usual, he asked what recipes I was working on. I mentioned the small, button-like oyster crackers I had baked earlier in the day and offered him a sample. His response: "Oh, they're really good, but they don't taste like oyster crackers." We laughed and I thanked him for his honesty. After discussing the crackers' merits, Burt and I decided that the recipe was well worth saving and re-inventing into a larger cracker to serve alone, with cheeses, or crumbled over soups, salads, or stews.

2 cups (9 oz./255 g) unbleached all-purpose flour + more for rolling
1¼ tsp. table salt
¾ tsp. baking powder
½ tsp. granulated sugar

½ tsp. freshly ground black pepper
3 Tbs. (1½ oz./42 g) unsalted butter, cut into small pieces and chilled

⅔ cup (160 ml) heavy cream, chilled
Coarse sea salt, for sprinkling

MAKE AHEAD

> The dough can be made, wrapped in plastic, and frozen for up to 1 month. Thaw for about an hour on the counter or in the refrigerator overnight before rolling, cutting, and baking as directed.

> The baked and cooled crackers can be layered between waxed paper or parchment and stowed in an airtight container at room temperature for up to 3 days or frozen for up to 1 month. Thaw at room temperature and warm for a few minutes at 325°F (165°C/gas 3) to refresh the flavors.

1. Whisk the flour, salt, baking powder, sugar, and pepper in a medium bowl until well blended. Add the cold butter pieces and, using your fingers, rub and smear the butter into the flour mixture; see the Essential Technique on p. 538. (You can also do this in a food processor using short pulses before scraping the mixture into a medium bowl before proceeding.)

2. Pour the cream over the flour and, using a silicone spatula, stir and fold until it forms a shaggy, moist dough with some floury bits remaining (I like to use one hand to help mix while keeping the other working the spatula). Using your fingers, gently press the crumbs together to form a cohesive dough. Scrape the dough onto your work surface and divide into two piles (about 8 oz./227 g each), wrap in plastic wrap, and keep at room temperature while the oven heats (this gives the dough a chance to relax before rolling).

For more about using your hand to help mix, see p. 85.

3. Position a rack in the center of the oven and heat the oven to 400°F (200°C/gas 6). Line two large baking sheets with parchment.

4. Arrange a large piece of parchment on the work surface, put one of the piles in the center, and cover with another piece of parchment. Using a rolling pin, roll the dough between the parchment until it is ⅛ inch (3 mm) thick, lifting, turning, and repositioning the parchment and lightly flouring throughout the rolling. If the dough resists rolling, cover with plastic and let rest for a few minutes before continuing.

For more about rolling dough between parchment, see p. 133.

5. Using the tines of a fork, score the dough all over. Cut rounds with a 2¼-inch (5.5 cm) plain or fluted round cookie cutter and arrange close together (they won't spread) on one of the prepared baking sheets. Repeat with the remaining dough.

For more about docking the dough, see below.

6. Bake, one sheet at a time, until the tops are pale golden brown, 11 to 13 minutes. Move the sheet to a rack, sprinkle with some coarse sea salt, and let cool for 5 minutes. Using a wide spatula, move the crackers from the sheet to a rack and let cool enough to eat or cool completely. While the first sheet is baking, repeat with the remaining dough.

FINISHING TOUCHES

Before baking, brush the tops with extra heavy cream.

TWISTS

Flavor swap

Plain: Omit the black pepper and proceed as directed.

Re-size it

> **Tiny soup or stew crackers:** Roll the dough as directed but do not score it. Cut rounds with a 1-inch (2.5 cm) fluted or plain round cookie cutter. Bake as directed.

> **Random shapes:** Roll the dough as directed, but instead of cutting with a cookie cutter, use a plain pastry wheel to cut random shapes (see p. 542).

BAKER'S WISDOM

Pricking (docking) dough

Also called "docking," pricking a pie, puff, pastry, or cracker dough with the tines of a fork creates vents for steam to escape while baking. This prevents the dough from bubbling or puffing up. There are docking rollers and other tools made specifically for this purpose, but, unless you make a ton of pastry dough, a table fork works just fine.

When making the smaller 1-inch (2.5 cm) crackers (see Twists above), I like them to puff up so I skip this step.

(continued)

Blending the dough

To blend the cold butter pieces into the dry ingredients, rub and smear between your fingers until the butter is broken up and scattered throughout the flour. A crumbly mixture will form.

Once the cream has been poured into the bowl, use a spatula and one hand to work it into the flour–butter mixture until it forms a shaggy dough.

Continue to work the dough until it becomes smooth and all crumbs are fully incorporated. Wrap in plastic and keep at room temperature before rolling out.

Using the tines of a fork, prick the dough all over. This is called docking the dough and doing so prevents the dough from puffing up when it bakes.

Sesame Seed Crackers

Makes about 50 crackers

At first glance, these crackers don't look all that interesting. To some, they look plain and, well, boring. But like most things, this cracker shouldn't be judged on looks alone. Paper thin, crisp, and loaded with sesame flavor, these salty nibblers are addictive and delicious. If you can resist eating them for a day or two after making and baking, the sesame flavor deepens. The double blast of sesame flavor comes from toasted sesame seeds—they add a nubby texture to the crackers along with sesame essence—and toasted sesame oil—a dark caramel-colored vegetable oil infused and pressed with toasted sesame seeds with an assertive flavor.

For extra-thin and even crackers, I use my pasta machine rollers. You can use a rolling pin, but the pasta machine is quick and efficient. It's also nice to use the machine for something other than making pasta.

2 Tbs. sesame seeds
1 cup (4½ oz./128 g) unbleached
    all-purpose flour

¾ tsp. baking powder
¾ tsp. table salt
½ tsp. granulated sugar

5 Tbs. water
2 Tbs. toasted sesame oil
Coarse salt, for dusting

1. Put the sesame seeds in a small nonstick skillet. Cook over medium heat, stirring occasionally (more frequently toward the end) with a heatproof spatula until the seeds are nutty brown and fragrant, 2 to 4 minutes. Scrape the seeds onto a plate to prevent overtoasting and let cool completely (see the Essential Technique on p. 540).

2. Secure a pasta rolling machine on the counter or secure the attachment to your stand mixer (read the manual thoroughly if this is your first time using it). Position a rack in the center of the oven and heat the oven to 425°F (220°C/gas 7). Line two large cookie sheets with parchment or nonstick liners.

3. Put the flour, toasted sesame seeds, baking powder, salt, and sugar in the bowl of a stand mixer (or in a large bowl using an electric handheld mixer fitted with wire beaters or dough hooks) and whisk until blended. Fit the mixer with the paddle attachment and mix on medium speed while pouring in the water and then the oil. Mix on medium speed until the flour is completely incorporated and the mixture forms a moist, crumbly dough, 2 to 3 minutes.

4. Scrape the dough onto the counter and knead a few times until a soft dough forms. Divide into 2 pieces and cover one with plastic. Using the palm of your hand, flatten the uncovered dough. Set the pasta rolling machine at the largest opening (#1) and crank the dough through the machine. It will be very rough and broken in patches. Use both hands to initially guide the dough into the machine, and then position them to guide the dough out of the machine as it comes through. Fold the dough in half and repeat rolling and folding until the dough comes out

MAKE AHEAD

The cooled crackers can be stowed in an airtight container for up to 1 week.

TWISTS

Re-size it

Instead of baking large strips of dough and breaking apart after baking, cut into triangles, strips, or random shapes before baking.

smooth. Adjust the machine to a narrower setting (#3) and pass the dough through. It should be smooth but, if not, fold in half and pass it through again. Adjust the machine to the next narrower setting (#5) and pass the dough through. Adjust the machine down to #6 and pass the dough through. It will be very, very thin and still slightly sticky.

For more about rolling dough through a pasta machine, see p. 552.

5. Arrange the dough strip on the counter and using a knife, fluted pastry wheel, or pizza wheel, cut crosswise into long strips and arrange close together on one of the baking sheets. Sprinkle with some coarse salt and bake until the crackers are golden brown, 10 to 12 minutes. Don't undercook or the crackers will be soggy. Move the sheet to a rack and let cool for about 5 minutes. Using a spatula, lift the crackers from the sheet and onto a rack to cool completely. Break the cooled strip into large or small pieces. Roll the remaining dough while the first sheet is baking.

BAKER'S WISDOM

Sesame seeds

Most commonly pale ivory in color, sesame seeds have a slightly sweet, nutty flavor that deepens when toasted. They add a nutty crunch to both sweet and savory dishes. Because of their high oil content, it's best to purchase in small quantities and store in the refrigerator. Before using, always give them the sniff test. If the aroma is off, they are most likely rancid.

Toasted sesame seeds are used to make tahini as well as sesame oil. The oil ranges in color from deep golden to dark brown and is primarily used as a flavoring. Not meant to be a cooking oil, use sparingly (the flavor is robust) as a seasoning in stir-fries or other Asian dishes. Like sesame seeds, the oil is perishable, so buy in small amounts, keep refrigerated, and make sure it passes the sniff test before using.

ESSENTIAL TECHNIQUE

Toasting sesame seeds

Untoasted sesame seeds (left) will brown quickly toward the end, so be vigilant as you cook. Put in a nonstick skillet and toast over medium heat, stirring occasionally (more frequently toward the end) with a heatproof spatula until they are medium brown (center). If they get too dark (right), they will taste burnt and very bitter.

Smoked Paprika Gouda Bites

Makes about 100 crackers

These little buttery, cheesy nibblers are very addictive, so unless you're planning to eat the whole batch yourself, make sure you have some pals around to save you from yourself. You can use sharp Cheddar for the cracker but, for a more sophisticated, enticing flavor, I prefer a combo of smoked Gouda and smoked paprika.

Using a similar technique to making pie dough, by hand or in a food processor, the dough comes together in minutes and can be stowed in the fridge or freezer. The fun comes in shaping these cheesy gems. After rolling the dough, you can cut them, as I have, into random shapes using a pastry wheel or knife or, if you like, use a small whimsical cookie cutter like a mini dog bone or shark.

4 Tbs. (2 oz./57 g) unsalted butter
¾ cup (3⅜ oz./96 g) unbleached all-purpose flour + more for rolling

1 cup (4 oz./113 g) coarsely shredded Gouda cheese (preferably a smoked variety)
2 Tbs. finely ground Parmigiano Reggiano cheese (see p. 38)

¾ tsp. ground smoked paprika
½ tsp. table salt
1 Tbs. very cold water
Coarse sea salt, for sprinkling

1. Cut the butter in half lengthwise and then cut each strip into 4 pieces. Pile the butter onto a plate and slide into the freezer until ready to use.

2. Whisk the flour, cheeses, smoked paprika, and salt in a medium bowl until well blended. Add the cold butter pieces and, using a pastry blender or two knives, cut the butter into the flour mixture until it resembles coarse meal, about 4 minutes. (You can also do this in a food processor using short pulses before scraping the mixture into a medium bowl before proceeding.)

For more about cutting butter into flour, see p. 502.

3. Pour the water over the flour and, using a silicone spatula, stir and fold until it forms a shaggy, moist dough with some floury bits remaining (I like to use one hand to help mix while keeping the other working the spatula). Scrape the dough and any remaining floury bits onto the counter and gather into a mound. Starting with the top of the mound and using the heel of your hand, smear a section of the dough down the side and along the work surface away from you to blend the butter pieces into the dough. Repeat with the remaining dough in sections. Using a bench scraper, fold the dough together (the mixture will be rough and crumbly). Turn the pile about 90 degrees and repeat the smearing process until the mixture just comes together into a cohesive dough (this is a technique called *fraisage*). Be careful not to overwork the dough because that will make the crust dense. Once the dough is just holding together with some crumbs left around the edges, roll it into a rough rectangle about 8 x 4½ inches (20 x 11 cm). It will be very rough around the edges. Using a bench scraper, fold the top third of the dough toward the middle, brushing off any excess flour, and fold the bottom third over the two layers

MAKE AHEAD

> The dough can be made, wrapped in plastic, and frozen for up to a month. Thaw for about an hour on the counter or in the refrigerator overnight before rolling, cutting, and baking as directed.

> The baked and cooled crackers can be layered between waxed paper or parchment and stowed in an airtight container at room temperature for up to 3 days or frozen for up to 1 month. Thaw at room temperature and warm for a few minutes at 325°F (165°C/ gas 3) to refresh the flavors.

TWISTS

Flavor swap

Cheddar: Instead of the Gouda, use the same amount of shredded sharp Cheddar.

Re-size it

Instead of making random shapes, cut the rolled dough with small cookie cutters and bake as directed.

ESSENTIAL TECHNIQUE

Cutting dough pieces

A

A fluted pastry cutter makes short work of cutting the dough into 1½-inch (4 cm) strips. You can also use a pizza wheel, but the fluted edges are a nice touch.

B

Continue cutting the dough into random pieces, then slightly separate on the parchment and sprinkle with coarse salt. Slide the parchment onto a cookie sheet and bake.

to make a rectangle (this is similar to folding a letter). Turn the dough so that the open edge is on the right side and repeat the rolling and folding. Divide in half, wrap in plastic, and refrigerate until firm, about 2 hours or up to 2 days.

For more about using your hand to help mix, see p. 85.

For more about *fraisage*, see p. 549.

4. Position a rack in the center of the oven and heat the oven to 375°F (190°C/gas 5).

5. Remove one of the doughs from the refrigerator and, if it's very cold, set it out at room temperature until it's just pliable enough to roll, 10 to 20 minutes. Arrange a large piece of parchment on a work surface, put the unwrapped dough in the center, and cover with another piece of parchment. Using a rolling pin, roll the dough between the parchment to a rough rectangle about ⅛ inch (3 mm) thick, lifting, turning, and repositioning the parchment and lightly flouring throughout the rolling. If the dough resists rolling, cover with plastic and let rest for a few minutes before continuing.

For more about rolling dough between parchment, see p. 133.

6. Using a pizza wheel or fluted pastry cutter, cut the dough into about 1½-inch (4 cm) random pieces (see the Essential Technique at left). Spread the pieces about ¼ inch (6 mm) apart, sprinkle with the coarse salt, and slide the parchment onto a cookie sheet. Bake, one sheet at a time, until golden brown around the edges, 12 to 14 minutes. Move the sheet to a rack and let cool for 5 minutes. Using a wide spatula, move the crackers from the sheet to a rack until cool enough to eat or let cool completely. While the first sheet is baking, repeat rolling and cutting with the remaining dough. Serve warm or at room temperature.

BAKER'S WISDOM

Smoked paprika

A cousin to Hungarian paprika, smoked paprika, also called Spanish paprika, is more than a simple garnish for deviled eggs or salads. Made from pimiento peppers that have been dried and oak-smoked, smoked paprika is mildly sweet and very fragrant. That said, the smoky flavor can easily overwhelm a dish, so use it sparingly. I like to add it to spice rubs, stews, and soups, and it is especially delicious in these bite-sized crackers.

Whole-Wheat Pitas

Makes eight 6-inch (15 cm) pitas

With so many store-bought options available in the bread aisle, it's easy to forget how simple most breads are to make at home; pitas are an excellent example. Pulled together with a few on-hand ingredients (and no preservatives or ingredients you can't pronounce!), making homemade pita bread is good family fun. I like making them with the young kids within my extended family. Everyone gets into the shaping action and, after I slap the dough onto the pizza stone, the kids gather round and watch through the oven window as they bake. The commentary is worthy of a televised sporting event play-by-play and, when the pitas puff up, the crowd roars with excitement. No need to set a timer when I have this group in the house!

1¾ cups (7⅞ oz./223 g) whole-wheat flour

1 cup (4½ oz./128 g) unbleached all-purpose flour

2 tsp. quick-rise (instant) yeast

1 tsp. table salt

1 cup (240 ml) water, warmed to between 115° and 125°F (45° and 52°C)

3 Tbs. olive oil + more for greasing the bowl

1 Tbs. honey

Make the dough

1. Put the flours, yeast, and salt in the bowl of a stand mixer and whisk until well blended. Fit the mixer with the dough hook and mix on medium speed while pouring in the warm water, oil, and honey. Mix on medium speed until the flour is completely incorporated, scraping the sides as needed. Increase the speed to medium high and beat until the dough is smooth and pulls away from the sides and bottom of the bowl, 5 to 7 minutes. If the dough climbs up the hook, stop the mixer and scrape the dough back down into the bowl as necessary. The dough will be soft and slightly damp to the touch.

For more about scraping dough from a dough hook, see p. 449.

2. Remove the dough hook, scrape the dough onto the counter, knead once or twice until it no longer sticks to the counter and passes the windowpane test, and shape into a ball. Lightly grease the sides of the bowl and put the dough, rounded side up, back in. Cover the bowl with a plate or plastic wrap. Let rise in a warm spot until doubled in size, 45 to 60 minutes.

For more about hand kneading, see p. 449.

For more about the windowpane test, see p. 470.

Shape and cook

1. Position a rack in the bottom third of the oven and set a pizza stone or Baking Steel on the rack. Heat the oven to 500°F (260°C/gas 10) for at least 20 minutes. Have ready an ungreased cookie sheet and a small spray bottle filled with water.

(continued)

MAKE AHEAD

The pitas can be cooked, cooled completely, wrapped in plastic, and stowed at room temperature for up to 2 days. Reheat in a warm oven, microwave, or toaster oven before serving.

FINISHING TOUCHES

After the dough is slapped onto the stone, sprinkle with a little coarse sea salt.

2. Scrape the dough onto an unfloured work surface and press down on the dough to deflate it. Using a bench scraper or knife, portion the dough into 8 equal pieces (about 2¾ to 2⅞ oz./79 to 82 g each); shape into rounds and cover loosely with plastic or a towel. Let rest for 5 to 10 minutes.

For more about deflating risen dough, see p. 477.

For more about working with plastic wrap, see p. 546.

For more about weighing dough, see p. 450.

3. Put one dough ball on an unfloured work surface. The dough should be tacky on the work surface; otherwise, it will be impossible to shape. Using your hands, press and deflate the dough and shape it into a 4-inch (10 cm) round. Using a rolling pin, roll the dough into a 6-inch round about ⅛ to ¼ inch (3 to 6 mm) thick, lifting and loosening the dough as you roll to prevent sticking. Using two hands, lift the round and place on an ungreased cookie sheet. Using a small spray bottle, spritz the tops of the pitas with a little water. Repeat with one more dough ball and then continue shaping while the first sheet is cooking.

4. With lightly dampened hands, lift one dough round and put it in one palm, water side down. Open the oven door and working quickly and carefully, slap the dough onto the hot stone in one motion, making sure not to touch your hand on the very hot stone (see the Essential Technique below). Close the oven door while you organize the second dough round and repeat. Bake until the pitas are puffed and the tops are pale golden, 3 to 4 minutes. Using a wide spatula, move the pitas to a clean towel or foil (this keeps the pitas warm and soft) and repeat with the remaining dough.

ESSENTIAL TECHNIQUE

Cooking on a pizza stone

A

Arrange the rolled and shaped dough on an ungreased cookie sheet. Using a small spray bottle, spritz the top with a little water.

B

With lightly dampened hands, lift one dough round and put in one palm, water side down. Open the oven door, pull out the rack, if possible, and carefully slap the dough onto the hot stone in one motion, making sure not to touch your hand on the very hot stone. Close the oven door while you organize the second dough round and repeat.

Roasted Red Pepper–Goat Cheese Whole-Wheat Focaccia

Makes 1 loaf (1¾ lb./794 g)   [PHOTO ON P. 415]

The secret to my chewy, airy, hearty focaccia lies in the addition of whole-wheat flour in the dough. Whole wheat contains wheat germ and bran, lending a deeper, more complex flavor and structure to the dough, and, when paired with softer all-purpose flour, the baked texture of this Italian classic is the perfect combination of airy yet hearty.

The dough is sticky and wet, so it's best to mix in a stand mixer. Once kneaded and risen, the dough is pressed into a freeform shape. There's no need to be precise or finicky, making it easy for beginning bread bakers. Focaccia's trademark dimpling requires little skill to shape and, frankly, it's fun to do. It's not often we have permission to randomly stick our fingers into our food.

Focaccia is often made and served unadorned, but I like it best when it's topped with a combination of strong flavors, like those in this recipe or in the flavor swaps (see p. 546). The bread can be served as is or it can be cut into squares or rectangles and split horizontally for sandwiches or paninis.

For the dough
2 cups (9 oz./255 g) unbleached bread flour
1⅓ cups (6 oz./170 g) whole-wheat flour
2 tsp. quick-rise (instant) yeast
2 tsp. granulated sugar
2 tsp. table salt

1½ cups (360 ml) water, warmed to between 115° and 125°F (45° and 52°C)
Nonstick cooking spray
Cornmeal, for dusting

For the topping
¾ cup (4½ oz./128 g) coarsely chopped, drained roasted red peppers

½ cup (2 oz./57 g) crumbled goat cheese
1 Tbs. chopped fresh rosemary
3 to 5 Tbs. olive oil, divided
Coarse sea salt and freshly ground black pepper

Make the dough

1. Put both flours, the yeast, sugar, and salt into a large bowl of a stand mixer and whisk until well blended. Fit the mixer with the dough hook and mix on medium speed while pouring the warm water into the flour mixture until the flour is completely incorporated. Increase the speed to medium high and beat until the dough is smooth and pulls away from the sides and bottom of the bowl, 9 to 11 minutes. If the dough climbs up the hook, stop the mixer and scrape the dough back down into the bowl. The dough will be soft and sticky to the touch.

For more about scraping dough from a dough hook, see p. 449.

2. Remove the dough hook, scrape the dough onto the counter, knead once or twice until it no longer sticks to the counter and passes the windowpane test, and shape into a ball. Lightly grease the sides of the bowl and put the dough, rounded side up, back in. Cover the bowl with a plate or plastic wrap. Let rise in a warm spot until doubled in size, about 45 minutes.

For more about hand kneading, see p. 449.

For more about the windowpane test, see p. 470.

(continued)

MAKE AHEAD

The bread can be baked, cooled, covered, and stowed at room temperature for up to 2 days.

TWISTS

Flavor swap

> Blue cheese, oregano, and pancetta: Instead of the goat cheese, substitute ½ cup (2¼ oz./64 g) crumbled blue cheese; instead of the red pepper, substitute ¾ cup (3 oz./85 g) coarsely chopped pancetta, lightly browned and not drained (use the rendered fat instead of olive oil for drizzling); instead of the chopped rosemary, substitute 1 Tbs. chopped fresh oregano.

> Thyme, olive, and Parmigiano Reggiano: Instead of the goat cheese, substitute ⅓ cup (1⅓ oz./39 g) ground Parmigiano Reggiano; instead of the red pepper, substitute ¾ cup (3¾ oz./106 g) coarsely chopped pitted Kalamata olives; instead of the chopped rosemary, substitute 1 Tbs. chopped fresh thyme.

Shape and bake the dough

1. Line a 13 x 18 x 1-inch (33 x 46 x 2.5 cm) half sheet pan with parchment and generously sprinkle with cornmeal. Scrape the dough onto the prepared pan. Using your hands and working from the center outward toward the edges, gently press out the gas while shaping the dough into an approximately ½-inch (12 mm) thick oval or rectangle (see the Essential Technique on the facing page). The shape doesn't matter; just make sure it's about ½ inch (12 mm) thick.

2. Scatter the red peppers, goat cheese, and rosemary evenly over the dough. Drizzle 2 to 3 Tbs. olive oil evenly over the top.

3. Cover the dough loosely (to allow for rising) but completely with plastic and let the dough rise in a warm spot (see the Baker's Wisdom below). After about 20 minutes, position a rack in the center of the oven and heat the oven to 400°F (200°C/gas 6); continue to let the dough rise.

4. When the oven is heated and the dough is puffy and about 1 inch thick, carefully peel away the plastic. Dimple the dough by pressing your three middle fingers down to the bottom of the dough at about 1-inch (12 mm) intervals. Sprinkle with about 1 tsp. of the sea salt and a few grinds of black pepper.

5. Bake until the bread is golden brown and sounds hollow when tapped, 20 to 25 minutes. Move the pan to a rack, drizzle with the remaining 1 or 2 Tbs. olive oil, and let cool for 20 minutes. Using a large metal spatula, move the loaf directly to the rack to cool. The focaccia is best served the day it's made, warm or at room temperature.

BAKER'S WISDOM

Working with plastic wrap

For shaped or freeform breads that are covered while rising, I find it's best to cover with plastic wrap that I have crumbled and re-shaped so it doesn't stick—as much—to rising dough. Tear away a large sheet of plastic wrap. Holding each end in opposite hands, crumble the plastic together in the center while still holding the ends. Pull the plastic apart in opposite directions and then loosely but completely cover the bread.

Shaping and topping the dough

A

Scrape the dough onto a half sheet pan lined with parchment and sprinkled with cornmeal. Using lightly floured fingers, gently press out the gas bubbles in the dough while shaping it into a ½-inch (12 mm) thick oval.

B

Scatter the toppings evenly over the dough, then drizzle with 2 to 3 Tbs. olive oil.

C

Cover the dough loosely but completely with plastic wrap and let the dough rise.

D

Dimple the risen dough by pressing your three middle fingers down to the bottom of the dough at about 1-inch (2.5 cm) intervals. Sprinkle the dough with sea salt and a few grinds of black pepper.

Spicy Pine Nut Kalamata Parmesan Sablés

Makes 32 crackers   [PHOTO ON P. 416]

In French, the term "sablé" means sandy. Normally the term is associated with a sweet, shortbread-like cookie, but the wonderfully tender, crumbly texture of these savory crackers so closely resembles that of its sweet cousin that I couldn't resist naming them "sablés."

Packed with the big flavors of Kalamata olives, Parmigiano Reggiano, and pine nuts, along with some cayenne for a kick, these crackers are an irresistible and slightly addictive hors d'oeuvre to serve with wine or cocktails. Make sure to bake them until the edges are nutty brown; otherwise, the flavors will be muted and the texture will be soft.

The technique of smearing just-blended dough with the heel of your hand to turn the crumbly mixture into flaky layers of butter and dough is called *fraisage*. The dough comes together quickly and the shaping options are endless, so you might want to double or triple the recipe and keep the extra dough in the freezer in case you have drop-in guests.

8 Tbs. (4 oz./113 g) cold unsalted butter
1⅓ cups (6 oz./170 g) unbleached all-purpose flour
½ cup (2 oz./57 g) ground Parmigiano Reggiano cheese (see p. 38)

2 tsp. chopped fresh rosemary
½ tsp. table salt
⅛ tsp. ground cayenne + more to taste
½ cup (2¼ oz./64 g) pine nuts, lightly toasted and cooled (see p. 33)

3 Tbs. chopped Kalamata olives, drained on paper towels
2 Tbs. ice-cold water

MAKE AHEAD

> The dough can be shaped, wrapped in plastic, and frozen for up to a month. Thaw for about an hour on the counter or in the refrigerator overnight before slicing and baking as directed.

> The baked and cooled sablés can be layered between waxed paper or parchment in an airtight container and kept at room temperature for up to 3 days before serving or frozen for up to 1 month. Thaw at room temperature and warm them for a few minutes at 325°F (165°C/gas 3) to refresh the flavors.

1. Cut the butter in half lengthwise and then cut each strip into 6 pieces. Put the butter on a plate and put it into the freezer until ready to use.

2. Whisk the flour, cheese, rosemary, salt, and cayenne in a large bowl until well blended. Add the butter and, using your fingers or a pastry blender, blend the butter into the flour mixture until it resembles coarse meal. (You can also do this in a food processor using short pulses and then scrape the mixture into a large bowl before proceeding.)

3. Add the pine nuts and olives and stir until blended. Pour the water over the flour and, using a silicone spatula, stir and fold until it forms a shaggy, moist dough with some floury bits remaining (I like to use one hand to help mix while keeping the other working the spatula). Scrape the dough and any remaining floury bits onto the counter and gather into a mound. Starting with the top of the mound and using the heel of your hand, smear a section of the dough down the side and along the work surface away from you to blend the butter pieces into the dough. Repeat with the remaining dough in sections. Using a bench scraper, fold the dough together (the mixture will be rough and crumbly). Turn the pile about 90 degrees and repeat the smearing process until the mixture just comes together into a cohesive dough (this is a technique called *fraisage*). Be careful not to overwork the dough because that will make the crust dense (see the Essential Technique on the facing page).

4. Using a bench scraper, put the dough on a piece of plastic wrap and shape it into an 8 x 2¾-inch (20 x 7 cm) rectangle; use the flat edge of the bench scraper to make the sides straight and wrap tightly in the plastic. Refrigerate until very firm, about 3 hours or up to 2 days.

5. Position a rack in the center of the oven and heat the oven to 375°F (190°C/gas 5). Line two large baking sheets with parchment. Using a thin, sharp knife, cut the rectangle into ¼-inch (6 mm) thick slices and arrange about 1 inch (2.5 cm) apart on the prepared sheets. Bake, one sheet at a time, until golden brown around the edges, 16 to 18 minutes. Move the sheet to a rack and let cool for 5 minutes. Using a large spatula, transfer the crackers directly to the rack and let sit until cool enough to eat, or let cool completely. Repeat with the remaining dough, using cooled baking sheets. Serve warm or at room temperature.

TWISTS

Flavor swap

Instead of the pine nuts, use ⅓ cup (1⅓ oz./38 g) chopped, lightly toasted walnuts or pecans (see p. 33).

Re-size it

Instead of shaping the dough into a rectangle, shape it into an 8-inch (20 cm) long log or square and proceed as directed, cutting into ¼-inch (6 mm) slices before baking (see p. 148).

ESSENTIAL TECHNIQUE

Fraisage

A

Working in sections and with the heel of your hand, push and gently smear a section of the dough away from you. Push all the way to the far edge of the pile.

B

Use a bench scraper to fold the dough on top of itself, folding from the farthest edge to the closest. Repeat until the dough is back in a rough pile and turn 90 degrees.

C

With the dough crumbles re-formed into a pile, use the heel of your hand to again push and smear the dough away from you. Repeat the smearing until all of the crumbles have been blended.

D

Straighten the sides and ends of the rectangle with the flat edge of the bench scraper. Wrap plastic around it, then straighten one last time before letting the dough chill until firm.

"Everything" Flatbread Crackers

Makes about 26 crackers   [PHOTO ON P. 417]

My daughter Tierney is a big fan of flatbread crackers with the "everything" topping, but she doesn't like the ones with caraway seeds. I couldn't agree more and, because those are hard to find, I decided it was time to make them at home—just the way us Dodge girls like 'em. The result is a hearty, low-fat cracker with just the right amount of crunch along with a good dose of our favorite toppings: sesame seeds, poppy seeds, and dried onions. At the risk of alienating caraway lovers, I have included them in the topping ingredients as optional.

These crackers are meant to be crispy with a slightly dry bite. To that end, the dough needs to be rolled thinly and evenly. I use a hand-crank pasta machine (stand mixer attachments work well, too) to roll and re-roll the dough until it's smooth and forms a long, thin strip similar to a length of pasta. In a pinch, you can use a rolling pin, but you'll need to put some serious muscle into the job to make the dough smooth and an even thinness.

As a side note: You've heard me chime in time and again on the importance of weighing the flour or, at the least, properly measuring for volume measures. This topic came up again when my friend, Janis Tester, tested this recipe in her home. I asked her how the recipe performed and she responded that she loved the baked cracker but had to add more water to make the dough. I knew right away that this was a flour measuring issue and, sure enough, Janis used the dip-and-swipe volume measure and not my spoon-and-swipe method, proving, once again, that how you measure really does matter.

2 Tbs. sesame seeds
2 Tbs. poppy seeds
4 tsp. dried minced onion
2 tsp. caraway seeds (optional)
Coarse salt and freshly ground black
   pepper

1 white (1 oz./28 g) from a large egg
   (see p. 371)
1 cup (4½ oz./128 g) whole-wheat
   flour
⅔ cup (3 oz./85 g) unbleached
   all-purpose flour

1 tsp. table salt
½ cup (120 ml) water
2 Tbs. neutral oil (safflower, canola,
   vegetable, or corn)

1. Secure a pasta rolling machine on the counter or secure the attachment to your stand mixer (read the manual thoroughly if this is your first time using it). Position a rack in the center of the oven and heat the oven to 425°F (220°C/gas 7). Line two large cookie sheets with parchment or nonstick liners. Put the sesame seeds, poppy seeds, minced onion, and caraway seeds (if using) in a small bowl and have the coarse salt and pepper at the ready. Put the egg white in another small bowl and, using a fork, mix until well blended.

2. Put the flours and table salt in the bowl of a stand mixer and whisk until blended. Fit the mixer with the paddle attachment and mix on medium speed while pouring in the water and oil. Mix on medium speed until the flour is completely incorporated and forms a moist, crumbly dough, 2 to 3 minutes.

3. Scrape the dough onto the counter and knead a few times until a soft dough forms. Divide into 2 equal pieces, covering one with plastic. Using the palm of your hand, flatten the dough. Set the pasta rolling machine at the largest opening (#1) and crank the dough through the machine. It will be very rough and broken in patches. Fold the dough in half and repeat rolling and folding until the dough comes out smooth. Adjust the machine to a narrower setting (#3) and pass the dough through. It should be smooth, but if not, pass it through again without folding. Adjust the machine to the next narrower setting (#5) and pass the dough through (see the Essential Technique on p. 552). It should be slightly thicker than ⅛ inch (3 mm). Arrange the dough strip (about 26 inches/66 cm long) crosswise on the counter. Repeat with the remaining piece of dough.

4. Using the tines of a fork, prick the dough all over. Brush the tops of the dough with the egg white and scatter the seed mixture evenly over the dough. Sprinkle with coarse salt and black pepper, pressing gently so the toppings stick to the dough. Using a knife, fluted pastry wheel, or pizza wheel, cut the dough into 2-inch (5 cm) wide strips.

5. Arrange the strips about ½ inch (12 mm) apart on the prepared cookie sheets. Do not press down. Bake, one sheet at a time, until the crackers are deep golden brown around the edges, 8 to 14 minutes (don't undercook or the crackers will be soggy). Move the sheet to a rack to cool for about 5 minutes. Using a spatula, move the crackers directly to the rack and let cool completely.

TWISTS

Re-size it
Instead of cutting the dough into rectangles, cut into triangles or random shapes before baking as directed.

(continued)

MAKE AHEAD

The crackers can be made and stowed in an airtight container for up to 1 month.

ESSENTIAL TECHNIQUE

Making the dough

A

Knead the dough on the counter a few times until softened, then divide into two pieces; cover one and set aside.

B

Working with a pasta rolling machine, feed the dough through the largest opening. It will be rough and break apart.

C

Lay the dough on the counter and fold it in half, then feed it through the machine again, passing it through a narrower setting.

D

Hold one hand underneath the dough as it comes out of the machine and use the other to guide it into the opening. As you continue the rolling and folding process and adjust the machine to a narrower setting, the dough will start to come out smooth.

E

The dough is ready when it's smooth with no holes, is just thicker than 1/8 inch (3 mm), and is about 26 inches (66 cm) long. Lay the dough on the work surface, then repeat the process with the other piece of dough.

Spicy Cheese Grissini

Makes 40 to 45 breadsticks   [PHOTO ON P. 418]

These crisp, crunchy breadsticks are my version of the Italian classic that my family devours at Centro, one of our favorite local restaurants, as we wait for dinner. These grissini are a staple on my counter. I stand a bunch of them in a tall glass or quart-sized canning jar for easy nibbling. They are a perfect grab-and-go snack for the family and, for me, a tasty nibbler as I work through the edits of this book.

Whether you make them plain, herbed, or cheesy with a spicy kick, these sticks are downright addictive. They are also remarkably easy to make due to their freeform, whimsical shapes. The dough is sticky so I recommend mixing in a stand mixer.

For this version, keep in mind that ½ tsp. cayenne makes a spicy breadstick (the heat builds as you eat the breadsticks). If you prefer your snacks on the milder side, try them first with the lower amount of cayenne and increase it the next time. Check out the other two flavors in Twists (see p. 554); I like to make all three for party snacks.

2½ cups (11¼ oz./319 g) unbleached all-purpose flour
2¼ tsp. instant (quick-rise) yeast
1¼ tsp. table salt
¾ tsp. sweet ground paprika

¼ to ½ tsp. ground cayenne
1 cup (240 ml) water, warmed to between 115° and 125°F (45° and 52°C)

¼ cup (60 ml) olive oil + more for greasing the bowl
½ cup (2 oz./57 g) ground Parmigiano Reggiano cheese (see p. 38)

Make the dough

1. Put the flour, yeast, table salt, paprika, and cayenne in a large bowl of a stand mixer and whisk until well blended. Fit the mixer with the dough hook, then mix on medium speed while pouring in the warm water and oil until the flour is completely incorporated, scraping the sides as needed. Increase the speed to medium high and beat until the dough is smooth and pulls away from the sides and bottom of the bowl, 9 to 11 minutes. If the dough climbs up the hook, stop the mixer and scrape the dough back down into the bowl. Add the cheese and mix until blended, about 1 minute. The dough will be soft and sticky to the touch.

For more about scraping dough from a dough hook, see p. 449.

2. Remove the dough hook, scrape the dough onto the counter, knead once or twice until it no longer sticks to the counter and passes the windowpane test, and shape into a ball. Lightly grease the sides of the bowl and put the dough, rounded side up, back in. Cover the bowl with a plate or plastic wrap. Let rise in a warm spot until doubled in size, about 45 minutes.

For more about hand kneading, see p. 449.

For more about the windowpane test, see p. 470.

(continued)

MAKE AHEAD

> The dough can be prepared, risen, and refrigerated (covered) for up to 4 hours before shaping and baking.

> Arrange the baked and cooled breadsticks in a single or slightly overlapping layer in a half sheet pan, cover with plastic, and stow at room temperature for up to 2 weeks.

Shape and bake the dough

1. After about 30 minutes, position a rack in the center of the oven and heat the oven to 400°F (200°C/gas 6); continue to let the dough rise. Have ready four cookie sheets lined with parchment or nonstick liners.

2. Scrape the dough onto an unfloured work surface and press down on the dough to deflate it. Using a bench scraper or knife, portion the dough in half and cover one half with plastic. Working with the other half and using your hands, work from the center outward toward the edges, gently pressing out the gas while shaping the dough into an 8 x 6-inch (20 x 15 cm) rectangle. With one long edge facing you, use a pizza wheel or a knife to cut the dough crosswise into ⅓- to ½-inch (8 to 12 mm) strips.

For more about deflating risen dough, see p. 477.

For more about weighing dough, see p. 450.

3. Hold one strip by the ends and gently tap it on the surface, stretching it to the length of the cookie sheet (about 16 inches/40.5 cm), keeping the shape as uniform as possible. To even out the strips, use your hands to gently roll the thicker parts against the work surface until the strip is even. If the dough is too sticky, very lightly flour your hands. Avoid too much flour as it prevents the strip from stretching well. Arrange the breadsticks on the prepared sheets, about 1 inch (2.5 cm) apart. They can be straight or one of the ends can be shaped into hooks or S-curves (see the Essential Technique on the facing page). Repeat with the remaining dough.

4. Bake, one sheet at a time and as they are filled and ready, until the breadsticks are deep golden brown, 15 to 20 minutes (the thicker the strips, the longer the baking time). (If some of the breadsticks are cooking faster than others, use tongs to remove them from the baking sheet and continue baking the remainder.) Move the sheet to a rack and let cool completely.

TWISTS

Flavor swap

> **Classic:** Omit the Parmigiano Reggiano and cayenne and proceed as directed.

> **Herbed:** Instead of the Parmigiano Reggiano and cayenne, substitute ½ cup (⅝ oz./18 g) chopped fresh herbs (a combination of chives, basil, rosemary, and thyme).

FINISHING TOUCHES

Sprinkle some crushed sea salt over the breadsticks when they are just out of the oven.

Cutting the dough and shaping the breadsticks

A

Working with one half of the dough, use your hands to shape it into an 8 x 6-inch (20 x 15 cm) rectangle, then use a pizza wheel to cut strips about ⅓ to ½ inch (8 to 12 mm) wide.

B

Hold one strip by both ends and gently tap it on the work surface as you gently stretch the dough to the length of the baking sheet. Keep the thickness as even as possible. If necessary, gently roll the thick parts on the counter until the strip is uniform.

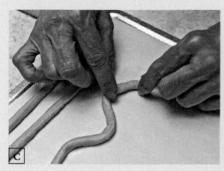

C

Place the breadsticks on the prepared cookie sheet, leaving them straight or shaping the top into an S-curve or hook shape.

Chapter 11

FRUIT DESSERTS

> > > >

Concord Grape Not-So-Dowdy

Serves 6 to 8

PB & J sandwiches have never been a favorite of mine, even in childhood. My sandwich of choice was always cream cheese and grape jam or jelly. I loved the big, bold flavor of Concord grapes paired with the silky smooth cream cheese. I still get a hankering for it, but, nowadays, I turn to this gloriously delicious version of my childhood sandwich. Instead of using jarred jam, I use fall's finest Concord grapes and a lightly sweetened, creamy, soft biscuit topping in place of the cream cheese and bread to soak up all the yummy, rich juices.

Working with Concord grapes is easy if a bit more time-consuming than other fruits. While some newer varieties are seedless, most grapes are filled with seeds hard enough to make your dentist happy, so the trick is to rid them of the seeds without sacrificing flavor and color-filled skins. If you've never worked with Concord grapes, the process is two-fold. After rinsing and draining, gather a few extra hands like I did when we shot the photo series on p. 559 (thanks Claire, Carolyn, and Sloan!) and squeeze the pulp out of the their skins while saving the latter for later. Once the pulp is soft, strain out those nasty seeds while extracting the pale green purée. Add the skins and cook until tender and the purée takes on its magical deep purple color and heavenly aroma. Add a topping and you're done!

3 Tbs. cornstarch
1 Tbs. water
1 Tbs. freshly squeezed lemon juice
4½ cups (about 1¾ to 2 lb./794 to 907 g with stems) Concord grapes, rinsed and well drained

1¼ cups (8¾ oz./248 g) granulated sugar + more as needed
Pinch of table salt
1 recipe single pie crust dough (see p. 313), chilled
2 Tbs. heavy cream

Heavy cream, vanilla ice cream, or Boozy Hard Sauce (recipe on p. 565; optional), for serving

1. Put the cornstarch, water, and lemon juice in a small cup or ramekin and stir until smooth. Set aside. Lightly grease an 8-inch (20 cm) square baking dish (I like Pyrex).

2. Working with one grape at a time over a medium bowl, pinch it at the end opposite the stem to push the center (pulp and seeds) out and slip off the skin. Put the skins in another medium bowl and set aside (see the Essential Technique on p. 559). Put the skinned grapes, sugar, and salt in a medium saucepan and cook, stirring occasionally, over medium-low heat until the sugar is dissolved and the fruit bursts when pressed against the pan, 5 to 7 minutes.

3. Strain the mixture through a fine-mesh sieve into a medium bowl, firmly pressing on the solids (you'll have about 2 cups/480 ml). Scrape the underside of the sieve into the bowl; discard the seeds in the sieve. Scrape the purée back into the same saucepan and add the reserved skins. Set over medium-low heat and cook, stirring and pressing on the skins, until just boiling. Taste and stir in more sugar, if needed. Slide the saucepan from the heat.

(continued)

TWISTS

Re-size it

> **Individual dowdies:** Portion the filling among six lightly greased 6-oz. (180 ml) ramekins (3½ inches wide x 1⅔ inches high; 9 cm x 4.2 cm), filling them about two-thirds full. Cut the rolled dough into six 3½-inch (9 cm) rounds and place on top of the fruit. Brush with the cream, sprinkle with the sugar, and bake as directed, 20 to 25 minutes.

> **Instead of the pie-crust topping, use a drop biscuit:** Whisk together 1½ cups (6 oz./170 g) unbleached all-purpose flour, ⅓ cup (2⅜ oz./ 67 g) granulated sugar, 1¾ tsp. baking powder, and ¼ tsp. table salt in a medium bowl. Add ⅔ cup (160 ml) heavy cream, 6 Tbs. (3 oz./ 85 g) melted unsalted butter, and 1 tsp. pure vanilla extract. Using a silicone spatula, gently stir the ingredients together until the flour is evenly moistened and the dough begins to form large, soft, moist clumps. Drop spoonfuls of the dough evenly over the top of the filling. Bake as directed until the filling is bubbling and a pick inserted in one of the center biscuits comes out clean, 28 to 32 minutes.

4. Stir the reserved cornstarch mixture until smooth and slowly add to the grape mixture, whisking constantly until well blended. Cook, whisking, over medium heat until the mixture is just boiling. Pour into the prepared pan and set aside.

5. Position a rack in the center of the oven, set a foil-lined half sheet pan on the rack, and heat the oven to 375°F (190°C/gas 5).

6. Pull the dough disk from the fridge and, if it's very cold, set it out at room temperature until it's just pliable enough to roll, 10 to 20 minutes. Arrange a piece of parchment on your work surface, put the unwrapped dough in the center, and cover with another piece of parchment. Using a rolling pin, roll the dough between the parchment to a ⅛- to ¼-inch (3 to 6 mm) thickness, turning, lifting, and repositioning the parchment and lightly flouring throughout the rolling.

For more about rolling dough between parchment, see p. 133.

7. Peel away the top parchment, cut the dough into a 9-inch (23 cm) square, and peel away and discard the excess dough. Make two 1½-inch (4 cm) long slits in the center of the dough square, forming an X through the dough. Carefully roll the dough around the pin, leaving the bottom parchment behind, and position over the filled baking dish. Unroll the dough onto the dish, allowing the excess to hang over the edges. Roll the overhang under itself to shape an edge crust that rests on top of the filling (don't worry about crimping). Brush the dough with some of the heavy cream and sprinkle evenly with more sugar.

For more about rolling dough around a pin and placing on a baking pan, see p. 364.

8. Set the dish on the baking sheet and bake until the pastry is browned and the filling is bubbling in the center, 35 to 40 minutes. Let cool for about 10 minutes, then serve. If you like, serve warm with a drizzle of heavy cream, a small scoop of ice cream, or Boozy Hard Sauce.

BAKER'S WISDOM

What's in a name?

A baked fruit dessert with a simple topping—like pastry or drop dumpling— is often referred to as a "pandowdy" due to its perceived simple and plain appearance, but I refuse to call any dessert, most of all this one, plain. Even with a pie-crust topping, any dessert with a sweetened, bubbling fruit filling and a homemade topping of any kind earns the right to a proud and honorable name. How about Baked_____ (fill in your fruit) Triumph?

Making the grape compote

A

Working with one grape at a time, pinch it between your thumb and index finger at the end opposite the stem. The grape will slip out of the skin. Continue with all of the grapes, keeping the flesh and skins in separate bowls.

B

Cook the skinned grapes with the sugar and salt until the fruit is tender and crushes easily when pressed with a silicone spatula against the side of the pan.

C

Once the grapes are tender, pour the mixture through a fine-mesh sieve into a medium bowl. Press firmly on the solids to push the pulp through the sieve, leaving the grape seeds behind. Use your spatula to scrape any pulp clinging to the bottom of the sieve into the bowl. Discard the seeds.

D

Return the pulp to the pan and add the reserved skins. Cook, stirring, until the skins are tender and beginning to break apart. When the purée comes to a boil, stir in the cornstarch mixture. The mixture will take on a beautiful jewel tone.

Rhubarb Red Berry Fool

Serves 6

A fruit fool is a classic British dessert and it's one of the quickest, easiest desserts out there. It's as simple as folding a well-seasoned fruit purée into whipped cream, piling into glasses, and serving. You can dress it up a bit by layering it with crushed cookies or, as I've done here, layering with extra fruit compote for a more intense fruit flavor.

The flavor of the fool depends on the quality of the fruit you use. Start with in-season rhubarb and ripe raspberries and make sure your purée is very flavorful, adjusting the sweetness levels along with the accent flavors (in this case, orange juice) before folding it into the whipped cream.

So what's up with the quirky name? Maybe it is named as such because it's so easy to make that any fool can do it or, maybe, because it's so scrumptious that you'd be a fool not to make it.

The compote makes 2½ cups (600 ml). Warm or chilled, it's delicious on its own or as companion to shortcakes, yogurt, or ice cream.

For the rhubarb–berry compote
⅔ cup (4⅝ oz./131 g) granulated sugar
3 Tbs. freshly squeezed orange juice or orange flavored liqueur (or a combination)
12 oz. (340 g) fresh rhubarb, trimmed and cut into ½-inch (2 mm) pieces (see the facing page)

8 oz. (227 g) strawberries, rinsed, dried, hulled, and quartered (halved if small) to yield about 2 cups
½ cup (2 oz./57 g) raspberries, rinsed and dried
Pinch of table salt

For the fool
1 cup (240 ml) heavy cream, chilled
⅓ cup (1⅜ oz./39 g) confectioners' sugar, sifted if lumpy
1 tsp. pure vanilla extract
Pinch of table salt

MAKE AHEAD

> The compote can be made and refrigerated for up to 4 days.

> The fool can be made and refrigerated for up to 1 day.

TWISTS

Flavor swap

Ginger: Add 2 to 3 Tbs. finely chopped crystallized ginger to the whipped cream along with the compote.

Make the compote
Put the sugar and orange juice in a medium saucepan. Cook, stirring, over medium-low heat until the sugar is dissolved. Add the rhubarb and cook, stirring gently and occasionally, until the rhubarb is barely tender and some juices are released, 5 to 7 minutes. Add the strawberries and continue cooking, stirring gently, until the berries have released some juices and are just tender and the rhubarb is beginning to break apart, about 3 minutes. Slide the pan off the heat, add the raspberries and salt, and stir gently until mixed. Scrape the compote into a medium bowl and set aside to cool to room temperature. Cover and refrigerate until cold, about 3 hours or up to 2 days. For faster cooling, set the bowl over a larger bowl filled with ice and a little water, stirring and scraping the sides frequently, until cooled to room temperature.

Make the fool and assemble
1. Put the heavy cream, confectioners' sugar, vanilla, and salt in a large bowl and beat with an electric handheld mixer fitted with wire beaters until firm peaks form. Add 2 cups (480 ml) of the chilled compote to the whipped cream and, using a large silicone spatula, gently fold together until just blended.

For more about beating cream to firm peaks, see p. 212.

For more about folding, see p. 270.

2. Have ready six 8-oz. (240 ml) glasses and the compote. Spoon about 1 Tbs. of the remaining compote into the bottom of each glass. Portion the fool evenly among the glasses (about ⅔ cup/160 ml per serving). Top with the remaining compote and serve immediately or cover the remaining compote and each glass with plastic and refrigerate for up to 3 hours.

FINISHING TOUCHES

Serve with a mint sprig and a Lemon Drop Snap (recipe on p. 189) or Toasted Coconut Meltaway (recipe on p. 201) on the side.

ESSENTIAL TECHNIQUE

Cutting rhubarb

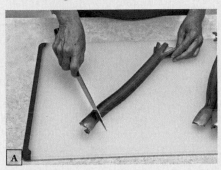

A

Trim the ends off the rhubarb and any bit of leaves that might be attached (the leaves are poisonous). Unless the rhubarb is very thick, there's no need to peel.

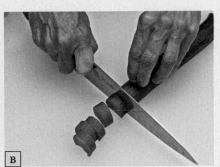

B

You'll cut rhubarb similar to how you cut celery. Hold the stalk with the rounded side up, securing it to your cutting board with your fingertips, and cut into pieces as directed.

C

D

For diced rhubarb, cut into 4-inch (10 cm) pieces, cut each stalk lengthwise into thick slices and cut each slice in half. Keeping your fingertips tucked behind your first knuckles, hold a few sticks together as you cut the rhubarb into the size needed for your recipe.

Left to right: ¼-inch (6 mm) slices, 2-inch (5 cm) pieces, ¼-inch (6 mm) dice.

>>>

Poached Citrus-Spiked Rosé Peaches

Serves 4

Two of my summer pleasures are perfectly chilled, crisp rosé wines and ripe, juicy peaches. In this twist on the classic, I've gone a step further and paired them together for a stunning and refreshing summer dessert.

The trick to poaching excellence lies in carefully monitoring the temperature of the poaching liquid for a gentle simmer. Just the slightest bit of boiling can injure the delicate fruit and cloud the ruby red broth. While this is not the end of the world nor the ruin of the finished dessert, you'll be happier with your results if you keep an eye on the cooking and adjust your flame accordingly.

For the poached peaches
3 cups (720 ml) rosé wine (I like Domaine Houchart from Provence)
1 cup (240 ml) water
¾ cup (5¼ oz./149 g) granulated sugar

2 strips of lemon zest (see p. 138)
½ vanilla bean, split (see p. 275) or 1 teaspoon pure vanilla extract or vanilla bean paste
Pinch of table salt
4 medium-sized firm-ripe peaches

For serving
1 cup (240 ml) heavy cream
1 to 2 Tbs. honey
2 to 3 Tbs. finely chopped pistachios (see p. 304)

MAKE AHEAD

The peaches and syrup can be made, cooled, covered, and refrigerated for up to 2 days before serving. Leftover peaches are delicious spooned over Greek yogurt and topped with a little granola.

BAKER'S WISDOM

Choosing ripe fruit

For the best flavor in all your fruit desserts, it's imperative to select the ripest fruit you can find. When buying stone fruit—peaches, nectarines, plums, and apricots—look for fruit without blemishes or soft or brown spots. The fruit should feel heavy in your hand and give slightly at the "shoulders" (near the stem end of the fruit). Most important, the fruit must pass the smell test. It should smell like what it is—for instance, a peach should smell like a peach. If there is no aroma, move on to a different fruit until you're successful.

Make the peaches

1. Using the tip of a small knife, cut an X through the skin at the pointed end (opposite the stem end) of the peaches.

For more about preparing peaches, see p. 108.

2. Put the wine, water, sugar, lemon zest, vanilla bean, and salt in a saucepan just wide enough to hold the peaches in a single layer. Bring to a boil over medium-high heat, stirring occasionally, to dissolve the sugar. Reduce the heat to low and add the peaches. They should be completely submerged; if not, add a little extra water—up to ½ cup (120 ml). Cover with a round of parchment placed directly on the liquid (see the Essential Technique on the facing page). Simmer very gently until the fruit is tender when pierced with a toothpick or wooden skewer (a knife tip would leave an unsightly gash), 20 to 40 minutes, depending on the ripeness of the peaches. Adjust the heat accordingly to keep the liquid at a gentle simmer. Slide the pan off the heat.

3. When the peaches are cool enough to handle, after about 15 minutes, lift them, one at a time, from the liquid and, using a small knife or your fingers, start at the X and carefully peel away the skin and put the whole peaches in a bowl.

4. Return the liquid to a boil over medium-high heat and cook until it is reduced to a thin, flavorful syrup, about 1½ cups (360 ml), 3 to 5 minutes. Fish out the lemon zest and the vanilla bean. Using the back of a small knife, scrape out the seeds and add to the liquid. If using extract or paste, add it now and stir until blended. Pour the syrup over the peaches and refrigerate until chilled.

Make the whipped cream

In a medium bowl, combine the heavy cream and honey. Using an electric handheld mixer fitted with wire beaters, beat until firm peaks form when the beaters are lifted. Serve immediately or cover and refrigerate until ready to serve or for up to 1 hour.

For more about beating cream to firm peaks, see p. 212.

To serve

Spoon some of the whipped cream into serving bowls or goblets (I like to use martini glasses), top with a peach, drizzle with some of the syrup, and sprinkle with some of the pistachios. Serve immediately. (Sipping the extra rosé syrup is optional but encouraged!)

TWISTS

Flavor swap

> Instead of whipped cream, use scoopfuls of white chocolate mousse (see p. 329) or vanilla ice cream.

> Instead of peaches, use the same amount ripe pears, peeled, halved, and cored.

ESSENTIAL TECHNIQUE

Poaching peaches

A

B

Place the peaches in the poaching liquid, adding them one at a time. Be sure you choose a saucepan just large enough to hold the peaches in a single layer and completely submerged in the liquid.

Cover the peaches with a parchment round. Place the parchment directly on the liquid, use your spoon to press gently onto the fruit, then let the peaches simmer until tender.

C

Test doneness by removing one peach and poking it with a wooden toothpick. Don't use a knife, which can leave a visible slit. Once the peaches are tender and cool enough to handle, remove one at a time and peel off the skin, using your fingers.

Baked Blueberry Crumble

Serves 6 to 8

Based on an old-fashioned classic, I've combined two of my favorite breakfast items—blueberry jam and English muffins—into one simple yet superlative summer dessert. I think it's even better than smearing homemade blueberry jam over a toasted and buttered English muffin. Yes, it's that good.

The technique is very straightforward. Crumbled muffins, sugar, and butter whiz together to form the bottom crust and crumb topping. The filling comes together even easier when you use summer's finest berries as the star of this show (I chose blueberries, but use whatever is ripe and delicious). I like to crush a small portion of the berries with the dry ingredients before mixing in the remaining fruit to help distribute the flour and sugar evenly through the filling. When baked until the topping is deep brown and crunchy and the fruit filling is bubbling, no garnish is needed. That doesn't stop me from adding a scoop of vanilla ice cream, cream, or hard sauce.

3½ (7 oz./198 g) English muffins, torn into pieces
¾ cup (5¼ oz./149 g) granulated sugar, divided
Pinch of table salt

4 Tbs. (2 oz./57 g) unsalted butter, melted
2 Tbs. unbleached all-purpose flour
4 cups (20 oz./567 g) blueberries, rinsed and dried, divided

1 tsp. pure vanilla extract
Heavy cream, vanilla ice cream, or Boozy Hard Sauce (recipe on the facing page; optional), for serving

TWISTS

Flavor swap

Instead of the blueberries, use raspberries, blackberries, or a mix of berries.

1. Position a rack in the center of the oven and heat the oven to 375°F (190°C/gas 5).

2. Put the torn English muffins in a food processor or blender and pulse until coarse crumbs form, about 1 minute. Dump the crumbs into a medium bowl, add ½ cup (3½ oz./99 g) granulated sugar and the salt, and, using a table fork, toss until blended. Drizzle the melted butter over the crumbs and toss until the crumbs are evenly coated.

3. Whisk the flour, the remaining ¼ cup (1¾ oz./50 g) sugar, and a pinch of salt in a large bowl. Add about 1 cup (5 oz./142 g) blueberries and the vanilla and, using a table fork, mash and stir the berries until they are mostly crushed and the mixture is well blended. This will help the flour mixture disperse evenly through and dissolve completely. Add the remaining blueberries and stir until well coated and blended.

4. Scatter about a third of the breadcrumb mixture evenly over the bottom of an 8-inch (20 cm) square baking dish (I like Pyrex) and spread evenly. Scrape the berry mixture evenly over the crumbs, then scatter the remaining topping evenly over the fruit. Don't press down. Bake until the topping is browned and the juices are bubbling in the center, 55 to 60 minutes. Let cool for 10 minutes. Serve warm, with or without a drizzle of heavy cream, Boozy Hard Sauce, or a small scoop of ice cream.

Boozy Hard Sauce

8 Tbs. (4 oz./113 g) unsalted butter, softened

1 cup (4 oz./113 g) confectioners' sugar, sifted if lumpy

1 Tbs. bourbon or brandy or 1½ tsp. pure vanilla extract

Put all the ingredients in a small bowl and mix with a spoon or electric handheld mixer fitted with wire beaters until smooth and well blended. Use immediately or cover and refrigerate for up to 2 weeks. Soften at room temperature before serving.

Assembling the crumble

Combine about a quarter of the blueberries with the flour mixture and blend and mash with a fork to release the berries' juices and moisten the dry ingredients. Add the remaining blueberries and stir until well coated.

With about a third of the breadcrumbs (4⅛ oz./117 g) lining the bottom of the pan, scrape the blueberries on top, spreading them evenly over the crumbs.

Sprinkle the remaining crumbs over top of the blueberries but don't press down.

Rhubarb Oatmeal Pecan Crisp

Serves 6 to 8

As I was working on this recipe, I wondered out loud to my good friend Gail Dosik whether or not I was including too many rhubarb recipes in this book. Her response? "There is no such thing as too much rhubarb!" I agree with Gail. After all, rhubarb's season is very short and its tart, tangy deliciousness should be thoroughly explored and enjoyed.

The oatmeal and pecans add a wonderfully nubby texture to the topping that offers a nice contrast to the soft, stewed rhubarb filling. Like all crisps, this is a homey dessert that is easily made and served for a weeknight family dinner as well as a late spring/early summer picnic or barbecue.

As I have mentioned in other rhubarb recipes, make sure to trim off and discard all the leaves—they are poisonous.

Nonstick cooking spray or softened butter, for preparing the pan

For the topping
8 Tbs. (4 oz./113 g) unsalted butter
⅔ cup (2 oz./57 g) old-fashioned oats
½ cup (2¼ oz./64 g) unbleached all-purpose flour
⅔ cup (4⅝ oz./131 g) firmly packed light brown sugar

¾ tsp. ground ginger
Pinch of table salt
⅓ cup (1⅜ oz./39 g) chopped pecans (see p. 304)

For the fruit
¾ cup (5¼ oz./149 g) granulated sugar
2 Tbs. cornstarch
1 Tbs. finely grated orange zest (see p. 138)

Pinch of table salt
1½ lb. (680 g) rhubarb, trimmed and cut into 1½-inch (4 cm) pieces (see p. 561)

Heavy cream, vanilla ice cream, or Boozy Hard Sauce (recipe on p. 565; optional), for serving

1. Position a rack in the center of the oven and heat the oven to 375°F (190°C/gas 5). Lightly grease an 8-inch (20 cm) square baking dish.

2. Cut the butter in half lengthwise and then cut each strip into 6 pieces. Pile onto a plate and slide into the freezer until ready to use. Whisk the oats, flour, brown sugar, ginger, and salt in a medium bowl until blended, then add the butter pieces. Using your fingers, rub the mixture together until the butter is completely incorporated and the mixture forms medium to large crumbs. Add the pecans and toss. Refrigerate the topping while the oven heats and you prepare the filling.

For more about rubbing butter into a dry mixture, see p. 572.

3. Put the sugar, cornstarch, orange zest, and salt in a medium bowl and whisk until blended. Add the rhubarb and toss. Scrape the mixture into the baking dish and spread evenly. Scatter the topping evenly over the fruit. Don't press down. Bake until the topping is browned, the rhubarb pieces are tender when pierced with a knife, and the juices are bubbling, 45 to 48 minutes. Let cool for 10 minutes. Serve warm, with or without a drizzle of heavy cream, Boozy Hard Sauce, or a small scoop of ice cream.

> The topping can be made and refrigerated for up to 5 days or frozen for up to 3 months.

> The crisp is best served warm. If you're not serving within 1 hour, let cool completely, cover, and refrigerate for up to 1 day; reheat in a 325°F (165°C/gas 3) oven until a fork inserted in the center is warm to the touch and the topping is crisp, about 20 minutes.

TWISTS

Flavor swap

Berry: Instead of the rhubarb, use the same about of berries (strawberries, blueberries, raspberries, or a combination of the three) and reduce the granulated sugar to 1/3 to 1/2 cup (2³/₈ to 3¹/₂ oz./ 67 to 99 g), depending on the fruits' natural sweetness.

ESSENTIAL TECHNIQUE

Types of oatmeal

Made from groats that have been steamed and flattened into flakes with large rollers, **old-fashioned or rolled oats** are used in most baking recipes, including this crisp.

Similar to old-fashioned oats, **quick-cooking oats** are cut into smaller pieces before steaming and rolling. While they cook up faster than old-fashioned and can be used in recipes as a substitute, their flavor is somewhat lackluster.

> >

Skillet Apple Pear Cobbler *with* Spiced Shortbread

Serves 8 to 10

Making cobblers in a skillet might seem like an extra and senseless variation on the classic but, as in this case, change is good! For me, the traditional method of mixing fruit and topping with the biscuit topping before baking always means that, while the tops of the biscuits are cooked through, the bottom part that sits on the fruit is soggy and unpleasant. To solve this problem, I start the fruit in a skillet on top of the stove, allowing the juices to release and the fruit to get very hot. This way, when I drop the biscuits on top, the underside begins to cook immediately, solving the soggy-bottom issue.

Fresh ginger adds a bright note to the apple and pear filling and, just for good measure, I've spiked it with applejack brandy (though you can also use cider) for a full-flavored finish. Served alone, the fruit makes a wonderful compote, but the addition of the deeply spiced, Linzer-like shortbread topping brings the dessert up to a new level of sophistication and deliciousness.

For the topping
1¼ cups (5⅝ oz./159 g) unbleached all-purpose flour
½ cup (2 oz./57 g) finely ground toasted hazelnuts (see p. 457)
½ tsp. baking powder
¼ tsp. ground cinnamon
¼ tsp. ground ginger
⅛ tsp. ground nutmeg
Pinch of ground cloves
¼ tsp. table salt
Pinch of ground white pepper
8 Tbs. (4 oz./113 g) unsalted butter, softened

½ cup (3½ oz./99 g) firmly packed light brown sugar
3 yolks from large eggs (see p. 371)
1 tsp. pure vanilla extract

For the filling
3 Tbs. unsalted butter
⅓ cup (2⅜ oz./67 g) firmly packed light brown sugar
1 Tbs. unbleached all-purpose flour
1½ tsp. finely chopped fresh ginger (see p. 312)
Pinch of table salt
½ cup (120 ml) applejack brandy or apple cider

1 Tbs. freshly squeezed lemon juice
1 lb. (454 g) firm, sweet-tart apples, peeled, cored, and cut into ½-inch (12 mm) thick slices (Honey Crisp or Golden Delicious are two of my favorites; see p. 363)
1 lb. (454 g) firm-ripe pears, peeled, cored, and cut into ¾-inch (2 cm) thick slices (see p. 122)

Vanilla ice cream or slightly sweetened whipped cream, for serving (optional) (see p. 367)

Make the topping

1. In a medium bowl, combine the flour, ground hazelnuts, baking powder, cinnamon, ground ginger, nutmeg, cloves, salt, and white pepper (see the Essential Technique on p. 570). Whisk until well blended.

2. Put the butter in the bowl of a stand mixer fitted with the paddle attachment (or in a large bowl and using an electric handheld mixer fitted with wire beaters). Beat on medium speed until well blended and smooth, about 1 minute. Add the brown sugar and beat on medium-high speed until well blended, about 2 minutes. Add the egg yolks and vanilla and beat until well blended, about 1 minute. Add the flour–hazelnut mixture and beat on medium-low speed until well blended, about 1 minute.

For more about scraping the bowl and beater, see p. 289.

3. Place a large piece of plastic wrap on the counter. Scrape the dough onto the plastic. Using the plastic as a helper, press and shape the dough into a 7½-inch (19 cm) long log. Wrap in a second piece of plastic and refrigerate until firm, about 4 hours.

For more about shaping dough into a log, see p. 148.

Assemble and bake the cobbler

1. Position a rack in the center of the oven and heat the oven to 375°F (190°C/gas 5). Unwrap the log and set on a cutting board. Using a thin, sharp knife, cut the log into ten ¾-inch (2 cm) thick slices, wrap again, and keep refrigerated.

2. Put the butter in a 10½ x 2 to 2½-inch (26.5 x 5 to 6 cm) ovenproof skillet (8- to 10-cup capacity) with an ovenproof handle. Set over medium-low heat and melt the butter, about 1 minute. Add the brown sugar, flour, fresh ginger, and salt and cook, stirring and smearing with a silicone spatula, until the sugar is melted and the mixture is smooth and fragrant, about 1 minute. Whisking constantly, add the brandy and lemon juice and cook until the mixture is smooth and boiling, about 2 minutes.

3. Reduce the heat to low and add the apple slices. Cook, tossing and stirring gently, until very hot and just barely tender, about 5 minutes. Add the pear slices and gently toss until coated and hot, about 3 minutes. Slide the pan off the heat and spread the fruit slices into a relatively even layer. Arrange the topping slices randomly over the fruit, leaving some space between them (carefully—the filling is hot).

4. Bake until the filling is bubbling in the center and a pick inserted in a dumpling comes out clean, 30 to 40 minutes. Move the pan to a rack and let cool for 10 to 15 minutes to allow the juices to settle before serving with ice cream or whipped cream, if desired.

MAKE AHEAD

> The spiced shortbread can be made and refrigerated for up to 2 days.

> The cobbler is best served warm. If you're not serving within 1 hour, let cool completely, cover, and refrigerate for up to 3 days; reheat in a 325°F (165°C/gas 3) oven until a fork inserted in the center is warm to the touch, about 20 minutes.

BAKER'S WISDOM

Choosing the right pan

It's best to make a fruit-filled cobbler in stainless or enamel-coated skillets with oven-proof handles. Cast iron skillets might seem to be a natural rustic partner, but they will discolor the fruits and impart a metallic taste to the filling.

TWISTS

Flavor swap

FOR THE FILLING
> Instead of the pear–apple combination, use a peach (p. 295) or berry (p. 567) filling.

> Instead of the pear–apple combination, make the filling all apples or all pears using the total weight listed for both fruits.

FOR THE TOPPING
> Instead of the shortbread, use the topping from one of these recipes: Apple Crisp (p. 571), Rhubarb Oatmeal Pecan Crisp (p. 566), or Skillet Ginger Plum Cobbler (p. 580).

(continued)

Measuring spices and mixing dry ingredients

It's important to measure ingredients accurately. When working with spices, spoon out enough of the spice to overfill the measuring spoon, then use the back of a knife blade or metal spatula to swipe the excess back into the jar, leaving you with the amount called for in your recipe. Some containers, such as baking powder, come with a built-in scraper. Fill the measuring spoon, then run the edge across the scraper on the can.

When measuring and adding a number of ingredients to be mixed together, spoon them into separate mounds in the bowl to help keep track of what you have already measured. When whisking dry ingredients together, use a whisk in a stirring/folding movement to pull the ingredients from the outer edge of the bowl into the center. Continue until the ingredients are well mixed.

Classic Apple Crisp

Serves 6 to 8

Growing up, apple crisp was part of my mom's fall dessert repertoire, but it wasn't until I was 21 and tasted Dica Smith's version of the classic that I truly fell in love with it. Could it have been her hard sauce—boozy and divine—or the crispy topping—buttery and sugary? Honestly, they were both heavenly. Dica's fall classic had me at hello and my version doesn't stray too far. Why change something that is already wonderful?

For my crisp, I prefer a combination of sweet and juicy Macintosh apples that break down during baking and sweet-tart Golden Delicious that soften but hold their shape. For yours, I suggest you visit the farmers' market and try out some of your local varieties. Taste for sweetness and ask about the baked texture, then dive in. Unlike apples for pies, which need to retain some structure after baking for cleanish slices, crisps are more stew- or pudding-like, so you have more freedom with your choices. Once home, if you find your apples are tart, toss them with 1 to 3 Tbs. granulated sugar before adding the water and topping.

For the topping
1 cup (4½ oz./128 g) unbleached
   all-purpose flour
⅔ cup (4⅝ oz./131 g) firmly
   packed dark brown sugar
¾ tsp. ground cinnamon
Pinch of table salt

8 Tbs. (4 oz./113 g) unsalted butter,
   cut into ½-inch (12 mm) pieces
   and chilled

For the fruit
2 lb. (907 g) (about 4 medium-large)
   firm, sweet apples
3 Tbs. water

Heavy cream, vanilla ice cream, or
   Boozy Hard Sauce (recipe on
   p. 565; optional), for serving

1. Put the flour, brown sugar, cinnamon, and salt in a medium bowl. Whisk until blended and add the butter pieces. Using your fingers, rub the mixture together until the butter is incorporated and the mixture looks like coarse crumbs (see the Essential Technique on p. 572). Refrigerate the topping while the oven heats and you prepare the apples.

2. Position a rack in the center of the oven and heat the oven to 375°F (190°C/gas 5).

3. Peel the apples and cut in half lengthwise. Scoop out the cores and cut the halves lengthwise into ½- to ¾-inch (12 mm to 2 cm) thick slices. You should have about 6 cups (1.4 liters). Scrape the apples into an 8-inch (20 cm) square baking dish (I like Pyrex) and spread evenly. Scatter the topping evenly over the fruit. Don't press down. Bake until the topping is browned, the apples are tender when pierced with a knife, and the juices are bubbling, 48 to 50 minutes. Let cool for 10 minutes. Serve warm, with or without a drizzle of heavy cream, a small scoop of ice cream, or Boozy Hard Sauce.

For more about cutting apples, see p. 122.

(continued)

MAKE AHEAD

> The topping can be made, covered, and refrigerated for up to 4 days or frozen for up to 3 months.

> The crisp can be baked, cooled completely, covered, and stowed at room temperature for up to 3 days before reheating.

TWISTS

Flavor swap

> Instead of apples, use all pears or a combination of the two.

> Add up to ¾ cup (3 oz./85 g) chopped nuts to the topping.

ESSENTIAL TECHNIQUE

Mixing the topping

A With the dry ingredients blended together in a bowl, add the chilled butter pieces.

B Mix the butter into the dry ingredients, using your fingers to pinch and rub the mixture together until the ingredients resemble coarse crumbs and no butter pieces are visible.

Individual Apple Tarte Tatin

Serves 6

As a pastry student in Paris, I was charged with championing many iconic French desserts, all of them heavenly and exotic to my maturing palate and culinary naiveté. The one that proved life-changing, a seminal moment in my baking life, was the Tarte Tatin. My roots firmly planted in American baking, I approached this tart with a yawn and a sigh. "Just a one-crust version of apple pie," I thought to myself. I couldn't have been more incorrect.

When making those first few Tatins, I discovered smells, textures, and flavor-filled nuances that I had yet to experience. I came to realize that baking was more than just steps that lead to a finished dessert. It was about the process, dare I say ritual, and every part of it layered together and built toward the success of the dessert. The caramel needed to be coaxed to just the right stage. The sweet-tart, firm apples eased into the thick, jewel-like sauce and turned lovingly before blanketing them with sweet, flaky dough. Baking and then the heart-stopping moment of flipping and removing the pan to expose the brilliance of simple ingredients prepared with caring purposefulness.

When deciding on recipes to include in this book, I argued against a Tarte Tatin, citing the many, many versions of Tarte Tatin already available online and in books. Instead, I elected to create an individual version that was more approachable for the home baker but mirrored the mastery and magic of the classic in appearance as well as flavor. My hope is that you find joy in these mini tartes and take away a glimmer of what I found all those years ago in a kitchen on Rue de la Varenne.

1 recipe single pie crust dough (see p. 313), chilled
½ cup (3½ oz./99 g) firmly packed dark brown sugar

3 Tbs. (1½ oz./42 g) unsalted butter
½ tsp. ground cinnamon
Pinch of table salt

3 small apples (about 6½ oz./ 184 g each), peeled, halved, and cored (see Baker's Wisdom on p. 363 for information on choosing a variety; see p. 122 for halving and coring)

1. Position a rack in the lower third of the oven, set a half sheet pan on the rack, and heat the oven to 450°F (230°C/gas 8). Have ready one extra-large, 6-cup muffin tin.

2. Pull the dough disk from the fridge and, if it's very cold, set it out at room temperature until it's just pliable enough to roll, 10 to 20 minutes. Arrange a large piece of parchment on your work surface, put the unwrapped dough in the center, and cover with another piece of parchment. Using a rolling pin, roll the dough between the parchment to a thickness between ⅛ and ¼ inch (3 to 6 mm), turning, lifting, and repositioning the parchment and lightly flouring throughout the rolling.

For more about rolling dough between parchment, see p. 133.

3. Peel away the top parchment and, using a 4-inch (10 cm) round cookie cutter, cut out as many rounds as you can and arrange them on a cookie sheet; cover with plastic wrap. Stack and reroll the scraps and cut out more

TWISTS

Flavor swap

> Instead of apples, use 3 small, round pears, peeled, halved, and cored.

> Instead of ground cinnamon, use the same amount of ground ginger or cardamom.

rounds. If your kitchen is warm, slide the sheet into the fridge while you continue with the recipe.

4. Put the brown sugar, butter, cinnamon, and salt in a medium bowl. Mix with a spoon, spatula, or electric handheld mixer until well blended. Portion evenly among the muffin cups (about 1½ Tbs. each). Arrange an apple half, rounded side down, into each cup and gently press into the sugar mixture. If needed, trim the apple with a paring knife to fit. Working with one pastry round at a time, center over the apple and gently fit the extra dough into and around the gap between the cup and the apple so that it goes down the inside of the tin.

5. Reduce the oven temperature to 425°F (220°C/gas 7) and bake until the top crusts are deep golden brown and the apples are tender when pierced with a long skewer inserted from the side and under the pastry, 19 to 21 minutes. Move the pan to a rack. Immediately place an upside down half sheet pan on top of the pan and, using pot holders, grip both the pan and the tin and invert. Let the inverted pan rest for about 2 minutes to let the topping settle. Gently remove the pan and, using a wide metal spatula, move the tartes to small serving plates (see the Essential Technique on p. 575). Scrape up any caramel from the pan and drizzle over the apples. Serve warm.

Assembling and unmolding the tartes

A

Arrange apples, rounded side down (this will be the top when unmolded), on top of the brown sugar–filled muffin cup and press in gently. If necessary, trim away a bit of the apple so it fits the cup.

B

Position a 4-inch (10 cm) pastry round on top of each apple, fitting the edges down around the gap between the apple and the edge of the muffin cup.

C

After baking, invert the muffin tin onto a sheet pan, then let the tartes rest for a couple of minutes. This will allow the caramel to settle on top of the tartes. Remove the muffin tin and use a wide, offset metal spatula to move the tartes to dessert plates. Scrape up any extra juices and caramel from the pan and drizzle over the apples.

Brown Sugar Hazelnut Fig Clafoutis

Serves 6 to 8 [PHOTO ON P. 419]

A classic French clafoutis is perhaps the simplest dessert to make but also one of the most flavorful. The rustic, country pudding is traditionally made with unpitted fresh dark cherries baked in a thick, egg-rich batter spiked with Cognac. Here, I've chosen to spotlight fresh figs, brown sugar, and dark rum. The juicy, tender figs caramelize slightly during baking, and the rum, brown sugar, and toasted hazelnuts added just before serving all lend themselves to a rich, earthy-flavored dessert that's easy enough to make during the week. Try and serve it straight from the oven, while it's fully puffed. Like a soufflé, it will quickly deflate—still delicious but not quite as spectacular to look at.

Nonstick cooking spray or softened butter, for preparing the pan

10 oz. (283 g) (about 9 small) ripe figs, trimmed and halved lengthwise (quartered if larger) (see the facing page)

¼ cup (1¾ oz./50 g) firmly packed light brown sugar

¼ cup (1⅛ oz./32 g) unbleached all-purpose flour

Pinch of table salt

2 large eggs, at room temperature

⅔ cup (160 ml) half-and-half or whole milk

2 Tbs. unsalted butter, melted

2 Tbs. dark rum

1 tsp. pure vanilla extract

¼ cup (1 oz./28 g) medium-fine chopped blanched hazelnuts, toasted, for garnish (see p. 457)

2 Tbs. granulated sugar, for garnish

1. Position a rack in the center of the oven and heat the oven to 350°F (180°C/gas 4). Lightly grease a shallow 6-cup (1.4 l) baking dish. Arrange the figs cut side up in the prepared pan to form an even layer.

2. Put the brown sugar, flour, and salt in a medium bowl and whisk until well blended. Add the eggs and whisk until blended. Add the half-and-half, melted butter, rum, and vanilla and whisk until well blended and foamy, about 1 minute. Pour the egg mixture over the figs and bake until the custard is puffed and browned around the edges, the fruit is bubbling, and a knife inserted in the center comes out clean, 24 to 27 minutes. Move to a rack, sprinkle the hazelnuts and granulated sugar over the top, and serve immediately. The clafoutis will deflate as it cools but will still be delicious served slightly warm or at room temperature.

MAKE AHEAD

The custard mixture can be prepared, covered, and refrigerated for up 2 days.

TWISTS

Flavor swap

Cherry-almond: Instead of the figs, use the same amount of pitted cherries. Instead of the rum, use the same amount of Cognac. Instead of the hazelnuts, use the same amount of sliced almonds.

FINISHING TOUCHES

Instead of the hazelnuts and granulated sugar, dust the top with sifted confectioners' sugar just before serving.

BAKER'S WISDOM

Fig varietals

Available from early summer into fall, fresh figs have a teardrop shape, velvety skin, and fleshy inside that's studded with crunchy seeds. Several varieties are widely available in the U.S. Black Mission figs are very sweet, with blackish-purple skin and pink flesh. Brown Turkey are large, with maroon skin and a mild flavor. Calamyrna are large, with golden skin, pinkish-white flesh, and a nutty flavor.

Look for fruits that are heavy for their size and soft, yielding to gentle pressure, and avoid ones with any signs of mold. Ripe figs have a short shelf life and are best when used within 1 or 2 days. There's no need to peel figs. Just give them a gentle rinse, then dry and trim off the stem.

Trimming and cutting figs

Working with one fig at a time, use a paring knife to cut away the stem close to the fruit, then cut the fruit in half lengthwise and slice through it.

> >

Double Chocolate–Cherry Shortcakes

Serves 8   [PHOTO ON P. 420]

My twist on classic strawberry shortcake begins with deeply chocolaty and decadently rich shortcake biscuits with a rustic, craggy appearance. They are stand-alone wonderful. Pairing them with a sparkling, fresh cherry compote and whipped vanilla bean mascarpone will put this dessert on the top of your list. It serves double duty as an easy-to-make casual weeknight dessert as well as a sophisticated summery sit-down dinner party finale.

For the shortcakes
8 Tbs. (4 oz./113 g) unsalted butter
⅔ cup (160 ml) buttermilk, chilled
1 tsp. pure vanilla extract
1¾ cups (7⅞ oz./223 g) unbleached
    all-purpose flour
⅔ cup (4⅝ oz./131 g) granulated
    sugar
⅓ cup (1 oz./28 g) unsweetened
    natural cocoa powder, sifted if
    lumpy (see p. 158)
1 Tbs. baking powder
½ tsp. baking soda

¾ tsp. table salt
½ cup (3 oz./85 g) chopped
    bittersweet, semisweet, milk, or
    white chocolate (see p. 380)
2 Tbs. coarse sanding sugar
    (optional)

For the sweetened whipped cream
1½ cups (360 ml) heavy cream
½ cup (4 oz./113 g) mascarpone
3 Tbs. granulated sugar
1 tsp. vanilla bean paste or pure
    vanilla extract

For the cherry compote
1 lb. (454 g) firm, ripe sweet cherries
    (a combination of dark and
    Rainier), washed and dried
⅓ cup (2⅜ oz./67 g) granulated
    sugar + more to taste
1 Tbs. orange liqueur
Pinch of table salt

(continued)

MAKE AHEAD

> The shortcakes can be baked, cooled, covered, and stowed at room temperature for up to 1 day or wrapped in plastic and frozen for up to 1 month. If frozen, thaw, unwrapped, at room temperature 30 minutes before proceeding with the recipe.

> The whipped cream can be made and refrigerated for up to 3 hours.

> The cherry compote can be made and refrigerated for up to 4 hours.

TWISTS

Flavor swap

> Instead of cherries, use the same amount of strawberries. Reserve 8 small whole strawberries and rinse, hull, and halve (or quarter if large) the remaining berries and proceed with the recipe.

> Instead of the whipped cream filling, use large scoopfuls of vanilla or cherry ice cream.

BAKER'S WISDOM

Working with cherries

Pitting cherries is a messy business, as the red juice can stain clothes, fingers, and counters. To keep things clean, I use a pitter that has an enclosed container to catch the cherries as they are pitted. Even then, you might want to wear an old shirt and apron and work over the counter covered with a few paper towels or parchment (see p. 322).

Make the shortcakes

1. Position a rack in the center of the oven and heat the oven to 400°F (200°C/gas 6). Line a cookie sheet with parchment or a nonstick liner.

2. Cut the butter in half lengthwise, cut each half lengthwise again, and then cut each strip into 8 pieces. Pile the butter onto a plate and slide it into the freezer until ready to use. Measure the buttermilk in a 1-cup (240 ml) Pyrex measure and add the vanilla. Using a fork, whisk until blended and refrigerate until ready to use.

3. Whisk the flour, sugar, cocoa powder, baking powder, baking soda, and salt in a large bowl until well blended. Add the cold butter pieces and, using a pastry blender or two knives, cut the butter into the flour mixture until the butter is pea-sized. (You can also do this step in a food processor using short pulses, scraping the blended mixture into a large bowl before proceeding.)

For more about mixing butter and flour together until the butter is pea-sized, see p. 80.

4. Add the chopped chocolate. Pour the buttermilk and vanilla over the flour mixture and, using a silicone spatula, stir and fold until it forms a shaggy, moist dough with some floury bits remaining. (I like to use one hand to help mix while keeping the other working the spatula; see the Essential Technique on the facing page.) Scrape the dough and any remaining floury bits onto the counter and knead a few times until the dough is evenly moist and holds together well.

5. Gently press the dough into a thick 8 x 4-inch (20 x 10 cm) rectangle. Using a large sharp knife, trim the edges to make a neat rectangle and cut into 8 equal squares. Arrange on the prepared cookie sheet about 2 inches (5 cm) apart. Sprinkle the tops with the sanding sugar, if using. Bake until the shortcakes are puffed and spring back when the tops are gently pressed, 16 to 18 minutes. Move the sheet to a rack and let the shortcakes sit until they're cool enough to handle, about 15 minutes. Serve warm or at room temperature.

Make the whipped cream

In a medium bowl, combine the cream, mascarpone, sugar, and vanilla. Using an electric handheld mixer fitted with wire beaters, beat until firm peaks form when the beaters are lifted. Serve immediately or cover and refrigerate until ready to serve.

For more about beating cream to firm peaks, see p. 212.

Make the cherry compote

Select 8 pretty cherries with stems and refrigerate until ready to serve. Pit the remaining cherries and cut in half. In a medium bowl, combine the cherries, sugar, liqueur, and salt. Toss until blended. Taste and add more sugar, if needed. Cover the bowl and refrigerate, stirring occasionally, until the cherries have released some of their juices.

For more about pitting cherries, see p. 322.

To serve

If made ahead, warm the shortcakes (in a toaster oven or an oven set on 300°F/150°C). Using a serrated knife, cut the shortcakes in half horizontally and put the bottom halves on serving plates. Spoon some of the cherries, including the juices, over each shortcake, top with a big dollop of the whipped cream, and cover with the shortcake lids. Top with a dollop of the whipped cream and the reserved whole cherries. Serve immediately.

FINISHING TOUCHES

> Drizzle chocolate sauce (see p. 501) over each serving plate before assembling and serving the shortcakes.

> Instead of serving with a cherry on top, sprinkle with chocolate shards (see p. 250) or curls (see p. 381).

ESSENTIAL TECHNIQUE

Mixing the dough and shaping the shortcakes

A With the dry ingredients mixed and the butter added, pour in the wet ingredients and then mix well, using a spatula and one hand to help form a shaggy dough.

B Scrape the dough onto your work surface and knead a few times until it holds together. Shape it into a rough 8 x 4-inch (20 x 10 cm) rectangle.

C Trim all edges to even up the rectangle before cutting the dough into squares.

D Cut the dough rectangle into 8 equal squares, slicing first down the center, then slicing across three times. Transfer the squares to the prepared cookie sheet, carefully using the blade of the knife to help move them.

Skillet Ginger Plum Cobbler *with* Poppy Seed Dumplings

Serves 8 to 10   [PHOTO ON P. 421]

The secret to this cobbler's bright flavor is fresh ginger and lemon juice in the jewel-like, multicolored plum filling. They brighten without overwhelming the plums. The poppy seeds in the drop biscuit topping add texture, and the light, airy texture soaks up the fruit juices. Use a light hand when mixing the dumpling dough or the topping will be tough. Leftovers, if you have any, make a delicious breakfast when gently heated in the microwave or on top of the stove. For more about skillet cobblers, see p. 568.

For the dumplings
2 cups (9 oz./255 g) unbleached all-purpose flour
½ cup (3½ oz./99 g) granulated sugar
1 Tbs. poppy seeds
1½ tsp. baking powder
½ tsp. table salt
¾ cup (180 ml) heavy cream
1 large whole egg, at room temperature

1 yolk from a large egg, at room temperature (see p. 371)
1 tsp. pure vanilla extract
8 Tbs. (4 oz./113 g) unsalted butter, melted and cooled slightly

For the filling
2½ lb. (1.2 kg) ripe plums, halved and pitted, each half cut into 3 wedges (see p. 587)
⅔ cup (4⅝ oz./131 g) granulated sugar

1 Tbs. minced fresh ginger (see p. 312)
1 Tbs. cornstarch
2 tsp. freshly squeezed lemon juice
Pinch of table salt
2 Tbs. (1 oz./28 g) unsalted butter
2 Tbs. coarse sugar (optional)

MAKE AHEAD

The cobbler is best served warm. If you're not serving within 1 hour, let cool completely, cover, and refrigerate for up to 3 days; reheat in a 325°F (165°C/gas 3) oven until a fork inserted in the center is warm to the touch, about 20 minutes.

Make the dumplings

1. Put the flour, sugar, poppy seeds, baking powder, and salt in a large bowl and whisk until well blended.

2. Put the heavy cream, egg, yolk, and vanilla in medium bowl (or measure the heavy cream in a 2-cup/480 ml glass measure, add the egg, yolk, and vanilla) and mix with a fork or small whisk until blended. Add the heavy cream mixture and the melted butter to the flour mixture. Using a silicone spatula, gently fold ingredients together until just blended. Refrigerate the dough in the bowl while preparing the fruit filling.

For more about folding, see p. 270.

Assemble and bake the cobbler

1. Position a rack in the center of the oven and heat the oven to 375°F (190°C/gas 5). Put the plums, sugar, ginger, cornstarch, lemon juice, and salt in a large bowl and toss until blended.

2. Put the butter in a 10½ x 2 to 2½-inch (26.5 x 5 to 6 cm) ovenproof skillet (8- to 10-cup capacity). Set over medium-low heat and melt the butter, about 1 minute. Add the plum mixture, including any juices, and cook, stirring gently, until the mixture is just boiling and the juices have thickened slightly, about 5 minutes.

3. Slide the pan off the heat and spread the fruit into a relatively even layer. Using a 2-Tbs. scoop, drop the dumpling dough randomly on top of the hot filling. The dough will almost completely cover the fruit. If desired, sprinkle the coarse sugar evenly over the dumplings.

4. Bake until the filling is bubbling and a pick inserted in a dumpling comes out clean, 30 to 40 minutes. Move the pan to a rack and let cool for 10 to 15 minutes to allow the juices to settle before serving.

TWISTS

Flavor swap

> Instead of plums in the filling, use the same amount of peaches or nectarines.

> Instead of ginger in the filling, use the same amount of finely grated lemon or orange zest (see p. 138).

> Instead of the poppy seeds in the dough, use ¼ cup (1 oz./28 g) toasted, finely chopped almonds and ½ tsp. pure almond extract along with the vanilla.

> Instead of the poppy seed dumplings, use the topping from the Apple Pear Cobbler (p. 568).

FINISHING TOUCHES

Serve plain or with a scoop of vanilla ice cream or lightly sweetened whipped cream.

ESSENTIAL TECHNIQUE

Dropping dough on the hot fruit

The plums will retain their jewel color as they cook. When the juice has thickened slightly and the mixture is just boiling, it's time to add the dough on top.

Scoop the dough with a 2-Tbs. scoop and drop on top of the hot plum mixture. While the position of the dough can be random, keep the scoops close together, so that the top surface of the plums is almost completely covered.

If you like, sprinkle coarse sanding sugar on top of the dough before baking. The sugar gives the topping a little sparkle and an extra sweet crunch.

Sparkling Mixed Berry Terrine

Makes eight 1-inch (2.5 cm) slices   [PHOTO ON P. 422]

Perfect for a summer brunch or dessert, every bite of this light and refreshing terrine is loaded with big, bright flavors of summer. Almost any wine or juice will work in this recipe, but I like to use a sparkling, ruby red, rosé dessert wine like Bigaro Elio Perrone. It's low in alcohol and acidity as well as sugar, and the flavors partner beautifully with the berries.

2⅓ cups (560 ml) rosé or white, lightly sweet Italian dessert wine (I like sparkling Bigaro Elio Perrone)

2 envelopes (¼ oz each) unflavored powdered gelatin

1 quart (16 oz./454 g) strawberries, rinsed, well dried, and hulled

1½ cups (7½ oz./213 g) raspberries (preferably yellow or a mix of yellow and red), rinsed and well dried

1 cup (5 oz./142 g) blueberries, rinsed and well dried

1 cup (5 oz./142 g) blackberries, rinsed and well dried

Mascarpone or fromage blanc, for serving

2 Tbs. thinly sliced mint leaves, for serving (see p. 484)

MAKE AHEAD

The terrine can be prepared, covered, and refrigerated for up to 2 days before serving.

TWISTS

Flavor swap

Add 2 Tbs. finely chopped crystallized ginger to the berry mixture.

1. Have ready an 8½ x 4½ x 2¾-inch (21.5 x 11 x 7 cm) (6-cup/960 ml) Pyrex or ceramic loaf pan and make room in the fridge. If your wine is sparkling, measure out 2⅓ cups (560 ml) and stir vigorously to release some of the bubbles and let settle.

2. Pour 1 cup (240 ml) of the wine into a small saucepan and sprinkle the gelatin evenly over the top. Let sit until the gelatin is absorbed into the wine and plumped, about 3 minutes. Cook over medium-low heat, stirring frequently, until the gelatin is dissolved and the liquid is clear, 1 to 2 minutes. Slide the pan off the heat, add the remaining wine, and set aside to cool slightly, stirring occasionally.

For more about softening gelatin, see p. 378.

3. Cut the strawberries in half (or quarters, if large). Put all the berries in a large bowl and gently toss to combine. Pile the berries into the loaf pan and spread evenly. Slowly pour the warm (not hot) gelatin liquid over the berries. Tap the loaf pan gently on the counter to release any air bubbles. Refrigerate until the top is no longer tacky and cover with plastic wrap. Refrigerate until very firm, at least 8 hours.

4. To unmold and serve, run a thin-bladed knife between the gelatin and the loaf pan and dip the pan into very hot water and hold for 1 minute. Place a flat serving plate over the top of the pan, grip both the plate and the mold, invert, and shake gently to loosen the terrine (see the Essential Technique on the facing page). Repeat if necessary. Using a serrated knife, cut into 1-inch (2.5 cm) slices and serve with a schmear of mascarpone on the plate and a sprinkle of sliced mint.

Gelatin dessert molds

Although some recipes advise lightly coating a mold with oil, I don't find it necessary. Instead, I simply rinse the mold with water, shake out the excess, then pour in the gelatin mixture. Gelatin desserts usually become firm within 3 to 4 hours of refrigeration. Small desserts set in simple molds may be unmolded at this point. However, gelatin terrines and large gelatins made in tall or complex molds should be refrigerated for at least 8 hours and preferably up to 1 day. Gelatin continues to stiffen over a 24-hour period.

To unmold, dip the mold into a sink or deep pan filled with very hot tap water. For this terrine, you can also run a thin-bladed knife between the gelatin and the sides of the loaf pan before dipping for a little head start. Dip metal molds for no longer than a couple of seconds; thick molds of glass or ceramic need to be dipped for up to 60 seconds before they release, depending on the water's temperature. Invert a plate over the top of the mold and then turn both over together. If the dessert is reluctant to come out, repeat dipping in the hot water.

Instead of serving with the mascarpone, serve with Double Raspberry Sauce (recipe on p. 215).

ESSENTIAL TECHNIQUE

Unmolding a gelatin dessert

A. Once the terrine is chilled and set, run a thin-bladed knife between the gelatin and the loaf pan. Place the bottom of the pan in hot water to loosen it from the bottom. If you've used a glass pan, as here, this can take up to 60 seconds; a metal pan should be dipped for just a few seconds.

B. With a serving plate over the top of the pan, quickly invert the terrine. Inverting is easier if you use a loaf pan with extended sides off the top, like this Pyrex.

C. Give the pan a little shake. You should see the terrine loosening from the pan (left side of the left picture). Once the terrine has released from the pan, lift off the pan. If it is stubborn, repeat the dipping process.

Boozy Mango Brûlée

Serves 4 [PHOTO ON P. 423]

This recipe is another example that dessert doesn't have to be complicated and that you don't need a culinary school degree hanging on your wall to wow your guests.

You'll use a kitchen torch to brûlée the mangos, and if you don't have one in your arsenal, I encourage you to get one. It is very safe to use and can be purchased online or at most culinary shops. You'll use it for this recipe plus many others in all of my books. And you'll find that your family and guests will get positively giddy with dessert anticipation every time you pull it from your pantry.

For the syrup
⅓ cup (80 ml) water
¼ cup (3½ oz./99 g) granulated sugar
1 to 2 Tbs. dark rum (I like Myers's®)

For the mangos
4 large, ripe mangos (preferably Tommy Atkins or Kent varieties)
Sea salt
4 Tbs. granulated sugar

Vanilla-flavored Greek yogurt, for serving (optional)
Lime wedges, for serving

MAKE AHEAD

The syrup can be made and refrigerated for up to 3 days.

TWISTS

Flavor swap

> Instead of rum, add tequila to the syrup.

> Instead of rum, add 1 split vanilla bean to the syrup.

> Instead of lime wedges, sprinkle ⅓ cup (1⅝ oz./46 g) chopped pistachios on the plate.

BAKER'S WISDOM

Choosing ripe mangos

Make sure you use ripe mangos. Look for ones that give slightly when you press gently near the stem with your thumb. They should be bruise- and blemish-free and have a spicy-citrus fragrance.

Make the syrup

Put the water and sugar in a small saucepan. Cook, stirring frequently, over medium heat until the sugar is dissolved and the liquid is boiling. Slide the pan off the heat, stir in the rum, and set aside to cool completely, stirring occasionally. Cover and refrigerate until well chilled.

Make and serve the mangos

1. Arrange 1 mango on one of its narrower sides (it should almost balance itself). Position a sharp or serrated knife just off center and cut down one wide side. If the knife meets resistance, you've hit the mango pit. Adjust the knife slightly farther from the center and try again. Repeat with the other wide side as well as the two narrow sides. Repeat with the other 3 mangos.

2. Arrange 1 mango half, skin side down, on a cutting board and, using a sharp paring knife, cut the mango in a ¾-inch (2 cm) crosshatch pattern, being careful not to cut through the skin. Using the paring knife or a curved, serrated grapefruit knife, cut between the mango and the skin to release the fruit but not tear the skin. Rearrange the chunks, if necessary, and move to a plate. Repeat with the remaining mango halves; cover and refrigerate until ready to serve.

3. Arrange the cut mango halves, skin side down, on four small dessert plates (2 halves per plate) and sprinkle with a little salt. Evenly sprinkle the tops with sugar (½ Tbs. per mango half) and slowly pass a handheld torch over the sugar until it's melted and caramelized. Add a dollop of yogurt (if using) to each plate along with a lime wedge. Spoon a little of the syrup over the caramelized mangos and serve immediately.

For more about brûléeing, see p. 386.

Cutting a mango

A

Mangos come in different shapes and colors. Small Ataulfo (left) are ripe when deep golden yellow and slightly wrinkly and give slightly when pressed. Medium-sized Francis' (center) greenish hue turns golden yellow and gives slightly when ripe. Tommy Atkins or Kent varieties are large and often more readily available. They are perfect for this recipe and are ripe when they give slightly when pressed around the "shoulders" or by the stem end.

B

To cut a mango, arrange on the cutting board with the flatter end down—it will stand almost by itself. Position a sharp knife just off center and cut down one side; if it meets resistance, it means you've run into the pit. Remove the knife and position it slightly farther from the center until you can cut straight through.

C

Reposition the mango and cut down the other side, then lay the mango piece flat and slice around the pit to release as much flesh as possible. Discard the pit and nibble on the small pieces.

D

Working with one mango half at a time, using a sharp paring knife to cut a crosshatch pattern in the flesh. Be careful you don't cut all the way through the skin. Release the mango from the skin by sliding a grapefruit knife between the flesh and skin. If you don't have a grapefruit knife, a paring knife works too.

Pecan Streusel-Topped Apricot Buckle

Serves 8 to 10

Named for the way the batter and fruit buckle while baking, the name alone conjures up old-school images of grandmas making use of every last bit of fruit before it spoils, by folding the chopped pieces into a spongy, vanilla-scented batter and telling the kiddies "waste not, want not." My grandmother didn't cook a lick, but if she had, I suspect she would have happily made this for Sunday suppers, with any leftovers served for breakfast.

I've used apricots here, but this type of cake lends itself beautifully to any juicy stone fruit or berry. Play around with the flavors and nuts in the streusel topping, too. There are so many wonderful combinations to pair with the fruity cake and all are well worth exploring.

Nonstick cooking spray or softened butter, for preparing the pan

For the pecan streusel
⅔ cup (3 oz./85 g) unbleached all-purpose flour
¼ cup (2⅜ oz./67 g) firmly packed light or dark brown sugar
¼ tsp. ground cinnamon
Pinch of table salt

4 Tbs. (2 oz./57 g) unsalted butter, chilled and cut into 8 pieces
⅓ cup (1⅝ oz./46 g) chopped pecans (see p. 304)

For the cake
3 to 4 ripe apricots (10 oz./283 g total)
1⅓ cups (6 oz./170 g) unbleached all-purpose flour
1¾ tsp. baking powder

½ tsp. table salt
12 Tbs. (6 oz./170 g) unsalted butter, softened
1 cup (7 oz./198 g) granulated sugar
3 large eggs, at room temperature
1 tsp. pure vanilla extract
¼ tsp. pure almond extract
1 tsp. finely grated lemon zest (see p. 138)

MAKE AHEAD

> The topping can be prepared, covered, and frozen for up to 1 month.

> The buckle can be cooled, covered with plastic, and stowed at room temperature for up to 3 days.

Make the streusel

Put the flour, brown sugar, cinnamon, and salt in a medium bowl. Whisk until blended and add the butter pieces. Using your fingers, rub the mixture together until the butter is incorporated and the mixture looks like coarse crumbs. Pop the bowl into the freezer while preparing the cake batter to allow the butter to firm up.

For more about rubbing butter into a dry mixture, see p. 572.

Make the cake

1. Position a rack on in the center of the oven and heat the oven to 350°F (180°C/gas 4). Lightly grease an 8-inch (20 cm) square pan (I use Pyrex). Cut the apricots in half, remove the pits, and cut into 1-inch (2.5 cm) chunks (see the Essential Technique on the facing page).

2. Whisk the flour, baking powder, and salt in a medium bowl until well blended. Put the butter in the bowl of a stand mixer fitted with the paddle attachment (or in a large bowl and using an electric handheld mixer fitted with wire beaters). Beat on medium speed until well blended and smooth, about 1 minute. Add the sugar and beat on medium-high speed until well blended, about 2 minutes. Add the eggs, one at a time, beating well after each addition. Add the vanilla, almond extract, and lemon zest with the last egg.

3. Add the flour mixture and gently fold with a silicone spatula until the flour is just blended. Add half of the apricots and fold a few more times until they are just incorporated.

For more about folding, see p. 270.

4. Scrape the batter into the prepared pan and spread evenly. Scatter the remaining apricots evenly over the batter. Remove the streusel from the freezer and crumble into small pieces with your fingertips. Add the pecans and toss to combine. Sprinkle the topping evenly over the cake. Bake until the top is browned and a pick inserted in the center of the cake comes out clean, 49 to 51 minutes. Move to a rack and let cool for at least 20 minutes. Cut into squares and serve warm or at room temperature.

TWISTS

Flavor swap

> Instead of apricots, use the same amount of one or a combination of two of the following: strawberries, blueberries, raspberries, peaches, or nectarines.

> Instead of pecans, use the same amount of one of the following: slivered almonds, chopped walnuts, or chopped hazelnuts.

ESSENTIAL TECHNIQUE

Cutting apricots and other stone fruit

To cut apricots, hold the fruit in one hand while you use a paring knife to cut into the flesh at the stem end. Cut around the pit (the knife won't be able to cut all the way through), turning the fruit as you cut. There's no need to peel apricots before cooking them because the skin is so thin.

Once you've cut all the way around the pit, release the fruit, opening up the halves like a book. Then use the tip of your finger to nudge and lift the pit from the fruit and discard. Continue cutting the fruit as needed for your recipe.

Peaches *and* Cream Pavlova

Serves 12   [PHOTO ON P. 424]

Years ago, I had the opportunity to talk with famed Aussie chef Nicky Major about Pavlova, a meringue dessert named after Russian ballet dancer Anna Pavlova. Nicky's description of the crunchy outside and soft, creamy interior won me over and, honestly, I've been obsessed with this dessert ever since that conversation. Here, with this recipe, I think I have made Nicky proud.

I've chosen a peach theme (purée folded into whipped cream with slices on top) for this Pavlova, but other fruit like mangos, kiwis, papayas, or berries would all be delicious. As you can see, the end result is almost too pretty to eat...almost.

For the Pavlova
1½ cups (10½ oz./298 g)
   superfine sugar (see the
   facing page)
2 Tbs. + 1 tsp. cornstarch
Pinch of table salt
5 whites from large eggs (5 oz./
   142 g), at room temperature
   (see p. 371)
½ tsp. cream of tartar
1½ tsp. vinegar (distilled white,
   white wine, or white balsamic)
1½ tsp. pure vanilla extract

For the peachy whipped cream
2 ripe, medium peaches, halved,
   pitted and cut into wedges
   (see p. 108)
1¼ cups (300 ml) heavy cream,
   chilled
⅔ cup (2⅝ oz./74 g)
   confectioners' sugar (sifted if
   lumpy)
½ tsp. pure vanilla extract

For the fruit topping
2 to 3 cups (480 to 720 ml) thinly
   sliced peaches of varying colors
   (from about 3 peaches)
⅓ cup (80 ml) pomegranate seeds
Small mint sprigs

MAKE AHEAD

> The baked and cooled meringue can be stowed in an airtight container at room temperature for up to 1 day.

> The peach purée can be made and refrigerated for 1 day or frozen for up to 3 months. Thaw before using.

> The finished Pavlova can be assembled and refrigerated for up to 1 hour.

Make the Pavlova

1. Position a rack in the center of the oven and heat the oven to 300°F (150°C/gas 2). Trace a 7-inch (17 cm) circle in the center of a piece of parchment and arrange it marked side down on a cookie sheet (nonstick liners don't work with this recipe). For the best meringue volume, start with super clean equipment (see p. 33).

For more about marking and cutting parchment, see p. 232.

2. Put the superfine sugar, cornstarch, and salt in a small bowl and whisk until well blended and no lumps remain. Set aside.

3. Put the egg whites and cream of tartar in a clean bowl of a stand mixer fitted with the whisk attachment (or in a large bowl using an electric handheld mixer fitted with wire beaters) and beat on medium speed until the whites are frothy, 30 to 45 seconds. Increase the speed to medium high and beat until the whites form soft peaks, 1½ to 2 minutes. Continue beating while gradually adding the sugar mixture by tablespoonful. This will take about 3 minutes, stopping and scraping down the sides twice. When all the sugar mixture is added and the whites are firm and glossy, add the vinegar and vanilla. Beat on high speed until blended, about 30 seconds.

For more about beating egg whites, see p. 212.

4. Scrape about half of the meringue into a mound in the center of the traced circle and spread to the edges. Scrape the remaining meringue onto the center in a mound and, using the back of a large spoon, spread to an even but very free–form thickness around the sides with some swirls and peaks. Make a shallow indentation in the center of the meringue.

5. Reduce the oven temperature to 200°F (95°C). Bake until the outside of the meringue feels firm and it moves only slightly when nudged with a fingertip (the center will still be soft), 2 to 2½ hours. Turn off the oven and let the meringue cool completely in the oven or up to 8 hours. Move the sheet to the counter. Carefully slide a long metal spatula between the parchment and the meringue to loosen. Using the parchment, move the meringue to a flat serving plate and gently nudge the meringue onto the plate; discard the parchment.

Make the cream and assemble

1. Pile the peaches into a food processor and purée until smooth, about 1 minute. Measure and reserve ½ cup (120 ml) and use the remaining for another purpose (it's delicious stirred into yogurt, mixed into a fruit smoothie, or saved for your evening cocktail).

2. Put the heavy cream and confectioners' sugar in a large bowl. Beat with an electric handheld mixer fitted with wire beaters on medium-high speed until it's thick enough to hold firm peaks when the beater is lifted, about 2 minutes. Add the vanilla and beat on medium speed until well blended.

For more about beating to firm peaks, see p. 212.

3. Add the peach purée and, using a large silicone spatula, fold until just barely blended with some large peachy streaks still very visible. Spoon the cream into the center of the meringue and top with the peach slices, pomegranate seeds, and mint sprigs.

4. To serve, use a serrated knife to cut into wedges.

TWISTS

Flavor swap

MAKE IT STRAWBERRY-LEMON

> For the Pavlova, add 1 Tbs. finely grated lemon zest (see p. 138) along with the vanilla.

> For the cream, instead of using the fresh, puréed peaches in the whipped cream, fold in ½ cup (4¼ oz./120 g) lemon curd as directed.

> Instead of topping with peaches and pomegranate seeds, use sliced strawberries and blueberries along with the mint springs.

(continued)

BAKING WISDOM

Superfine sugar

If you can't find superfine sugar at your grocery store, make your own by whizzing the same amount of granulated sugar in a food processor until the granules are pulverized. These finely ground sugar crystals dissolve quickly in whipped whites to make silky, sweet meringues.

ESSENTIAL TECHNIQUE

Making the pavlova

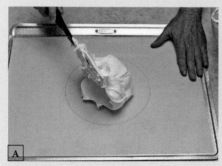

Scrape about half of the meringue in the center of a 7-inch (17 cm) circle drawn on parchment (be sure the parchment is drawn side down) on a cookie sheet. Using an offset spatula, spread it to the edges.

Pile the other half of the meringue in the center, then use the back of a tablespoon to spread it out to the edges, mounding it at the edges with plenty of swirls and peaks and forming an indentation in the center.

After the meringue has baked and then cooled, it will be crispy on the outside but fluffy on the inside.

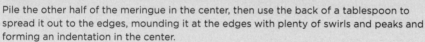

Melon Compote

Serves 6 to 8   [PHOTO ON P. 425]

Dessert and recipe inspiration comes from everywhere, and a recent trip to the Mexican Riviera was no exception. Between the warm breezes, rich tropical vegetation, and salty sea spray, I was awash with ideas. This dessert is my homemade take on a glorious fruit tower my hotel served for breakfast each morning. The stacked, thick discs of ripe melons, pineapple, and papaya formed a breathtaking explosion of color and tropical flavor.

Once home and back to work on this book, my challenge was to re-create the same beauty and flavor in a way that every home cook could prepare and serve with ease. While I can't promise you the salty sea smells or the warm rays of Mexican sunshine, I can promise that these flavors will brighten your summer days and nights.

For the syrup
¾ cup (180 ml) water
¾ cup (5¼ oz./149 g) granulated
  sugar
6 sprigs fresh lemon thyme + more
  for serving
1 to 2 Tbs. light rum (I like Bacardi®)

2 tsp. freshly squeezed lemon juice
Pinch of table salt

For the compote
5½ cups fresh melon slices,
  preferably in assorted colors
  (from about 1 medium or 2 halves)

1½ cups fresh pineapple slices
  (from about ½ small)

¼ cup (60 ml) pomegranate seeds,
  for serving

Make the syrup

Put the water and sugar in a small saucepan. Strip the thyme sprigs (see the Essential Technique on p. 592) and add the leaves to the pot. Cook, stirring frequently, over medium heat until the sugar is dissolved and the liquid is boiling. Continue cooking until the liquid is slightly thick and reduced to ¾ cup (180 ml), about 4 minutes. Slide the pan off the heat, stir in the rum, lemon juice, and salt, and set aside to cool completely, stirring occasionally. Cover and refrigerate until well chilled. The longer it sits, the stronger the flavors become.

Make the compote and serve

About 1 hour before serving, arrange the melon and pineapple slices on a large serving plate. Drizzle half of the syrup over the fruit and refrigerate the rest. Just before serving, drizzle the remaining syrup over the top, sprinkle with the pomegranate seeds, and add a few fresh thyme sprigs for garnish.

(continued)

MAKE AHEAD

The syrup can be covered and refrigerated for up to 3 days.

TWISTS

Flavor swap

> Instead of the thyme sprigs and lemon juice, add 1 split vanilla bean to the syrup.

> Instead of the thyme sprigs and lemon juice, add 2 Tbs. finely grated orange zest to the syrup.

> Instead of the pomegranate seeds, sprinkle with ½ cup (2½ oz./71 g) pistachios just before serving.

> >

Mixed Berry Summer Pudding

Serves 4 to 6   [PHOTO ON P. 426]

The sophisticated look of this "pud," as the Brits would call it, belies its down-home, comfort food roots. A simple way to use up berries before they spoil, this pudding is traditionally made in a deep bowl or charlotte mold with stale bread slices lining the sides and filled with a lightly sweetened collection of juicy berries, topped with more bread, and then weighted overnight or longer to compact the fruit.

I've veered only slightly from the classic with a few modern twists and, dare I say, improvements. I chose a 4-cup (960 ml) Pyrex measure instead of a deep bowl or charlotte mold because it is the perfect depth to ensure the correct ratio of cake to berries; plus it's in every home baker's arsenal (if it isn't, it should be). Lightly greasing the bowl makes it easier to line with plastic wrap and it also makes quick work of unmolding. Instead of the bread, I like to use my cornmeal pound cake. The slices' slightly coarse texture soaks up the berry juices without losing their sturdiness, allowing this pudding to stand tall and proud. Lastly, I've added a good dose of Grand Marnier—why not?

Nonstick cooking spray, for
preparing the pan

1 recipe Cornmeal Pound Cake
(recipe on p. 274; made without
the blueberries)

1 quart (16 oz./454 g) strawberries,
rinsed, well dried, and hulled
(about 4 cups)

⅔ cup (5¼ oz./149 g) granulated
sugar

½ cup (120 ml) water

1 Tbs. finely grated orange zest
(see p. 138)

Pinch of table salt

1 cup (5 oz./142 g) blackberries,
rinsed and well dried

2 cups (10 oz./283 g) raspberries,
rinsed and well dried, divided

2 to 3 Tbs. Grand Marnier or water

2 Tbs. freshly squeezed lemon juice

1. Lightly grease a small (4- to 5-cup/960 to 1183 ml), deep bowl (I use a 4-cup/960 ml Pyrex measure) with cooking spray. Line with 2 long pieces of plastic wrap crossed in the center, letting the excess hang over the sides (see the Essential Technique on p. 594). Make room in the fridge.

2. Trim the brown edges from the pound cake and cut into ½-inch (12 mm) thick slices. Arrange the slices snugly next to each other to cover the bottom and sides of the bowl completely. Using your fingers, push the slices together and fill any gaps with smaller pieces so that all the slices fit tightly and there are no openings.

3. Cut the strawberries into halves (or quarters, if large). Put the strawberries, sugar, water, orange zest, and salt in a medium saucepan. Bring to a boil over medium heat, stirring frequently. Add the blackberries and half of the raspberries and reduce the heat to low; simmer, stirring constantly, until the strawberries are barely tender and the liquid is syrupy, about 2 minutes. Slide the pan off the heat. Add the remaining raspberries, the Grand Marnier, and lemon juice; gently stir until just blended and set aside to cool slightly.

4. Spoon about ½ cup (120 ml) of the berry juice into the lined bowl to cover the bottom. Spoon the berries with as little juice as possible into the bowl. Cover the berries with some of the remaining pound cake, fitting the slices together tightly and filling in any gaps with small pieces (see the Essential Technique on pp. 594–595). Spoon the remaining juice over the pound cake and around the edges. Wrap the excess plastic wrap over the bowl. Set the bowl on a rimmed plate (to catch any drippings), put a flat plate or bowl directly on top of the pudding, and set a 2- or 3-lb. (1 to 1.4 kg) weight (like a large can of tomatoes or applesauce) on top. Make sure the plate/bowl sits directly on top of the pudding and doesn't rest on the rim—it is meant to compress the pudding. Refrigerate for at least 8 hours or up to 2 days.

5. To serve, unwrap the mold and place a shallow serving bowl or plate on top of the mold. Grip both the plate and the mold and invert. Gently pull on the plastic while lifting off the bowl. Wipe the edge of the plate clean if necessary. Using a serrated knife, cut into wedges. Don't worry if the slices crumble a bit—the pudding is meant to be a homey dessert and the flavor won't suffer a bit.

(continued)

MAKE AHEAD

> The pudding can be prepared, covered, and refrigerated up to 2 days before unmolding and serving.

> The unmolded pudding can be refrigerated for up to 1 hour before serving.

TWISTS

Flavor swap

> Instead of orange zest, use 2 tsp. finely grated lemon zest.

> Instead of Grand Marnier, use the same amount of freshly squeezed orange juice.

> Instead of the cornmeal pound cake, use one 16-oz. (454 g) store-bought pound cake (thawed if frozen); 24 slices firm white bread (preferably on the stale side), about ⅓ inch (8 mm) thick, crusts removed; or 2 packages (3 oz./85 g each) soft ladyfingers.

FINISHING TOUCHES

Serve with lightly sweetened whipped cream or a scoop of vanilla bean or berry ice cream.

Assembling and unmolding the pudding

A

Prepare the pan (I like to use a 4-cup/ 960 ml Pyrex measure) by greasing, then covering with plastic wrap. Place two pieces of plastic wrap across the top of the cup or bowl so they cross in the middle, then use your hand and fingers to press them against the bottom and sides of the cup. Be sure there is ample overhang on all sides.

B

The more cooked, browned edges of the pound cake will mar the finished look and won't absorb the juices as well as the interior. Using a serrated knife, carefully cut away the brown edges.

C

It's important that the cake slices are all ½ inch (12 mm) thick so that they readily absorb the juice and are sturdy enough to hold their shape when unmolded. Measure the pound cake and make tick marks to ensure the slices are even.

D

Working with one slice at a time, cut to fit the bottom of the cup, placing pieces snugly so the bottom is completely covered with cake, then arrange slices along the side of the cup. Use your finger

to push the slices into each other tightly, then cut smaller pieces as needed to tightly fill any gaps. The cup should be completely covered with cake.

E

The tops of the slices will extend slightly beyond the cup and be uneven.

F

Fill the bottom of the cake-lined cup with ½ cup (120 ml) of berry juice, then fill the cup with berries. Try to get as little juice with the berries as possible for now.

G

Cover the top of the cup with more cake slices, positioning them tightly together and cutting as needed to fill all holes. Trim the tops of the cake slices as needed.

H

Spoon the remaining juice over the top and edges of the cake. It's important that the top of the cake is completely soaked, so pull up on the overhanging plastic wrap and use it as a barrier to add more juice to all exposed areas of the cake. This is a messy—but necessary—process.

I

Wrap the top of the cake with the overhanging plastic—pull it over tightly to help the juice settle into the cake. Set a plate or bowl directly on top of the cake to weigh it down, then add a large can to add pressure. Let sit in the fridge for 8 hours.

J

Peel back and unfold the plastic wrap from the top of the pudding.

K

Place a large plate on the unwrapped pudding, then, holding the plate and the cup, quickly invert the pudding onto the plate. Don't worry about all the juice drips and splatters from the plastic—you can clean up the plate before serving if you like. Gently pull down on the plastic while lifting off the cup.

L

Pull off the plastic wrap and discard. If needed, wipe any drips from the edges of the plate before slicing and serving.

Toasted Walnut–Allspice Shortcakes
with Dried Fruit Compote

Serves 8

While shortcakes are a well-known and loved summer classic, when coupled with the right spices and fruit, they make for an all-star fall and winter dessert. For my wintery version, I've chosen the warm, earthy flavors of allspice, whole-wheat flour, and toasted walnuts in the shortcakes, paired them with an apple cider and mixed dried fruit compote, and topped with a whipped sour cream and light brown sugar cream. It's sure to be your new go-to cool-weather dessert.

For the shortcakes
6 Tbs. (3 oz./85 g) unsalted butter
⅔ cup (160 ml) heavy cream, chilled
1 tsp. pure vanilla extract
1 cup (4½ oz./128 g) unbleached all-purpose flour
¾ cup (3⅜ oz./96 g) whole-wheat flour
½ cup (3½ oz./99 g) firmly packed light brown sugar
5 tsp. baking powder
½ tsp. ground allspice
½ tsp. table salt

⅓ cup (1⅜ oz./39 g) chopped walnuts, toasted (see p. 33)
2 Tbs. coarse sanding sugar (optional)

For the dried fruit compote
3 cups (720 ml) apple cider
10 dried figs (6 oz./170 g), trimmed and cut into quarters or eighths, if large (see p. 598)
⅔ cup (6 oz./170 g) lightly packed dried apricots, coarsely chopped or snipped (see p. 598)
⅔ cup (4⅝ oz./131 g) firmly packed light brown sugar

Pinch of table salt
1 cup (4½ oz./128 g) dried cranberries
1 cup (5 oz./142 g) golden raisins
1 tsp. pure vanilla extract

For the whipped cream
1½ cups (360 ml) heavy cream
¼ cup (1¾ oz./50 g) firmly packed light brown sugar
1 tsp. vanilla bean paste or pure vanilla extract
⅓ cup (2⅝ oz./74 g) sour cream

Make the shortcakes

1. Position a rack in the center of the oven and heat the oven to 400°F (200°C/gas 6). Line a cookie sheet with parchment or a nonstick liner.

2. Cut the butter in half lengthwise, cut each half lengthwise again, and then cut each strip into 8 pieces. Pile the butter onto a plate and slide it into the freezer until ready to use. Measure the heavy cream in a 1-cup (240 ml) Pyrex measure and add the vanilla. Using a fork, whisk until blended, then refrigerate until ready to use.

3. Whisk the all-purpose and whole-wheat flours, brown sugar, baking powder, allspice, and salt in a large bowl until well blended. Add the cold butter pieces and, using a pastry blender or two knives, cut the butter into the flour mixture until the butter is pea-sized. (You can also do this step in a food processor using short pulses, scraping the blended mixture into a large bowl before proceeding.)

4. Add the chopped walnuts. Pour the cream and vanilla over the flour mixture and, using a silicone spatula, stir and fold until it forms a shaggy, moist dough with some floury bits remaining. (I like to use one hand to help mix while keeping the other working the spatula.) Scrape the dough and any remaining floury bits onto the counter and knead a few times until the dough is evenly moist and holds together well.

For more about mixing shortcake dough, see p. 579.

5. Gently press the dough into a rectangle slightly larger than 8 x 4 inches (20 x 10 cm). Using a large sharp knife, trim the edges to make a neat rectangle and cut into 8 equal squares. Arrange on the prepared cookie sheet about 1½ inches (4 cm) apart. Sprinkle the tops with the sanding sugar, if using. Bake until the edges are deep golden brown and a pick inserted in the center of a shortcake comes out clean, 19 to 21 minutes. Move the sheet to a rack and let the shortcakes sit until they're cool enough to handle, about 15 minutes. Serve warm or at room temperature.

For more about shaping shortcakes, see p. 579.

Make the compote

Put the apple cider, figs, apricots, brown sugar, and salt in a large saucepan. Bring to a boil over medium-high heat, reduce the heat, and simmer, stirring occasionally, until the juices are thick and syrupy and the fruit is barely tender, 8 to 10 minutes. Add the cranberries and raisins and continue to cook until the fruit is tender. Slide the pan off the heat, stir in the vanilla, and set aside, stirring occasionally, until warm. If the juices are very thick, add a little more cider.

Make the whipped cream

In a medium bowl, combine the cream, brown sugar, and vanilla. Using an electric handheld mixer fitted with wire beaters, beat until medium-firm peaks form when the beaters are lifted. Add the sour cream and beat until blended and firm peaks form. Serve immediately or cover and refrigerate until ready to serve.

For more about beating cream to firm peaks, see p. 212.

To serve

If made ahead, warm the shortcakes (a toaster oven set on 300°F/150°C is great for this). Using a serrated knife, cut the shortcakes in half crosswise and place the bottom halves on serving plates. Spoon some of the dried fruit compote, including the juices, over each shortcake, top with a big dollop of the whipped cream, and cover with the shortcake lids. Top with a dollop of the whipped cream and a little compote. Serve immediately.

(continued)

MAKE AHEAD

> The shortcakes can be baked, cooled, covered, and stowed at room temperature for up to 1 day or wrapped in plastic and frozen for up to 1 month. If frozen, thaw, unwrapped, at room temperature for 30 minutes.

> The compote can be made, cooled, covered, and refrigerated for up to 1 week before reheating and serving. Add more cider if the juices are too thick. Leftover compote is delicious spooned over hot oatmeal.

> The whipped cream can be made and refrigerated for up to 3 hours.

TWISTS

Flavor swap

> Instead of the whipped cream filling, use scoops of white chocolate mousse (see p. 328) or vanilla ice cream.

> Instead of the vanilla extract in the compote, use the same amount of aged balsamic vinegar.

> Instead of the dried fruit compote, use fresh, ripe figs, trimmed and quartered.

ESSENTIAL TECHNIQUE

Trimming the fruit

A

B

Kitchen shears are a must-have tool in your baking arsenal. Use them to snip dried apricots.

When cutting dried figs, first trim the stem off the fruit, then cut in half and quarters if the fruit is large. When making the compote, it's important to start cooking the thicker dried fruit, like apricots and figs, first and then add the smaller, more delicate fruits like dried cranberries and raisins.

C

When cooked, the compote will be thick and syrupy; the dried fruit will be tender and plumped.

METRIC EQUIVALENTS

Liquid/Dry Measures

U.S.	METRIC
1/4 teaspoon	1.25 milliliters
1/2 teaspoon	2.5 milliliters
1 teaspoon	5 milliliters
1 tablespoon (3 teaspoons)	15 milliliters
1 fluid ounce (2 tablespoons)	30 milliliters
1/4 cup	60 milliliters
1/3 cup	80 milliliters
1/2 cup	120 milliliters
1 cup	240 milliliters
1 pint (2 cups)	480 milliliters
1 quart (4 cups; 32 ounces)	960 milliliters
1 gallon (4 quarts)	3.84 liters
1 ounce (by weight)	28 grams
1 pound	454 grams
2.2 pounds	1 kilogram

Oven Temperatures

°F	GAS MARK	°C
250	1/2	120
275	1	140
300	2	150
325	3	165
350	4	180
375	5	190
400	6	200
425	7	220
450	8	230
475	9	240
500	10	260
550	Broil	290

INDEX